44

Johannes Reuchlin and the Campaign to Destroy Jewish Books

Johannes Reuchlin and the Campaign to Destroy Jewish Books

DAVID H. PRICE

OXFORD
UNIVERSITY PRESS

2011

OXFORD
UNIVERSITY PRESS

Oxford University Press, Inc., publishes works that further
Oxford University's objective of excellence
in research, scholarship, and education.

Oxford   New York
Auckland   Cape Town   Dar es Salaam   Hong Kong   Karachi
Kuala Lumpur   Madrid   Melbourne   Mexico City   Nairobi
New Delhi   Shanghai   Taipei   Toronto

With offices in
Argentina   Austria   Brazil   Chile   Czech Republic   France   Greece
Guatemala   Hungary   Italy   Japan   Poland   Portugal   Singapore
South Korea   Switzerland   Thailand   Turkey   Ukraine   Vietnam

Copyright © 2011 by Oxford University Press, Inc.

Published by Oxford University Press, Inc.
198 Madison Avenue, New York, New York 10016

www.oup.com

Oxford is a registered trademark of Oxford University Press.

Library of Congress Cataloging-in-Publication Data
Price, David, 1957–
Johannes Reuchlin and the campaign to destroy Jewish books / David H. Price.
    p. cm.
Includes bibliographical references.
ISBN 978-0-19-539421-4
1. Reuchlin, Johann, 1455–1522. 2. Judaism—Relations—Christianity.
3. Christianity and other religions—Judaism.
4. Jewish literature—Censorship—Germany—History—16th century.
5. Humanism—Germany—History—16th century.
6. Scholasticism—Germany—History—16th century. I. Title.
B785.R64P75 2010
261.2'609031—dc22   2010001092

For Samuel Price Hotchkiss

Acknowledgments

Research and writing often seem to be solitary endeavors. The countless hours reading in the library, the days framing paragraphs, the weeks or even months working out an argument—these tasks are all done on one's own. Yet, when one looks back on the project, it becomes clear that the solitary scholar depended at nearly every stage upon the goodwill and good work of many people, both friends and strangers.

This book would not exist in this form were it not for the kind support and wisdom I received from several friends and colleagues, above all, Jeremy Adams, Kirsten Christensen, Glenn Ehrstine, David Gilner, Arthur Groos, Ralph Keen, Wilhelm Kühlmann, Steven Ozment, Wayne Pitard, Anita Seitz-Jakubik, and Bonnie Wheeler. I am especially grateful to Donald Weinstein and Volkhard Wels for their painstaking review of drafts of this book and the many improvements that resulted from their efforts. I also wish to thank several people at Oxford University Press, especially Theo Calderara, who expressed enthusiasm for this project from the start and has been an engaging editor throughout. Charlotte Steinhardt, Liz Smith, and Rene Leath made many important contributions to the demanding task of turning an author's manuscript into a book.

Samuel Johnson had it just about right when he said that a writer "will turn over half a library to make one book," and I thank the many librarians who assisted me in that enjoyable sport of hunting down books. I used the collections of the Beinecke Rare

Book and Manuscript Library at Yale University (supported by a visiting scholar's fellowship), and I am grateful for the assistance of the staff of the Herzog August Bibliothek in Wolfenbüttel, Germany. In the midst of this undertaking, my scholarly life changed thanks to the (ever-expanding) wonders of the Munich Digitisation Centre at the Bayerische Staatsbibliothek, which enabled me to turn over hundreds of Renaissance books from the comfort of my home study. I thank Gundula Niemeyer and Gertrud Friedl in particular for their help with my navigation of the Web sites of the Bayerische Staatsbibliothek. Michael Matthäus offered generous and expert assistance with the remarkable manuscripts documenting the book controversy that are housed at the Institut für Stadtgeschichte Frankfurt am Main.

For years, I have felt deeply indebted to the staff at the Klau Library of the Hebrew Union College-Jewish Institute of Religion (Cincinnati), where I have spent untold happy days using the magnificent collections. Lee Raubvogel, Daniel Rettberg, Arona Rudovsky, and Laurel Wolfson have always been welcoming and supportive. Above all, I have had the good fortune to benefit from the scholarly advice and encouragement of David Gilner, Director of Libraries at Hebrew Union College-Jewish Institute of Religion. Although I have been using the Klau Library for some thirty years now (and I was, in part, willing to undertake this project because it has such extensive holdings in early Renaissance Christian-Jewish relations), my admiration for it grows with each new visit. Most of the pages of this book were conceived, drafted, or written there.

Ordinarily, it might seem unnecessary to express gratitude to previous scholars in such a preface, since, after all, my notes and bibliography will provide sufficient indications of specific indebtedness. Yet even if this study is grounded in a fresh, comprehensive reevaluation of all the primary historical sources, I nonetheless feel an acute need to acknowledge that I have repeatedly profited from the perspectives of scores of studies, especially sharply focused analyses in recent publications. The overarching interpretations of such venerable scholars as Heinrich Graetz, Ludwig Geiger, and Max Brod will be mentioned throughout this book, but investigations of particular aspects of Reuchlin's career, anti-Jewish agitation, and the book controversy (several of which originated as doctoral dissertations), taken as an aggregate, have had an even greater impact on my understanding and the development of my approaches. I especially wish to acknowledge the magisterial edition, with historical commentary, of Reuchlin's correspondence. That project, undertaken by Matthias Dall'Asta and Gerald Dörner, is laying a secure foundation for future research on Reuchlin.

Finally, I thank my wife Valerie Hotchkiss and our son, Samuel Price Hotchkiss. Over the years, they have been unfailingly thoughtful and engaging in many discussions about Reuchlin and early modern Jewish life, and have always been willing to read yet another draft of this book. I dedicate this book to Sam in appreciation of the many ways he has helped and also in the hope that someday I might be able to support him on a project as much as he has supported me on this one.

Contents

Johannes Reuchlin
and the Campaign to
Destroy Jewish Books

I

"Impermissibly Favorable to Jews?"

I would prefer...that the entire Old Testament be destroyed rather than that the peace of Christendom be broken on account of the books of the Jews.

—Desiderius Erasmus, writing to Johannes Caesarius, a humanist in Cologne, on 3 November 1517

An unprecedented effort to end the practice of Judaism in the Holy Roman Empire began in 1509. Until then, campaigns against Jews, though numerous and often effective, had been limited to individual territories within the complex empire. The goal of the 1509 persecution was to weaken Judaism everywhere it remained by confiscating and destroying all Jewish writings except the Hebrew Bible. This aggressive strategy, carefully formulated to be compatible with standing imperial law, was initially spearheaded by Johannes Pfefferkorn,[1] a recent convert to Christianity who had been agitating against Jewish communities in Germany since 1505. With strong backing from the Franciscan and Dominican orders, and armed with a personal endorsement from the emperor's sister, Pfefferkorn managed to persuade Maximilian I to authorize the extraordinary measure of seizing and burning Jewish books throughout the empire. The ultimate purpose, as expressed in the emperor's mandate, was clear. The action would "defend" Christianity against alleged blasphemies in the books and, more important, end Judaism through conversion.[2] Faced with the loss of their books, especially their prayer books and the Talmud, the "people of the book" would succumb more easily to conversion or, as the Jews themselves soon protested, simply would be unable to observe their religion.[3] The new policy, the only known campaign with the goal of undermining Judaism everywhere in the empire,[4] was first implemented energetically in Frankfurt am Main, beginning in September 1509.

The action occurred at a time when all of Europe was contemplating the end of Judaism. After the expulsion of the world's largest Jewish community from Spain in 1492 and the forced Portuguese conversion of 1497,[5] European Judaism was tottering at the edge of the abyss. Jews had long since disappeared from England (expulsion 1290) and France (expulsion from crown territories, 1394). Expulsions had also been mandated in many individual territories across the Holy Roman Empire—Vienna (1420/21), Cologne (1424), Bavaria (1442/50), Würzburg (1453), Passau (1478), Mecklenburg (1492), Magdeburg (1493), Württemberg (1498), Nuremberg (1498–99), Ulm (1499), and Brandenburg (1510), to name but a few.[6] During the second half of the fifteenth century, the area open to Jewish residency contracted with virtually every passing year. Various jurisdictions in Italy, the only major homeland to western European Jewry outside of the empire in 1509, were following suit. As a result of the spread of Spanish rule, Jews were banished from Sicily in 1492 and from the Kingdom of Naples through a series of expulsions, with the strongest intensity during 1511–14, that concluded in 1541.[7] This moment in history, which instigated a strong exodus to eastern Europe and the Ottoman Empire, marks the nadir of Jewish life in western and central Europe prior to the Holocaust.

While this curtain was falling on European Jewry, act one, scene one of a new Christian-Jewish drama began. A tiny number of Christian scholars were starting to cultivate contacts with learned Jews for a very different purpose— they were seeking Hebrew and Jewish scholarship, hoping to acquire new methods for theological education and research. Ultimately they would succeed, for the embrace of Hebrew in the Renaissance would invigorate Christian scholarship and lay a permanent foundation for the modern study of the Bible. This started in the 1480s, when suddenly the Renaissance ideal of returning "to the sources" of ancient culture and Christianity, the methodology that would soon undergird the religious reform movements, expanded to include the recovery of Hebrew Scriptures.[8] Despite explicit repudiations of Judaism, this development amounted to implicit acknowledgment by Christians that Jewish tradition and learning possessed value for them. A few Christians, virtually for the first time in the history of their religion, expressed enthusiasm for Jewish studies.[9]

By 1506, a watershed in the history of Christian scholarship, a prominent German lawyer named Johannes Reuchlin had learned enough from Jewish scholars to publish the first Hebrew grammar and dictionary written for Christians, his *Rudiments of Hebrew*.[10] No less an authority than the modern Jewish historian Gershom Scholem aptly described him as "the first scholar of Judaism, its language and its world, especially the Cabala…the man who, nearly five centuries ago, brought to life the discipline of Jewish studies in Europe."[11] Reuchlin's grammar was just the first step in a sweeping movement. In the 1510s and 1520s, scholars in the leading centers of humanist culture— Florence, Venice, and, above all, Rome—promoted Hebrew scholarship as one of the great promises for a renewal of Christianity. In the 1520s, the inchoate Protestant movement decisively embraced Hebrew philology, and, by the 1530s, Hebrew studies were established at universities throughout western Europe.[12]

The worlds of academia and anti-Jewish agitation were not separate realms in medieval and early modern Europe. Soon the founder of Christian Hebrew studies was at the center of a maelstrom that engulfed European intellectual life for nearly a decade. This crisis resulted directly from the turmoil of the ambitious anti-Jewish campaign of 1509–10, when Maximilian I sought evaluations of the confiscation policy from four universities and three individual scholars, including Reuchlin. To everyone's surprise, the lawyer-scholar argued strenuously against the predatory action of Maximilian's mandate, forcefully contending that it did not accord with imperial law, was not justified on religious grounds, and threatened to cause more harm than good.[13] He copiously explained his position in *Recommendation Whether to Confiscate, Destroy and Burn All Jewish Books*, a legal analysis he sent the emperor in October 1510 and later published in 1511, under extreme provocation, as part of a controversial pamphlet entitled *Eye Glasses (Augenspiegel)*.

Reuchlin's pamphlet, which effectively stymied the new and dangerously potent method of persecution, plunged Christian Europe into a wrenching controversy. Inquisitor General Jacob Hoogstraeten and the University of Cologne brought heresy charges against him, alleging on the basis of forty-three statements that his *Recommendation* was "impermissibly favorable to Jews."[14] In 1512, the university published these charges, under the authorship of Arnold van Tongern, as part of its effort to discredit Reuchlin and restart the book pogrom.[15] While the heresy trial was wending its way through ecclesiastical courts, the inquisitor general escalated the stakes for academia by securing formal condemnations of Reuchlin's defense of Jewish writings from major theological faculties, including Paris, Cologne, and Louvain. By 1513, the controversy was being discussed everywhere across Europe in part because it implicated the champion of the new Renaissance humanist methodology for biblical studies and in part because destruction of European Jewry was then such a burning issue. Many authorities tried to influence the outcome of the case, one way or the other—the emperor (Maximilian I), the future emperor (Charles V), the current pope (Leo X), a future pope (Adrian VI), two kings of France (Louis XII and Francis I), other princes, secular and ecclesiastical, some fifty cities in the Holy Roman Empire, university faculties, professors and scholars all over the Continent and even in England. The resulting trials, which persisted until Pope Leo X handed down a final ruling in 1520, reveal some of the most unstable fault lines in European intellectual culture, ones that would shift violently as the century progressed. After all, Reuchlin's writings and the chain reaction they touched off mark the first time in European history that some Christians sought accurate knowledge of Judaism and its history. That development, of course, was a critical element in the Christian reexamination of its own history and its own sacred texts, a process that began with the Renaissance scholars discussed in this book.

Despite some historical precedents, Reuchlin's position on Judaism struck many of his contemporaries as an unacceptable innovation; for some, it even provoked outrage. His defense of Jewish rights in the face of a ruinous persecution was a disappointing blow to the anti-Jewish agitators. They now saw no way to achieve their goal of complete—and legally implemented—destruction of Jewish writings without answering Reuchlin's powerful counterarguments. Initially, Reuchlin's opponents were motivated by their resolve to annihilate Judaism but soon some began to express additional concerns about where Renaissance humanism might lead—not only to increased toleration of Jews but also to new approaches to Christian theology, and perhaps even to a different conceptualization of Christianity. On the other hand, Reuchlin's pathbreaking research in Hebrew elicited admiration from many enthusiasts of the humanist movement. The ability to associate his position on Jewish writings with humanist scholarship, specifically to the process of Christianity returning to its Bible in the original languages, immediately mustered an elite cohort of supporters for his cause. This configuration not only created a public forum for debate on the proper or acceptable Christian attitude toward Judaism but also led to a major confrontation between scholasticism and humanism.[16] Together, these two conflicts made up the Reuchlin Affair.

"A Miracle within a Miracle"?

The phenomenon of Reuchlin was so unusual that several commentators, even among his contemporaries, hyperbolically invoked the "miraculous" or preternatural in their attempts at explanation. What stands out for us now, as we look at the Reuchlin Affair, is the fact that no European Christian scholar, certainly not one of such distinction, had ever before been accused of favoring Judaism and Jews.

When the controversy broke out in full force in 1511, the most prominent Renaissance humanist, Desiderius Erasmus, was initially uncertain about how to respond. Reuchlin, arguably *the* pioneer in the northern European recovery of Greek, was Erasmus's precursor as advocate of the direct study of Greek sources for theology, including the Christian Bible in Greek. Not satisfied with Greek alone, Reuchlin had also mastered that other language crucial for biblical research, the one that sometimes made Erasmus shudder with unease—Hebrew. Perhaps it was partly an unconscious need to compensate for his failure to learn the language that prompted Erasmus to express disdain for Hebrew and even a willingness to jettison the Old Testament: "I would prefer...that the whole Old Testament be destroyed rather than that the peace of Christendom be broken on account of the books of the Jews."[17] But Erasmus also had substantive questions about Reuchlin's scholarly enterprise, especially his promotion of Kabbalah (which, in his opinion, could make Christianity too Jewish). Moreover, like Luther, Erasmus felt that a historical, grammatical, or literal approach to reading Hebrew Scriptures would render them insufficiently Christian.[18] A spiritual or allegorical approach, one that could uncover Christ in the text, was necessary for the Old Testament.

Yet despite his deep anti-Jewish biases, Erasmus ultimately supported Reuchlin as a way of defending fledgling humanist biblical studies. Upon Reuchlin's death in June 1522, Erasmus rushed a lavish eulogy into print—*The Apotheosis of Reuchlin*[19]—canonizing him as the patron saint of Renaissance Hebrew studies. In this flattering vision of the scholar's reception in heaven, St. Jerome ushers the Hebrew scholar into paradise to spend eternity as his celestial colleague, in close proximity to God. Casting Reuchlin as the eternal alter ego of St. Jerome was the highest monument Erasmus or any other humanist could have erected,[20] for Jerome, the ranking biblical scholar among Christian saints, had faithfully translated Hebrew and Greek Scriptures into Latin. Moreover, Erasmus venerated St. Jerome as the apotheosis of theological study, a pious scholar who trained his thought not on speculation or logic but rather on faith and the text of the Bible. According to Erasmus, St. Jerome was not the medium for any supernatural events; his saintly "miracles" were the writings and translations he produced. Similarly, "St. Johannes Reuchlin" earned a special place in Erasmus's heaven by virtue of his academic "miracle," by becoming the first modern European to achieve expertise in all three sacred languages—Latin, Greek, and Hebrew.

There was another way of perceiving Reuchlin as a miracle. Many have venerated him as the spirited and resourceful defender of humanism against the inquisition. That was the idea behind a famous Reuchlin tribute by the romantic poet Johann Wolfgang von Goethe. For Goethe, Reuchlin was "zu seiner Zeit ein Wunderzeichen"[21] ("the mark of a miracle in his own time") because of his courage, determination, and largely agile combat against the bigotry and anti-intellectualism of churchmen. This was a common reaction among Reuchlin's supporters during his lifetime, as expressed most humorously in the satire *The Letters of Obscure Men* (1515).[22] Reuchlin's aggressive defense against the heresy cases ultimately won support from Maximilian I (who, as we will see, would change his position on the Jewish question dramatically), Ulrich von Hutten, Erasmus, and many others, including a then unknown professor of Bible, Martin Luther. Soon, Germans would interpret the conflict as the first salvo fired against scholasticism in the name of the new cultural movement of Renaissance humanism. In their opinion, Reuchlin exposed intellectual (and even moral) weakness in the church, especially within the inquisitional church and among theology professors. In this way, the Reuchlin Affair conditioned an academic environment for reception of Luther's challenges beginning in 1517.

A sixteenth-century rabbi, Josel of Rosheim, also detected a miracle.[23] To Josel of Rosheim, the most influential Jewish leader in the Holy Roman Empire during the Renaissance, God showed a "miracle within a miracle" ("נס בתוך נס") when one of "the scholars of the nations" helped restore the Torah to its proper place in Frankfurt.[24] This does sound like a great miracle, especially when considered in light of the reactions to Reuchlin from Renaissance Christians. Indeed, many of his Christian defenders left the Jewish question out of the equation altogether. As far as I can determine, not a single Christian in the Renaissance claimed that Reuchlin was a great man for having defended civil rights for Jews. His detractors, though, did condemn him outright as a Judaizing enemy of the Christian faith, repeatedly charging that his research—his advocacy for Jewish scholarship, his championing of the Kabbalah, his defense of Jewish prayer books and the Talmud—not to mention the temerity of once publishing these ideas in a German-language work, rather than in a Latin tract for scholars only, undermined Christian orthodoxy, dispirited average Christian believers, and ruined efforts to convert Jews.

Historical Judgments

His contributions to scholarship were so significant and the controversies that swirled around him so great that Reuchlin has been the subject of continual evaluation since around 1510. His was the most important heresy trial since the condemnation of Jan Hus at the Council of Constance in 1415. His trials roiled European academic waters because the inquisitors had targeted the prime advocate of the new biblical studies movement. Just as his case was highly controversial during the Renaissance, modern historical studies, especially the major biographies, have evinced considerable disagreement, perhaps most frequently over the degree to which Reuchlin advocated toleration of Judaism and whether the controversy pertained primarily to the advancement of humanism or the preservation of Jewish legal rights.

The Reuchlin Affair became a commonplace in partisan Protestant scholarship because, as a proponent of the humanist movement, he was at the head of a group that resisted the authority of the inquisition and several faculties of theology, including such powerhouses as Paris and Cologne, and this occurred literally on the eve (and during the early hours) of the Reformation. Moreover, as we will see, Luther at first attempted to link his fledgling protest to the storms of the Reuchlin controversy. The Protestant embrace of him, which was so adamant that he received a place of honor in the 1868 *Luther Monument* of Worms,[25] has nonetheless always looked rather strained since Reuchlin ultimately rejected Luther's movement. Reuchlin's bedrock position was that all of his work on Judaism and Hebrew was fully compatible with the doctrine of the Catholic Church. Goethe and many others suggest that he was opposing intolerant theologians in general, whereas he was usually specific in his objections, however vehement and unrelenting. His quarrel was not with the inquisition in general but primarily with the Dominican prosecution of the issues raised in the controversy. However wrenching the heresy trial was, Reuchlin never wavered in his faith that true salvation could be found only within the protective mantle of the church.[26]

Moreover, contrary to the thrust of many treatments that cast him as a sort of "honorary Lutheran" rebel,[27] a major dynamic of the controversy was Reuchlin's alliance with humanist prelates in Rome, the goal of which was not only to exonerate him but also to advance humanist Hebrew studies everywhere. Influential men in papal Rome, including Pope Leo X himself, embraced Reuchlin as an embodiment of Renaissance ideals and promoted him as the pioneer of humanist studies in the Holy Roman Empire. Reuchlin remained loyal to Rome not out of any cynical pragmatism but because of many long-standing religious and intellectual affinities: to a great extent the Roman curia was his ally both politically and intellectually—an important fact that the subsequent outbreak of the Reformation has obscured.[28]

Another cataclysmic event in German history has also had a decisive impact on the representation of Reuchlin: the Holocaust. Since World War II, scholarship on Reuchlin and the controversy over Jewish books has been prolific if highly fragmented. This is partly the unintended result of an unusual development: a politically created demand for continuous Reuchlin research in Germany. Since 1955, the major impetus in Reuchlin studies has come from his birthplace of Pforzheim, a regional cultural center on the edge of Germany's Black Forest. Pforzheim had always taken pride in Reuchlin as its favorite son and even organized a tribute for the four-hundredth anniversary of his death in 1922. In 1955, it was time to celebrate the five-hundredth anniversary of his birth, but now the intervening disaster of the Holocaust lent tremendous significance to the task of finding "Germans We Can Be Proud Of." (That was the title of a book published in 1957 that included a celebratory biography of Reuchlin.[29]) Pforzheim, which had endured more than its share of horror in World War II (including total incineration in a British firebombing raid), possessed something whose value increased after the Holocaust—a man, a German, who had become the center of a European-wide scandal in the Renaissance because he dared to defend Jewish rights. The city has provided funds and guidance for numerous Reuchlin conferences over the years. It maintains a Reuchlin Archive and has awarded a "Reuchlin Prize" every other year since 1955 for distinguished contributions to the humanities. In conjunction with the Free University of Berlin and the University of Heidelberg, the city has also supported an ongoing project to produce a critical edition of most of Reuchlin's works. In 2008, Pforzheim opened the ambitious Johannes Reuchlin Museum as a cultural shrine in its most prominent ecclesiastical building, the St. Michael's Church. The result of such intense patronage of Reuchlin scholarship has been an impressive accumulation of specialized investigations of particular aspects of this history but also, paradoxically, the absence of overarching reassessments of the man and his culture. Indeed, with the exception of one book, which was completed in Israel in 1965, there has not been a comprehensive study of Reuchlin since 1871. All told, Pforzheim conferences have sponsored the creation of well over 100 scholarly articles that have increased our knowledge of Reuchlin exponentially, even if the context of this research may have contributed in some instances to a propensity to portray Reuchlin in primarily heroic terms.

During the past two centuries, German-speaking Jewish historians have produced the major comprehensive assessments of Reuchlin. It was one of the founders of Jewish historiography, Heinrich Graetz,[30] who wrote an extensive tribute to Reuchlin's regard for Jewish traditions and for Jews in his epochal *History of the Jews* (1853–76).[31] In a way, this provoked Ludwig Geiger's effort of 1871, a book that remains the most important biography of Reuchlin, though it is woefully antiquated and sometimes inaccurate. Trying to achieve the proverbial balanced view, Geiger documented occasions where Reuchlin appeared to deprecate Judaism. Geiger was able to conclude that Reuchlin's major work, *Recommendation Whether to Confiscate, Destroy and Burn All Jewish Books*, "displays pure and tolerant principles, a kind and beautiful point of view," even if some elements are "not in harmony with the demands of complete religious equality."[32] Unlike Graetz and the later historian Isidor Kracauer,[33] Geiger ultimately focused on the turmoil caused by humanist challenges to scholastic theology (and faulted Graetz for having placed the book controversy in the center of the Reuchlin Affair).[34] Even if the subsequent discovery of hundreds of relevant sources for Reuchlin has made his work obsolete (Geiger did not have the archival material necessary for an accurate description of the controversy over Jewish books), Geiger was able to shape a compelling narrative of Reuchlin's life. He was in a fine position to achieve this success, for his father, Abraham Geiger, appropriately hailed as "one of the three most important Jewish scholars in Germany in the nineteenth century,"[35] had also studied Reuchlin extensively.

In some ways, Max Brod's biography of 1965, a book burgeoning with wide-ranging and fascinating vignettes on Renaissance and twentieth-century culture, offers the most hagiographic presentation.[36] Brod was a German speaker from the multicultural world of Prague. Though ethnically Jewish, he identified with German culture. He is remembered now as the friend of Franz Kafka, the literary executor who ignored the author's deathbed wishes and saved the unfinished works—including *The Trial*—from destruction.

Brod was as skeptical of Geiger as Geiger had been of Graetz. Geiger, he felt, had been too stingy in his assessment and, in particular, had appeared biased against Reuchlin's Kabbalistic mysticism.[37] Brod was writing in the context of a revival of Kabbalah under the inspiration of Gershom Scholem. In a manifestly liberal mind-set, Brod developed an impressively empathetic appreciation for Reuchlin's religious life. But above all, Brod was writing about himself, especially about himself as someone who had escaped the Holocaust but remained intellectually anchored in German high culture. The biography repeatedly portrays Jewish statehood as the answer to many of the problems Jews faced in earlier times (and implicitly conveys optimism about the future of Ashkenazi culture in Israel). As was sometimes the case for adult Holocaust survivors, Brod presents himself as a Jew violently betrayed by the German culture he cherished so dearly. Almost as a gesture of reconciliation, he takes comfort in finding a "good German" in his subject, for to Brod it was obviously not Reuchlin but his opponents who manifested the mentality that can turn Christianity into such a destructive cultural pathogen.

Reuchlin's unusual position in the historiography of German culture has disposed many to venerate him, a phenomenon that began during his own lifetime and continues with vigor in Germany. Distortion of his positions on Judaism occurs in some studies, as do serious factual mistakes about what he actually did and wrote. The preeminent twentieth-century historian of the Reformation, Heiko Oberman, was in this respect justified when he wrote impatiently of a need to "shatter...the modern image" of Reuchlin, though his attempt to portray Reuchlin as an opponent of Judaism is also a distortion of the historical context.[38] It is, moreover, exceedingly difficult to assess Reuchlin from the perspective of Jewish history—did Reuchlin and the controversy abet Judaism's survival in Germany?—because many other unrelated factors were also decisive for gradual improvement in the political and legal position of European Jewry (detectable by the last quarter of the sixteenth century). Above all, the Reuchlin controversy created a context for the formulation of various Christian religious attitudes toward Judaism, some of which were new and, I will suggest, benevolent. In a sense, his trial, especially as it played out in ten years of intense controversy, was a trial of Christianity's stance on Judaism.

As we will see, this trial had more than one verdict.

2

Humanist Origins

I was the first to bring Greek studies back to Germany and the first to present and teach the art and study of the Hebrew language to the universal church.

—Johannes Reuchlin, writing to Pope Leo X, 1517

Although one of the first northern Europeans dedicated to the revival of classical learning, Johannes Reuchlin was at a deeper level a man of intense piety devoted to Christian doctrine and culture. Not the study of antiquity in isolation but the ideal of a seamless unity of classicism and Christianity is what made his perspective compelling to scholars and students of his time. When Reuchlin contemplated the historical beginnings of Christianity, he conceptualized it as an inherent element of the eternal grandeur of the ancient classical world. For Reuchlin and other humanists, the Renaissance "imitation" of ancient Greco-Roman culture was fully compatible with the creeds and traditions of Christian faith, even if some humanists, preeminently Erasmus, might sound the occasional cautionary note about ancient paganism creeping into Renaissance writing.

What does it mean when we label Reuchlin, Erasmus, or other Renaissance scholars as humanists? Humanism was in essence an educational reform movement that, after establishing deep roots in Italy around 1400 and gradually spreading throughout the rest of Europe, exerted a lasting influence on culture and politics. Although scholars can identify a few proto-humanists in the generation preceding his, Reuchlin was among the founders of humanism in northern Europe, often even acclaimed Germany's first humanist.[1] Humanist curricula began appearing in some northern European schools and universities around 1480 and became entrenched by around 1530. Generally speaking, humanist teachers emphasized five subject areas for instruction: Latin grammar, rhetoric, poetry, moral philosophy, and history.[2] These subjects, which belonged to the domain of the arts faculty at universities (as did dialectics or logic), were mastered by students pursuing the baccalaureate and the master of arts degrees. By "grammar" and "rhetoric," humanists meant the revival of classical Latin and Roman literary styles. Their textbooks for these disciplines, moreover, were based on actual classical usage rather than on abstracted systems of grammar (called "modalism"),[3] as was typical in the Middle Ages.

Humanist Latin was a brusque rejection of medieval Latin, still the primary language of church, government, and schools in fifteenth-century Europe. The humanist word for medieval Latin was "barbaric," which was both a technical term for nonstandard Latin usage and a favorite term of abuse. In 1492, the poet Conrad Celtis complained that German students had to listen to professors speaking "brokenly and crudely against all art and rule of speech like quacking geese or lowing oxen, disturbing the ear, pouring forth common, vile, and corrupt words and whatever enters their mouth, pronouncing harshly and barbarously the smooth Latin tongue."[4] *The Letters of Obscure Men*, one of the most enduring satires from the Renaissance, offered a scathing caricature of late-medieval, professorial Latin. This masterpiece, first published anonymously in 1515 by Johannes Crotus Rubeanus and others to support Reuchlin during the heresy trial, was a major contribution to the effort to turn the Reuchlin controversy into a battle between humanism and an old guard of scholastic theologians mired in both medieval language and logic.

If humanists worshiped a golden calf, it was ancient literary style. Humanists wrote in the manner of the ancients, revived the use of the ancient meters, restored the ancient genres of literature, studying and imitating the structures and strategies of ancient rhetoric. They called themselves *"poetae,"* so much so that scholastic theologians would dismiss the biblical research of Erasmus and Reuchlin as the work of mere "poets." Humanists strove to use words and phrases that resonated with ancient culture. Reuchlin, for instance, would be the first German to use the five-act structure of Roman comedy in a play, and his Latin, though perhaps not as elegant as Erasmus's, was polished and steeped in classical allusion.[5] His final statement in his epochal *Rudiments of Hebrew*, the first Christian guide to Hebrew Scriptures, is taken not from the Bible but from Horace's *Odes*: "I have erected a monument more lasting than bronze" ("Exegi monumentum aere perennius").[6] When Reuchlin had the honor of delivering an oration in the Sistine Chapel before Pope Alexander VI on 7 August 1498, it was in the idiom of classical Latin and was one of the first times a German satisfied the rhetorical expectations of the more advanced (and fastidious) Italian humanists.[7] Reuchlin also published a concise rhetorical manual for the composition of homilies that adopted the concepts of Ciceronian oratory,[8] intended primarily for use by the Dominican Order (and dedicated to Peter Wolff, the prominent prior of the Dominican house in Denkendorf).[9]

For the most part, history was a new discipline for education. Humanists stressed the study of ancient history (as recorded by the ancient historians themselves), and they also wrote histories of medieval and modern times, often in imitation of classical styles, frequently in order to draw moral lessons about political life.[10] One of the leading humanist writers of the fifteenth century, Leonardo Bruni (ca. 1370–1444) specialized in history, devoting the last twenty years of his life to composing the magisterial *History of the Florentine People*. Reuchlin's teacher Robert Gaguin followed in Bruni's footsteps with his *History of the Franks*, as did Reuchlin's later colleague at Tübingen, Johannes Nauclerus, with the *History of the World* (1500). In 1516, Reuchlin had the honor of composing the preface to a reprint of Nauclerus's history.[11] There, expressing a typically humanist position, he wrote that the study of history instills values (which he calls "virtue") in people and inspires them to seek honor, in particular by providing examples of greatness from ancient history. In a distinctive assertion about Jewish studies, Reuchlin not only claimed that Moses invented the art of writing and that Jews were the first to record history but also that "knowledge of antiquity must be sought from the Jews" (i.e., Jewish sources).[12]

Renaissance humanists cultivated a special interest in the early history of the Christian church. Within this field, their new methodology of source criticism possessed a marked propensity for stirring controversy. For example, Lorenzo Valla demonstrated that the *Donation of Constantine*, a document previously used to support papal claims to sovereignty in Italy, was a forgery,[13] and Erasmus's revolutionary biography—as opposed to hagiography—of St. Jerome from 1516 rejected all sources that claimed the saint performed miracles.[14] More important, humanists began revisiting early Christian writings with a new question: what do they tell us about the practices of the early church? And, to give the question a critical dimension, do current practices and dogma agree with those of the ancient church?

Moral philosophy was also a distinctively humanist subject. As a group, humanists did not uniformly eschew Aristotelian logic, the mainstay of late-medieval philosophy and theology,[15] but they did place considerably less emphasis on dialectics than had been the case in the late-medieval curriculum, sometimes even rejecting dialectics as a basis for biblical exegesis and theology. Instead, humanists sought to expand philosophical studies by focusing also on a selection of ancient moral philosophers such as Cicero, Plato, Plutarch, and Xenophon. In an early teaching experience, Reuchlin gave lectures at the University of Orléans on Cicero, who was revered in the Renaissance as a moral philosopher; one of Reuchlin's translations into German was of a philosophical work by Cicero (the *Tusculan Disputations*).[16] An early work in Greek philology, completed by 1477, was a Latin translation of Xenophon's *Apology of Socrates*,[17] an accessible introduction to Socratic ethical thinking (which also has the virtue of being written in Greek that is somewhat easier to construe than that of Plato's *Apology*). The humanist shift beyond logic also informs Erasmus's distinctive approach to Jesus of Nazareth as, among other things, a moral philosopher: Erasmus would label Jesus' teachings in the New Testament "the philosophy of Christ,"[18] a designation that would make little sense within the scholastic systems grounded in Aristotle. Nonetheless, no standard or even typical "humanist philosophy" ever emerged. Humanists were not uniformly Platonists; they did not all reject Aristotelian logic. And, most assuredly, they did not place "man" at the center of the universe. God and God's redemption of the created world were still what mattered most.

Humanists, especially Christian humanists, rallied to the academic battle cry of "back to the sources" ("*ad fontes*") in their literary, historical, philosophical, and theological studies. This meant going back to the sources in the original languages. Thus, there is nothing necessarily wrong in a theologian's use of Aristotle so long as he is using Aristotle in the original Greek,[19] as Reuchlin himself would insist.[20] For western European theology, the biggest change—a revolution that arguably altered the political map of the Continent—was study of the Bible (and other historical sources) in the original Hebrew and Greek versions, the fundamental goal of humanist studies for Reuchlin. In this respect, as we saw in chapter 1, he was the "trilingual miracle," for many a veritable hero of the founding generation of northern European humanism; as Erasmus would write in 1517, Reuchlin was "the glory of our modern Germany."[21]

A Humanist Family?

Information about Reuchlin's domestic life is severely limited,[22] although members of his immediate family were just prominent enough to leave behind a faint trail of archival evidence. His parents were Georg Reuchlin and Elisabeth Reuchlin (née Eck), and they had at least two other children, a daughter, Elisabeth, and another son, Dionysius. Elisabeth Eck was from a well-established, property-owning family; Georg was administrator for the Dominican Order in Pforzheim, a highly respected position that would have required an excellent basic education in addition to knowledge of legal and business affairs. The irony of Georg Reuchlin's career is that the crisis of his son's life would be a searing legal war with the Dominican Order. But until the controversy erupted, Johannes Reuchlin was inspired by his parents' affiliation and actually gravitated to the Dominicans in his own religious devotions. He was member of a Dominican-sponsored lay fraternity and had planned to be buried in the Dominican Hospital Church in Stuttgart. Moreover, as a lawyer, he represented the Dominican Order pro bono for over two decades. In 1519, as yet another response to the Dominican attack, Reuchlin published a set of letters from Dominicans thanking him for his generous legal assistance in past years.[23]

As a boy, Reuchlin was a prodigy on a significant instrument—Latin. Prodigies usually have the good fortune to be born to families able to nurture genius, and it would appear that Reuchlin's parents encouraged their children to value education. Reuchlin's sister, who married a certain Johannes Reuter, the mayor of the nearby city of Bretten, assumed partial responsibility for the education of Philipp Melanchthon, who, in turn, would become one of the most influential figures in the history of education in Germany. Johannes's brother, Dionysius, enjoyed a first-rate education, including tutorials at the Florentine Academy in 1491–92, where he studied Greek under the legendary émigré scholar Demetrios Chalcondyles. Both Chalcondyles and Marsilio Ficino wrote to Reuchlin with assurances that Dionysius and his companion, Johannes Streler, would be warmly welcomed at the Florentine Academy, with Ficino saying he had arranged for the youths to study under Giorgio Antonio Vespucci and that Lorenzo the Magnificent would also look after their progress.[24] Dionysius earned a BA degree from Basel in 1490 and an MA from Tübingen in 1494. Johannes managed to get Dionysius an appointment at the University of Heidelberg to teach Greek in 1498, but apparently the position lasted less than a year.[25] Dionysus also taught Greek in Tübingen, but not as a member of the faculty. He eventually became a priest and schoolteacher and may have left the priesthood under cover of the Lutheran movement.[26] It is possible that Dionysius was the father of Anton Reuchlin of Isny, a renowned Hebrew specialist of the mid-sixteenth century.[27] In a rather odd but suggestive poetic epistle of 30 June 1494 (which survives only in manuscript and was not intended for publication), Johannes cautions Dionysius about neglecting the grinding labor of research and indulging in soft living.[28] It is hard to know if this is merely the sort of thing an older brother might write to a university student or if it reflects an actual problem.

Johannes twice married into patrician families in Stuttgart. His first marriage was to a woman named Müller (her first name is unknown), the daughter of a wealthy family with close relatives on the Stuttgart city council and municipal court.[29] When they married is also unknown, although it was before early 1485,[30] and Reuchlin was still married to her during his political exile in Heidelberg (1496–99). In 1486, as a representative of Württemberg at the Diet of Frankfurt, Reuchlin recorded that he had written a love letter to his wife, or as he put it, *"peri erotos"* (concerning love),[31] thus giving the personal jotting a classical aura. Despite Ludwig Geiger's contentions, there are no indications that he ever considered divorcing her.[32] She died around the year 1501, probably in her early fifties, leaving Reuchlin substantial property. In addition to a house in Stuttgart, he had several parcels of land around Ditzingen,[33] a nearby village in the Swabian Alb (a volcanically formed range of hills known for its vineyards) where he ultimately planned to retire.

At yet another unknown date he remarried, this time a certain Anna Decker, the daughter of another prominent Stuttgart family. According to a seventeenth-century genealogy, the couple had a child who died in infancy, but it is not known if this late document is trustworthy.[34] Anna Decker probably died in 1519.[35] Since so many important details have vanished from the record, we will never know very much about the particulars of his family life. Reuchlin's two wives were apparently from families significantly more prominent than his own, but his doctorate and his position at the Stuttgart court would have allowed him to marry up. Moreover, his literary and political accomplishments earned him the distinction of being raised into the nobility, as a count palatine ("comes palatinus"), by Emperor Friedrich III in 1492.[36]

His most famous relative was Philipp Melanchthon (1497–1560). Melanchthon was the *Wunderkind* of Wittenberg, the young professor who, at the age of twenty-one, taught Greek to his senior colleague, Martin Luther. (During the 1510s, Greek emerged as a new wonder drug, a potential panacea for ecclesial ills, and Luther consumed it eagerly.) Melanchthon achieved renown both as Luther's successor and as the "teacher of Germany" ("praeceptor Germaniae"), perhaps the greatest educational reformer in German history. All told, he revised the curriculum in accord with humanist principles at some fifty-six known schools.[37] He was also the author of the first systematic Protestant theology (*Loci communes*, 1521) and the most enduring Protestant confession of faith, the *Augsburg Confession* (1530); he was always on hand to assist Luther with his scholarly tasks, most important perhaps, with the translation of the Bible from the original languages.

Melanchthon was very much Reuchlin's protégé. When Elisabeth Reuter, Reuchlin's sister, became his unofficial guardian in Pforzheim, he was a boy of ten. She certainly consulted with her famous brother on her gifted charge's education, and Reuchlin guided him through his studies in Pforzheim and especially later at Tübingen. It was even Reuchlin who landed him the appointment to the Wittenberg faculty.

Although both men paraded the connection, the precise nature of their kinship is not known. In the surviving letters, they address each other as "relative," using the fairly vague Latin terms of "cognatus" or "propinquus." As early as 24 July 1519, Johannes Eck, Luther's opponent at the Leipzig Debate, referred to Melanchthon as "an extremely arrogant nephew of Reuchlin" ("nepos Reuchlini multum arrogans").[38] That he was his nephew became common biographical opinion in the nineteenth century, especially in light of a 1574 designation of Melanchthon as Reuchlin's "nephew through his sister" on the assumption that "nephew" ("nepos") stood for "great nephew."[39] Yet even this designation is problematic, in part because it would mean that Reuchlin's sister Elisabeth would need to have been older than previously believed. Melanchthon's most recent biographer has postulated that Elisabeth was Melanchthon's great-aunt by marriage; that her husband was the great-uncle by blood.[40] If this is true, it matters little, for Reuchlin and Melanchthon regarded each other as close relatives. At the age of seventeen, Melanchthon wrote a preface to *The Letters of Distinguished Men* (1514), a major work that celebrated Reuchlin's intellectual prominence in Germany and throughout Europe.[41] For his part, Reuchlin gave Philipp the cognomen "Melanchthon." He had been born Schwartzerdt, a surname that cannot be easily parsed in Latin, the idiom of scholarship. Reuchlin translated it into a Latinate Greek: "Melan-chthon" is Greek for "black earth," which is what "Schwartz-erdt" suggests.[42]

A Humanist Hometown?

Apparently, it was not desirable to a Renaissance-minded German to live in a city that did not have a connection to classical antiquity. Reuchlin removed that blemish by "discovering" that his hometown had been founded (in Germany's Black Forest!) by ancient Trojans fleeing the wrath of Achilles. Reuchlin began his first major publication, *Miracle-Making Word* of 1494, with a panegyric description of Pforzheim, claiming that the town's name ("Phorcensis" in Latin) derived from its founder, a certain Phorcys, who was a minor figure in Homer's *Iliad*.[43] (Needless to say, Reuchlin does not mention that, according to the *Iliad*, Ajax slew Phorcys before the topless towers of Ilium.) Creating mythic genealogies that stretched back to antiquity was fashionable during Reuchlin's lifetime. Largely through the efforts of Emperor Maximilian I, the Hapsburg dynasty traced its lineage directly back to Aeneas, the Trojan hero who, in the imperial Roman version of things, ended his wanderings in Italy, where his descendants established the great civilization. Reuchlin would do something similar for Friedrich the Wise of Saxony, creating a genealogy for the elector's family that extended back to Homeric Greece.[44] Renaissance humanists derived pleasure from this kind of ornamentation. Contemporary culture shined brighter when reflected in the mirror of antiquity.

Whether or not Reuchlin really believed in its Trojan origin, he truly was born in Pforzheim on 29 January 1455.[45] The city was in the Margraviate of Baden in the southwest of what is today Germany.[46] Then Baden was part of the Holy Roman Empire, a chaotically complex confederation of over 2,000 territories, each with a high level of sovereignty. As the old saw aptly puts it, the Holy Roman Empire was neither holy, nor Roman, nor an empire. The last element of the witticism, which acknowledges the intricate puzzle of sovereignty, causes historians enormous trouble.

Even if he would live in his hometown for only about fifteen of his sixty-seven years, Reuchlin remained deeply attached to Pforzheim throughout his life. Upon his death in 1522, he bequeathed his most cherished possession, his library, to the city, specifically to St. Michael's collegiate church. This library, which he called "half of my soul,"[47] had some extraordinary items, including rare and precious Hebrew and Greek manuscripts, several of which survive today, mostly in the State Library of Baden in Karlsruhe.[48] Melanchthon praised the terms of the bequest as exemplary civic philanthropy, especially because "he did not want his heirs to disperse the collection."[49] The tribute has a certain poignancy since it was Melanchthon himself who would have inherited the books,[50] had he and Reuchlin not parted ways so fundamentally over the great issue of the 1520s—adherence to the Catholic Church or the evangelical movement. Three decades later, in a brief biography, Melanchthon would express profound respect for the heroic struggles of his mentor, and even attempt to connect the Reuchlin controversy to the beginnings of Luther's movement.[51]

Pforzheim is in a valley in the Black Forest, where the Würm and Nagold rivers converge to form a stream that, after flowing just a few more meters, empties into the Enz. At the end of the Middle Ages, it was a small city with a population of around 3,000, but so attractive that the margraves of Baden maintained an official residence there throughout the fifteenth century. While no detailed images of the city survive from the sixteenth century, Matthias Merian's engraving from 1643 conveys a good sense of how the city must have looked during the early Renaissance (see Figure 2.1). The city was small but dignified. The ensemble of

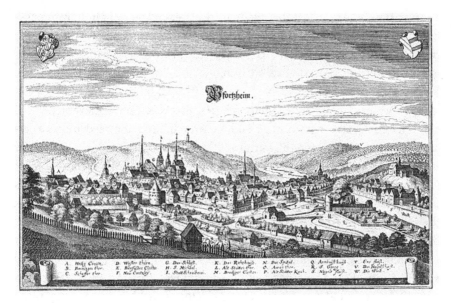

FIGURE 2.1. Matthias Merian, *Pforzheim* (engraving, published in 1643).

buildings created a gentle vertical lift that visually connected the stream-cut valley to the surrounding hills. Its beauty alone was sufficient to instill lifelong devotion in Reuchlin. The architecture of Reuchlin's youth was reduced to rubble on 23 February 1945 in a massive bombardment carried out by some 368 planes of the British Royal Air Force (RAF). According to RAF records, the planes dropped 731 tons of explosive and 820 tons of incendiary bombs on the city.[52] It is thought that as many as 18,000 people may have died in less than thirty minutes.[53]

In one respect, Reuchlin resembles the typical provincial who scored success in the larger world: he remained insufferably proud of his modest hometown. An innocent listener to his panegyrics would have thought Pforzheim was the Cambridge of the Holy Roman Empire. Although Reuchlin always insisted that it was a place of learning and culture, the city only had four monasteries and one Latin school, and is now remembered only as the birthplace of Reuchlin and the site of Melanchthon's grammar schooling. To his credit, even after he became renowned all over Europe, Reuchlin kept in touch with residents of Pforzheim, including Georg Simler, the principal schoolteacher. Apparently, Simler had schoolboys perform Reuchlin's play *Henno* in his honor during a visit,[54] and it was on that occasion that Reuchlin bestowed the Greek name Melanchthon on his beloved protégé.

When Reuchlin was still a child in Pforzheim, there had been an unsuccessful attempt to found a university there. Margrave Karl (r. 1453–75) petitioned Pius II for a papal privilege authorizing a new university in his residential city.

So important was this goal that the margrave personally went to Italy to negotiate with Pius (whom he had known since the 1454 Diet of Frankfurt). He received the papal charter on 7 December 1459 as well as permission to reorganize Pforzheim's St. Michael's Church as a collegiate church (*Stiftskirche*). Since new German universities typically depended on the benefices in a collegiate church to cover some faculty salaries, this was a key achievement.

But disaster struck from an unlikely quarter. In 1462, the need to elect a new archbishop of Mainz brought war to southwest Germany, with the Palatinate supporting one candidate, and Baden, Württemberg, and the Bishop of Metz (who happened to be Karl of Baden's brother) another. Friedrich the Victorious of the Palatinate, so named from this conflict, crushed the invading army at the Battle of Seckenheim. The three princes were captured and imprisoned under harsh conditions. Karl spent a year in shackles in a Heidelberg dungeon, apparently even enduring the stocks for a few weeks. Baden had to pay an indemnity of 20,000 gulden and the margraves were to rule in Pforzheim henceforth as feudal dependents of the elector of the Palatinate. After 1462, without resources for a university, Pforzheim could only look with envy to the regional intellectual centers of Tübingen, Freiburg, and Heidelberg.[55]

A special aspect of Reuchlin's lifelong custom of returning to his own source in Pforzheim was the symbiotic relationship that developed between him and the city's first printer, Thomas Anshelm (ca. 1465/70–1523).[56] Anshelm, who started printing only about thirty-five years after Gutenberg invented the technology, is a significant example of the small-time, early printer taking considerable risks on the production of new scholarship. His first known imprint was done in 1488 in Strasbourg. He is also known to have studied in Basel. Thus, we can imagine him as a printer's devil and apprentice in two of the most sophisticated printing centers of the 1480s and 1490s, before setting up a full-scale operation in the provinces. He worked in Pforzheim from ca. 1496 (certainly as of 1500) until 1511. His first project in Pforzheim, an imprint of thirty picture poems by the medieval writer Hrabanus Maurus, required the arduous task of setting type for poetry in such a way that the outline of the printed text formed images.[57] Anshelm used a fine Italian antiqua font, the style that signified humanist Latin (as opposed to medieval Latin) in this early period, and, more important, was willing to acquire Greek and Hebrew type.[58] His first Hebrew font appeared in Reuchlin's *German Epistle: Why the Jews Have Lived So Long in Exile* of 1505, and, with his Hebrew letters, he may have been the only German printer in 1506 capable of producing the *Rudiments of Hebrew*. Anshelm remained loyal to his principal author when the lawsuits and polemics made their joint ventures seem even riskier, becoming a major supplier of munitions, so to speak, in the explosive "battle of the books" between Reuchlin and his opponents. This was bold not only because it promised to make permanent enemies for him in some academic and ecclesiastical circles but also because imperial mandates imposed silence on Reuchlin.

Most of Anshelm's publishing in Pforzheim was of humanist textbooks—some forty known imprints fall into this category. Pforzheim, as we have seen, had failed to become a university town and had only the one good Latin school. Thus, with no local market to speak of, Anshelm depended on fairs, especially the international Frankfurt Fair, to move his stock. Some books could run into commercial difficulty, as did Reuchlin's *Rudiments of Hebrew*, which he produced in a large print run of 1,500 copies. To be sure, the book had a huge impact, with hundreds of scholars, including Erasmus, Luther, and Ulrich Zwingli, acquiring it to begin their study of Hebrew. But Hebrew would not be a standard part of the curriculum at universities for another two decades. In the absence of ready sales to students, Anshelm had to warehouse a few hundred copies of the book for several years, and Reuchlin had to negotiate a sale of 600 copies to the wealthy Basel printer Johannes Amerbach to relieve the financial strain on Anshelm.[59] After 1511, Anshelm moved his operation to Tübingen, where the university guaranteed a fairly healthy local consumption of his textbooks, and then in 1516 to Hagenau (in Alsace),[60] where his specialty remained theology and humanist textbooks, especially the works of Reuchlin. Perhaps the biggest success in the final stage of his career was the publication of Melanchthon's Greek grammar in 1518, a book that would go through some forty-four printings.[61]

Anshelm felt such a strong connection to Reuchlin that he altered his printing device to evoke Reuchlin's Hebrew research. As of 1506, the device displayed five Hebrew letters: Jhsvh (יהשוה; see Figure 2.2). Reuchlin had claimed that the insertion of a "ש" ("shin") in the tetragrammaton (Jhvh; יהוה)—the name of God in Hebrew Scripture—gave it a Christian substance, the effable name of Jesus (interpreted in this contorted effort as "Jeshua").[62] This device signifies the printer's profound identification with Reuchlin's innovative Hebrew humanism and the general expansion of Christian humanist studies.

Pforzheim had Jewish residents during the Middle Ages and Renaissance, although little is known of the community's history. As in many European cities, large and small, the Jews of Pforzheim had a long history of persecution. It is likely that Pforzheim Jews were murdered in the hysteria of the Great Plague of 1348/49.[63] When bubonic plague swept across Europe, many communities blamed the Jews for the disaster. Jews were murdered in riots, executed after show trials, or banished from many towns. Many of these expulsions, however, were quickly rescinded, as likely happened in Pforzheim.

FIGURE 2.2. Device of the printer Thomas Anshelm, which displays
Reuchlin's proposed alteration of the tetragrammaton (YHVH, יהוה) into
a pentagrammaton representing Jesus' name (YHSVH, יהשוה). Reuchlin,
Letters of Distinguished Men (Tübingen: Thomas Anshelm, 1514), final leaf.
Courtesy of the Klau Library, Hebrew Union College-Jewish Institute of
Religion, Cincinnati, Ohio.

Pforzheim was also the site of a blood libel case in 1267. In the Middle
Ages and the Renaissance (and even, albeit rarely, as late as the twentieth
century), Christians alleged that Jews used the blood of Christian children
in their rituals.[64] In the Pforzheim incident, some Jews were accused of
having murdered a Christian girl named Margaret, who had apparently
drowned. As far as we can tell, the case of Margaret of Pforzheim was typical. An explanation was needed for the death, often clearly the murder, of a
small child. Local Jews were apprehended on the charge that they tormented
and murdered the child in their nefarious rituals; authorities subjected the
accused Jews to brutal torture until a confession was extracted. Then several

Jews were executed. At Pforzheim, the Jewish victims were broken on a wheel and hanged.

That was not the end of the Pforzheim case. The body of the child Margaret became the object of a local cult that lasted for centuries and was still thriving in Reuchlin's lifetime. She was interred in a sarcophagus, known to have been on prominent display in St. Michael's Church until the Reformation era. The inscription read: "Margaret, murdered by the Jews, died happily on Friday, the first day of July in the year of the Lord 1260."[65] In 1507, her sarcophagus was opened in the presence of Cardinal Bernardino López de Carvajal, soon to be a powerful opponent of Reuchlin during his heresy proceedings in Rome.[66] Her remains were declared to be intact—convincing proof of her sanctity. Thus it would appear that a prominent religious observance in Reuchlin's Pforzheim served to arouse hatred of Jews. Moreover, several Pforzheim Jews were implicated in a 1470/71 blood libel case in nearby Endingen and suffered martyrdom under Margrave Karl.[67]

Humanist Education

Reuchlin attended the Latin school in his hometown, probably until he was fourteen or fifteen. In the 1460s, no northern school, certainly not Pforzheim's, had teachers trained in a humanist curriculum. Moreover, pupils did not yet enjoy the advantages of printed textbooks. Printing would become the major catalyst in the explosion of educational opportunities beginning in the generation immediately following Reuchlin's. Among the profound transformations that Reuchlin experienced was that he used manuscripts as a pupil, but printed books as a teacher. In 1488, Peter Jacobi wrote to Reuchlin from Pavia, resorting to a worn-out wordplay to tell him that he could find "many Greek children ('liberos') but no Greek books ('libros')."[68] The first decades of Reuchlin's mature Greek studies, in the 1470s through the 1490s, and even much of his work in the 1510s, depended heavily on manuscript sources. Greek printing before the sixteenth century is rare. Reuchlin's friend Aldo Manuzio, the most important printer of Greek, did not produce his first book until 1494 or 1495.

On 19 May 1470, as a boy of fifteen, Reuchlin registered for study at the University of Freiburg, which was the nearest university to his hometown, although it was then in Austrian (Hapsburg) territory. Founded in 1457 by Archduke Albrecht I of Austria, it was one of only ten universities that existed in the entire German-speaking world of 1470.[69] In the surviving documents, Reuchlin never mentioned his university experiences at Freiburg, which we should probably interpret as an indication that they were unexceptional. He did not study Greek or Hebrew there, for no one at the university had any competence in those subjects. He probably studied Aristotle in Latin translations (some of which were derived secondhand from Arabic translations), the *Summulae logicales* of Peter of Spain, and the medieval Latin grammar that was called the "Donatus." There was no glimmer of new learning in any of this.

In 1473, at the age of eighteen, Reuchlin enrolled at the University of Paris, probably a decisive opportunity in his life. It was there that he saw the first traces of what was happening in the Italian Renaissance and began the process of breaking away from the provincialism of Baden. In general, the French universities were so superior to the German start-ups that it was natural for a youth with Reuchlin's promise to matriculate at a university west of the Rhine. In addition to studying at the Sorbonne, Reuchlin would take a BA degree in Roman law at Orléans (1479) and an advanced degree in civil law in Poitiers (Licentiate degree, 1481). He first went to Paris as the companion of Friedrich of Baden, the third son of the Margrave Karl, who was pursuing an ecclesiastical career (and would ultimately attain the office of Bishop of Utrecht, 1496–1517). In a way, this early preferment set a course for Reuchlin's career, for he spent much of his life, comfortably and effectively, in the entourage of the powerful.

Among his teachers was Johannes Heynlin von Stein (Joannes a Lapide), a German probably originally from Stein, a village in the Black Forest not far from Pforzheim.[70] Though a scholastic philosopher of the Realist school, Heynlin showed considerable interest in humanist studies, which were then just beginning to spread from Italy to the rest of Europe. He served as Reuchlin's instructor for grammar, a course that typically included such matters as the construction of poetry in ancient meters, and Reuchlin later paid tribute to him as a pious Carthusian, prolific theologian, and as his first teacher in the humanities.[71] In collaboration with Guillaume Fichet, Heynlin von Stein also established the first printing press for the University of Paris, a small operation that was begun in the Rue St. Jacques, in the very building where Reuchlin found lodgings during his Parisian studies (thus affording him daily contact with the typesetters, all of whom were German).[72] Reuchlin studied rhetoric under another proto-humanist at Paris, Robert Gaguin. Gaguin wrote an extensive handbook for classical Latin versification that Thomas Anshelm would later reprint, perhaps on Reuchlin's recommendation,[73] and was best known as a Latin prose stylist and as a historian, in particular for his chronicle of the history of the Franks.[74] Later, in the 1480s, Gaguin would even translate some works by Pico della Mirandola into French.[75]

This first residence in France lasted only a year, after which he transferred to the University of Basel (founded in 1460), probably to continue his studies under Heynlin von Stein, who had accepted an ecclesiastical position there.[76] Although it was no Paris, Basel's culture was flourishing and, for a German city, rather cosmopolitan. (It did not secede from the Holy Roman Empire and join the Swiss Confederation until 1501.) A major church council, which lasted some eighteen years (1431–49; schismatic as of 1437), had brought hundreds of the best-educated Europeans to the city. At its peak, attendance at the Council of Basel may have reached the astonishing level of 3,500 clerics from all over Europe, especially from Italy. The city, which was already a commercial hub, also had the great fortune of having a paper-manufacturing industry in place before Gutenberg, which allowed Basel to develop into a major center for printing in the fifteenth century. Reuchlin completed his first two degrees there, the BA in 1475 and the MA in 1477. At a much later date, he would trace the formation of his humanist identity back to his Basel years: "As a young man, while contemplating barbarous and uncultivated philosophy [i.e., scholasticism] in Basel during the last century, I turned my thoughts to the elegance of Latin prose and poetry."[77] Indeed, Reuchlin's earliest surviving letters indicate that he offered courses on Vergil's *Aeneid* and rhetoric during his tenure there.[78]

In Basel, he befriended fellow student Sebastian Brant, who later became famous as the author of *Ship of Fools* (1494). Frequent correspondents, they were united by their enthusiastic promotion of humanist studies and their careers in government. It is also possible that he studied in Basel under the innovative theologian Wessel Gansfort (ca. 1419–89), one of the few professors of the fifteenth century who had managed to learn at least some Hebrew.[79] According to a mysterious comment from Reuchlin, Gansfort once discouraged him from studying Hebrew.[80]

During the Basel years, Reuchlin spent time in the shops of some of the great printers. He collaborated with Johannes Amerbach, perhaps the most ambitious Basel printer of the incunabular age, to produce a Latin dictionary. The resulting work, called the *Vocabularius breviloquus* (Concise Dictionary), was a publishing success, going through twenty-two printings from 1478 until 1504,[81] by which time it was woefully obsolete. The work, which was never published under Reuchlin's name, prefigures his future approach to philological research, namely, to compile work by other scholars. Markus Raphael Ackermann demonstrated that nearly all the legal entries in *Vocabularius breviloquus* were derived from *Vocabularius iuris utriusque* ("Dictionary for Each Law," i.e., ecclesiastical and Roman law), a work that Reuchlin did not acknowledge as a source.[82] Many other sources are given credit, the most important of which is the *Papias vocabulista*, a medieval word list. *Papias* is noteworthy for the high number of Greek and Hebrew words (all transliterated in the Roman alphabet).[83] All the Hebrew words in *Breviloquus* are from *Papias*, which in turn derived most of them from the Vulgate Bible. Thus, there is little original analysis in the lexicon, even if the attested interest in Greek and Hebrew is remarkable for this early date. There is also evidence that Amerbach and Reuchlin were planning a revision of the Greek-Latin dictionary of Joannes Crastonus.[84]

Learning Greek

As a university student, Reuchlin broke away not only from German cultural provincialism but also from Latin linguistic parochialism. This second step, which entailed a concerted effort to learn classical Greek, set him apart from other students of his generation. On the face of it, mastering ancient Greek would seem to be an insignificant accomplishment. But the rediscovery of Greek in the European Renaissance became a strong catalyst for the religious reforms of the sixteenth century. Some serious challenges to the dogma of the church arose when western Christians—the recognized pioneers in this movement were Valla and Erasmus—compared the Latin translation of the New Testament with the original Greek formulations. No one had done that in the west for nearly a millennium. Sure enough, the Greek text did not support many elements of doctrine as well as did the Latin translation. However predictable this result now seems to us, since doctrine had been derived largely from that Latin translation, it came as bad news, even a shock, in the Renaissance. The massive structure of the church, which was already in need of numerous repairs, had an unexpected foundation problem. When Luther attacked the penitential system of the church and specifically the misuse of indulgences, he could also use a novel weapon, the new science of the humanists—biblical philology, the study of the Bible in its original formulations. What did John the Baptist and Jesus say in Matthew's Gospel? Did they say "do penance" or "repent"? The Latin translation stated the former, suggesting that acts of satisfaction—performance of penance—were required. The original Greek said the latter, suggesting that a new state of mind—one of repentance—was necessary. One might well wonder if Luther could have conceptualized the *Ninety-five Theses* of 1517, had it not been for Erasmus's first edition of the New Testament in Greek in 1516. At the very least, the new humanist philology, with its new text of the Bible, justified subjecting the Latin church's doctrine to reevaluation.

A high point in Reuchlin's academic *cursus honorum* occurred in 1482 during his first trip to Rome. A young, unknown student in the entourage of

Eberhard the Bearded of Württemberg, he entered the classroom of the venerable Joannes Argyropoulos (1415–87) in Rome. This was a Greek seminar in the Vatican, frequented by Renaissance Italian elites, including an occasional bishop or cardinal. Argyropoulos was a Greek émigré teacher, a major force in the effort to introduce Italians to the study of Greek language and culture. When the famous scholar, known for his hauteur, made inquiry as to the visitor's identity and purpose, Reuchlin explained that he was "a German not entirely ignorant of Greek" and eager to perfect his knowledge.[85] In 1482, a German not entirely ignorant of Greek was a strange beast, and, perhaps sensing a chance to put down a northerner, Argyropoulos asked Reuchlin to read a passage from Thucydides in Greek and translate it into Latin. To the apparent astonishment of the professor, Reuchlin performed the task flawlessly, prompting Argyropoulos to proclaim: "Because of our exile, Greece has flown across the Alps."[86]

How had Reuchlin, back in 1482, come to be that strange German beast? Precisely as Argyropolous reportedly said, he had managed to study under Greek émigrés, with some of the very few who had crossed the Alps. In the mid-1470s, Paris and Basel were the only universities in northern Europe where Greek émigrés taught. Reuchlin began his Greek studies during his first year in Paris under some students of a certain Gregorios Tiphernas.[87] At best, this was a timid and certainly a truncated beginning, for serious instruction in Greek at Paris really began only with the arrival of Georgios Hermonymos (d. after 1508) in 1476, after the breakup of the scholarly circle that had formed at Rome around Cardinal Bessarion (d. 1472). Reuchlin's studies advanced when, in 1473, he transferred to the University of Basel and commenced three years of study under Andronicos Contoblacas (d. after 1477). Basel had the distinction of housing one of the largest collections of Greek manuscripts north of the Alps. The Dalmatian Cardinal Johannes Stojković of Ragusa (ca. 1390–1443), who spent many years in Basel during the council, bequeathed his Greek manuscripts to the Dominican convent of Basel in 1443.[88] Reuchlin had in his custody several manuscripts from Ragusa's gift, including a nearly complete New Testament in Greek from the twelfth century.[89] Contoblacas was an outstanding scholar and one with a measure of independence from the Greeks in Italy. He used a somewhat unusual grammar based on the system of the contemporary theologian Georgios Scholarios (ca. 1400–ca. 1473), who advanced to Gennadios II, Patriarch of Constantinople, under the Ottomans in 1454. Reuchlin's personal library included a Greek grammar by Scholarios, almost certainly a remnant of his tutelage under Contoblacas.

Thanks to Contoblacas, Reuchlin left Basel with an excellent basic knowledge of Greek. Thereafter he advanced his Greek knowledge "piecemeal"[90] through a series of encounters with other important émigré scholars. After Reuchlin returned to France in 1477 for his legal studies, he resumed his Greek studies briefly at the University of Paris, remaining for only one semester probably because he decided to study civil law, which was not taught in Paris. (Paris offered law degrees only in canon law.) Nonetheless, his Greek studies reached a very advanced level under the guidance of Georgios Hermonymos, who is now remembered as the instructor of Erasmus and Guillaume Budé. Likely, it was during this time that Reuchlin began composing his own Greek pedagogical works. The first one was probably his tract on the four dialects of ancient Greek, which survives in a manuscript copy made by one of Reuchlin's learned correspondents, the Benedictine monk Nikolaus Basellius.[91] Like the *Breviloquus*, this tract is more a compilation of older views, excerpted largely from a single Byzantine source,[92] than a fresh investigation of the subject. Using a corpus of ancient pedagogical works now labeled "Pseudo-Dositheus," Reuchlin also compiled an important set of conversations in Greek about everyday topics. Though made in France, these colloquies proved useful in Heidelberg when Reuchlin later taught Greek to a distinguished group of learners in 1496–99. The use of Greek colloquies was modeled on the pedagogical practice of memorizing Latin dialogues on ordinary topics in order to foster speaking ability in Latin. Reuchlin also assembled a manuscript of the Greek-language liturgy for St. Denis, a saint of tremendous significance in Paris. St. Denis was supposed to have been Dionysius the Areopagite mentioned in the Acts of the Apostles. At the time, most scholars in Europe thought that this very early Christian—an apostolic figure par excellence—had left behind a sizable corpus of writings, including mystical tracts and a treatise on the sacraments of the church. It was a blow to the historical anchor for the doctrine of the seven sacraments when humanist scholars, beginning with Valla, proved that these tracts were much too late to have been the work of the first-century Dionysius and were therefore not apostolic. Although Valla was authoritative as one of the founders of humanist textual criticism (and a major arbiter of literary style), Reuchlin never acknowledged any doubts about the apostolicity of the writings attributed to Dionysius the Areopagite.[93] He would ultimately portray (pseudo) Dionysius's mysticism as being compatible with aspects of Jewish Kabbalah.[94]

Spreading the Gospel of Greek

Reuchlin taught Greek privately while studying civil law in Orléans and Poitiers perhaps in order to pay his bills but also with a certain amount of missionary zeal. His émigré teachers gave the neophyte instructor their blessing, with Contoblacas writing an endorsement in Greek that reads a little bit like Jesus' Great Commission, though in this case the charge is to spread the Greek language among northerners.[95] Reuchlin was among the first non-Greeks to teach Greek, just as he would later be one of the first non-Jews to teach Hebrew. For his part, Hermonymos sent the young man a manuscript copy of Theodore Gaza's Greek grammar, a work that would end up in print and have an impact on early generations of students of Greek. But probably because it was rather too complex for rank beginners, Reuchlin composed his own grammar, the *Micropaedia*, which, as the title suggests, was probably a brief outline of Greek grammar.[96] It has not survived the centuries.

His subsequent journeys to Italy included important efforts to establish contacts with major Greek philologists. It is hard to tell if Reuchlin learned much more Greek under anyone's tutelage, though there is no reason to doubt that he really did attend Argyropoulos's seminar in Rome. Unquestionably, he was most eager for Italians or Italian Greeks to give their blessing to him as a philologist. In 1490/91, while on a long sojourn in Italy, he made contact with Demetrios Chalcondyles, then famous as the editor of Homer (1488). In a later, and highly significant, effort at self-promotion, Reuchlin published a complimentary letter Chalcondyles had sent him in Greek.[97]

It was in Rome in 1490 that Ermolao Barbaro, a Venetian scholar, bestowed the Greek sobriquet "Capnion" on Reuchlin.[98] "Capnion" means "little smoke" in ancient Greek, with the "*ōn*" ending being a common diminutive suffix. This is supposed to capture the German sense of "Reuchlin" as "little smoke." The "lin" would be the diminutive ending, more familiar in the High German "lein," with "Reuch" being understood as an umlauted "Rauch," meaning "smoke." Reuchlin was exorbitantly proud that a famous Italian humanist had rechristened him with a Greek sobriquet. Reuchlin had already been using a Roman tripartite form of his name—Joannis Reuchlinus Phorcensis—and now he could airbrush away the Germanic element of his identity and replace it with Greek. Humanists wanted to connect everything possible—especially themselves—to ancient Greek and Roman culture. After he was ennobled, Reuchlin began using a coat of arms that depicted an altar with a little curl of smoke rising; this bore the Augustan sounding label "Ara Capnionis," the Altar of Reuchlin (see Figure 2.3).

Reuchlin was respected for his Latin style, but unlike many humanists who avoided their native vernacular he also wrote German with elegance and ease. (Erasmus, for example, did not publish a single word in his native Dutch or any other vernacular language.) It is rather distinctive that Reuchlin translated a few Greek texts into German for circulation at German courts. The fact

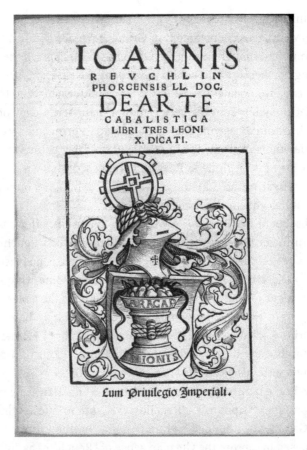

FIGURE 2.3. Johannes Reuchlin's coat of arms, showing the "altar of little smoke" (i.e., of Reuchlin). Reuchlin, *Art of the Kabbalah* (Hagenau: Anshelm, 1517), title page. Courtesy of the Klau Library, Hebrew Union College-Jewish Institute of Religion, Cincinnati, Ohio.

is that, while rulers such as Eberhard the Bearded and Philipp of the Palatinate desired polished humanists for various court functions, they themselves and most of the German nobility around 1500 did not know much Latin. For Eberhard, Reuchlin translated the first two Philippics of Demosthenes, which are lost,[99] as well as Demosthenes' first Olynthian speech, which has survived in a manuscript.[100] All of these works belong to Demosthenes' famous attempts to rouse the Athenians in 349/8 B.C.E. to oppose the growing might of Philip of Macedon before it was too late. Reuchlin recreated them for the Imperial Diet of Worms in 1495 in an attempt to support an imperially sponsored crusade against the Ottoman Turks.[101] It is one of the first cases in modern times that an ancient Greek tract was used in an effort to frame a discussion of political policy. Reuchlin also translated some Greek classics for the court of Philipp of the Palatinate, the most astonishing of which was a German verse translation of the duel between Menelaus and Paris in the third book of the *Iliad*.[102] One of Reuchlin's patrons would express amazement that such a thing was even possible. But this miraculous translation has been lost too.

Only his Latin translations of Greek made it into print during the Renaissance. He translated the *Battle of Frogs and Mice*, a work then thought to be by Homer, and published it in 1510.[103] In 1512, Anshelm printed Reuchlin's translation of a Pseudo-Hippocrates tract on the four humors, a theory of the human body that dominated learned circles in the early Renaissance.[104]

A special category in Reuchlin's Greek studies was early Christian writers, including the authors of the New Testament. Above all else, the return to the historical sources for Christian culture was the goal that animated his study of Greek as well as Hebrew. As early as 1488, he wrote the following passage in a letter to Jacob Lauber, the prior of the Carthusian Charterhouse in Basel and former rector of the university:

> I have decided that we must take refuge in the saving statutes of the new law [i.e., the New Testament], finding, as it were, asylum there. Writers of every other genre, be they historical, poetic, rhetorical, philo-sophical, or prophetic, are of secondary rank. There is nothing I would prefer more than that every professing Christian consider that kind of writing to be the most important which the first followers of Christ, inspired by the Holy Spirit, wrote down. Otherwise, let every law be inferior. Let the volumes of the apostles alone live and grow in us.[105]

He had in his custody some extremely significant Greek Christian manu-scripts, including the best Basel codex of the New Testament,[106] the very man-uscript that would be a major source for Erasmus's first edition of the Bible in Greek. Even more distinctive was his manuscript of the *Acts of the Council of Ephesus* (431), which included Proclus's sermon to the heretic Nestorius, a work that he translated into Latin for Jacob Lauber.[107] Proclus's sermon, a laudation of the Virgin Mary, features a defense of the term "God-bearer" as opposed to the heretical Nestorian term "Christ-bearer," concepts newly relevant in the west because of the controversy over Mary's nature. Was she conceived "immacu-lately," without original sin? Reuchlin also translated Nestorius's second letter to Cyril, a work that still survives in manuscript.[108] In 1513, Reuchlin published a Latin translation of an otherwise unknown Greek biography of Constantine, the emperor who made Christianity the quasi-official religion of the empire. Like its subject, the biography is a little mysterious—it was probably written in the fifteenth century—and Reuchlin seems to have overrated its value.

Toward the end of his life, Reuchlin also completed two major translations of Athanasius (d. 373), in part inspired by presumed parallels between his struggles and those of Athanasius, who during the long controversies over Arian theology was repeatedly accused of heresy and persecuted by some eastern Christians, but ultimately vindicated.[109] The first work was Athanasius's popular commentary on the Psalms, *Epistle to Marcellinus on the Psalms*,[110] which offers a comprehensive approach to Christian exegesis of Jewish Scripture (even though Athanasius accomplishes this exclusively through analysis of the Psalms). Reuchlin dedicated the publication to Jacob Questenberg at the Vatican court in recognition of their lifelong scholarly affinities and also in order to strengthen support for his case before the Roman curia.[111] The other is a lesser-known work attributed to Athanasius, *On Various Questions*, which is a miscellany of explanations of important doctrines in Christianity.[112] The extensive annotations to this work contain Reuchlin's final effort to use Jewish theology and philosophy (especially Maimonides) to elucidate Christian thought. He dedicated it in 1519 (before the final adjudication of his own case) to Albrecht of Brandenburg, archbishop of Mainz, to commemorate the archbishop's elevation to the College of Cardinals and to celebrate his patronage of German humanism.[113]

Reuchlin also attempted to establish an academy for advanced Greek study in the Holy Roman Empire. He may have seen this as a possible new vocation for himself when political upheavals in Württemberg forced his first voluntary exile. He spent the years 1496–97 and 1499 mostly in Heidelberg, where he conducted Greek seminars for some prominent scholars, including Johannes von Dalberg, bishop of Worms, and Johannes Trithemius (1462–1516), abbott of Sponheim. On 23 April 1499, Reuchlin wrote an intriguing reply to a lost letter from Aldo Manuzio, the most important printer of Greek texts in the early Renaissance.[114] (Reuchlin's library would ultimately have at least thirty-two Greek Aldine imprints.[115]) The letter indicates that Manuzio had enlisted Reuchlin's support in an effort to establish a Greek academy in Germany under the patronage of Emperor Maximilian, even though it would entail the relocation of his press.[116] Apparently, Reuchlin sought an audience with Maximilian to discuss this grandiose scheme but the emperor was preoccupied fighting a French army at the time. Reuchlin held out some hope that this military emergency explained his lack of progress, but overall his reply was pessimistic: "you know Germany. It hasn't stopped being uncultured....We are not worthy of you."[117] And, indeed, Germany did not get the Aldine press. Nothing more came of this effort, even though Maximilian would soon establish a humanist college at Vienna in 1501, but under the direction of Conrad Celtis.

Reuchlin promoted Greek studies until the very end of his life. In 1519, a political meltdown in Württemberg, including several military occupations of Stuttgart, forced Reuchlin into another "voluntary" exile. This time he went to Ingolstadt, where he became professor of Greek and Hebrew for three semesters in 1520–21. According to Reuchlin, more than 300 students jammed the Greek seminar. In the aftermath of Erasmus's publication of the New Testament in Greek in 1516, interest in Greek surged. In April 1520, Reuchlin published a Greek edition of some works by Xenophon, including his version of the *Apology of Socrates*.[118] Xenophon is an ideal author for neophyte Greek students because he wrote a clear and plain Greek, an approach to style that Reuchlin very much emulated. This work, which actually goes back to Reuchlin's first efforts in Greek,[119] was printed initially for students at Ingolstadt. Then, fleeing the plague in Ingolstadt, he became professor of Greek and Hebrew at the University of Tübingen in 1521. In April 1522, just weeks before his death, he published a Greek edition of the famous exchange of speeches between Aeschines and Demosthenes,[120] intended for his students at Tübingen, also among the last works Thomas Anshelm would print in his distinguished career.

Looking back on his career in 1513 (in a letter to Jacques Lefèvre d'Etaples), Reuchlin boasted that he had been teaching Greek for forty years, and had single-handedly laid the foundation for Germans to study Greek.[121] His point, besides self-promotion, was that his inauguration of Greek studies in Germany and of Hebrew studies for all Christians was undertaken as a service to the church. Ludwig Geiger made the claim that Reuchlin's study of Greek in Basel under Contoblacas was the first time a German ever learned Greek in Germany. This deserves emphasis because, while Reuchlin has gone down in history as the father of Christian Hebrew philology, he has not received adequate recognition as a primal force behind the meteoric rise of Greek studies in northern Europe. He also gave Greek humanism a meaningful compass, one with its orientation pointing to ancient Christian writers, even as it navigated the wider sea of classical culture.

3

Humanism at Court

The pride of our country and our letters.
                    —Sebastian Brant, addressing Johannes Reuchlin,
                                                  1 October 1495

Separating Reuchlin's scholarly and literary aspirations from his stellar career at the highest level of German politics would run the danger of introducing an unnecessary and even false distinction. At every stage of professional life, Reuchlin's success depended equally on his legal expertise and his distinction as a humanist scholar and writer. Consequently, as we will see, his lifelong efforts at academic advancement were an inherent component of his offices as governmental minister and jurist. In addition to its immediate relevance to the study of civil law, humanism was rapidly laying a common foundation for elite European culture and politics. Governments needed representation from highly cultured emissaries and advocates, professionals who had not only mastered the complexities of Roman law but also attained the academic and literary sophistication to interact effectively with other courtiers and lawyers throughout the empire and Europe. While it is easy to see the direct advantages of rhetoric, moral philosophy, and history as preparatory courses for careers in government, it is perhaps even more important to observe the indirect impact of humanism as it came to inform the culture of European governments in the broadest terms.

Reuchlin was a powerful and innovative scholar but also a deeply political animal. During nearly fifteen years as councilor to the duke of Württemberg (1482–96), he was concerned with maintenance or repair—and occasionally redesign—of the machinery of interterritorial relations, a demanding occupation because the Holy Roman Empire had so many parts. Moreover, while the devil of his world was the empire's complexity, his adopted home of Württemberg labored under the additional challenge of being a divided territory engaged in an arduous struggle over reunification. To compound the difficulties, Eberhard the Bearded of Württemberg had no legitimate male heirs, no trivial matter for an early modern state.

The Holy Roman Empire was less an empire with centralized power and more a congeries of largely sovereign territorial entities. In many ways, the imperial constitution was functioning reasonably well, but the boundaries of territories were not particularly stable, nor were the levels or types of governmental authority within the territories at all uniform. By the end of the fifteenth century, there had been many outbreaks of violence between members of the empire, and some were mired in a near constant state of hostility. A few important territories experienced division, as in the major split between Electoral Saxony and Ducal Saxony that was formalized in 1485, while others, especially dynastic families with multi-territorial interests such as the Wittelsbachers (in Bavaria and the Palatinate) and the Hapsburgs, aggressively sought to acquire additional territories, often through peaceful means such as purchase or dynastic marriage, but also by military might. In one such event that disrupted Reuchlin's life, Duke Ulrich of Württemberg (1487–1550) paid a heavy price for his occupation of the free imperial city of Reutlingen in 1519, losing control of his duchy to the Hapsburgs until 1534.

With the constant irritant of conflict within the empire and a growing threat from foreign powers, many territorial governments accepted the need for constitutional reforms, even as they remained wary of augmenting the emperor's authority. Historians now refer to this diffuse but pervasive effort as the "Reichsreform" movement.[1] A significant constitutional reform during Reuchlin's career was the formation in 1495 of the Imperial Chamber Court, which, as the supreme court for arbitrating disagreements between territories, was designed to support the "permanent peace"—the *Ewiger Landfriede*—that Maximilian declared between all entities of the empire that same year. Prior to 1495, territories of the Holy Roman Empire, legally permitted to wage warfare against each other, often got into destructive disputes, as befell Reuchlin's homeland of Baden when it foolishly invaded the Palatinate in 1462. In the late fifteenth century, parts of the empire formed regional leagues, typically called "circles," in order to help preserve the peace by providing for mutual defense and for judicial arbitration of disputes. Even after the reforms of 1495, the circles continued to function as the main mechanisms for keeping the peace, for most cases of arbitration were settled within the court of an imperial circle, even if appeals to the Imperial Chamber Court were allowed. In Reuchlin's southwest, territories formed the powerful Swabian League in 1487, which, among other functions, sponsored a court of arbitration and enforced its rulings.[2]

These larger political developments in the Holy Roman Empire also impacted policies on Jewish residency. As territories increased their sovereignty, the Jewish question frequently attained more urgency on the local level. A general trend around 1500 was for the territories and cities to resent imperial authority over Jews within their boundaries. Sometimes territories managed to acquire from the emperor the right to regulate Jewish life in their jurisdictions but this was not always the case and, even when it was, the territories had trouble retaining those regalian powers. The prospect of ending the possibility of imperial meddling (which included imperial taxing authority over Jews) within their boundaries emerged as yet another reason for individual territories to desire an end to their Jewish communities.[3]

The House of Württemberg

In the early 1480s, as Reuchlin was completing his university studies, the demand for highly educated governmental ministers was increasing dramatically. The aristocratic knight of the Middle Ages, with his military prowess, was now taking his seat on the privy council next to a powerfully educated commoner armed with law books. In particular, diplomacy was rapidly becoming acutely dependent on legal expertise, as territories were increasingly obliged to settle their differences in court. With his licentiate degree in law from Poitiers and, then, his doctorate from Tübingen, Reuchlin was able to enter governmental service in a relatively high orbit, serving as minister/councilor ("Rat") in the government of Württemberg (1482–96) and as judge for the Swabian League (1502–13); for a one-year span (1497–98), he also held an important appointment as councilor to Elector Philipp of the Palatinate (1448–1508).

From both cultural and political perspectives, Reuchlin and Eberhard the Bearded of Württemberg (1445–96) were exceedingly well matched. Eberhard, count and duke of Württemberg, is still best remembered for the visionary act of founding the University of Tübingen in 1477,[4] an institution destined for greatness in European history. Eberhard supported humanist studies at the university and, although he never learned Latin,[5] developed an abiding interest in the classics in German translation. A modern scholar has even claimed that Eberhard's was the first systematic program of translating the classics in

German cultural history.[6] He was drawn especially to ancient history and was such an avid Bible reader that he commissioned a new translation, even though several German Bibles were available, including, since 1466, several in the new print format. Eberhard, however, was in all likelihood no lover of Jewish learning, for Reuchlin once noted that he avoided displaying his Hebrew studies at court.[7] He also expelled the Tübingen Jewish community on the occasion of the foundation of the university.

While Eberhard admired classical learning, his initial motivation for founding the university was pragmatic: to educate clergy and lawyers in order to enhance the stability and stature of Württemberg.[8] Eberhard knew the cultural sophistication of the Italian Renaissance courts firsthand in part from his marriage to Barbara Gonzaga (1455–1503),[9] daughter of Marquis Ludovico II Gonzaga (1412–78) of Mantua, and in part from his journeys to Italy, including the wedding trip to Mantua in 1474, where he witnessed the flowering of Renaissance culture. Consequently, he was one of the first northerners to grasp that the administrative and diplomatic corps at European courts were expected to contribute to the advancement of humanist arts and scholarship. By the mid-1480s, even though his noble ministers still wielded the most influence, Eberhard had assembled a court with the largest number and highest percentage of educated, non-noble ministers in Germany, as Johannes Trithemius wrote: "Among all the German princes of our time that I know, there was none who adorned his court with so many educated people of every type with doctorates in so many disciplines as did the count of Württemberg."[10] A statistical study of the entourages of the various princes and free imperial cities at the 1495 Diet of Worms has indicated that Trithemius's claim was, if anything, an understatement.[11]

Eberhard's ambitions translated into a general expansion of the court's political activities. Among his goals were unifying Württemberg, reforming the Swabian monasteries, founding the university, cultivating strong ties to the Hapsburgs, and even helping to form the Swabian League. Eberhard also introduced legal reforms for Württemberg and reconstituted its central court of law (the "Hofgericht"), the legal court of highest appeal within the territorial state, implementing its first procedural code in 1475.[12] His capstone achievement was the 1495 elevation of Württemberg from a county to a duchy.

Prior to that, Eberhard succeeded in reuniting Württemberg, which since 1442 had been divided into two entities, Württemberg-Urach and Württemberg-Stuttgart. He achieved this consolidation as a result of superior military strength and patient diplomacy, gradually forcing his cousin Eberhard the Younger (1445–1504), count of Württemberg-Stuttgart, into the Münsingen Treaty of 1482, which granted Eberhard sovereignty over most of the Württemberg lands and allowed him, as of 1483, to rule from Stuttgart. In return, the Münsingen Treaty mandated that Eberhard the Younger would succeed Eberhard the Bearded.

Reuchlin entered the service of Eberhard of Württemberg because of his unusual accomplishments in humanist rhetoric. His earliest known contacts with the court resulted from his matriculation at the University of Tübingen on 9 December 1481. Although Tübingen awarded him the doctorate of law in 1484 or early 1485, Reuchlin became a member of the university probably in order to accept an innovative position, defined by Eberhard's statues for the university, as lecturer in the humanities.[13] According to Melanchthon, three leading scholars and ministers associated with the University of Tübingen, Gabriel Biel (ca. 1420/25–95), Peter Jacobi (ca. 1459–1509), and Johannes Nauclerus (ca. 1425–1510), immediately urged the count to name Reuchlin to his 1482 embassy to Rome.[14] Biel was a famous theologian who as a close advisor to Eberhard had directed the establishment of the Brethren of the Common Life in Württemberg,[15] and Johannes Nauclerus, apparently Reuchlin's mentor at the time, was professor of canon law, founding rector, and, as of 1482, chancellor of the university. Nauclerus's brother, Dr. Ludwig Nauclerus (ca. 1425/30–1512), was provost at the collegiate church (Stiftskirche) in Stuttgart and chancellor at Eberhard's court.[16] According to Melanchthon, Reuchlin was appointed to the embassy primarily because he spoke Latin more elegantly than the other Swabian academics.[17]

Although Eberhard, who had undertaken a much publicized pilgrimage to Jerusalem in 1468, journeyed to Rome at least in part as an act of faith and obedience, his political goal was to secure papal endorsement for revising the statutes for the University of Tübingen and adjusting the charter of the St. George Chapter in order to integrate the collegiate church, with its substantial endowments, into the operation of the university. In that regard, the embassy was a complete success, and Sixtus IV even saw fit to honor Eberhard with the *Golden Rose*, a distinction bestowed on princes for their loyalty to the Holy See. Sixtus IV's Rome was probably an inspiring confirmation of the political ascendance of humanism to the twenty-seven-year-old Reuchlin and the entire Swabian court. During the reign of Sixtus (1471–84), progress on the task of reviving the city of Rome was visible for the first time. In addition to important improvements to the infrastructure, such as constructing the Borgo Sant'Angelo and the eponymous Ponte Sisto across the Tiber, Sixtus commissioned several new churches in a recognizably Renaissance style, including Santa Maria del Popolo (begun ca. 1472), Ospedale di Santo Spirito (1475), and the epochal Sistine Chapel (completed 1481), forever after the symbol of papal preeminence. It was Sixtus, too, who established the Vatican Library (after Nicholas V first articulated the need for such an institution).[18] It was in the Vatican Library that Reuchlin, as recounted in chapter 2, represented the ascending cultural power of Württemberg so brilliantly at Argyropoulos's Greek seminar.[19]

Upon returning to Germany, Reuchlin embarked in earnest on his career as councilor to Eberhard. Although this meant that henceforth he would work primarily in administrative, juridical, and diplomatic capacities from a base in Stuttgart, it hardly divorced him from the academic world of the University of Tübingen. Initially, he continued to hold a teaching position for law at Tübingen, but in 1483, he was appointed associate justice at the Württemberg central court of law ("Hofgericht") in Stuttgart, a position that permitted him also to serve Eberhard as councilor. A record of those in the employ of the County of Württemberg, the so-called "Book of Servants" ("Dienerbuch"), formally lists him as of 1484/85 as a councilor or minister ("Rat"). His annual salary grew steadily. In 1484–86, it was 50 gulden; in 1487, 70 gulden; in 1488–89, 90 gulden; in 1490–92, 96 gulden; and as of 1494, it was 100 gulden.[20] Other ministers with doctorates in law tended to have salaries of around 150 gulden and permanent appointments, whereas Reuchlin's were for one year. Thus it is likely that Reuchlin's stature was initially just outside the innermost circle of Eberhard's advisors, but that was probably no longer true after around 1486, when he was increasingly assigned to highly sensitive matters.

The surviving records for Reuchlin's career as minister indicate that he traveled frequently for the court.[21] In the years 1483–86, he is known to have handled matters in the following places, sometimes on loan as a councilor to another court: Weil, Ravensburg, Munich, Eichstätt, Landshut, Pforzheim, Heidelberg, and the Benedictine abbey at Murrhardt (about twenty-five miles northeast of Stuttgart).[22] In 1483, Reuchlin endured the misadventure of being incarcerated by the imperial city of Ravensburg, furious that he, as the city's plenipotentiary for a case before Emperor Friedrich's court, agreed to a settlement the city deemed insufficient. In order to secure Reuchlin's release, the emperor had to threaten Ravensburg with force.[23] An embassy to Munich in 1484 was an important assignment, for Reuchlin was to consult with Duke Albrecht IV over Count Eberhard the Younger's attempts to undermine the Münsingen Treaty.[24] Albrecht's wife, Kunigunde, would later play a pivotal role in the anti-Jewish agitation of 1509–10.

One of Reuchlin's specialties was judicial arbitration of disputes between Württemberg and other territories. In 1490, he represented Württemberg in a contest of the feudal-lordship, here defined as stewardship ("Kastenvogt"), over the large monastery of Zwiefalten. With the support of the monastery itself, Austria was claiming overlordship. The surviving court records show that Reuchlin, assisted by other lawyers, mounted a vigorous defense of Württemberg's claim. After formal presentations of the case, the arbitrators suspended deliberations, pending collection of further evidence. As frequently happened in fifteenth-century civil litigation, the parties then settled out of court, in this case as part of the Nuremberg Treaty of 1491. Probably in the interest of strengthening ties with Württemberg, Austria surrendered its claim to Zwiefalten without any compensatory consideration.[25]

Reuchlin also represented Württemberg in several cases involving the Wittelsbach dynasty in the Palatinate, then an aggressive force that Eberhard had to reckon with in his every move. One case concerned road access for Württemberg traders passing through the Palatinate. In contravention of a regulatory treaty, the Palatinate unilaterally changed the trade route from Stuttgart to Frankfurt, a disruptive provocation because Frankfurt was the center of commerce and trading in the Holy Roman Empire. Württemberg prevailed in this case, although it did not recover its court expenses. The other case was a challenge from Württemberg over hunting rights in a particular area (Heuchelberg), the outcome of which is not known.[26] Although these are rather petty affairs, any dispute between Württemberg and the Palatinate was sensitive.

As Eberhard's trusted councilor, Reuchlin was frequently called upon to resolve internal dynastic issues in the House of Württemberg. Württemberg's greatest political liability was that none of the men in line to succeed Eberhard were fit to govern. Count Heinrich of Württemberg (ca. 1446–1519), Eberhard's cousin, developed serious psychological disabilities, as did his other male cousin, the future Duke Eberhard II, called the Younger (1445–1504; r. 1496–98), and Count Heinrich's son, the future Duke Ulrich (1487–1550; r. 1498–1519, 1534–50). The brutality and incompetence of Eberhard's two immediate successors undid almost all the progress he had achieved for the duchy. On 24 December 1489, Eberhard assigned Reuchlin the task of notifying Heinrich that he was being removed from the line of succession (where he evidently stood as second in line after his brother Eberhard the Younger, who, like Eberhard the Bearded, had no legitimate heirs).[27] In that same year, Heinrich viciously assaulted an official of the Palatinate, a certain Jacob von Rathsamhausen, leaving the victim crippled for life and Württemberg liable for damages of 3,900 florins.[28] Reuchlin, who also shouldered the impossible task of defending Heinrich in the resulting trial on 27 February 1490 in Heidelberg,[29] wrote to Eberhard on 12 April 1490 to lay out legal arguments for having Heinrich declared mentally incompetent, enclosing German translations of sections from the Corpus iuris civilis regulating the removal of rulers suffering from mental incapacity.[30] To make matters worse, Eberhard received a report in

July 1490 that Heinrich was surreptitiously trying to sell Württemberg territory in Alsace (Reichenweiler) to the Palatinate, Eberhard's bitter rival.[31] In August 1490, Eberhard arrested Heinrich and incarcerated him in the castle-keep at Hohen Urach. In October 1492, in response to Reuchlin's petition, Emperor Friedrich III ratified all the measures taken to declare Eberhard the legal guardian of Heinrich on grounds of mental incompetence.[32]

Eberhard the Younger, first in line to succeed Eberhard the Bearded, was also unfit to rule and had gradually lost authority over various small entities within Württemberg. In 1486, utterly discredited, Eberhard the Younger was stripped of his last territorial authority after he harassed a Dominican convent in Kirchheim. The Münsingen Treaty of 1482 had placed the diplomatic seal on Württemberg-Urach's hegemony over Württemberg-Stuttgart and established a de facto unified territory, which Eberhard the Bearded ruled from his new residence in Stuttgart. Now, fearing for the future of Württemberg, Eberhard the Bearded compelled Eberhard the Younger to enter into another treaty on the permanent unification of the territory, the Esslingen Treaty of 2 September 1492. According to the Esslingen agreement, the succession was set for Eberhard the Younger followed by Heinrich's son Ulrich, but with the imposition of a governing council during the term of Eberhard the Younger's reign. By 18 October 1492, Reuchlin had secured the necessary imperial ratification of the treaty, a major accomplishment.

Previously, Reuchlin had played an important role in Eberhard the Bearded's efforts to restrain his cousin. In 1488, Eberhard the Bearded discovered that Conrad Holzinger, a dissolute Augustinian friar who served as Eberhard the Younger's chief councilor, happened to be in Mainz.[33] With Reuchlin's aid, Eberhard persuaded the archbishop of Mainz to authorize Holzinger's incarceration on charges of clerical improprieties and to have him extradited to Württemberg, where he was imprisoned at Hohen Tübingen, the fortress castle on the hills above the Neckar River. When Eberhard the Younger became duke in 1496, he rehabilitated his advisor, an action that drove Reuchlin from Stuttgart into voluntary but necessary exile in the Palatinate.

Reuchlin was also assigned the case of the lapsed nun Katherine of Württemberg (1441–97), the half-sister of Eberhard the Younger. With the possibility that she would undermine the process of unifying Württemberg, it fell to Reuchlin to secure a signed affidavit renouncing all claims to any territorial inheritance. When she refused to cooperate, Reuchlin resorted to strong-arm tactics, securing papal authorization for her arrest as a runaway nun and holding it over her head as a palpable threat. Finally, in February 1489, Katherine complied.

The excellent legal reputation of his court, moreover, put Eberhard the Bearded in demand as an arbitrator of disputes between territories in the empire. We know of Reuchlin's involvement in three such cases, two of which involved some of the most powerful princes in the empire: a conflict between the elector-archbishop of Trier and the elector-archbishop of Cologne in 1487; and a dispute between the elector-archbishop of Trier and the elector-count of the Palatinate over feudal rights in two small locals (Winnenberg and Bilstein) in 1488.[34]

Diplomacy and Humanist Culture

Reuchlin's embassies allowed him to participate directly in the international culture of humanism, often called the *res publica literaria*.[35] In the early Renaissance, contact between governmental ministers was a major conduit for the spread of the new learning. Taking advantage of his three trips to Rome, Reuchlin developed a network of acquaintances among Italian humanists, including such famous men as Joannes Argyropoulos, Ermolao Barbaro, Demetrios Chalcondyles, Marsilio Ficino, Aldo Manuzio, Lorenzo de' Medici, and Giovanni Pico della Mirandola. Reuchlin's correspondence offers something of a Who's Who of early German humanism as well—Rudolf Agricola, Heinrich Bebel, Sebastian Brant, Conrad Celtis, Johannes von Dalberg, Desiderius Erasmus, Conrad Peutinger, Jacob Wimpfeling number among his correspondents. Among his Paris contacts were the humanists Guillaume Cop, Robert Gaguin, Georgios Hermonymos, and, above all, Jacques Lefèvre d'Etaples.

The primary goal of his nearly yearlong embassy to Rome in 1490 was educational, but he also represented Württemberg at Pope Innocent VIII's "Turk Congress," an assembly that convened on 25 March 1490 to assess the viability of launching a crusade in southeast Europe, but produced no tangible results. Reuchlin's principal charge was to assist Ludwig Wirtemberger, the illegitimate son of Eberhard the Bearded, during his advanced university studies in Rome.[36] Ludwig possessed the intellect and character that would have made him a worthy successor to his father. And, although succession was extremely unlikely, Eberhard the Bearded nevertheless expended considerable effort on behalf of his son, carefully supervising his legal education in France and Italy and arranging for Ludwig to be declared legitimate by the emperor in 1484. Under Reuchlin's guidance, he was awarded the doctorate in both canon and civil law in Rome in 1490, but all these efforts came to naught, as Ludwig predeceased his father in spring 1495.

During the 1490 residency in Rome, Reuchlin pursued his own studies with several Italian humanists, devoting himself in particular to Latin and Greek literature with the renowned scholar Ermolao Barbaro. Barbaro, who was serving as the Venetian ambassador to the Vatican, performed Reuchlin's "humanist baptism" in Rome, giving him the new Greek identity of "Capnion" as a translation of "Reuchlin" (see chapter 2).

In the context of his cultural-political embassy in Rome, Reuchlin was not only deepening his knowledge of Greek but also emerging as an internationally recognized scholar. While he remained virtually unpublished until 1494,[37] he had immersed himself since 1484 in the humanist literary cult of epistolary friendship. In 1514, he would publish *The Letters of Distinguished Men*, a volume of elegant letters from his erudite humanist friends to display his cultural and political prominence throughout Germany and beyond. During this embassy to Rome, he struck up a friendship that would last more than two decades as a literary letter exchange with a young German humanist named Jacob Questenberg, who then worked in the papal chancellery and would steadily advance in the curia to be papal secretary in 1504 and *clericus collegii*, head of the secretariat for the College of Cardinals, by 1514.[38] Questenberg venerated Reuchlin, addressing him as "Magnifice vir et doctor excellentissime" ("Magnificent man and most excellent doctor"),[39] and Reuchlin, generous senior scholar that he was becoming, always wrote encouragingly to the younger man. Over time, the value of this friendship increased since Questenberg later worked with the ecclesiastical princes who would decide Reuchlin's heresy case at Rome.

About a year after returning to Stuttgart from Rome, Reuchlin was dispatched to the imperial court at Linz, Austria, this time leaving Swabia behind for well over a year, from early 1492 until the autumn of 1493. Even though Friedrich III was slowly dying and the court was in decline, imperial business had to proceed.[40] Initially, Reuchlin's mission was to manage negotiations on behalf of Württemberg and the entire Swabian League concerning the territorial aggression of Duke Albrecht of Bavaria-Munich.[41] In 1486 Albrecht seized the free imperial city of Regensburg and declared it Bavarian territory. Regensburg was a wealthy city, albeit in decline, as well as home to one of the most important Jewish communities in the empire. The Swabian League was finally preparing to drive Albrecht out by force, for Emperor Friedrich agreed to place the duke, who was also his son-in-law, under imperial ban in early 1492, thus legalizing any military action against him. Fortunately, on 25 May 1492 through Maximilian's arbitration, Regensburg's independence was restored without the Swabian League resorting to invasion.[42]

But once again the most lasting achievement of Reuchlin's lengthy embassy lay in his humanist studies, this time in his goal of advancing biblical research. Reuchlin devoted nearly an entire year at Friedrich's court to the systematic study of Hebrew under his revered teacher, Jacob ben Jehiel Loans, a prominent rabbi and personal physician to the emperor.[43] Reuchlin was still in Linz, still studying under Loans, when Friedrich died on 19 August 1493, making Rabbi Loans, so to speak, attending physician at the end of one age and at the birth of another. But before that, Loans had arranged for Friedrich to honor Reuchlin with a sumptuous gift: a late twelfth-century manuscript of the Tanakh, certainly the most valuable book Reuchlin would ever own.[44] According to Melanchthon, "The old and wise emperor took delight in the scholarship of the German man."[45] Linz also became a milestone in Reuchlin's life when the emperor elevated him to the nobility as a "Count Palatine" on 24 October 1492. In an unusual gesture of favor, Reuchlin's ennoblement was declared hereditary, his brother Dionysius was included in the patent, and the emperor empowered Reuchlin to create ten further counts on his own authority.[46]

Reuchlin also represented Württemberg at two of the most important imperial diets of the fifteenth century, Frankfurt in 1486 and Worms in 1495. The Hapsburg dynasty scored a major success at the Diet of Frankfurt: the election of Maximilian as king of the empire, even though his father, Emperor Friedrich, was still alive.[47] Although the election proceeded smoothly, with all six electors in attendance casting their vote for Maximilian, it was highly irregular since, according to the Golden Bull, a new king was to be elected once the emperor had died. (At the time, the electors' choice for emperor received only the title of king, "rex Romanorum"; the king, also known as the emperor-elect, was raised to the title of emperor by papal coronation.) Apparently, bribes partially accounted for this success, so many that the electors were relieved of the obligation to swear a customary oath that they had received no assurances or gifts in return for their vote.[48] Ironically, another incentive for the six electors was that the only viable alternative to Maximilian, Matthias Corvinus, king of Hungary and king of Bohemia, appeared more powerful than Maximilian and therefore more threatening to the princes' interests. Corvinus was then waging a successful war against the Hapsburg home territories ("Erbländer") in the southeast and, in a painful blow, had managed to take Vienna, the unofficial capital, in June 1485. He planned to mount a challenge to the Hapsburgs and stand for election to succeed Friedrich. Again acting unconstitutionally, Friedrich simply did not invite Corvinus to the diet, even though the king of Bohemia was, ex officio, one of the seven imperial electors.[49] Reuchlin did not acknowledge that Emperor Friedrich took any liberties with the Golden Bull, composing instead a highly favorable account of all Hapsburg machinations. In that regard, he was reflecting the policy of Count Eberhard's court, which had aligned itself strategically with Friedrich and Maximilian.[50]

Reuchlin created an extensive narrative of the Diet of Frankfurt (and its aftermath) in his dispatches to Stuttgart.[51] Written in an appealing style, the reports are factual and descriptive, largely free of interpretive commentary. For example, Reuchlin noted the scandal of Bohemia's absence from the election by poignantly writing, without further comment, that "Bohemia's place was empty."[52] It had been a very long time (some forty-six years) since the last election and coronation of a Roman king, which may have motivated Reuchlin to devote special care to his accounts of the ceremonies, especially the coronation in Aachen, the jousting, and, most vividly, Maximilian's Burgundian-style entry into Frankfurt,[53] all of which had the power to evoke Emperor Maximilian's moniker as "the last knight" of the Middle Ages. According to Reuchlin, the jousting, which took place later in Cologne, did not go particularly well for Maximilian. Against his father's adamant wish, he entered the lists surreptitiously against Elector Philipp of the Palatinate, who knocked the emperor-elect nearly senseless from his mount.[54]

Nine years later, Reuchlin also participated in the historic 1495 Diet of Worms, one of the most important and contentious legislative assemblies in the thousand-year history of the empire.[55] In this, Maximilian's first diet as sole ruler after Friedrich's death, nothing less than reform of the constitution and defense of the empire stood on the agenda. Maximilian wanted to tighten his hold on the empire, in part through regularizing taxation and forcing the estates to submit their conflicts to courts for binding judgments. The estates, which were partially opposed to these ideas, also wanted to strengthen their own prerogatives and favored further limiting imperial authority by establishing a governing council for the empire (something that did happen after the 1521 Diet of Worms). Everyone agreed that real reforms were necessary, however contentious, yet the princes feared upsetting the delicate balances of power among the territories and the emperor.

The diet's legislative achievements were numerous, including establishment of the so-called "permanent peace" (*Ewiger Landfriede*) within the empire, creation of the Imperial Chamber Court as a supreme court, and a bold attempt to reform taxation. The "Common Penny," as the legislation was called, was ultimately little more than a first effort to establish an effective mechanism of uniform taxation, based on each individual's wealth.[56] For example, those with a worth of fewer than 500 gulden were assessed one shilling (1/24 of a gulden) per year; those with 500 gulden paid 1/2 of a gulden; those with 1,000 gulden paid 1 gulden; all Jews, moreover, were assessed 1 gulden (the understanding being that Jewish communities would raise the money to cover an aggregate assessment based on total population). The tax failed in large part because it could not be collected. The *Ewiger Landfriede*, however, was a turning point, and the Imperial Chamber Court (which replaced a less independent court under the king's authority) would function effectively as the court of final appeal until the dissolution of the empire in 1806. Overall, the Diet of Worms began a process (which was fairly complete by the recess of the 1555 Diet of Augsburg) that protected the rights and sovereignty of the estates of the realm. The princely estates were developing into full-fledged territorial sovereignties within the empire, but not directly under the aegis of the Hapsburg dynasty.

Worms addressed a new international crisis, one that would roil the waters of European politics for years to come. In late summer 1494, Charles VIII of France launched a military intervention in Italy, which managed, indirectly, to topple the Medicis in Florence and to strengthen French claims to sovereignty over the Kingdom of Naples. French-Hapsburg hostility had already boiled over into war over the Burgundian inheritance of Maximilian's first wife, Mary of Burgundy. In 1495, the specific rub was Maximilian's decision, formalized on 31 March 1495, to join the Holy League in an effort to drive Charles out of Italy. Charles's fortunes in Italy gave high drama to the early weeks of the diet, as reports on battles kept coming in. The estates assembled at Worms were, as a whole, not prepared to join Maximilian in waging a foreign war against Charles. They arrived at Worms with a different understanding, namely that the diet would be a brief prelude to a crusade against the Ottomans. Maximilian's announced goal was to rally the princes in Worms, proceed to Rome for the formal imperial coronation, and then liberate the Holy Land from the Turks. Such a path to imperial glory no longer looked passable once Charles VIII invaded Italy and announced his own intention of proceeding to the Holy Land. As things turned out, neither Maximilian nor Charles would ever mount a crusade to retake Palestine for Christianity.

On 26 March 1495, Maximilian opened the Diet at Worms with a speech in which he called on the estates to support him in war, first against the French and then against the Turks. This touched off bitter and chaotic disagreement, with a majority of the princes uncertain about this declaration and opposed to the empire joining the Holy League. Nor would the princes commit troops, though eventually they did authorize considerable financial support for the Italian campaign. A compelling diplomatic gesture came from the duke of Württemberg, who, drawing upon the wisdom of the Greeks to frame discussion of this troubling matter, circulated a German translation of Demosthenes' *First Olynthian Oration*, a thunderous attempt to rouse the Athenians to arms against Philip of Macedon. The moral lesson of this reference to Greek history

was that the empire should face the Turks sooner rather than later. The translator was Johannes Reuchlin, one of the very few Germans then capable of such
a feat.[57]

Reuchlin also supplied Eberhard with German versions of Demosthenes'
first two *Philippics* (also speeches opposing Philip of Macedon), which prompted
Hans von Hermansgrün, a leading diplomat at the diet,[58] to write that possibly
the princes would have acted more expeditiously to support Maximilian, "if
only you had sent your translations to each of the princes at the beginning of
the diet."[59] Even if he could be mildly critical of Maximilian, Hermansgrün
was waving a flag with the imperial double eagle, carping at the hesitancy of
the princes to act in concert with Maximilian against foreign foes. Reuchlin
also backed Maximilian in many basic ways, but seems to have been advocating financial assistance for Maximilian's Italian campaign, not participation
in it. Reuchlin thought that Maximilian, by joining the Holy League (then a
pact between the Papal States, Venice, Milan, Spain, and Maximilian), had
already exerted enough pressure to dislodge the French from Italy.[60] Though
expressed with circumspection, concern about Maximilian's politics seems
to emerge in one of Reuchlin's rhetorical sighs to Hermansgrün: "must we
always wage war?"[61] No doubt Reuchlin and the princes, for the most part, supported strengthening the empire, but not at the cost of weakening the power
of the estates.

During the diet, Reuchlin produced other German translations of Greek
works. One was a version of a dialogue by the ancient Greek writer Lucian, a
humorous debate over political rank in the Elysian Fields between Alexander
the Great, Scipio Africanus, and Hannibal. It was Reuchlin's archly humanist gift to Eberhard as Maximilian elevated him to the rank of duke on 21 July
1495.[62] The dignity would adhere henceforth to the territory of Württemberg,
and Eberhard could now take his place among the princes, voting with them
in the second estate of the diet. (The first estate consisted of the seven elector
princes, the second of the secular and ecclesiastical princes, and the third of
the free imperial cities.)

Reuchlin, however, did not attend all of the Diet of Worms, not even
the ceremony that elevated Württemberg to a dukedom. He was managing
governmental business in Stuttgart and Tübingen, perhaps pressing issues
at the Württemberg judicial court or possibly matters connected to Ludwig
Wirtemberger's unexpected death in May.[63] Reuchlin's name appears on an
official list of participants, probably an indication that he attended the first
weeks of the diet.[64] A letter from Johannes von Dalberg indicates that Reuchlin
had returned to Worms by 5 October at the latest,[65] almost certainly in order to
attend to final details of the diet, despite the earlier date of the official recess.

But by the time Worms was over and the Württemberg court had reas-
sembled in Stuttgart, Reuchlin enjoyed a new level of prestige, far beyond the
immediate ambit of his friends and colleagues. His renown as a governmental
minister was unusual for a German of his social origin. He had connections
at the highest levels of the empire and also in Italy and, to a lesser degree, in
France. More important, he had firmly established a public identity as a man
of the law, politics, and humanist scholarship.

Humanist Exile in Heidelberg

The coherence of humanist political culture is especially evident in Reuchlin's
tenure at the Heidelberg court of Elector Philipp of the Palatinate. In an unfortu-
nate turn of events for both Württemberg and Reuchlin, Eberhard the Bearded
was able to use his ducal title for but a few months. His death on 25 February
1496[66] initiated a long period of hardship for his duchy and Reuchlin's immediate flight into exile. Having earned the enmity of Eberhard II's closest advisor, Conrad Holzinger, for whose eight-year incarceration Reuchlin was partly
responsible, the scholar prudently left Württemberg before his enemies could
act. It was a mark of Reuchlin's political prominence that several German
courts were eager to welcome him. Two of Maximilian's councilors offered
to help in any way possible, with recommendations from the emperor or with
employment in an imperial capacity.[67]

But Reuchlin had established numerous scholarly and political ties to
the Heidelberg court of Elector Philipp of the Palatinate,[68] harking back at
least to 1484 when he exchanged letters with the newly appointed Heidelberg
professor Rudolf Agricola. Reuchlin's most prominent patron, however, was
Johannes von Dalberg, bishop of Worms, chancellor of Philipp's court, and
leader of the University of Heidelberg. Dalberg was renowned for his humanist education, his support of Greek studies, and, last not least, his library. As
councilor to Philipp, Dalberg contributed to the expansion of the University
of Heidelberg, decisively promoting humanist studies there. It was, in fact,
Dalberg who appointed Agricola in 1484 as one of the first professors of Greek
at a German university. In the 1484 letters to Reuchlin, Agricola had stressed
the value of studying the Bible in the original Greek and Hebrew texts, probably confirming Reuchlin's resolve to pursue, above all, a biblical humanist
focus in his future research.[69]

Dalberg exerted considerable influence over the early humanist movement
in Germany through his patronage of the Rhenish Literary Sodality, an association of humanist scholars centered in Heidelberg but with corresponding

members in other parts of the empire. Originally established in ca. 1495 by the poet-professor Conrad Celtis,[70] the Rhenish Sodality was the most elite scholarly-literary association in Germany, with such prominent members as Heinrich Bebel, Conrad Peutinger, Willibald Pirckheimer, Johannes Trithemius, Jacob Wimpfeling, and Ulrich Zasius. Among the active local members were several humanists who would not achieve fame but would be strong supporters of Reuchlin: Jacob Dracontius, Jodocus Gallus, and Joannes Vigilius. In 1489, Reuchlin sent Dalberg a treatise on the four principal dialects of ancient Greek[71] and a set of Greek dialogues designed to help students learn to speak ancient Greek.[72] In 1491, Dalberg acknowledged receipt of the unique gift of a German poetic translation of passages from Book 3 of the *Iliad*, the famous duel between Paris and Menelaus. Reuchlin's Homeric effort does not survive but it elicited a lengthy tribute from Dalberg, who was particularly impressed with Reuchlin's facility in German meter and rhyme.[73] This letter, an exemplary exhibition of the unity of humanist scholarly and political culture, also addressed a serious diplomatic problem: the escalating tensions between the Swabian League and Württemberg, on the one side, and the Wittelsbacher (in Bavaria and the Palatinate), on the other. Astutely, Dalberg was using his friendship with Reuchlin to keep open channels of communication. At the close of the letter, Dalberg even offered Reuchlin his court as a refuge, should the political situation in Württemberg ever turn dangerous—he was obviously already aware of the likely consequences of the enmity between Reuchlin and Eberhard's designated successor.[74] In 1494, Reuchlin dedicated his *Miracle-Making Word*, his inaugural Kabbalistic study, to Dalberg as well. In 1494 and 1495, moreover, Dalberg gave Reuchlin several Hebrew books, including a manuscript of Joseph Gikatilla's *Ginnat Egoz (Nut Garden)*,[75] a book of fundamental importance for Reuchlin's own *Art of the Kabbalah* (1517), and a version of Yom-Tov Lipmann's *Sefer ha-Nizzahon (Victory)*,[76] an anti-Christian polemic that Reuchlin would discuss in his *Recommendation Whether to Confiscate and Destroy All Jewish Books* (1510).

With his many accomplishments in 1496–97, Reuchlin contributed more than anyone else to increasing the prestige of Dalberg's circle. During his time in Heidelberg, he completed several translations, including a Latin version of a Greek biography of Emperor Constantine the Great, and some renderings of Latin works into German, most important the first book of Cicero's *Tusculan Disputations*, which he later presented to Elector Philipp to console him as he mourned his wife's death.[77] As early as 13 May 1496, a colleague wrote to Conrad Celtis that "Reuchlin's duty is to translate whatever the bishop (i.e., Dalberg) wishes from Greek into Latin."[78] Above all, Reuchlin offered Greek courses (and possibly some Hebrew) to students and professors alike. Among his most notable students were Johannes Eck and Franz von Sickingen, both of whom would play major roles later in his life, as well as Johannes Cuno, Thomas Truchseß,[79] and Jacob Dracontius.[80]

Reuchlin had composed surprisingly little poetry during his tenure as councilor for Württemberg.[81] Shortly before his hasty departure from Stuttgart, he claimed he felt incapable of writing a heroic poem in Eberhard's honor[82] "because the Neckar and the Swabian Alb always shun the muses, and there can be no place in Swabia for poets."[83] Although also on the Neckar River, Heidelberg proved to be a congenial home for Reuchlin's muse, for it was there that he composed his most important literary works, the Latin plays *Sergius, or the Head of the Head* (1496) and *Henno* (early 1497). *Henno*, so named for one of the main characters, became one of the earliest literary sensations of the Renaissance in Germany and is still considered canonical by literary historians. In the imprint itself, Sebastian Brant hailed Reuchlin as a German Terence, a perspective echoed by other contemporary writers, one of whom described Reuchlin as "the first and only poet among the Germans to write a comedy."[84] *Henno* would go through an impressive twenty-eight printings between 1498 and Reuchlin's death in 1522. Ten more would follow until 1615 and the play would be translated into German at least four separate times, including a spirited version by the Nuremberg shoemaker-poet Hans Sachs.[85] The bibliographic historian Josef Benzing recorded some fifteen separate printings of *Sergius* in the sixteenth century as well as a German translation from 1538 by Martin Roet.[86] In 1504, Hieronymus Emser, professor at the University of Erfurt, gave lectures on *Sergius* that the young Luther, then pursuing his bachelor's degree, attended. Although *Henno* had a few (decidedly minor) precursors, many literary historians see it as the genesis of the highly influential genre of school drama in the empire. The Pforzheim schoolmaster Georg Simler edited the play with a commentary for schoolboys. The unprecedented success of *Henno* depended on a number of factors, including the strong evocation of the Roman comedian Terence, whose plays provided the basic model for the language, versification, structure, and, above all, comic character types. Although unquestionably humanist, Reuchlin's Latinity displays a certain flexibility as well, for he allowed himself the liberty of combining Terentian and nonclassical diction and inserting non-Terentian entr'acte songs written in rhythmic medieval verse forms.[87]

Originally, Reuchlin intended both plays for production by humanist students at the university, but only *Henno* would have its premiere in Heidelberg. *Sergius* was initially held back from production on the advice of Dalberg because it satirized the mendicant orders and the cult of the saints. The comic anti-hero, a certain Buttubatta, proposes that a group of drunkard lowlifes promote the creation of a new saint's cult in order to swindle naive worshipers. Buttubatta produces a severed, decomposing human skull (later cleaned up), which is to serve as the relic of the fraudulent saint. In reality, the head belonged to a debauched monk, who at one time was the chief councilor of a ruler, therefore the subtitle *The Head of the Head*. This would-be saint thus invites comparison with Conrad Holzinger, the friar who advised Eberhard II. Nonetheless, the grotesque caricature of the corrupt monk is drawn so generally that Dalberg feared it could also anger a Heidelberg Franciscan (whose identity is no longer traceable).[88] Displaying the severed skull for most of the play, Buttubatta finally arouses the disgust of his dissolute coconspirators when he reveals the full biography of the "saint," including the lapsed monk's conversion to Islam. Reuchlin managed to slip a tribute to humanism into the play, as one student, abhorred by Buttubatta's plot and his coconspirators, expresses outrage that "you have dared to profane the sacred offices of the poets."[89]

Henno was first performed by students of the University of Heidelberg on 31 January 1497, in the presence of the rector of the university, Adam Werner von Themar, and under the auspices of Bishop Dalberg. Reuchlin designed the imprint to commemorate Dalberg's humanist circle: it begins with an introductory poem dedicating the play to the bishop and ends with a *didascalia* (program notes in the manner of Terentian comedy) celebrating Dalberg as the patron of humanist poetry at the "Heidelberg Lyceum."[90] Based in part on *Maître Pathelin*, a medieval French farce, Reuchlin's plot unfolds in a swift series of deceits perpetrated by a crafty servant named Dromo. Dromo steals eight gold florins from his master, the farmer Henno (Henno had already stolen the money from his own greedy wife), and several bolts of fine wool from a usurious cloth merchant, and then prevails over the merchant in a law case with representation from a deceitful lawyer. After cheating the lawyer out of his fee, Dromo is reconciled with Henno at the play's end when he says the stolen money can be used as the dowry for Henno's daughter, whom Dromo wished to marry. Scholars have observed that the miniature play—it runs to only 470 lines in a modern edition—touches on two social issues causing anxiety in early modern Germany: the growing entrenchment of a money-based economy and the expansion of the norms of Roman law to lower courts (thereby creating the need for professional representation even in petty civil litigation).[91] Even though this was designed to be a school play, Reuchlin openly acknowledges all manner of vices—drinking, prostitution, theft, and fraud—and does not impose a heavy-handed moral lesson on the play. The deceitful lawyer and the "evil usurer" are duped, but the comic hero prevails in his quest for money and marriage through his own dishonesty, stressing a secular ethic of success, however dubious the means. As Henno says, "We need gold no less than life."[92]

On the other hand, Martin Luther, who would quote a chorus from *Henno* in one of his letters, managed to extract a message that sounds somewhat more compatible with Christian views: "The man who is poor fears nothing and can lose nothing."[93] Above all, the lyrics of the choruses urge students to flee the acrimony of the courts—no doubt a reflection on Reuchlin's recent tribulations in Württemberg—and find refuge in a life of humanist letters.[94]

On 31 December 1497, after more than a year under the patronage of Dalberg, Elector Philipp appointed Reuchlin as his councilor and supervisor of his children's education.[95] The appointment as councilor specifically stated that Reuchlin would represent the court in domestic and foreign matters, a likely indication that an embassy to Rome was already being contemplated.[96] The position, which was limited to one year, brought Reuchlin several advantages, including a salary of 100 gulden (and some living expenses, such as use of two horses) and the opportunity to study in Rome. One of Reuchlin's princely charges, moreover, was Philipp's son Georg, the future bishop of Speyer, who would convene the court that issued the first verdict in the trials over Reuchlin's defense of Jewish writings.

Reuchlin's 1498 embassy to the Vatican gave him another important stage for his humanist writing. Elector Philipp dispatched him to Rome to resolve two significant matters for the Palatinate. First, a dispensation was needed for a dynastic marriage between Ruprecht, Philipp's son, and his first cousin, Elisabeth of Bavaria. While that was resolved, probably easily, the second matter was exceedingly problematic: Elector Philipp had been excommunicated as the result of a refusal to transfer territory (Berwartstein) to the Benedictine abbey of Weißenburg pursuant to an agreement of 1474. Instead, the Palatinate had enfeoffed the land to Hans von Dratt and had treated Weißenburg harshly, impounding crops and even threatening war.[97] Thus, Reuchlin had a difficult case to make. Nonetheless, after months of preliminary negotiations, Reuchlin was accorded the honor of petitioning the pope directly in a Ciceronian oration delivered in the Sistine Chapel. With relatively little substance to support his case, Reuchlin resorted to a largely rhetorical strategy in the oration. He attacked the Weißenburg monks aggressively, repeatedly claiming that they were corrupt and had stooped to a game of legal chess, in which they had merely outmaneuvered Philipp. Reuchlin carefully framed the diatribe against the monks with an unconditional endorsement of papal authority. Directly addressing Alexander VI in the Sistine Chapel, with its ample illustrations of the "power of the keys" (as, most famously, in Perugino's brand new *Christ Giving the Keys to St. Peter*), Reuchlin said that Christ "conferred on these, your spiritual and heavenly keys authority over not only some tiny clod of earth but, indeed, over the entire expanse of the world."[98] The panegyric to papal power reached such rhetorical heights that some fifteen years later Reuchlin's lawyer, now pleading the heresy defense at Rome, would label his client the "Orator of Papal Holiness," an epithet earned by this speech.[99] Reuchlin paid even stronger tribute to Philipp, stressing his enormous power as the ranking secular prince in the Holy Roman Empire after the emperor. Finally, Reuchlin introduced the argument that the Weißenburg monks had inappropriately appealed to the curia, thereby breaching the constitutional order of the newly reformed empire. Since the matter concerned the temporal authority of the monastery and since the monastery held its temporalia from the emperor, the proper jurisdiction for this case was an imperial tribune (Reuchlin probably means the newly formed Imperial Chamber Court), the legal course that, as Reuchlin stressed, the emperor himself had requested. Whether or not he was moved by Reuchlin's theatrical rhetoric, Alexander VI did not remove Philipp's excommunication immediately. That was accomplished in 1502 probably through the intervention of Cardinal Raimund Peraudi, who requested a copy of the speech from Reuchlin possibly as part of his effort.[100]

Regardless of its political impact, the papal address of 1498 was celebrated as a rhetorical triumph of such literary refinement that Aldo Manuzio, the most elite publisher of his generation, printed it immediately as an honor to Reuchlin. This was a distinction of the first order, for Reuchlin's papal address is one of only two works by a northern humanist that would receive an Aldine imprimatur.[101] (The other northerner so honored was Erasmus.) The ultimate result of the embassy, capped by the papal oration delivered before His Holiness in the Sistine Chapel, and printed by Manuzio, was to put Rome's imprimatur, as it were, on Reuchlin as the model for northern European humanist culture. As we will see in chapter 4, Reuchlin's third residency in Rome also provided his biblical scholarship with an immense boost: the opportunity to study Hebrew with the legendary Rabbi Obadiah Sforno and to acquire several crucial books that laid the foundation for his epochal publication of the *Rudiments of Hebrew*.

Judge for the Swabian League

After Eberhard II was removed from power by a governing council and his nephew Ulrich became duke of Württemberg (initially as a minor under the authority of a governing council), Reuchlin decided to return to Stuttgart.[102] Although he would never again hold an official appointment as councilor to the duke of Württemberg, there is evidence that Reuchlin served Ulrich on a few important occasions in the 1510s.[103] It is, however, not known what Reuchlin did during his first years back in the duchy, although it is sometimes thought that he worked for a while at the central Württemberg court (Hofgericht). He returned as early as October 1499, and in January 1500 he received a letter from Sebastian Brant congratulating him on being free from the "wretched annoyance of the court,"[104] a confirmation that Reuchlin then had no official capacity in the government. By early 1502, however, he had been appointed one of three judges for the court of the Swabian League, a distinguished position— with the title "Triumvir Suaviae"—that he would hold until his resignation in early 1513. Created in 1500 as part of the reorganization of the league, this was a standing court with the authority to settle disputes between the member territories. The court was not the final instance for interterritorial litigation, for its decisions could be appealed to the Imperial Chamber Court and its jurisdiction over specific cases could be challenged at the assemblies of the estates of the Swabian League. Each of the three chambers of the league—the princes, nobles, and free imperial cities—named one judge to the court. As the judge appointed by the princes, Reuchlin served as presiding judge in those cases where a princely territory was defendant and as an assessor ("Beisitzer") in all other cases. The few records that survive for his work as presiding judge attest a careful, professional discharge of his duties and above all indicate that cases could drag on to extraordinary lengths. One suit brought by Count Wolfgang of Oettingen against Duke Georg of Bavaria over the sale of feudal overlordship for a small village occupied Reuchlin's court for some six years (1506–12), whereupon his decision was appealed to the Imperial Chamber Court, which needed an additional four years to forge a final settlement.[105]

In addition to being highly respected, Reuchlin's Swabian judgeship was well remunerated. His annual salary was 200 florins along with some expenses, roughly double the ordinary pay of a professor at the University of Tübingen.[106] Except for a brief period in Ulm (1502–3),[107] the court met in Tübingen, which afforded Reuchlin easy access from Stuttgart and ample opportunities to participate in university life. Reuchlin's printer, Thomas Anshelm, even relocated his press to Tübingen during Reuchlin's tenure on the bench. Reuchlin resigned from the court in 1513, probably because it was being moved to Augsburg, although contributing factors may have included his declining health and possible awkwardness arising from Württemberg's 1512 withdrawal from the Swabian League. In 1506 a Tübingen professor, Michael Köchlin, addressed his tract, *The Transfer of Imperial Power from the Greeks to the Germans*, to the three judges of the Swabian League—Reuchlin, Johannes Streler, and Heinrich Winckelhofer—in recognition of their formation of an active humanist circle in Tübingen.[108] Reuchlin had also arranged for the learned converso Matthäus Adriani, who would later collide with Luther at

Wittenberg, to teach Hebrew in Tübingen in 1512.[109] Reuchlin had much to do in his position as Swabian triumvir, but it also allowed him to begin a highly productive period of scholarly writing, including, most important, the 1506 publication of the Hebrew grammar book, as well as a humanist rhetorical manual for preachers (1504), a Latin translation of the pseudo-Homeric *Battle of Frogs and Mice* (1510), a Latin translation of a Hebrew wedding poem by Joseph Ezobi (1512), an edition, translation, and commentary of the seven penitential Psalms in Hebrew (1512), and a Latin translation of a pseudo-Hippocratic tract on the four humors (1512).

Reuchlin was the senior triumvir of the Swabian League when he was asked to evaluate the imperial mandate authorizing the confiscation of Jewish writings. Some accounts, with too narrow a focus on the Reuchlin Affair, leave the impression that he stumbled from a scholarly advocacy into a political hornet's nest when he defended the legal rights of Jews in 1510. When Emperor Maximilian solicited his opinion, he knew the Hebrew scholar as a diplomat, judge, and doctor of law, and probable already recognized him as "our councilor."[110] Moreover, it was Reuchlin's legal expertise and especially his many powerful political connections—he was the consummate political insider who had served "on the councils of the most powerful princes of Germany"[111]—that enabled him to sustain his defense so effectively in the 1510s, as we will see. Few jurists in the empire had attained greater stature, and challenging legal questions, raised in politically contentious settings, were everyday matters for him.

4

Discovery of Hebrew

The language of the Jews is simple, pure, uncorrupted, sacred,
concise, and eternal, in which, it is said, God spoke in person with
humans and humans with angels, not through an interpreter but
face to face...as a friend speaks to a friend.

—Johannes Reuchlin, 1494, in
Miracle-Making Word

Ludwig Geiger called an encounter in Linz, Austria, between
Rabbi Jacob ben Jehiel Loans and Johannes Reuchlin "a moment of
world-historical importance."[1] However sweeping (not to mention
Eurocentric) this claim may sound now, it correctly identifies a
turning point for European Christianity—one that few historians
have taken stock of—in the simple agreement on the part of a
learned rabbi to give instruction in Hebrew to a Christian scholar.
Lessons began on 25 September 1492, and, as the pupil's proficiency
increased, this event would be recognized as the first consequential
step in Christianity's rediscovery of the Hebrew language and its
own roots in Judaism. In a way, it was the theological equivalent
of the 1492 discovery of the continent that was already inhabited.
The "discovery" of this continent of Hebrew, which for all intents
and purposes was previously unknown to Christians, created
new connections between the bifurcated theological worlds of the
two faiths, and, as such, would eventually form a new context for
Christian-Jewish coexistence.

For the most part, prior to Reuchlin's career, the few medieval Christians with a grasp of Hebrew used their knowledge in determined efforts to destroy Judaism. A tiny number of Christians, most of them former Jews, effectively attacked the Hebrew literary and theological heritage in their debates with Jews.[2] Even Nicholas of Lyra and Paul of Burgos,[3] virtually the only medieval scholars who used Hebrew to assess Latin renderings in the Vulgate, were also energetic anti-Jewish controversialists whose works, once they were printed in the fifteenth century, helped harden the anti-Jewish temper of the early Renaissance.

With Reuchlin, the goal for learning Hebrew entered uncharted waters, for he wanted to promote research on Christianity and was not concerned with bolstering anti-Jewish campaigns. Moreover, as his command of the Hebrew language improved, Reuchlin's admiration of Jewish research on the Bible and Kabbalah grew. There is more than a grain of truth in the later accusations by his Christian enemies that he held Jewish scholars in higher regard than medieval Christian theologians. While the question of Reuchlin's representation of Judaism and Jews has always been raised in studies of his legal repudiation of the book pogrom, a larger historical question is how the Christian scholarly study of Judaism impacted representation. Did immersion in Jewish studies foster the development of new Christian perspectives on contemporary Judaism and Jews?[4]

Despite the novelty of his respect for Jewish writing, Reuchlin took pains to justify Christian Hebrew studies as much as possible on the basis of older positions taken by the church. His favorite decree in canon law was a mandate issued by the Council of Vienne in 1312 that required leading universities to offer instruction in Hebrew.[5] Ultimately, he would use this canon to promote his pioneering Hebrew textbook of 1506[6] and, more significantly, as the crowning argument in his defense of Jewish writing in 1510.[7] In the Hebrew textbook, Reuchlin combined expressions of empathy for the plight of Jews suffering expulsion with a plea to implement the church's theoretical endorsement of Jewish studies:

> Indeed, I am aware of the deplorable plight of the Jews in our own
> time. They have been expelled not only from Spain but also from
> the borders of our Germany, forced to find homes for themselves
> elsewhere and even to emigrate to the Ottoman Empire. Therefore
> we can expect that the Hebrew language, along with a great loss
> of Holy Scriptures, will disappear and vanish from our midst. For
> this reason, in order to bring knowledge of the Hebrew language to
> Christians, I have decided to lay the first foundation with this book
> [i.e., *Rudiments of Hebrew*], as is provided for in the Constitutions of
> Pope Clement V [i.e., decrees from the Council of Vienne].[8]

While Reuchlin always viewed his scholarship as a challenge to the practices of Christian theology, until the outbreak of the book controversy he did not conceive of his research as a threat to the anti-Jewish campaigns sweeping across the empire. He feared that his Hebrew research would "expose him to barking dogs that would bite," [9] not because of a benign attitude toward Judaism but because he was advocating a new methodology for Christian theologians.

Above all, his research raised a basic question about the status of the Latin Vulgate, the Bible that European Christianity had used so intensively and exclusively during the previous millennium. Reuchlin admitted that, despite his high regard for the scholarship of St. Jerome, he could no longer accept the Vulgate as an authoritative and reliable foundation for establishing doctrine. In particular, his Hebrew-Latin lexicon—which constitutes by far the largest segment of his *Rudiments of Hebrew*—rejected Jerome's text in several hundred places, sometimes caustically brushing aside his renderings as sheer nonsense. The root issue was not so much that the venerable Jerome may have nodded now and then, but rather that no translation should ever serve as the basis for Christian theology, and glaringly so, as Reuchlin observed, now that the printing press was making the Hebrew Bible increasingly available. Fundamentally, Reuchlin was calling for the adoption of a new Bible for Christianity: "it will be necessary for the ancient dignity of the Holy Scriptures to be restored to a new appearance which is unknown to the Latin world."[10] While Jerome had argued that the translation of the Bible (and its canon) should be grounded in the Hebrew text, which he famously championed as the "Hebrew truth"' (as opposed to the Greek Septuagint translation), Reuchlin went further and insisted on the primacy of the Hebrew Bible without the mediation of a Christian translation. He expressed this memorably as "I revere St. Jerome as an angel, and I respect Nicholas of Lyra as a great teacher, but I worship the (Hebrew) truth as God."[11]

Varying degrees of regard for Jerome, Nicholas of Lyra, and the Hebrew text of the Bible are not altogether astonishing claims. Reuchlin's methodology, however, was also grounded in the study of medieval Jewish scholarship since it, unlike the Christian, had never lost touch with the "Hebrew truth." The elevation of Jewish scholarship was a purely academic judgment but it ultimately fostered Reuchlin's creation of a distinctive discourse of Christian admiration of the Jewish tradition and individual Jews. When, in 1514, he published a letter that addressed his first Hebrew teacher, Rabbi Loans, as "My Lord, dear master Jacob, my companion, and my good friend,...with deep longing I wish to see your blessed face to delight in the radiance of your bright countenance by hearing your most pure doctrine,"[12] Reuchlin was redefining the boundaries for Christian representation of Jews and Judaism, and defiantly so since he was already embroiled in the heresy trial. He included the letter to Loans in an anthology that featured correspondence with such eminent

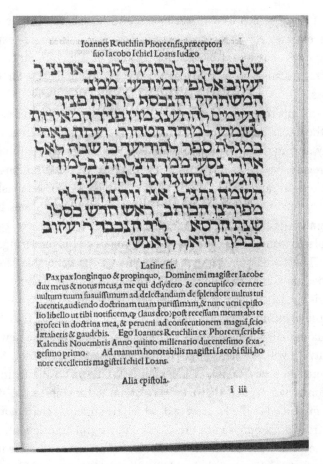

FIGURE 4.1. Johannes Reuchlin, letter to Rabbi Jacob ben Jehiel Loans. From Reuchlin, *Letters of Distinguished Men* (Tübingen: Thomas Anshelm, 1514), fol. i3ʳ. Courtesy of the Klau Library, Hebrew Union College-Jewish Institute of Religion, Cincinnati, Ohio.

Christian scholars as Erasmus, Willibald Pirckheimer, Giles of Viterbo, and Aldo Manuzio (see Figure 4.1). After this letter appeared, Johannes Pfefferkorn attacked it as another intolerable example of Reuchlin's favorable treatment of Jews and Judaism.[13] Despite that and despite the travails of the ongoing heresy trial, Reuchlin republished the letter with a Latin translation in 1519.[14]

Learning Hebrew

How did Reuchlin gain a sufficient command of Hebrew to launch Christian Jewish studies? He claimed that his Hebrew studies commenced under Loans, which would mean he was thirty-seven years old when embarking on the defining project of his life. This assertion, however, contradicts other evidence, although perhaps we should construe it as little more than an admission that his progress before Loans had been modest.

The earliest surviving record of Reuchlin's interest in Hebrew is in an impressive epistolary exchange with Rudolf Agricola from 1484–85.[15] Agricola, a revered eminence among the early humanists in the north, had apparently managed to learn a smattering of Hebrew from another famous theologian, Wessel Gansfort, whose knowledge was also very limited. Reuchlin's letter is remarkable in two respects. First, it addresses an issue that would pertain to his prime interest in Hebrew studies—Christianization of the Kabbalah. Reuchlin asks Agricola's opinion on a passage from Psalm 54 ("Save me, O God, by thy name"): what does "thy name" refer to? Is it the tetragrammaton (the name of God, i.e., YHVH [יהוה]) or because of the prominence of "save," which in Hebrew is a component of Jesus' name "Jehoshua" ("יהושע", yod-heh-vav-shin-ʿayin), might it be an evocation of Jesus (which he later construed as the pentagrammaton that supplanted the tetragrammaton)?

Before continuing this discussion, I should point out that Reuchlin ultimately adopted a defective spelling of Jesus' name in order to claim that it constituted the effable version of the ineffable tetragrammaton. He was probably inspired by the actual Hebrew name of Jesus, "Jehoshua," which is based on the root "yoshaʿ" (yod-shin-ʿayin; ישע) and does mean "YHV(H) is salvation." Probably because he was aware that Jehoshua does not contain all four letters of the tetragrammaton (it lacks the final heh), Reuchlin proposed that Jesus' name be spelled "יהשוה" (yod-heh-shin-vav-heh), an orthography that makes no sense etymologically and has no basis in Hebrew usage. Though unsalvageable, this catachresis informed both of Reuchlin's tracts on Christian Kabbalah.

The other remarkable element in Reuchlin's letter is that it contains two passages from Psalms quoted in the original Hebrew, written in Hebrew script and in Reuchlin's hand.[16] Hardly proof that Reuchlin could already read Scripture in Hebrew, these quotations may indicate little more than that, by the time he wrote this letter (ca. 1484–85), he owned an edition of the Psalms in Hebrew and was comparing it with the Vulgate text. The first part of the Hebrew Bible ever to be printed was the Psalms, issued probably in Bologna in 1477; two further printings of Psalms appeared by 1480.[17] The letter to Agricola was written during the time that Reuchlin later claimed he "heard" Flavius Mithridates lecturing.[18] Mithridates, who is thought to have toured universities in France and Germany in 1484–85,[19] was a tutor to Giovanni Pico della Mirandola and translated a large corpus of Kabbalistic tracts for Pico into Latin.

Reuchlin never explained what moved him to begin dipping so zealously into Hebrew Bibles. Perhaps, some have thought, it was Wessel Gansfort with his modicum of Hebrew. Gansfort taught (though not Hebrew) at Paris and Basel during Reuchlin's tenure at both institutions. Curiously, Agricola's letter to Reuchlin suggests that, on the contrary, Gansfort discouraged the eager student from taking up Hebrew. It is probably best to assume that Reuchlin had become aware of a few scholars making tentative efforts in that area. While, with the help of expert instruction, he was able to achieve a very high level of proficiency in Greek during his university studies, he could do little more than keep his eyes peeled for small opportunities to learn about the other biblical language.

We know that Reuchlin met Lorenzo de' Medici and toured the magnificent Palazzo Medici in 1482, as part of the retinue of Eberhard of Württemberg. He surely became aware of Marsilio Ficino's Academy and the budding interest in Hebrew there but made no reference to it in any of his reflections on the first Italian embassy. The moment of recognition probably occurred later, with the 1490 trip to Italy when, according to his own accounts, he came under the spell of Ficino and the charismatic Pico della Mirandola, both of whom by that date were extolling the significance of Hebrew and, specifically, of Jewish Kabbalah. Pico himself published an analysis of Jehoshua as the effable version of YHVH in his *Nine Hundred Theses* of 1486 (i.e., after Reuchlin's surviving letter on this subject). Reuchlin probably originally derived his concept of the pentagrammaton from the biblical commentary of Paul of Burgos,[20] which Reuchlin admired throughout his career, but it was Pico's enthusiasm that stirred his imagination so deeply. When publishing the *Rudiments of Hebrew*, Reuchlin wrote that Pico's promotion of Hebrew (and Kabbalah) as the receptacle of hidden knowledge of the divine made study of the language imperative for him:

> To this (idea) a most weighty authority gives his support, the noble
> and refined Count of the Roman Empire, the philosopher Giovanni
> Pico della Mirandola, who says, "whoever masters the grammar of
> the Hebrew language profoundly and from the roots and knows how
> to use it to the right degree in his research, he will have the rule and
> guide for accurately finding anything knowable."[21]

Reuchlin claimed that a major reason for the creation of his own Hebrew handbook was the reluctance of German Jews to teach Christians.[22] Interestingly, his teacher Loans was not originally from Germany, but a native of Mantua or Ferrara. Reuchlin also indicated that he had had only limited contact with Jews in Germany prior to 1492 in large part because very few lived in Württemberg under Eberhard the Bearded.[23] In 1512 (in his *A Clear Explanation*), he wrote that no Jews at all remained in the duchy.[24]

Despite the alleged unwillingness of German Jews to offer instruction to Christians, there is reliable evidence that Reuchlin studied Hebrew under an otherwise unknown Jew named Calman, apparently a learned Jewish scribe, in the mid-1480s. Reuchlin recorded this in the first Hebrew book he is known to have acquired, a copy of a medieval Hebrew lexicon he commissioned from Calman in 1486: "Calman the Jew, the Hebrew grammar teacher of Johannes Reuchlin of Pforzheim, copied this dictionary for him, his pupil, for pay."[25] The work itself is Menahem ben Saruq's dictionary (*Mahberet*), a pioneering medieval effort in Hebrew lexicography, but one that was superseded by the work of David Kimhi. Calman, moreover, copied a version of *Mahberet* that included Yiddish translations of the definitions and explanations, which would have increased the book's usefulness to Reuchlin exponentially. It is also known that, prior to meeting Loans, Reuchlin was trying to acquire a complete Hebrew Bible. In June 1492, he received word from Florence that Joshua Solomon Soncino's printed edition of the Hebrew Bible was available for purchase.[26] That lead apparently did not work out, though Reuchlin did acquire a complete Hebrew Bible later in 1492 (which happened to be the first edition of 1488, printed by Israel Nathan Soncino).[27]

An Italian by birth, Jacob ben Jehiel Loans had been serving as physician to Emperor Friedrich III for at least seven years when Reuchlin met him. Unfortunately, no works by him, if there were any, survive; we also have only very limited sources for his life beyond what Reuchlin wrote. According to Reuchlin, the emperor raised Loans into the lower nobility, which, if true, is the only fifteenth-century case of such an honor being bestowed on a Jew in Germany. In remarks scattered throughout the *Rudiments of Hebrew*, Reuchlin paid tribute to Loans as "my teacher, in my opinion the powerfully learned Jacob Jehiel Loans, a Jew" ("praeceptor meus, mea sententia valde doctus Jacobus Jehiel Loans Hebraeus") and as "my most humane teacher, the excellent doctor" ("humanissimus praeceptor meus ille Iacobus iehiel loans doctor excellens").[28] For the deceased Loans, Reuchlin prayed in 1506 "may God's mercy come over him."[29] While Loans left no comment on the achievements of his Christian pupil, Loans's nephew, Josel of Rosheim, would later herald Reuchlin as a "miracle within a miracle"[30] for having defended Jewish books in 1510.

Reuchlin spent the better part of an entire year as Loans's student. Significant diplomatic matters—containment of the duke of Bavaria and ratification of a new treaty governing succession in Württemberg—brought him to Linz and his fortuitous encounter with Loans. After concluding the difficult negotiations by October 1492, Reuchlin was able to remain in Linz for nearly a year (until after the emperor's death in August 1493) and devote himself primarily to learning Hebrew, an accomplishment that the emperor honored by presenting Reuchlin with a magnificent manuscript of the Hebrew Bible.[31] The first fruit of his studies with Loans (and his first independent publication) was *Miracle-Making Word* of 1494, a tentative effort to apply some elements of Jewish Kabbalah to Christianity (see discussion below), and, according to Max Brod, the first publication by a Christian author that portrayed Jews and Judaism favorably.[32] The Hebrew scholarship in *Miracle-Making Word*, however, was amateurish, and Reuchlin was keenly aware of his shortcomings and the need to advance his Hebrew studies.

No less a place than Rome, the heart of Latin Christendom, turned out to be the ideal venue for acquiring a firmer grasp on Hebrew. Reuchlin took advantage of a 1498 embassy to the Holy See, on behalf of Elector Philipp of the Palatinate, to devote his energies afresh to Jewish studies.[33] In 1498, Rome had one of the largest, most stable, and most ancient Jewish communities in Europe. It was an exceedingly attractive place for Reuchlin in part because he was able to make some major book acquisitions there. Because of the expulsions of Jewish communities throughout Europe, Hebrew books were becoming hard to find.[34] Reuchlin frequently complained that Hebrew books were difficult to acquire, sometimes lamenting that Jews were reluctant to sell their books to Christians, although one reason for the difficulty was that the devastating expulsions had stymied the growth of Jewish printing. Three complete Hebrew Bibles were printed by Jews between 1488 and 1494. But only one more edition would appear, also printed by the venerable Jewish house of Soncino, before Christians began printing the Hebrew Bible as of 1516.[35] By the time the Roman book hunt was over, Reuchlin's quarry bag was stuffed with trophies, including David Kimhi's *Sefer Mikhlol*, the twelfth-century grammar and lexicon that would form a basis for his *Rudiments of Hebrew* of 1506.[36] He acquired the *Sefer Mikhlol* in two parts: a 1282 manuscript of the grammar section, usually entitled *Diqduq*,[37] and an imprint of the massive Hebrew lexicon section (Naples: Azriel ben Joseph Ashkenazi, 1490).[38] Among the other prizes were David Kimhi's commentary on the Prophets (Soncino: Joshua Solomon Soncino, 1485),[39] a commentary on Jeremiah, falsely attributed to Joseph Kimhi (*Codex Reuchlinianus* 12),[40] a Pentateuch with Nahmanides's commentary (Naples, 1490),[41] and the spectacular manuscript of the Prophets from 1105 (*Codex Reuchlinianus* 3).[42] On the very day that he delivered a speech before Alexander VI, the book hound acquired a rare manuscript of the ancient Aramaic paraphrase of the Prophets (the Targum of Jonathan).[43] No less a dignitary than Lawrence Behem, who served as the Vatican majordomo under Alexander VI, assisted Reuchlin on his quests for Hebrew books in Jewish Rome.[44]

Were it not for this final trip to Rome, Reuchlin could not have written the Hebrew grammar. Even more important than the book acquisitions were Hebrew lessons with Obadiah Sforno, one of the most revered biblical commentators in the Jewish tradition[45] and still a living voice because his commentary on the Torah appears in rabbinic Bibles.[46] The prodigy Sforno, then only in his early twenties, cultivated ties with Christians in Rome, especially at the papal court, and was distinctive for being a rabbi who was also equipped with humanist Latinity, an exceedingly rare attainment in 1498. According to Reuchlin, "He [i.e., Sforno], as if a professor of the humanities, gave me lessons every day during the entire embassy."[47] Indeed, Sforno's 1501 diploma for his doctorate in medicine from the University of Ferrara refers to his previous studies in the "faculty of the arts" at the University of Rome,[48] which is the likely context of his association with Reuchlin. We also know that later in life he created a Latin-Hebrew grammar (now lost) at the urging of a Christian patron[49] and that he produced an elegant Latin translation of his own most important philosophical work, Or 'ammin ("Light of the Nations"), which he rendered as Lumen gentium in 1548.

Sforno probably left an imprint on Reuchlin's attitude toward Jews for other reasons as well. For example, deeply impressed, Reuchlin cited the rabbinic teaching that righteous people outside of the covenant of Israel would find redemption[50] as a powerful argument against the assumption that Jews were hostile to the Christian religion. Although there are many possible sources for Reuchlin's knowledge of this teaching,[51] Sforno was noteworthy for stressing it.[52] Sforno even urged Jews to teach Christians Hebrew and Jewish learning, contrary to the restriction of the Talmud tractate Hagigah. In his commentary on Exodus 24:12, he contended that God wants both Jews and non-Jews to study Torah and the Mishnah, and therefore that it is imperative that non-Jews learn Hebrew. He occasionally suggested that gentile knowledge of Hebrew could improve Jewish-Christian relations.

None of the sources gives an exact account of what Sforno and Reuchlin accomplished or how they conducted the tutorial. In his tribute to Reuchlin from 1552, Melanchthon claimed that Sforno charged one gold piece for every lesson, a detail intended to underscore Reuchlin's commitment to Hebrew philology and, perhaps, to evoke the stereotype of greedy Jews,[53] but Reuchlin confirmed that his studies with Sforno were costly.[54] Reuchlin started the lessons on 13 June 1498 and continued probably until sometime in the early months of 1499 when he left Rome for Germany. He claimed that the lessons took place every day during the lengthy legation. One could easily suppose that

Reuchlin and Sforno worked through the lexicon and grammar of the Kimhis, perhaps even turning their sources into Latin versions as they proceeded. That kind of effort would have created a foundation for Reuchlin's 1506 lexicon and grammar. In the *Rudiments of Hebrew*, Reuchlin displays a near perfect understanding of David Kimhi in his Latin renderings of the lexicon, an accomplishment that may have relied to a significant degree on consultation with a profound expert in Hebrew and Latin, such as Sforno.

There is evidence that Reuchlin possessed—and may have commissioned—a translation of Moses Kimhi's *Mahalakh*, the Hebrew textbook that exerted the greatest influence on the grammar parts of Reuchlin's *Rudiments of Hebrew*. Reuchlin's own copy of a Hebrew-German manuscript of the *Mahalakh* does not survive, though a copy of it does in the Bavarian State Library in Munich.[55] Moreover, Conrad Pellican attested that in 1501 Reuchlin allowed him to consult "a handwritten exemplar of the grammar of Rabbi Moses Kimhi, which he had had translated into German by the same Jew who had translated some other fragments for a priest in Ulm."[56] Such a volume would have been of extreme value to Reuchlin as he composed his grammar.

Christian Hebrew

More than just the first Hebrew book written for Christians, *Rudiments of Hebrew* is also a complex manifesto for the biblical humanist movement (published a full decade before Erasmus's Greek New Testament) that challenged the authority of the Vulgate Bible and, equally daring, presented Jewish scholarship as the key to resurrecting the moribund Christian study of the Bible. In order, however, to accomplish these goals, especially to facilitate Christian appropriation of Jewish learning, Reuchlin pursued a strategy of structuring biblical Hebrew as a Christian language. This methodology, which probably is not self-consciously hostile to Jewish interests, gives rise to contradictory impulses, as Reuchlin alternates between distorting and celebrating the Hebrew-Jewish tradition.

In some important ways, *Rudiments of Hebrew* was a determined effort to square a circle. The square peg that Reuchlin pounded into the circle of Hebrew was humanist Latin. The specific results of this approach to Hebrew are, as one would predict, torturous but not entirely without an occasional charm. For example, though written in Latin, the imprint adopts the direction of Hebrew pagination, with pages running from right to left.

Reuchlin employs the terminology and categories of classical Hebrew philology (especially as used by the medieval scholars David and Moses Kimhi) and classical Latin philology (as exemplified by the sixth-century grammarian Priscian).[57] Unsurprisingly, the Latin terminology (and therefore structure) informs the organization of the presentation of grammar and morphology; Reuchlin often adheres to the Latin paradigms even when corresponding forms are essentially missing in Hebrew. The result may be highly artificial, but it would have made the paradigms seem familiar to a Christian readership.

The textbook is divided into three books. Book 1 has a brief introduction to the Hebrew alphabet and vocalization (pp. 5–31) and the first half of a massive lexicon for biblical Hebrew, organized by Hebrew roots (32–259; *alef* through *kaf*); book 2 completes the dictionary (260–545; *lamed* through *tav*); book 3 is an extensive presentation of Hebrew parts of speech (nouns, verbs, syntax; 550–620).

Reuchlin was not exaggerating when he wrote "I reduced the language of the Jews to Latin rules, an accomplishment never previously conceived of."[58] To accomplish this mission impossible, he manufactured Hebrew equivalents to fill out Latin paradigms (adapting most of the examples from Moses Kimhi's medieval Hebrew primer, *Mahalakh*[59]). For instance, he dutifully declined nouns so as to form nominative (which he sometimes calls the "absolute," a more appropriate label for the Hebrew form), genitive, dative, accusative, and ablative cases. For example, on pages 556–57, he declines "אִישׁ," "man," as follows:

Nominativo	אִישׁ	vir (i.e., man)
Genitivo	הָאִישׁ	viri (i.e., of the man)
Dativo	לְאִישׁ	viro (i.e., to man)
Accusat[iv]o	אֶת אִישׁ	virum (i.e., man)
Ablativo	מֵאִישׁ	a viro (i.e., from man)

All of the Latin cases are arguably the same Hebrew "absolute," the only real possibility for an exception being the accusative case. The particle "אֶת" indicates that the noun it precedes is functioning as the object of the verb (and thus evokes the accusative case in Latin); it also occurs frequently in the Bible, even though it is not necessary for indicating a direct object. Reuchlin's dative and ablative cases are simply the noun + prefixed preposition (" לְ," i.e., "to" and " מִן," i.e., "from"). This alignment with Latin, though unnecessary for learning Hebrew, might have provided some comfort to the neophyte student, since, after all, Latin was the foreign language most carefully studied (often the only one) and its paradigms were inscribed in every student's mind.

The "genitive case" best illustrates the hazards of Reuchlin's system. His equivalent for the genitive case is merely the article + noun in absolute state— "the man" ("הָאִישׁ"). This is hardly a genitive form, even if the combination of article and noun in the absolute state is the correct form for a noun that follows a noun in the construct state. Hebrew is starkly different from Latin and English in this regard. For the phrase "horse of the man," the form of the word for "horse" is altered to connect it to "the man"—and the form of the word for "the man" remains in the absolute state preceded by the simple article. The point that needs explanation (and Reuchlin fails to provide it here) is that the form of the first noun is altered to the construct state. Thus, the Latin noun system will not accommodate this Hebrew structure, something that Reuchlin might have helpfully pointed out. To his credit, he did explain the construct case elsewhere.[60] Moreover, most of Reuchlin's paradigms are of basic importance for construing (and recognizing) pronouns and nouns correctly. For instance, based largely on Moses Kimhi's grammar, he carefully compiled paradigms of pronouns used with inseparable prepositions and as suffixes on verbs and nouns. He also explained the need to remove prefixes from words in order to find the roots used for lexicon entries.[61]

The verbal system represents a similar, yet vastly more complex (and imaginative) attempt to provide Hebrew forms for all the standard paradigms of Latin. To cite Reuchlin's first example, for the present tense (which does not occur in Hebrew), he simply provides a paradigm of the active participle. This approach would usually yield an accurate translation of a Hebrew participle, but it is a confusing presentation, all the more so because Reuchlin does not explain what he is doing. In general, he does not use standard Hebrew terminology for the verbal stems, even though he was familiar with it.[62] Reuchlin sorted out the seven stems of Hebrew verbs—Qal, Niphal, Piel, Pual, Hithpael, Hiphil, and Hophal—as follows: Qal is called first conjugation; Piel second; Hiphil third; and Hithpael fourth. Reuchlin then, reasonably enough, labels the Niphal stem the passive of the first conjugation (Qal)[63]; Pual the passive of the second conjugation (Piel)[64]; and Hophal the passive of the third conjugation (Hiphil).[65] As a reflexive (or passive) stem, Hithpael lacks a corresponding passive. All of this (and more) creative grammatics may amount to a serious distortion of Hebrew but we should understand it, more appropriately, as the result of Reuchlin's effort to find Latin, the Christian language, in Hebrew. Obviously, this approach, despite its impeccable Latinity, could never make sense and it was dropped by subsequent Christian grammarians.[66]

In several respects, though, Reuchlin followed his Jewish sources closely. He offered extensive paradigms of irregular (or weak) verbs and also lists of pronominal suffixes on verbs (pp. 612ff.) The sections on weak verbs, which he calls "verba defectiva," and on pronominal suffixes are derived from Moses Kimhi's *Mahalakh*.[67]

The final part of the grammar, which Reuchlin labels "de consignificativo," is a grab bag of miscellaneous observations on syntax from the perspective of such parts of speech as prepositions, conjunctions, adverbs, interjections, and so on.[68] It is for the most part little more than a word list of conjunctions, prepositions, and adverbs with terse Latin translations.

For instance, Reuchlin explains a form of comparison this way: "Comparandi יוֹתֵר magis" ([word] of comparison יוֹתֵר more).[69] This would be rather hard to understand since Reuchlin does not describe the ordinary Hebrew form of comparison, the *"min* of comparison" (adjective followed by *min* + noun), nor does he explain that יוֹתֵר [more] would need to be followed by a *"min* of comparison." Elsewhere (but without cross-referencing) he did explain that Hebrew does not have a comparative declination of adjectives or adverbs but identified the *min* + noun construction, confusingly, as an ablative of comparison.[70]

Somewhat more successful is Reuchlin's explanation of the *vav*-consecutive (i.e., *vav* ["and"] prefixed to a verb), which changes the valence of the Hebrew perfect and future forms. It is the very last item in his grammar, tacked on as if an afterthought despite its extreme significance for reading the Bible. He correctly notes "for when a *vav* pointed with a *sheva* is prefixed to a verb in the preterite tense, which transfers its accent to the last syllable, then that same verb is changed into the future tense."[71]

I have mentioned grammar first, but *Rudiments of Hebrew* actually begins with a massive Hebrew lexicon preceded only by a brief introduction to the Hebrew alphabet and vocalization. Reuchlin envisioned zealous students eager to master a comprehensive biblical lexicon of some 500 pages before undertaking the study of morphology and syntax. To assist those industrious students, he designed a tutorial for vocalization based on a Hebrew genealogy of Jesus,[72] thus providing an entry into Hebrew that proceeded through the doorway of the New Testament Gospels. For the dictionary proper, which runs from page 32 all the way to 545 (from "אָב" [father] to "תֵּשַׁע" [nine]), Reuchlin composed felicitous Latin definitions of Hebrew roots and connected most of the Hebrew words to actual Bible passages. The copious Bible references, however, are given exclusively in Latin, even though they serve to illustrate the usage of Hebrew words. Geiger complained, rightly, that Reuchlin's quotation of the Bible in Latin only diminished the usefulness of the lexicon as a reference work,[73] but he failed to observe that this section is intended as an exercise for the neophyte student who has not yet studied Hebrew morphology or syntax. Moreover, the lexicon tends to provide morphological notes such as the forms of Hebrew nouns in the plural and construct cases, and includes examples with pronominal suffixes. In an act of filial piety, Sebastian Münster issued a new edition of Reuchlin's grammar in 1537, for which he provided the original Hebrew for quotations from the Bible.

Every entry of Reuchlin's lexicon is based on David Kimhi's *Book of Roots* (*Sefer ha-Shorashim*), which is part of his *Sefer Mikhlol* (roughly, *Book of Completion*).[74] Reuchlin did not explain that he was adapting the *Book of Roots*, stating instead that "I made the Hebrew dictionary by myself through great and hard effort."[75] The likely reason for this concealment was his determination to present a Christian discourse with Christian authorship. In part, he accomplished that by emphasizing his own persona throughout the book in the novel role of a Christian teacher of Hebrew. The *Rudiments of Hebrew* is actually a letter addressed to his brother, Dionysius, albeit a long one that manages to quote a 600-page lexicon and grammar. The letter, which emerges at various junctures throughout the book, defends the value of Hebrew studies for Christian scholars and plainly states that instruction should be conducted by Christian teachers: "Indeed with good cause I would hope that everyone interested in Christianity would rather receive these rudiments [i.e., instruction in Hebrew], from you, a priest, and even from me, though a married man, rather than from the Jews."[76] Similarly, at the end of the book, Reuchlin explains to Dionysius that Christians must offer instruction in the Jewish language in part because Jews are concealing the language:

> Misled either by hatred or ignorance, the Jews in our country do not
> want to instruct any Christian in their language and they refuse to
> do this on the basis of a certain Rabbi Amos who said the following
> in the Talmud: "These words of the Bible should not be explained to
> any unbeliever because it is written, 'He revealed his word to Jacob,
> his laws and legislation to Israel He did this for no other people'"
> (Psalm 147, 19). We, however, who are in a state of grace are urged
> otherwise in Matthew 10—"Whatever someone whispers in your ear,
> proclaim that from your rooftops," which is what I am doing.[77]

Thus, it comes as no surprise that Reuchlin concluded the lexicon with a Christianized invocation to the muse, addressed to Jesus, giving the Christian God, but not David Kimhi or Moses Kimhi, credit for inspiring the book: "It is most fitting to thank our lord, the great messiah, to whose marvelous name, which is Jesus, I dedicate this most laborious work on collecting the roots of Hebrew words, done by night and by day in vigilant study."[78]

Given this concerted effort to Christianize Hebrew, it is all the more notable that Reuchlin did acknowledge Jewish sources at many points for specific information. The lexicon does in fact have scores of individual references to David Kimhi[79] and to some twenty other Jewish scholars as well (including about a dozen medieval writers). Reuchlin also derived most of his references to other Jewish scholars from David Kimhi's *Book of Roots*. For instance, he embraces the authority of the following Talmudic sages, none of whom he knows directly from the Talmud: Rabbi Akiva, Rabbi Nahman ben Isaac, Rabbi Yohanan (Johanan ben Nappaha), Rabbi Eliezer, Rabbi Simeon ben Gamaliel, and Rabbi Simeon ben Lakish. Among the other citations pilfered from Kimhi are several to the famous biblical scholars Abraham ibn Ezra and Saadiah ben Joseph Gaon as well as others from a host of savants, such as Jonah ibn Janah (whom Reuchlin calls Rabbi Jonah),[80] Judah ben David Hayyuj (whom Reuchlin calls Rabbi Judah), Jacob ben Eliezar (a lexicographer now known through David Kimhi's references to his lost works),[81] Moses Gikatilla, Isaac Benvenisti, and the Jewish history called *Josippon*,[82] which Reuchlin attributes to Joseph ben Gorion. These references are sufficiently numerous and sufficiently diverse to give the impression that Reuchlin has absorbed a very broad swath of Jewish scholarship, whereas, in reality, he appropriated them from Kimhi.

Reuchlin did, however, add some material, apparently collected by himself, from a few notable sources. Most appropriately, he occasionally included material from Kimhi's Bible commentaries.[83] Impressively, he quoted several Masoretic notes, presumably on the basis of a manuscript Bible.[84] (The Masoretic Bible would not be printed until 1524–25, a triumph achieved by the Christian printer Daniel Bomberg, albeit in reliance on the Jewish editor Jacob ben Hayyim.) He also apparently derived material from the following works on his own: Moses Maimonides' *Guide for the Perplexed*,[85] Judah Halevi's *Kuzari* (*The Khazars*), Joseph Gikatilla's *Ginnat Egoz* (*Nut Garden*), Moses Nahmanides' commentary on the Pentateuch, Rabbi Levi ben Gershon's commentary on Daniel, and the Aramaic Targums (both the Targum Onkelos and Targum Jonathan). Above all, Reuchlin made heavy use of the biblical commentaries by the great medieval scholar Rashi, unquestionably the leading Jewish exegete for Reuchlin. On rare occasion, he records specific indebtedness to oral instruction from his Jewish teachers. For example, he explicitly gives credit to Jacob ben Jehiel Loans for the explanation of the *vav*-consecutive.[86]

The net result of all these references to Jewish sources is not that they provide a appropriate acknowledgment of the extent of Reuchlin's indebtedness but rather that they propound the authority of the rabbinic tradition and, thereby, establish Jewish research as authoritative for Christian scholars. Whenever Reuchlin used a vague but affirmative tag such as "as the Jewish teachers say" or in his scores of references "according to David Kimhi," he was elevating Jewish philology to the highest level for Christian students.

Reuchlin was careful, however, to wrap the Jewish philology of the Kimhis in a heavy mantle of Christianity. Above all, he created a pervasive

Christian presence in the lexicon section by substituting Jerome's Latin translations for the hundreds of original Hebrew texts that David Kimhi had cited. The result of this is paradoxical. The sheer quantity of quotation from Jerome transformed the lexicon into an overwhelmingly Christian book. But this modification established the context for Reuchlin's sustained effort to correct the Vulgate text and reject its authority on the basis of Jewish biblical research.[87] *Rudiments of Hebrew* included several observations on Hebrew words as explained in the commentaries of Nicholas of Lyra and Paul of Burgos. Despite a high regard for his commentary, Reuchlin quarreled with some of Lyra's interpretations of Hebrew phrases and, overall, he qualified Lyra's accomplishment on the grounds that he borrowed all his observations from Rashi. Thus Lyra emerges as a precedent for Reuchlin's valorization of the Jewish tradition. For Reuchlin, the most reliable Christian exegete of the Middle Ages was Paul of Burgos: "The distinguished teacher Paul, Bishop of Burgos, formerly the most learned man among the Jews, whose later conversion to our faith brought salvation to many people. I am not ashamed to grant him preeminence above all the other [scholars]."[88] Obviously, Reuchlin championed Paul of Burgos as the scholar who united Jewish learning and Christian faith. That the converso received his highest scholarly accolade was certainly not disingenuous but it also reflected the mentality of Christian conversion that we will encounter in our discussion of the 1494 *Miracle-Making Word*. But Reuchlin's views were still developing. In his next major work after *Rudiments of Hebrew*, *Art of Kabbalah* (1517), it is no longer necessary for the ideal Jewish scholar to convert to Christianity, even if Kabbalah is still perceived as a repository of Christian truths.

According to Reuchlin, the *Rudiments of Hebrew* was designed to function as a textbook for students working on their own without classroom guidance from a professor. That after all was the only possible scenario for the book since no universities offered Hebrew instruction in 1506. Indeed, the complete absence of Hebrew instruction is the reason Reuchlin's book did not sell briskly.[89] According to Reuchlin, students should work through the *Rudiments of Hebrew* and portions of the Hebrew Bible simultaneously: "Although the volume of my *Rudiments* contains a nearly complete instruction for understanding Hebrew, it can only be applied directly, if some volumes of the Bible are used, since they are entirely in that language."[90] Eventually, Reuchlin came to realize that it had become difficult to acquire biblical texts in Hebrew; he blamed Maximilian's wars in Italy for drying up the sources of printed Jewish books.[91]

Therefore, in 1512 he published a pedagogical edition of the seven penitential Psalms to give students a practice text for reading biblical Hebrew. In the introduction to the *Seven Penitential Psalms* (which is dedicated to Jacob Lemp, a leading professor of theology and canon law at Tübingen),[92] Reuchlin explains his purpose:

> Thus in order that my instruction in the *Rudiments of Hebrew*, which was printed many years ago, should have this material,...after having put my adversaries aside, I edited the seven penitential Psalms for every student of Hebrew. They should be thoroughly studied, which will be all the easier because we are already accustomed to reciting them in our daily prayers. To me and to many others, especially the humanistically minded, this thing seemed most useful for developing the ability to read, pronounce and understand [Hebrew]. It [i.e., this edition of the Psalms] will be as follows: First, the Hebrew text of the Psalms is given; then my word-for-word translation; lastly, a grammatical explanation, written in an ordinarily, common, everyday style so that students will more easily understand what I mean; and everything will have cross-references to the books of my *Rudiments*.[93]

In fact, Reuchlin's *Seven Penitential Psalms* features a Hebrew text for Psalms 6, 31, 37, 50, 101, 129, and 142,[94] a literal Latin translation, and copious notes that parse every Hebrew word in the texts. Sebastian Münster wrote that the notes were so detailed that they would enable "a seven-year-old boy to learn Hebrew."[95] Although considerably older than seven, Martin Luther used Reuchlin's *Seven Penitential Psalms* to create his first German translation of original Scripture, the *Sieben Bußpsalmen* of 1517.

Reuchlin's final contribution to Hebrew philology was his 1518 publication of *Accents and Orthography of the Hebrew Language*, a work that he dedicated to Cardinal Adriano Castellesi, who, as we will see in chapter 8, served on the Roman commission that passed judgment in 1516 on Reuchlin's heresy case. The work's most significant contribution to the Christian study of the Hebrew Scriptures lies in its description of the extensive system of accents used in biblical manuscripts and printed books to indicate various kinds of word stresses and musical cantillation. En route to identifying where the ordinary word accent falls and explaining changes in vocalization, it also offers an extensive overview of Hebrew paradigms, for both nouns and verbs. In part, it reinforces the paradigms of the *Rudiments of Hebrew*.

Accents and Orthography of the Hebrew Language is divided into three parts, each of which covers different types of Hebrew accentuation. Book 1, by far the most extensive, is a general presentation of *ta'amai ha-miqra'* (i.e., accents of Scripture).[96] The organization conforms roughly to that used in the

Rudiments: nouns—numerals—nouns with suffixes—prepositions—prepositions with pronouns, followed by a review of verb paradigms and verb forms
with suffixes.[97] Book 2 includes an extensive description of the Hebrew *meteg*
(מתג; "bridle"), a vertical stroke written under a letter that indicates a pause,
and the *dagesh* ("piercing"), a dot placed in the center of a letter to indicate
that the pronunciation should be harder (often called "*dagesh lene*") or that
the letter should be doubled (often called "*dagesh forte*"). Book 2 concludes
with a surprisingly lengthy account of the difference between "*sin*" (שׂ) and
"*shin*" (שׁ).[98] Book 3, which Reuchlin titles "נגינת," offers a valuable description of the *neginot*, the accent marks for cantillation. Understanding of these
accents, which like the vowel points were systematized by the Masoretes, is
important for fully understanding Hebrew manuscripts and printings of the
Bible. (Obviously, like vowel points, they do not appear in Torah scrolls.) This
is the context of Reuchlin's use of musical notation to give tonal equivalents for
the *neginot*, making this the first known book to feature Hebrew printed with
western musical notation. Musical notation (including four-part harmony) is
given for each of the Hebrew *neginot*.[99]

An important subtext in *Accents and Orthography of the Hebrew Language*
is Reuchlin's determination to sanction the Christian use of Jewish authorities. In it, he continued to give lavish credit to the Jewish scholarship he drew
on: "I have written all of this according to the teaching of the Jews in the way
in which they have analyzed this material in their grammatical and musical
books."[100] Once again, his major source was David Kimhi and most of the additional authorities that he had used in the *Rudiments of Hebrew*.

As we will see later (in chapter 8), Reuchlin composed *Accents and
Orthography of the Hebrew Language* at the height of the international controversy over his defense of Jewish books. Especially in light of the long history of
bitter attacks on his integrity, it is understandable that Reuchlin's anxiety concerning the acceptance of rabbinic authorities is, if anything, even higher than
it was when he published the *Rudiments of Hebrew* a decade earlier: "Greed did
not drive me to learn the Hebrew mysteries—indeed, I lavished gold liberally
on the expenses of those studies—nor did a vain desire for fame, for those
studies had to be concealed publicly, in so far as they would seem indecent for
a man established in such high regard."[101]

The impact of Reuchlin's research was seismic. German universities
scrambled to hire Hebrew professors in the 1510s. A letter of 30 March 1518
to Reuchlin gives the impression that the greatest concern of Friedrich the
Wise, elector of Saxony, was not to decide how to respond to the controversy
of the *Ninety-five Theses* (posted 31 October 1517) but something vastly more
significant—how to find suitable professors of Greek and Hebrew for the

University of Wittenberg.[102] In his reply, Reuchlin declined the professorship on the grounds that he was now too old to move so far away and instead proposed a short list of outstanding young Hebraicists who had studied under him—Johannes Oecolampadius and Conrad Pellican—as well as Paulo Ricci, a convert from Judaism who had recently published a Latin translation of the Kabbalistic *Gates of Light* (1516).[103] The letter includes an interesting disqualification of most Jewish converts on the grounds that they would typically have an insufficient command of Latin for university teaching.[104] Ultimately, Reuchlin recommended his protégé Philipp Melanchthon, who indeed began his momentous career in Wittenberg teaching both Greek and Hebrew, before Matthäus Adriani commenced rigorous Hebrew instruction in Wittenberg in 1520.[105]

In his final two years of life, however, Reuchlin did leave retirement to take successive professorships at the University of Ingolstadt (1520–21) and at the University of Tübingen (1521–22). According to his own accounts, a flood of students swamped his classes—in one letter he says 400 students were jamming the lecture hall for Hebrew and Greek. No doubt, such popularity resulted in part from the professor's fame but it also indicates the immediate success of his advocacy of Hebrew studies. His *Rudiments of Hebrew* demonstrably inspired scores of influential scholars to change their approach to theological study. Ulrich Zwingli and Martin Luther, to name just two, are known to have acquired Reuchlin's textbook and to have used it as a basis for their unusually consequential encounters with the Bible.[106] Several important professors of the next generation passed through his classroom, perhaps most famously Conrad Pellican, Sebastian Münster, Johannes Oecolampadius, Johannes Cellarius, Jacob Ceporinus, and Johann Forster. Münster, moreover, followed Reuchlin's lead by basing his own publications on those of the great rabbis, including, above all, David Kimhi and Moses Kimhi. Although Münster would dominate Christian Hebrew studies in the next generation, mainly because of his phenomenally influential publication of the Bible in Hebrew and Latin, no less a figure than Luther would accuse him of "Judaizing."[107] Indeed, Christian Hebrew scholarship would have more than one trajectory. Later Protestant Hebraists in the sixteenth century fiercely rejected Reuchlin's endorsement of rabbinic scholarship. In 1557, one of Reuchlin's students, Johann Forster, produced a Hebrew lexicon that proclaimed on the title page that it had been compiled directly from Holy Scripture "without the lies of the rabbis."[108]

When Reuchlin developed his Hebrew courses for Ingolstadt and Tübingen he did not order the *Rudiments of Hebrew* for his students. (Maybe it was an act of mercy, for his textbook was expensive.) Instead he based his instruction on Moses Kimhi's succinct *Mahalakh*, a book he had used extensively for his

Rudiments, which as of 1519 was available in a Hebrew-only pamphlet published by Reuchlin's printer Thomas Anshelm.[109] This new edition, which was dedicated to Elector Friedrich the Wise of Saxony, lacked any Christian reworking or even a Christian translation, though Reuchlin's student Münster would soon provide one. This was Reuchlin's last known effort to embrace the rabbinic tradition and his final assertion of the value of medieval Jewish writing to Christianity.

Christian Kabbalah

Thus far we have dealt almost exclusively with Reuchlin's Hebrew philology, a new beginning for Christianity that has remained foundational for theologians ever since. The founder of Christian Hebrew studies has also been recognized, along with Pico della Mirandola, as the founder of Christian Kabbalah, the Christian attempt to appropriate the methods and teachings of this esoteric and mystical element in Judaism. Although Kabbalah would have a persistent existence in Christianity over the next two centuries after Reuchlin, it never approached the high level of significance it had in early-modern Judaism. Joseph Leon Blau characterized Christian Kabbalah as an "intellectual fad" with a wide but thin diffusion.[110] Even though his contribution to Christian Kabbalah was foundational, if anything, this accomplishment carried the potential to undermine the credibility of his advocacy of Hebrew studies, for ever since Pico della Mirandola's 1486 publication of the *Nine Hundred Theses* Christian Kabbalists faced suspicions of heresy. As we will see in chapter 8, Reuchlin's opponents published strong condemnations of his Kabbalistic research beginning in 1518 (as a direct response to his *Art of the Kabbalah*). Many humanists, moreover, chose to see Reuchlin exclusively as a philologist, entirely ignoring his identity as a Kabbalist.[111] In his booming tribute to Reuchlin as Christian philologist, as we saw in chapter 1, Erasmus did not so much as mention his research in Kabbalah. There were many reasons for this, not the least one being Erasmus's fear that accusations of doctrinal error could taint the biblical philology movement. Reuchlin himself even stressed the more basic importance of biblical philology in his Kabbalistic tracts,[112] and his *Rudiments of Hebrew* eschewed any endorsement of Kabbalistic practices.

Reuchlin's two Kabbalistic tracts mark both the dawn and the dusk of his scholarly career. His *Miracle-Making Word* appeared in 1494 as his first major publication, strategically dedicated to Johannes von Dalberg, the ambitious patron of Christian humanism at the University of Heidelberg.[113] The work is an attempt to synthesize Kabbalistic theosophy with Greek philosophy and Christianity, a goal that also informs his *Art of the Kabbalah* (1517), where Reuchlin claims that Kabbalah is the source (and, therefore, the most authentic form) of Greek Pythagoreanism.[114] More important, *Art of the Kabbalah* offers a competent introduction to an eclectic array of Kabbalistic concepts drawn from Spanish and Italian sources. Even if Reuchlin's eclecticism may result in a simplification of Kabbalistic thinking,[115] the work is impressive because of the breadth of his innovative research. Reuchlin dedicated *Art of the Kabbalah*, much as Erasmus did the Greek Bible of 1516, to Pope Leo X as a humanist contribution to theological studies, one on a par, he thought, with his *Rudiments of Hebrew.*[116]

It is not surprising that Reuchlin's Kabbalistic studies encountered a mixed reception during his own lifetime, stirring opposition from the anti-Jewish movement at Cologne and also from some of his humanist supporters. Kabbalah has also occasioned disagreement of various types in the scholarship on Reuchlin. Several twentieth-century writers—Scholem, Brod, and Zika among them—have castigated the classic treatments of Reuchlin for undervaluing the importance of Kabbalah, while others have clashed over defining the substance of Reuchlin's Kabbalah. For some scholars (Geiger and Spitz), Reuchlin's Kabbalah was largely concerned with explanation of the mystical union between God and human as well as uncovering the mystical meanings of Scripture, whereas other scholars have contended that Reuchlin embraced the goal of performing magic through Kabbalah.[117] Many Kabbalists did claim that miracles were worked through knowledge of the names of God and the names of God's emanations,[118] but Reuchlin, especially in his mature treatise, described study of the names of God and the *sefirot* as ways of knowing God. The authors of some of the most comprehensive treatments of Reuchlin—Heinrich Graetz and Ludwig Geiger—probably were convinced that Kabbalah held little real value for the Jewish tradition generally (despite its historical importance),[119] but they rightly emphasized that Reuchlin did not advocate approaching Kabbalah primarily from the perspective of magic in the manner of Johannes Trithemius or even Cornelius Agrippa von Nettesheim. Even in the fledgling *Miracle-Making Word*, Reuchlin emphasized God's agency as the source of miracles: "Every human miracle, whose substance is true and not imaginary, whether it be great or modest, or slight, if the prescribed order of sacred things is followed, must always be attributed to glorious God, whose name may be blessed in all eternity."[120] Thus, while humans may petition divine intervention or work toward union with God, every miraculous action, even if suggested through the "miraculous word," originates in God's power and depends on belief in the saving force of the incarnation. In 1517, he expressed this orthodox position more forcefully: "Proper Kabbalists...affirm that miraculous works are from God alone and depend on the faith of man."[121] Reuchlin unquestionably absorbed the hermeticism of Ficino and the Kabbalistic enthusiasm of Pico, but his primary interests, certainly by 1517, were religious (mystical), philological, and exegetical. Moreover, Kabbalah and Jewish studies excited his interest because he wanted to uncover the *prisca theologia* (ancient, original theology) that, he felt, informed disparate religious traditions. Theurgistic Kabbalah was of little interest to him by 1517.[122]

While Kabbalah exists in a multitude of forms in Judaism, several of its central themes possessed considerable affinity to a Christian theological out-look. Among the elements of deepest interest to Reuchlin and other Christian Kabbalists were the transcendence of God and God's relationship to human-ity, a subject that Kabbalah explored in its theory of divine emanations called *sefirot* ("numbers" or "emanations"); the mystical (hidden) meaning of Holy Scripture and methods for uncovering those meanings; and the redemption of the world through the messiah.[123] In a basic way, God's transcendence—God is often identified as *"Ein Sof"* ("without end"; אֵין סוֹף) in Kabbalah—raised the theological problem of understanding God's relationship to humanity (and nature), a question that the Kabbalists answered in various ways, sometimes with a gnostic, Neoplatonic system of divine emanations, and sometimes, as in Maimonides, with a neo-Aristotelian approach to positing a relationship between the human and divine intellect.[124] These were engaging concepts to Christians seeking unity with God and, as we will see, it also allowed Christians to speculate on the relationship of their doctrine of the trinity to the theory of emanations. Karl Grözinger, moreover, was able to demonstrate Reuchlin's distinctive focus on messianism, which he adapted from the approaches of Abraham Abulafia and Azriel of Gerona, even though messianism was not a major concern in Jewish Kabbalah before Isaac Luria (1534–72).[125]

Like Jewish Kabbalists in the Renaissance, Reuchlin labored under the misconception that significant Kabbalistic sources were ancient. For example, he thought that the *Zohar*, a work of the late thirteenth century from Spain, was composed by the Talmudic sage Simeon ben Yohai in the second cen-tury. Moreover, again like Jewish Kabbalists, Reuchlin believed that God had revealed Kabbalistic teachings to Moses on Mount Sinai along with the written Law (much as the Mishnah is still traditionally viewed as the oral comple-ment to the Torah, also revealed on Mount Sinai). Reuchlin derived the term "Kabbalah" from "'Mose kibel,' i.e., Moses heard and accepted the Law from Sinai, from which Kabbalah is called acceptance (reception) through."[126] The Sinaitic revelation was an important premise because it allowed Christian Kabbalists to argue that the many observations in Kabbalah on the messiah to come pertained to Jesus and the development of the Christian faith. In other words, that Kabbalah, like the Hebrew Bible (according to Christian exegetes), was capable of demonstrating the validity of Christianity.

As we have seen, a powerful impetus for Reuchlin's embrace of Hebrew came from Giovanni Pico della Mirandola, even if Reuchlin's direct contact with Pico was extremely limited. He probably met him in 1490 but never managed to exchange letters with him, perhaps because Pico died by 1492. Nonetheless, Reuchlin immersed himself in Pico's writings, especially the *Nine Hundred Theses*, *Oration on the Dignity of Humanity* (which served as a kind of prelude to the *Theses*), and the widely read *Apology*. Pico had studied with a number of Jewish scholars (Elijah Delmedigo and Johanan Alemanno) and had commissioned Flavius Mithridates to translate Kabbalistic tracts into Latin. That his firsthand knowledge of Hebrew texts remained minimal did not temper the boldness of his assertions that Kabbalah effectively demonstrated the validity of basic Christian beliefs. In the *Nine Hundred Theses*, he famously said that "no science gives us stronger certainty about the divinity of Christ than do magic and Kabbalah,"[127] thereby becoming the first in a long line to claim that Kabbalah was concerned with Jesus, the messiah to come, and that the Jews had carefully preserved these revelations, even though they could not understand them. According to Pico's lapidary theses, Kabbalah proved the validity of the trinity, the incarnation, messiahship of Jesus, and even original sin. He therefore concluded that Christians not only need to study Kabbalah but also should use it as a weapon against Jews. Christian truths transmitted in Kabbalah, once explained to Jews, will offer a compelling argument for conversion. In this respect, Pico was expressing the same anti-Jewish rationale offered in the fifteenth century for the Christian study of the Talmud.

Miracle-Making Word

The first publication to result from Reuchlin's study of Hebrew and the esotericism of Pico (as well as Marsilio Ficino) was *Miracle-Making Word* (1494). Though lengthy, it demonstrates only modest familiarity with Hebrew and Kabbalah; very few Hebrew words are quoted and nothing is printed in Hebrew characters. Even more disappointing, in the hundreds of quotations from ancient sources, including the Bible, classical literature, philosophy, history, hermetic texts, and early Christian writers, there is not a single reference to a specific Jewish Kabbalistic text. It is an impressive demonstration of deep reading in many topics (especially in such recent scholarship as Ficino's translations of Hermes Trismegistos), but not in Kabbalah or any other Jewish works except the Bible. While the actual discussion of the Hebrew names of

God evokes Kabbalah, it is, in fact, drawn heavily from Dionysius the (Pseudo-) Areopagite's mystical tract *On the Divine Names* and a miscellany of ancient, non-Jewish sources.

Miracle-Making Word was composed as a dialogue—one set in Reuchlin's hometown of Pforzheim—between Reuchlin (bearing his newly minted Greek cognomen "Capnion"), Sidonius, a humanist philosopher with proclivities for Epicureanism, and Baruch, a learned Jew, with an astonishing command of classical culture. While his overarching purpose is to show commonalities between various ancient discourses on God, Reuchlin carefully conducts his analysis from the basis of two premises: (1) Judaism preserved the original discourse between God and humanity; and (2) Christianity now expresses the most perfect form of religion. These two principles guide the effort to fathom the meaning of "hidden words," to uncover the secrets of ancient philosophies (especially ancient theosophies such as Pythagoreanism) and, in particular, to reveal the names that Jews, various pagan writers, Pythagoras, and, of course, Christians have used for God and God's attributes.

As the title suggests, it did at least sketch the contours of Kabbalistic expositions on the names of God. Besides the tetragrammaton, Reuchlin (using the voice of the Jewish interlocutor Baruch) focused at some length on three names of God found in Kabbalah: *Ehyeh* ("I am," from Exodus 3:14: "ehyeh asher ehyeh"; I am that I am); *Hu* ("he," from Isaiah 13:8); and *Esh* ("fire," derived from God's appearance to Moses in Exodus 3:2). Instead of grounding these names in specific Kabbalistic sources, Reuchlin meticulously quoted biblical proof texts and cited pagan Greco-Roman and Christian mystical texts to document his claims.[128] For example, he linked *Ehyeh* to Plato's discussion of God in *Timaios*;[129] equated *Hu* with a description of Jupiter in Vergil's *Aeneid*;[130] and also found *Esh* in *Timaios*.[131] Dionysios the (Pseudo-) Areopagite is Reuchlin's principal source for Christian mystical definitions for these names. Using passages from his tract *On the Divine Names*, Reuchlin identifies the three Hebrew names with mystical discourse on God's being (and separation from humanity), God's glory and power, and the action or workings (*operatio*) of God. Although Dionysios does not use the terminology of *Hu*, Reuchlin described the qualities of *Hu* with a lengthy quotation from the Greek mystic.[132]

Capnion arranges the names in the order of *Hu, Ehyeh,* and *Esh* (which he consistently misspells as "*Esth*") to project the Christian trinity of God the Father, God the Son, and God the Holy Spirit as "Substance (being), power, and action."[133] He rounds out this association of Jewish, orthodox Christian, and Christian mystical terminology with an equation of the trinity to the Greek poet Homer's depictions of Jupiter, Athena, and Aphrodite. While we might dismiss this as an overly imaginative as well as an overly deterministic effort to establish a theosophic syncretism, Reuchlin considered his work to be solid evidence that these divergent religious perspectives derive from an authentic (and common) ancient theology (the *prisca theologia*).[134]

Baruch's descriptions of the Kabbalistic emanations of God—the *sefirot*—are unusually chaotic and even partially erroneous.[135] He describes the attributes of God that emanate from God's being as expressions of the three names *Hu, Ehyeh,* and *Esh.* The correct names and the standard order of the *sefirot* are: (1) *Keter* (crown), (2) *Hokhmah* (wisdom), (3) *Binah* (understanding), (4) *Hesed* (mercy), (5) *Gevurah* (strength; also called *Pahad*), (6) *Tiferet* (glory), (7) *Netsah* (victory), (8) *Hod* (honor), (9) *Yesod* (foundation), and (10) *Malkhut* (kingdom; now usually called *Shekhinah,* "divine presence"). In *Miracle-Making Word,* Reuchlin omitted the *sefirah* of *Yesod* from his list and misunderstood *Gevurah* and *Pahad,* which are variants of the fifth *sefirah,* as separate emanated attributes. He also got the order wrong.[136] All of this would be corrected twenty-three years later in his *Art of the Kabbalah.*[137]

Judaism ultimately has only limited validity in this first attempt to synthesize ancient religious and theosophic beliefs under the aegis of Christian orthodoxy. Reuchlin may be attempting to appear well-disposed to Judaism when he acknowledges that the ancient Jewish religion practiced the true worship of God: "The Jews have made great contributions to our ability and often with greater justification we should imitate them more than other cultures, since according to the testimony of our forefathers their religion had a closer relation to divinity and worshiped God correctly."[138] But, he also emphasizes the church's position that the beliefs and liturgy of contemporary Judaism are now no longer attuned to the true God.

While Judaism has lost its relevance, Hebrew has not, and much of the tract is devoted to propounding the special status of the Hebrew language. As indicated in the epigraph to this chapter, Reuchlin celebrated Hebrew as the first language God created, the very medium for the union of God and people. Thus the embrace of Kabbalistic ideas of language, especially the connection of the names of God to God, elevates Hebrew to the ultimate status of being the salvific mediation between God and the human. According to Reuchlin, an existential unity between the transcendent God and the human is possible in the Hebrew word. This unity occurs in the articulation of the name of God for there is a "bond of words" between God and humans, which is possible because "God is the breath ("spiritus"), the word is the breathing ("spiratio"), and the human is the breather ("spirans").[139]

Formerly this unity could be invoked through the tetragrammaton, but now that name of God has become ineffable (the *Shem ha-Meforash*). Reuchlin attributes this demise to the defective development of Judaism (by which he means the failure to embrace Jesus as the messiah). According to the interlocutor Capnion (speaking to Baruch):

> Believe me, we must understand that an important reason is
> standing in the way so that the miracle-working words have stopped
> responding to your Jews, as you say.[140] ...The saving power of words,
> which has deserted you and has chosen us, accompanies us and, as
> can be observed, obeys our will. This power of the perfect religion,
> given and presented by divine will and not by human council,
> has changed its venue not by chance but rather with diligence
> and purpose because you altered the legitimate form of worship.
> Therefore you mumble in vain, in vain you invoke God, whom you
> do not worship as he desires, but rather you coax with your own
> fabrications. Moreover, you hate us, the true worshipers of God, with
> an eternal passion.[141]

Despite this deprecation of Judaism and Jews, Hebrew remains for him the proper language for the invocation of God and for functioning as the medium that unifies God and the human.

Hebrew may be the language of God-human union, but the names of God have shifted within that discourse to reflect the development, from the Christian perspective, of God's covenants. Thus, in the following passage, Reuchlin identifies different names for God before the covenant, during the covenant with Israel, and, according to Christians, during the second covenant:

> Connect all these statements and you will easily perceive that
> the greatest force at every time and the most efficacious action
> was always through the trigrammaton of the forefathers, the
> tetragrammaton of the patriarchs, and the pentagrammaton of
> the sons, that is, in the state of nature it was SDI [i.e., "*Shaddai*"];
> under the law it was ADNI [i.e., "*Adonai*," the usual vocalization for
> *Yhvh*]; and under grace it was IHSVH. We are now the sons of God.
> Therefore we use five letters for him in whom we believe and whom
> we invoke as the mediator of God and humans, he who is both God
> and human.[142]

This passage comes in the aftermath of Capnion's revelation of the miracle-making word—*Ihsvh*—the pentagrammaton created by the addition of a *shin* to the tetragrammaton. Capnion concedes that his revelation is little more than a confirmation of the validity of Christianity and that all the powers that proceed from this miracle-making word are already known to Christianity, even if he does continue to connect it as much as possible to the *unio mystica*: "Does it seem a small thing that you are going forth with such profit, having gotten your wish? This is that miracle-making word, which you have been hoping for for so long, the marvelous word, the deifying word, indeed, God as word and word as God, the name of the word *Ihsvh* and the word of the name *Ihsvh*, the same *Ihsvh*, word and name, who is the Lord of Lords."[143]

So what is the power of the pentagrammaton, according to Reuchlin? It is wholly consistent with Christianity's view of God's being and power and of humanity's relationship to God. Reuchlin's central thesis turns out to be a recasting of Jesus' own proclamation in the Gospel of John 14:12–14, a passage that offers the ultimate explanation of the miracle-making word:

> And let us depend on God and let us have unshakable, genuine, and simple faith in the son of God through whom we live, are moved, and exist. From his own lips of truth, he infallibly promised us with the assurance, saying: "Amen, amen, I say to you, whoever believes in me, he will do the works which I do and he will do things greater than these because I am going to the father, and whatever you pray for from the father in my name, I will do it, so that the father will be glorified in the son. If you pray for anything in my name, I will do it." These are the divine testimonies, these are the monuments of our mysteries, these are the sacerdotal memorials, these are the purest signs, these are our ceremonies, which are completed with little effort, easy to do, and with little pomp.[144]

Thus, Reuchlin's conclusion is that the Christian worship of God, its prayers and liturgies offered "in the name of Jesus," constitutes the correct discourse of salvation. In a rhetorical barrage, Capnion fires off a long list of miracles achieved through the miracle-making word, all of which are taken from the New Testament or other early Christian writings.[145]

Readers have often observed Reuchlin's favorable representation of Baruch in this dialogue (and the even more impressive characterization of Simon in *Art of the Kabbalah*). From this, they have concluded that Reuchlin had an unusual capacity for respecting Jewish scholars for their accomplishments. But to what degree does this imply tolerance for Judaism? It certainly establishes a tone that could mitigate hatred of Jews as people in public discourse. But it does not necessarily recognize any value in the continued practice of Judaism. When in 1494 Reuchlin emphasized that Judaism had formerly been the true worship of God he was obviously recognizing a standard Christian position but at the same time urging his contemporaries to consider adopting a more benign outlook on Jews. But in *Miracle-Making Word*, he also consistently maintained that Judaism had been entirely superseded by Christianity. The value of Jewish writings is historically contingent; those historical writings do not necessarily elevate the status of contemporary Judaism.

In *Miracle-Making Word* there are several statements on the humiliation and the historical demise of Israel, an act that Reuchlin unquestionably associates with divine will. At one point, Capnion even sighs loudly that there is little hope for ever converting the "stiff-necked" Jews.[146] In fact, Capnion insists that Baruch must repudiate the Talmud and undergo an elaborate "washing" ceremony,[147] quoting Isaiah 1:16 to make his point: "Let this be your change of mind. Baruch, abandon the Talmud, and, you, Sidonius, abandon your Epicurus and Lucretius. 'Wash yourselves; make yourselves clean.'"[148] Even though he wistfully calls the Talmud the source of "the greatest pleasure" and "sweeter than all that remains in life," Baruch agrees "to reject the Talmud" so as "not to remain ignorant of the miracle-making word."[149]

Art of the Kabbalah

Twenty-three years later, with his publication of *Art of the Kabbalah*, Reuchlin took a long stride forward. This is a major work of Christian scholarship on Judaism, one that is richly nourished by Jewish sources. Indeed, many pages are heavy with Hebrew quotations, printed with great confidence, though in a roughly cut font, by Thomas Anshelm. As would become customary for sixteenth-century Christian humanists, Reuchlin helpfully translated each Hebrew passage into Latin.

Pico may have been the first Christian to use the term "Kabbalah" and to champion the validity of the *sefirot* but he did not explain any Kabbalistic principles in much detail. Reuchlin has pride of place in historical surveys of Christian Kabbalism because he was the first to explain many basic Kabbalistic principles and adapt them to Christianity. His influence was pervasive until the end of the seventeenth century, even if Christians after him had access to vastly more Jewish sources. As Reuchlin himself conceded, there were "countless Kabbalists"[150] to study. Even so, in *Art of the Kabbalah*, he was able to use several major medieval sources—the *Zohar* (*Book of Splendor*) by Moses de León[151] and the works of Joseph Gikatilla, especially his *Ginnat Egoz* (*Nut Garden*), *Sha'arei Orah* (*Gates of Light*), and *Sha'arei Tsedeq* (*Gates of Righteousness*),[152] and perhaps the *Sefer Yetsirah* (*Book of Formation*; anonymous work from the third or fourth century).[153] He also knew the *Gates of Light* through the 1516 Latin translation by Paolo Ricci, a prominent Jewish convert to Christianity, as well as in the Hebrew original.[154] Nonetheless, although Reuchlin certainly had complete copies of some of his Kabbalistic sources, Gershom Scholem discovered that he relied greatly on an anthology of Kabbalistic texts similar (or identical) to a manuscript in the Jewish Theological Seminary (MS Halberstam 444).[155] An interesting feature of Reuchlin's sources, as we can see in the following list, is that he absorbed such an eclectic mixture of diverse approaches to Kabbalah. Reuchlin explicitly cited his sources at the beginning of Simon's exposition of Kabbalah in book 1; that list includes the following authors and works (given in Reuchlin's order): Rabbi Akiva (ca. 40–135); the *Zohar* (which Reuchlin attributes to Simeon ben Yohai); *Sefer ha-Bahir* (*Book of Brightness*, a foundational text of the late twelfth century); Abraham Abulafia (thirteenth century); Moses Nahmanides (1194–1270); Menahem Recanati (ca. 1250–ca. 1310); Moses Maimonides (1135–1204; specifically his *Guide for the Perplexed*, which Reuchlin frequently cites); Joseph Gikatilla (1248–ca. 1325); Saadiah Gaon (882–942); Abraham ibn Ezra (1089–1164); Azriel of Gerona (thirteenth century); Todros Abulafia (ca. 1220–98); Judah Halevi (ca. 1075–1141); and Joseph Albo (ca. 1380–1444).[156] It was fitting that he concluded his catalog with a tribute to a principal source, Joseph Gikatilla:

> But in my opinion no one up to this time has ever written about that art more scientifically, more distinctly, and more lucidly than has Rabbi Joseph ben Abraham of Castile, a citizen of Salem. He studiously built up three volumes on this discipline, in which he clarified the entire teachings of the Kabbalists—the first volume is on words, the second on letters, and the third is on points [i.e., diacritics and punctuation]. The title of his book is גנת אגוז, i.e., *Nut Garden*, based on the Song of Songs, 'I went down to the garden (orchard) of nuts.'"[157]

He also frequently cites other Jewish authorities (as in his *Rudiments of Hebrew*), including the Talmud, David Kimhi, and, especially, Rashi. Many elements of the Jewish tradition, including the writings of several medieval rabbis, appear in this book as authorities both for investigating theology and, more significantly, for leading a spiritual life in accord with God's will.

As in the earlier work, Reuchlin is determined to connect divergent religious worlds—Judaism, Islam, Christianity, and ancient paganism, especially the esotericism of Hermes Trismegistos and, above all, Pythagoras.[158] This time, two philosophers—one is Philolaus, a Christian with expertise in Pythagoreanism, hermetic writings, and Christian mysticism; the other is Marranus, a Muslim from Constantinople eager to learn about Pythagoreanism[159]—hope to take advantage of their journey to Frankfurt during one of the great commercial fairs to study Kabbalah under a local scholar named Simon ben Eleazar. Philolaus claims that this Simon is a descendant of Simeon ben Yohai, the famed Talmudic rabbi and the supposed author of the *Zohar*.[160]

Like the 1494 work, Reuchlin organized *Art of the Kabbalah* into three books. Book 1 is Simon's introduction to the Kabbalah, with strong emphasis on doctrines about the messiah to come. Book 2 records a dialogue between Philolaus and Marranus on the commonalities between Pythagoreanism and Kabbalah. (Simon is absent because he must observe the Sabbath.) Book 3, by far the most significant source of Kabbalistic information, addresses the following topics: the Sabbath,[161] the goals of Kabbalah,[162] the "fifty gates of understanding,"[163] the "thirty-two paths of wisdom,"[164] the seventy-two angels,[165] the ten *sefirot*,[166] the "art of Kabbalah" (meaning techniques of Bible exegesis),[167] a loosely organized discourse on angels and demons, followed by a closing discussion of Jesus as the messiah.[168]

Why should a Muslim and a Christian interested in Pythagoreanism seek out a Jewish Kabbalist? Contact with the renowned Kabbalist is of great significance because Reuchlin pronounces Pythagoras the Greek embodiment of Kabbalah, "for it is said that Pythagoras derived nearly all his dogmas from it."[169] And, indeed, that all subsequent forms of esoteric thought derive from Kabbalah. Clearly, the connection to antiquity has great meaning for Reuchlin, the quintessential Renaissance humanist. He would certainly prefer being labeled "Christian humanist Kabbalist" rather than the now standard "Christian Kabbalist." Frequently, he described himself as the scholar who recovered "Pythagoreanism" but never as the founder of "Christian Kabbalah." The classical moniker would have been less jarring than the Jewish one, but, inspired by Eusebius of Caesarea's *Preparation for the Gospel* (*Praeparatio evangelica*), Reuchlin genuinely believed that Pythagoreanism was an estuary of Kabbalah[170]:

> Pythagoras [drew] his stream [of knowledge] from the boundless ocean of Kabbalah....For what purpose does either Kabbalah or Pythagoras have other than to bring the souls of men back to God, that is, to move them forward to a state of perfect blessedness. Something else they have in common is their way of handing down knowledge and their practice, common to both, through symbols, signs, sayings, proverbs, numbers and figures, and letters, syllables, and words.[171]

Reuchlin did not stop at acclaiming Kabbalah the source for Pythagoreanism; according to him, Judaism is the ultimate source for all philosophy, and ancient philosophical and theological systems simply plagiarized the Jews:

> Everything the Jews have, both their traditions [i.e., the revelations they have received] and their discoveries have been published by

foreign plagiarisms first committed by the Greeks and then by the Romans. And we have nothing in our philosophy that was not originally Jewish, even though in our age the glory they deserve is taken from them and now everything of theirs is held in the lowest regard.[172]

With striking acuity, Max Brod wrote that "Reuchlin is simultaneously a mystic and a philologist,"[173] thereby boldly identifying two elements in Reuchlin's approach to theology that may seem contradictory to us. These two poles certainly characterize his study of Kabbalah for he understood Kabbalah as the path to salvation and unity with God and as the ultimate art for studying divine language. According to his most basic definition, "Kabbalah is a symbolic reception of divine revelation, handed down for the salvific contemplation of God and the separate forms [i.e., emanations]."[174] Indeed, Reuchlin admitted that it was necessary to be "equipped with many skills, an immense knowledge of the humanities," in order to contemplate the divine emanations and "creep into the deepest recesses of God."[175]

Despite the presentation of a tremendous amount of recondite and technical matters of Kabbalah, Reuchlin never loses sight of something more basic: the need to develop piety and spirituality. Perhaps the most noticeable feature of the tract is the steady flow of encouragement to lead a godly life as part of the Kabbalah. These many, often elegantly formulated passages have a special significance because they are either quotes from Jewish writers or are spoken by the Jewish interlocutor Simon. The Jewish voice takes the lead in urging godliness throughout the tract. It is important to reflect on the fact that it is not a Christian but the Jew Simon who says such things as "we conceive an intense and burning love for God,"[176] or "that man who controls his thoughts in his heart to the extent that, after conquering the flesh, he can meditate on the divine law, that man, I say, is blessed since he will see God because of his pure heart."[177]

The sheer quantity of Kabbalistic information and the sheer number of Kabbalistic themes are overwhelming. Especially book 3 is a whirlwind tour of the world of Kabbalistic research and thinking, delivered in ways evocative of Gikatilla. Reuchlin was the first to introduce to Christian thought the Kabbalistic categories of the "work of creation" (*ma'aseh bereshit*), cosmological speculations on creation and the divine emanations, and the "work of the chariot" (*ma'aseh merkavah*), eschatological speculations, especially on the coming of the messiah, that were inspired initially by the book of Ezekiel.[178] Without using a Jewish source (as far as I can tell), he tried to differentiate Talmud and Kabbalah on this basis, implying that the Talmud offers a guide for life in this world; Kabbalah for attaining salvation hereafter.[179] He also claimed that the two discourses had different concepts of salvation: the Talmudists are interested in the salvation of Israel (as is traditional for Jewish messianism), whereas the Kabbalists focus more generally on the redemption of fallen humanity, thus making Kabbalah sound more familiar to a Christian ear. There is, however, no expression of hostility toward the Talmud whatsoever; the Talmud is frequently cited as a rich treasury of religious thought.

The most sustained exposition is accorded to Kabbalistic approaches to scriptural exegesis, which Reuchlin labels "the art of the Kabbalah."[180] In book 1, Simon had already explained the scriptural basis of Kabbalah:

> Nothing could connect us more intricately to God…than the
> Scriptures, which lead us first to admiration of divine things, then
> to recognition of them and finally to a burning love of divinity
> recognized in this way.…This [i.e., Scripture] is the only field for
> true contemplation, the individual words of which are all mysteries,
> every phrase, syllable, diacritic, punctuation mark are full of hidden
> meanings.[181]

This sounds like a hopeful philologist-mystic speaking. The Kabbalist assumption that every aspect of Scripture bears meaning drew upon the medieval Jewish (and Christian) view that Scriptures were the result of literal inspiration. For the Christian humanist this carried a special burden—the necessity of returning to the literally inspired Scriptures in their original forms. Every aspect of the language of Scripture was now subject to analysis.

Reuchlin introduced Christianity to *gematria*, *notarikon*, and *temurah*, the three Kabbalistic methods for ascertaining hidden meanings in the Hebrew Scriptures. As Reuchlin indicates, his presentation of the topic draws extensively on the outstanding synthesis Gikatilla composed in his *Nut Garden*. The Hebrew word for garden in Gikatilla's title creates an acronym (g-n-t) for the three methods: "As Rabbi Joseph the Younger of Salem entitled the books he wrote about this art, the *Garden*, גנת, because of the three letters of this word [i.e., in the construct state], each one of which designates one part of the art of the Kabbalah, for *gimel* signifies גימטריא [i.e., *gematria*], *nun* נוטריקון [i.e., *notariqon*], and *tav* תמורה [i.e., *temurah*]."[182]

Gematria is the manipulation of words based on their numerical value, usually arrived at through adding up the values of their letters. (As in Greek, Hebrew letters also function as numbers and, therefore, Kabbalists were able to say that words had numerical values.) Using the code of *gematria*, the exegete substitutes other words of an equal numerical value for the word in Hebrew

Scripture, thus revealing a new hidden meaning in the Bible.[183] Often the process has a homiletic quality. For instance, the *gematria* analysis of *hokhmah* (wisdom) creates an association between "wisdom" and the commandments of the Torah. Simon explains that the numerical value of *hokhmah* is 613, the very number of the commandments that tradition (as recorded in the Talmud) claims are expressed in the Torah.[184] This confirms the wisdom of the commandments themselves and the wisdom of living in accord with them.[185]

Interpretation by *notarikon* (i.e., "shorthand") usually extracts a moral lesson encoded in an acronym. Often, the letters of entire words are treated as acronyms; sometimes, the initial or final letters of words in a phrase are used to form a new word as well. For example, "amen" can mean *"Adonai Melekh Ne'eman"* ("God is a righteous king"). Reuchlin locates this special sense specifically in Isaiah: "Read Isaiah, chapter 65, 'He will be blessed in God, amen.' Who is that God? The Kabbalists respond that it is אדני מלך נאמן, that is, 'The Lord is a faithful king,' for the three letters of amen denote the three first letters of those words."[186]

Reuchlin introduces his explanation of *temurah* (which means transposition or exchange) by labeling it a "much more occult" technique.[187] This system, which can be complex and arbitrary in equal measure, uses anagrammatic rearrangements of letters and substitution of letters according to a flexible code (or table) called a *tsiruf* (צירוף).[188] *Temurah* often gives the appearance that virtually any desired result of substitution can be achieved. As we will see below, Reuchlin uses *temurah* to extract a trinitarian message from the letters of the tetragrammaton.

Representation of Judaism

Art of the Kabbalah provides insight into Reuchlin's mature position on the status of Judaism. The representation of Judaism in this work differs significantly from that of *Miracle-Making Word* because it does not unfold as a triumphalist discourse of "adversus Judaeos": *Art of the Kabbalah* features neither the defeat nor conversion of its Jewish hero. Moreover, nearly every page contains an implicit statement of important commonalities between Christianity and Judaism, and, while Reuchlin's premise is that all philosophy has been derived from Judaism, he does not limit the value of Judaism to its status as historical precursor to Christianity. *Art of the Kabbalah* is a depiction of the history of Jewish scholarship and piety, including Judaism of 1517, as an ongoing story of God's people. The Jewish search for God, be it in biblical study, meditation, or devotion, has integrity and differs from that of Christianity only in its historical accidents, not in its essence. The net result of Reuchlin's new Christian Kabbalism is that Judaism and Jews are defended, not castigated.[189]

The portrayal of the Jewish interlocutor Simon suggests that Reuchlin intended to represent contemporary Jewish scholars as humanist ideals.[190] To some readers today, Simon may appear as a prefiguration, though a full 250 years earlier, of Gotthold Ephraim Lessing's Nathan the Wise. Reuchlin probably intended him as an evocation of his Jewish teachers Sforno and Loans. Simon is a man of moral probity, godly wisdom, theological expertise, and, above all else, humanist eloquence; as one interlocutor says, he commands "Nestorian eloquence."[191] A good place to appreciate the warmth of this representation is at the beginning of book 2, where the non-Jewish interlocutors express their amazement that such a man, from the despised race of the Jews, has such magnanimity and knowledge. Marranus wishes he could have stayed up all night gazing on the divine countenance of Simon and listening to his words.[192] The final words of the tract can be read as an indication of an emerging innovation of Christian-Jewish relations, as Christians and Jews join in a quest for knowledge of God. All good things, even 200-page Kabbalistic tracts, have to come to an end. As the gentiles bid farewell to Simon, they acclaim him, very much from the perspective of Christianity, as "decus nostrum,"[193] meaning "our glory," or "our pride." This foundational work of Christian Kabbalah ends without Jewish conversion, suggesting instead the possibility of enriching Christianity without defacing Judaism.

The representation of Judaism is even more unusual. The work, written in the "Christian language" of Latin, gives Judaism a voice that Christians can hear and comprehend. The great Jewish sages and the medieval rabbis are powerful theologians and philosophers who have taught a way of life and a love of God that befit all humanity. Hundreds of quotations from Jewish sources espouse godly teachings as in the following brief example, which is typical for many pages of the book: "'Whoever teaches the people to walk in the way of the Lord,' writes Rabbi David Kimhi..., 'he will be saved; whoever contemns this, he will perish.'"[194] For the first time, Reuchlin presents Kimhi's piety, quite apart from his scholarship, for the edification of the Christian reader.

Without any chauvinism or disdain, and with only limited qualification, Reuchlin portrays Jewish piety and Jewish mysticism as exemplary for Christians. The one qualification pertains to the issue of the messiah, which Reuchlin handles in a complex and subtle fashion, but without the blunt tone of Judaism-bashing that he had lapsed into in 1494. Nonetheless, as before, Reuchlin expressly values Kabbalah as a Jewish repository of teachings on Jesus as the messiah. Apparently not realizing the implications of his words, Simon presents the pentagrammaton as authentic Kabbalistic teaching (which, of course, it is not). In Simon's narrative, the angel Raziel informs the fallen Adam that the new Adam, the messiah, will bear the tetragrammaton (the ineffable name of God) altered by the insertion of a *shin*.[195] This *shin* will represent the "mercy" of the messiah.

Moreover, as the work builds to a climax, Simon offers a trinitarian analysis of a powerful name of God—a name of forty-two letters—that he has derived through the technique of *temurah* (manipulation, transformation of letters). Once again, despite the use of an authentic technique, this result is not a part of the Kabbalistic tradition:

> Rabbi Hakadosh [i.e., Judah ha-Nasi] says that from the
> tetragrammaton flows the name of twelve letters, אב בן ורוח הקדש,
> i.e., father, son, and holy spirit, from which the name of
> forty-two letters is derived, which is pronounced as follows,
> אב אלהים בן אלהים רוח הקדש אלהים שלשה באחד אחד בשלשה, i.e., God the
> Father, God the Son, and God the Holy Spirit, three in one, and one
> in three.[196]

Once again, this analysis is described by Simon as if it belonged to authentic Jewish Kabbalah, and he does so without making any comment on its obvious relevance to Christianity.

At the very end of the work, *Jhsvh* as the name of God emerges as challenge to Judaism. It is, however, Marranus, the Muslim, who tells Simon that everything the Kabbalists can do through the ineffable name of God, the Christians can do more effectively through the effable pentagrammaton—*Jhsvh*. Marranus quotes the same passage mentioned in *Miracle-Making Word*—now identified as coming from the Midrash on Psalms—that ponders if God does not hear Jewish prayers because Jews can no longer articulate the *Shem ha-Meforash*.[197] To this one challenge to the validity of Judaism, Simon replies with an ironic "perhaps." But then Simon shows yet another Kabbalistic way to connect Judaism and Christianity, this time by associating the Hebrew word for "cross" with the Hebrew word for "wood" as used in the Exodus account of the bronze serpent set up in the desert to restore the Jewish faith. This is an innovative use of *gematria* (the two words are associated because each has a numerical value of 150),[198] but it is actually just derived from a traditional association (typology) for Christian Bible exegetes. (The bronze serpent in alignment with the cross would soon appear as an image on many a Renaissance Protestant Bible.) But Reuchlin, speaking through the Jewish Kabbalist Simon, once again wishes to demonstrate that the methods and revelations of Kabbalah can have a special relevance to Christianity.

And that is the penultimate note of *Art of the Kabbalah*. The dialogue ends without any conversion, or even any pressure on Simon to convert. Apart from

Marranus's brief challenge, as noted above, there is no overt rhetoric "against the Jews." The final note is one of joy as Simon explains that he must depart the next day (making further discussion impossible) to attend his uncle's wedding, which will be celebrated in the great Jewish center of Regensburg. The friends bid farewell, acclaiming Simon as "our glory" ("decus nostrum").

This representation of the Jew as "our glory" marks a major departure from the Kabbalistic tract of 1494. Max Brod characterized *Art of the Kabbalah* as "a work in which he dared to say more and more substantial things to benefit the persecuted Jews and their disdained and misunderstood intellectual champions than in all of his earlier works combined."[199] It is, moreover, an especially daring representation for 1517, a time when Reuchlin's heresy trial was nearing its dramatic conclusion. The narrative frame for *Art of the Kabbalah* is actually Reuchlin's trial, for the book begins and ends with a letter to Pope Leo X, who was then deliberating his final judgment on the question of whether or not Reuchlin expressed ideas that were "impermissibly favorable to the Jews." Reuchlin's address to Leo closes with a brief account of the state of his trial at the Roman curia. He confidently announces that a Roman commission of cardinals and other prelates—he refers to them as "the lights of the world"[200]— has just vindicated him (an event of summer 1516). But he acknowledges that a final decision now rests in the hands of the pope.

This, of course, brings us to the topic of the following chapters—the campaign against Judaism and Reuchlin's defense of Jewish writings.

5

Johannes Pfefferkorn and the Campaign against Jews

Therefore take the path of books away from them. Burn the books.
Then it will be that much easier to bring them to the path of truth.
—Johannes Pfefferkorn, in *Mirror of the Jews* (1507)

He [i.e., Pfefferkorn] can hardly be castigated as a half-Jew for his
actions indicate that he is a Jew and a half.
—Erasmus, writing to Willibald Pirckheimer on
2 November 1517

Johannes Pfefferkorn probably endured more barrages of anti-
Semitic hate speech than any other person in the Renaissance.
According to his foes, he was an ignorant, corrupt, criminal, even
stinking Jewish butcher. In several letters (one of which Reuchlin
published in 1519), Erasmus suggested that he was masterminding a
Jewish plot to destroy Christianity.[1] On the surface, this is puzzling
because, after 1504, he was certainly no longer a Jew and, in fact,
had dedicated himself, body and soul, to annihilating his former
faith.

The anti-Semitism of those who opposed Pfefferkorn is an important facet of the Reuchlin Affair for it blatantly reveals how readily
many of Reuchlin's supporters were able to square hatred of Jews and
scorn for Judaism with promotion of Jewish studies among Christians.
As for Pfefferkorn, Reuchlin and his supporters were willing to stoop
to almost any level in their efforts to discredit him.[2] Despite waging an

unflagging battle against Judaism, the newly Christian pamphleteer remained vulnerable to innuendos of insincerity, of being a "half-Jew," or, in Erasmus's unsavory attempt at humor, a "Jew and a half."[3] The anti-Judaism of some Reuchlin supporters was so misplaced that it provoked a Catholic historian, Georg Weislinger, to compose a defense of Pfefferkorn against the Reuchlinists some 200 years after the fact.[4] Weislinger's main point was that Pfefferkorn was a good and devout Christian, while the Reuchlinists in question would soon show their true colors by becoming supporters of the renegade friar Martin Luther.

As the embodiment of the plight of the Jewish convert, Pfefferkorn has elicited an occasional expression of limited sympathy from modern historians. Heiko Oberman saw him, the traitor to his native culture and the suspicious newcomer to Christians, as an "absolute outsider."[5] In contrast to Spain or Portugal, the number of Jewish converts to Christianity in the Holy Roman Empire was relatively small; there is also no evidence that a distinctive converso culture ever developed in Germany, or that insincere conversion (and, therefore, crypto-Judaism) was ever a worrisome issue for Christian authorities there. Nonetheless, the Ashkenazi converts adopted a complex social identity. They may have been welcomed in a festive baptism celebration (and deeply mourned by the Jewish community), but they would also frequently face suspicions of being inauthentic Christians. Pfefferkorn himself complained of disingenuous conversion: "One finds many a bad Jew who goes to a place and gets baptized, not that he wants to be a good Christian, but only because he wants to acquire money and property."[6] In one very unusual statement, he chastises himself for lapsing into "the old evil habits" from which only the sacrament of confession can offer restoration.[7] In a basic way, the new Christian was still partly a Jew, even if there was no social network for nurturing such an identity in Germany as there was in Spain. Elisheva Carlebach evocatively defined the Ashkenazi conversion as the formation of "a divided soul."[8]

Nonetheless, as evidenced by many documents, including the imperial mandate of August 1509, Pfefferkorn had earned the trust of Christian authorities. We can also see similar evidence of acceptance in the records of other (admittedly prominent) Jewish converts from the period. For example, Victor of Carben,[9] a rabbi who became a Dominican friar, was a contemporary of Pfefferkorn (as well as fellow resident of Cologne) who also achieved renown as an author of anti-Jewish books. Emperor Maximilian called upon him, too, in 1510 to evaluate the mandate against Jewish writings. If anything, Pfefferkorn inspired unusually great confidence in the educated and elite Christians he encountered, that is, until the publication of his harsh pamphlets against Johannes Reuchlin made him a polarizing figure in the Christian world.

Johannes Pfefferkorn did not act alone and certainly not in a vacuum, yet initially he was the most prominent figure in the campaign against Jewish books. Shortly after his conversion to Christianity in 1504 or 1505,[10] he developed extensive contacts with houses of Observant Franciscans and seems to have become involved in conversionary missions to Jewish communities. In a 1516 account, Pfefferkorn credited the Franciscans with conceiving the book campaign:

> I did not start this affair on my own initiative. For the honorable and reverend priestly fathers and lords of the Observant Franciscan Order incited me to do it. During confession, they taught and instructed me that I could accomplish nothing better on earth that would be more pleasing to God and would be more beneficial to me in eternal life than that I should pave the way and work assiduously that their false and blasphemous books be taken away (as indicated previously) and destroyed. Also that they should not be allowed to practice shameful usury and that they should earn their bread among Christians with menial labor and that they should be compelled to hear the word of God at appropriate times from our preachers. I received such instruction and direction with the help and assistance of the same fathers of the Observant Franciscans, from such convents as those in Mainz, Oppenheim, Heidelberg, Ulm, and Munich. They also recommended me to the most noble, high born princess, duchess, sister of his imperial majesty [i.e., Duchess Kunigunde of Bavaria]. Moreover, in the presence of the emperor and the princess several of the same fathers made the request in this matter along with me.[11]

His early actions probably resembled anti-Jewish campaigns that mendicant preachers had been mounting since the thirteenth century, sometimes with the assistance of Jewish converts. In 1507, Pfefferkorn's effort gained prominence as he began publishing innovative pamphlets that recast elements of scholarly anti-Judaism in vernacular, popular forms. Pfefferkorn appears to have taken pride in the rhetorical accomplishment of his pamphlets: "Thus I exposed their evil, their perfidy, and their blasphemy of God, which before my day no one had done so clearly and understandably."[12] Even after 1509, when leadership of the campaign was being assumed by other authorities (including the archbishop of Mainz, the inquisitor general of Teutonia, the University of Cologne, and even Emperor Maximilian), Pfefferkorn continued to be a prominent agitator, publishing additional pamphlets against Jews and their supporters, above all Reuchlin, until 1521.

A key to Pfefferkorn's success was his skillful and unrelenting advocacy of the new stratagem of complete suppression of Jewish books. Pfefferkorn and his allies proposed many different policies for destroying Jewish life—forced menial labor, forced baptism, compulsory attendance at Christian missionary sermons, and expulsion—but none of them were likely to be implemented or successful. Mandatory attendance at sermons was a common anti-Jewish measure that clearly harassed Jews but led to few conversions. Forced baptism was explicitly illegal under existing law, and there were many historical precedents for allowing Jews to return to Judaism, after they "accepted" baptism in the extreme duress of a pogrom. Expulsion, which certainly was being used effectively against German Jewish communities, was fraught with difficulty because it could only be carried out on a territory-by-territory basis through agreements negotiated between territorial authorities and the emperor. Many territories of the empire had driven out Jews, but each expulsion was a slow, inefficient process that entailed an extensive political campaign without guarantee of success. The city of Nuremberg, for example, had lobbied for twenty-five years to gain permission to expel all its Jewish citizens, in return for which it ended up having to pay the emperor a heavy tax.[13] Furthermore, as Pfefferkorn complained, Jews expelled from one place could often receive permission to settle in an adjoining territory.[14] For example, since 1425, Jews could not reside in Cologne, but were allowed to live in nearby Deutz, from which they continued to conduct business in the city.

In order to undermine the practice of Judaism across the empire in every city and village, Pfefferkorn's pamphlets agitated for a legal ban on all Jewish writings—not just the Talmud, as is often erroneously stated in historical accounts. This strategy had two advantages for the anti-Jewish agitators. One was that a propaganda campaign against Jewish writings would stoke the fires of Christian anti-Semitism since it would repeatedly "prove" that the Jews, with their hateful and blasphemous prayers and writings, deserved to be reviled by Christians. The other was that this tactic did not require any new imperial legislation or negotiations between the emperor and the estates, for Pfefferkorn claimed that several legal justifications for destroying Jewish writings were already in place. The official position, as recorded by Pfefferkorn and in the mandates themselves, was that confiscation would end illegal Jewish blasphemy and abet conversion. The ultimate goal, however, was to make it impossible to practice Judaism within the empire. Without the written guidance of the rabbis, the record of the oral tradition, and liturgical prayers and other devotions, there could be no Judaism.

Johannes Pfefferkorn

Surprisingly little is known with certainty about Johannes Pfefferkorn.[15] Born Joseph Pfefferkorn, he lived from around 1469 or 1470 until after 1521.[16] The

year of his birth can be estimated based on a statement that he received baptism, which occurred in 1504 or 1505, after having lived "for thirty-six years
in Jewish error."[17] The last record of Pfefferkorn is the 1521 appearance of his
pamphlet *An Impassioned Protest* against Jews and Reuchlin (in which he even
called for the distinguished scholar's execution).[18] It is possible that he was
originally from the thriving commercial city of Nuremberg and suffered the
devastating expulsion of 1498–99. In a character reference dated 20 August
1506, the city council of Nuremberg certified that "he had previously led
an honorable existence among us" but did not say when.[19] He is sometimes
thought to have come from Bohemia, where he may have received at least part
of his schooling under the tutelage of his uncle, the otherwise unknown Rabbi
Meir Pfefferkorn.[20] (Even after conversion, Pfefferkorn would express great
admiration for his uncle's Talmudic learning.) He and his wife, Anna, had
several children and lived, at least for a while, in the Jewish community of
Dachau, Bavaria.[21] Anna also converted, as did at least one child who was baptized as Lawrence. Lawrence studied the humanities at a university, though it
is not known where.[22] In 1521, Pfefferkorn wrote that Lawrence had an MA and
had advised him as he wrote his pamphlets.[23]

As a young man, Joseph Pfefferkorn probably made his living in business,
possibly as a merchant and, by his own admission, as a moneylender, the occupation he would later characterize as the Jewish scourge of Christian society.[24]
Pfefferkorn's enemies, both Jewish and gentile, dismissed him as an uneducated Jewish butcher, but he denied ever having pursued that trade.[25] The
issue of his alleged ignorance looms large in documents from the sixteenth
century and in much of the early scholarship on Pfefferkorn.[26] He was not a
scholar, and his lack of bookishness has made him vulnerable to disparage-
ment. Moreover, his rhetoric is often so harsh and hateful that it has been easy
for historians to fall into the trap of imagining that the author was deficient
in every intellectual respect. But his pamphlets suggest, on the contrary, that
he had a solid basic education and was a skillful writer of German. In the first
imperial mandate, Maximilian confidently declared him an "educated" man.[27]
He knew biblical Hebrew reasonably well, although, according to Reuchlin,
Pfefferkorn conceded that he was not well versed in the Aramaic-Hebrew language of the Talmud.[28] Although he was not capable of translating them, he
did claim responsibility for the content of the Latin versions of his pamphlets
(which do have a few added statements not present in the German originals).[29]
In a general way, the quality of his writing reflects the level of ability found in
the most skillful artisan writers of his period, such as the Nuremberg barber-
surgeon Hans Folz (who also published anti-Jewish pamphlets).[30] Pfefferkorn
once wrote that, until his conversion, he had enjoyed prominence in the Jewish

community of the entire empire: "Several times in the conduct of its affairs, the Jewish community dispatched me as a legate to kings, princes, and lords."[31] It is unlikely that he would have printed this boastful statement in a pamphlet of 1516, by which time his every word was subject to hostile criticism, if it was completely without substance. Moreover, his adept execution of the anti-Jewish campaign itself proves that he was a man of formidable political talent.

Joseph Pfefferkorn converted to Christianity in the ancient archdiocese of Cologne. He took the Christian name Johannes and thereupon became active in missions against the Jews, certainly sponsored by the Observant Franciscans and perhaps by Dominicans as well. Anti-Jewish agitation, which may have been a full-time occupation from 1504 until 1513, took him to many places in the Holy Roman Empire, especially in Bohemia, Bavaria, and the Rhineland. He probably resided most frequently in Cologne since the first imperial mandate of 1509 identifies him as Johannes Pfefferkorn "of Cologne." As early as August 1506, Philipp, Elector of the Palatinate and Duke of Bavaria, issued a patent to Pfefferkorn that urged all the elector's subjects to grant him special privileges in furtherance of his mission to the Jews.[32] Pfefferkorn boasted that he managed to convert fifteen Jews and that he would have converted more if a certain Johannes Reuchlin had not undermined him.[33] From 1513 onward, Pfefferkorn was the warden ("meyster im Spital") of the hospital of St. Ursula in Cologne,[34] an important position and a mark of the respect he commanded there.[35]

Mission to Jews and Christians

While there is no reason to doubt that Pfefferkorn was an effective anti-Jewish agitator or that Jews dreaded encounters with him,[36] probably the most effective aspect of his campaign was its exploitation of the printing press. Before Maximilian authorized destruction of Jewish books in August 1509, Pfefferkorn published a series of four illustrated anti-Jewish tracts: *Mirror of the Jews* (1507), *Confession of the Jews* (1508), *How the Blind Jews Observe Their Easter* (1509), and *The Enemy of the Jews* (1509), all of which appeared in both German and Latin editions. Each of the German pamphlets, moreover, appeared in two separate dialects—the language of the Cologne area and (early) high German—which gave his propaganda a very large potential audience.[37] Counting the German originals and the Latin translations, these four works went through twenty-one editions within three years,[38] an astonishingly large number and an indication that, by 1509, Pfefferkorn had emerged as a leading authority on Judaism in the Holy Roman Empire. His only Christian peers were Reuchlin and Victor of Carben. Pfefferkorn's pamphlets must have helped build the political momentum that enabled the formerly obscure convert to get an audience with the emperor to press the case against Jewish books.

While the German-language tracts are notable for delivering a strong and clear message to a wide audience, the Latin versions were probably equally significant, as they appear to have created a significant following among academics. A major reason for Pfefferkorn's success was that he could combine popular, vernacular rabble-rousing with the ability to attract strong backing from theologians at German universities. In this way, his campaign, albeit on a much smaller scale, looks like a prefiguration of the German-Latin bilingualism of Martin Luther's religious pamphleteering with its simultaneous appeal to popular and academic audiences. With the exception of his 1510 *In Praise and Honor of Emperor Maximilian* (which was translated by an otherwise unknown Andreas Kanter of Frisia[39]), it is not known who translated the pamphlets. Scholars have often attributed the Latin versions of *Confession of the Jews*, *How the Blind Jews Observe Their Easter*, *The Enemy of the Jews*, and *Defense of Johannes Pfefferkorn* to Ortwin Gratius, professor of the arts at the University of Cologne. Gratius certainly put his imprimatur on the Latin versions of *How the Blind Jews Observe Their Easter* and *The Enemy of the Jews* by contributing a signed title-page poem to each. Written in an ostentatious humanist style, the poems suggest an alliance between the anti-Jewish campaign and the faculty, including the fledgling humanists at the university. In one of the poems, Gratius writes that "the mother of eternal Jove [i.e., Mary] rejoices," as does everyone else in heaven, because with Pfefferkorn's book "the circumcised cohort is being laid low by its own sword" [i.e., Pfefferkorn's descriptions of Jewish practices].[40] Similarly, *The Enemy of the Jews* begins with a "refined epigram on the stubbornness of the Jews by Ortwin Gratius of Deventer, professor of the liberal arts."[41] In a letter signed by Professor Gratius, *How the Blind Jews Observe Their Easter* is dedicated to Professor Arnold van Tongern (a theologian at the University of Cologne who in 1512 would publish the first set of heresy charges against Reuchlin).[42] Gratius praises Tongern with humanist-fired hyperbole as "the most profound interpreter of literature (humanities)....Therefore it happens that students of the humanities rush to your college in large numbers as if to a kind of Delphic oracle of Apollo."[43] Whether or not the principal translator, Gratius was clearly trying to associate Pfefferkorn's campaign with the beginnings of humanism at the University of Cologne. In 1509, Gratius also supervised the Latin publication of Victor of Carben's anti-Jewish book, *A Beautiful and New Work...in Which All the Errors of the Jews Are Revealed.*[44] Soon, Professor Gratius would become infamous throughout Europe as the hapless and corrupt recipient of *The Letters of Obscure Men* , which, moreover, features several satires of attempts by Gratius and other Pfefferkorn supporters at the University of Cologne to put their humanist learning on ostentatious display.

While at first Pfefferkorn really did proselytize Jewish audiences, at some point, probably early on in his missionary career, his purpose shifted from encouraging conversion to fomenting anti-Jewish public opinion. One of his first works was apparently a translation of one of the Gospels into either Hebrew or Yiddish (perhaps, in this case, merely German in Hebrew characters),[45] probably an earnest attempt to make the Christian Bible appear more authoritative to Jews. Unfortunately, this text is no longer extant, and quite possibly it was only a paraphrase of the sense rather than a direct translation of a Gospel.[46] He also produced Hebrew translations of the *Lord's Prayer*, the *Hail Mary*, and the *Apostles' Creed*, which were printed together on a broadside, only a single copy of which has survived from 1508.[47]

His first pamphlet, *Mirror of the Jews* of 1507, features a lengthy direct address to Jewish audiences that likely incorporates material used in actual sermons. Occasionally, Pfefferkorn lapses into a dismissive or even a harsh, fire-and-brimstone outburst, but overall he addresses his Jewish audience benevolently as "my most beloved brethren" ("myn hertzallerliebsten bruder!"),[48] in a fashion suggestive of a genuine interest in encouraging conversion. In this first part of *Mirror of the Jews*, he also raises topics that were either commonplace or suitable for authentic Christian sermonizing to Jews: the reliability of the Christian gospel,[49] the dissolution of the covenant with Israel, Christ as the messiah, the trinity,[50] the refutation of charges that Christians worship idols,[51] accusations that some Jews live knowingly in error, attempts to allay Jewish concerns that some Christians have manifestly fallen into lives of sin, and the veracity of the resurrection. Most of these subjects are argued on the basis of copious quotations from Hebrew Scriptures (in German translation), with much of the material drawn from traditional Christian polemics against Judaism, as is most evident in the extensive mustering of Old Testament prophecies of the messiah. Some original material is also used, as in a discussion of a recent false messiah, a certain Asher ben Rav Meier, an Ashkenazi Kabbalist who appeared in northern Italy in 1502 and mesmerized a following with his penitential preaching.[52] Pfefferkorn mocks the Jews' gullibility in that instance and, conversely, questions their stubborn rejection of Jesus. Nonetheless, he also considers Jewish objections to Christian practices, especially the Jewish perception of idolatry in Christian religious art and the veneration of Mary and the saints.[53] These were traditional concerns of Jews and Pfefferkorn appears to take them seriously.

It is, however, only the first part of *Mirror of the Jews* that may contain vestiges of sermons to the Jews. The remainder, which speaks directly to

Christians (quite possibly also reflecting actual speeches), is intended to motivate Christians to take action against Jews. There is some external evidence that Pfefferkorn, although a layman, did deliver sermons (or sermon-like addresses) to Christians. Johannes Reuchlin once objected strenuously to Pfefferkorn's unusual license to preach.[54] In a comment on "a sermon that I gave in Frankfurt," Pfefferkorn responded that he did not preach about the word of God or the Christian faith in the manner of a priest, "but only about three matters: that the Jews be forced to work so that they may not charge interest; that they be forced to hear the word of God; that they not keep possession of their horrendous books."[55] *Mirror of the Jews* advocated this very program, namely that Christian governments outlaw Jewish usury,[56] mandate Jewish attendance at sermons,[57] and burn their books.[58] Pfefferkorn's first tract is especially adamant about the need to suppress Jewish books, "whose hideous contents are lies against Christ and Mary"[59]: "Therefore you who hold power must take the books from them and leave them nothing more than the text of the Holy Scriptures, i.e., the Bible."[60]

Mirror of the Jews features harsh denunciations of German Jews, including a remarkable assertion that they murder Christian children out of spite and envy but not, as most Christians think, to use their blood in rituals.[61] His strongest criticism, in a way, is reserved for governing authorities, "princes, lords, and cities," that permit Jewish residency. He inveighs against Christian princes who tolerate Jews in order to exploit poor Christian subjects, claiming that wealth "will be wretchedly sucked out of the sweat and blood of your subjects" by the Jews.[62]

With this criticism, Pfefferkorn was addressing a difficult issue for anti-Jewish agitation in the Holy Roman Empire: expulsion could result in loss of tax revenues. The emperor, above all, profited from the ability to tax Jews directly, for Jews were legally classified as the emperor's "cameral servants," subject to his policies and exactions in return for his protection of their lives and property. Pfefferkorn once complained that Jews were unable to convert because, upon relinquishing their protected status as Jews, they were required to forfeit their assets to offset future tax losses for the emperor.[63] Naturally, rulers worried about financial matters when expelling Jews. In 1492, King Ferdinand of Spain required banished Jews to pay future tax assessments on their way out. Pfefferkorn, however, insisted that rulers simply had a higher obligation, that faith and piety compelled them to end the alleged Jewish blasphemy of God, no matter what the cost and, if necessary, that commoners must make governing authorities aware of this obligation. Furthermore, the princes' shortsighted gains in tax revenues collected from Jewish usurers were actually undermining Christian society by increasing levels of pauperization.

An historian once claimed that "Pfefferkorn's 'plan of salvation,' to which he owes his place in our histories, was integrated with a bold critique of the view that Jews could be arbitrarily taxed and exploited as the state's *Kammerknechte* ('cameral servants')."[64] But Pfefferkorn's message was much more volatile than that: while taxes may have been extorted directly from the Jews, he claimed the money ultimately came from the pockets of impoverished Christian borrowers. Pfefferkorn's tracts are bold because they implored the masses of poor Christians to stand up to their rulers to end Jewish money lending as exploitation of Christians.

Pfefferkorn's subsequent pamphlets eschew any pretense of addressing Jews. His next two works, *Confession of the Jews* (which first appeared in February 1508) and *How the Blind Jews Observe Their Easter* (3 January 1509), use derisive descriptions of Jewish holidays as points of departure for making sweeping condemnations of Judaism. *Confession of the Jews* turns so profoundly away from addressing potential converts that the title page expresses the wish that the pamphlet "not fall into Jewish hands."[65] The first two parts of *Confession of the Jews* explain various rituals of atonement associated with Rosh Hashanah and Yom Kippur in order "to hold up the Jews to ridicule."[66] Pfefferkorn also emphasizes the accusation that Jewish prayers foment hatred of Christianity, especially *Avinu Malkenu* ("Our Father, Our King"), which is recited during the Ten Days of Repentance, the time from Rosh Hashanah to Yom Kippur: "the curse you have just heard [i.e., an imprecation in *Avinu Malkenu* against enemies of Israel] is especially against us and no one else. Therefore it is my sincere advice according to my slight understanding that such books of curses should be taken from them."[67] After his disparaging review of atonement rituals,[68] Pfefferkorn begins a general attack against tolerating Jews in Germany, contending that "the presence of Jews is worse than the presence of the devil" because they not only undermine the Christian faith through their blasphemy (as does the devil), but also corrode Christian society through economic exploitation.[69] This prompts Pfefferkorn to attack Jewish money lending again[70] and to unleash a barrage of accusations concerning Jews blaspheming Christianity. The purpose of all this vitriol becomes clear in the fifth part of the tract, an address to political authorities urging expulsion: "Drive them out of your lands or forbid them to take interest. Let them labor as we Christians have to do and compel them, if they want to or not, to hear the word of God....Is it not true that many Jews were living in many places, cities, and lands, such as France, Spain, Denmark, and others besides, and recently also in Nuremberg, Ulm, Nördlingen, etc. who have now all been expelled? I ask you, what loss, opposition, or complaint has resulted from that? If they [i.e., governmental authorities] have acted well in this matter, you should rightly follow their example for the sake of your own soul's salvation."[71] *The Confession of the Jews* also calls for the destruction of Jewish writings, especially the Talmud.[72]

Similarly, *How the Blind Jews Observe Their Easter* expands from a narrow focus on the observation of a Jewish holiday, in this case Passover, into a broad-brush defamation of Judaism. Like other anti-Jewish polemicists, Pfefferkorn adopts the inconsistent strategy of both interpreting Jewish rituals as symbols of Christian doctrine and of ridiculing practices as signs of religious decadence. For example, the matzah, bitter herbs, and red wine of the Passover Seder become symbols of Christ (which the blind Jews cannot see), for "the Jewish Easter [i.e., Passover] is nothing other than an allegory and announcement of our Easter."[73] This form of anti-Jewish allegorese has deep roots, reaching all the way back to late antiquity, most notably to the approach of St. Augustine.[74] On the other hand, Pfefferkorn also finds Jewish agitation against Christianity in the Seder, as, for example, in the recitation of Psalm 79, for "with the words, 'O Lord, pour out your wrath over the people who have not recognized you,' we Christians are being referred to."[75]

An important element in the discourse of *Confession of the Jews* and *How the Blind Jews Observe Their Easter* is the contention, expressed with considerable emphasis in the latter tract, that Jews are heretics within Judaism: "They do not adhere to the law of Moses as they are commanded."[76] This accusation offers a way to circumvent the traditional legal immunity to charges of heresy on the grounds that Jews were outside the Christian faith and therefore could not be heretics. Pfefferkorn, however, alleges that the rabbis had so perverted the Jewish law over the years that Jews now deviated from true, biblical Judaism. In this respect, he is echoing traditional Christian attacks on the Talmud, in particular the accusation that the Talmud makes Judaism something other than the faith of the Old Testament.

How the Blind Jews Observe Their Easter even announces on the title page that Judaism should not be tolerated because Jews have become "heretics of the New and Old Testament."[77] After a Christological description of the Seder, Pfefferkorn changes focus and lists ten ways in which contemporary Judaism is a heresy, contending that Jews should be "answerable to the courts, according to the law of Moses," in other words that Jews should be subject to heresy prosecutions. While the first few allegations are trivial objections to the observance of Passover,[78] he also charges that Jewish money lending contradicts Torah and that Jews willingly murder Christians. The fourth section is a rabble-rousing invective against Jewish money lenders who deceive their Christian victims (after enticing them with loans that are initially interest-free), and the fifth part is a strident call to action, in which he urges Christians to become "crusaders"[79] against Judaism and repeats his tripartite mantra that authorities should outlaw Jewish money lending, compel Jews to attend Christian sermons, and confiscate all Jewish books except the Bible for "their books are the mother of their criminality."[80] The final pages include an endorsement of forced baptism of Jewish children[81] and a plea that recalcitrant Jews be driven from the empire like "criminal dogs."[82]

The rhetoric of *How the Blind Jews Observe Their Easter* is so inflammatory that, in the following year, Reuchlin accused Pfefferkorn of fomenting insurrection against the rule of the princes throughout the empire.[83] Reuchlin was referring above all to the final segments of the pamphlet, where Pfefferkorn uses direct discourse in (fictional) dramatizations of demands from the common people to the princes who protect Jews. The following is a typical example:

> If, however, the lords reproach you and say "we have to tolerate the Jews and admit them; for the laws admit them." To that you might answer, "It is true that the laws admit them. But they [i.e., the laws] strongly forbid usury and blasphemy of God. Therefore our request and desire are in accord with the law. For we are not requesting that they be eradicated but that usury and blasphemy of God be ended and that the false books be taken from them."[84]

The historical irony of these pamphlets is that they are a first step in offering a Christian readership information about Jewish customs, even if Pfefferkorn's "interpretations" of Passover and Yom Kippur are designed to ridicule and distort.[85] By 1512, the learned Franciscan Thomas Murner would offer a more detailed and more neutral description of the Passover Seder.[86] Pfefferkorn's polemical approach, however, would reappear with a vengeance in Antonius Margaritha's 1530 pamphlet *The Entire Jewish Faith*, a book that influenced Martin Luther's anti-Semitism.[87]

The last pamphlet to appear before the confiscations began was *The Enemy of the Jews* (1509). As the title suggests, this tract essentially devolves into a take-no-prisoners discourse against Judaism. Every pretense of explaining Jewish beliefs or of encouraging conversion has vanished and Jewish blasphemy has become the defining trope. As Pfefferkorn says in the dedication of the Latin version to Archbishop Philipp of Cologne, "Indeed, that race of people is cursed and it cannot be moved by words or prayers, or reason, or logic, as Ortwin Gratius explained with such learning in his epigram"[88] (referring to the title-page epigram "On the Stubbornness of the Jews"). The first section of the pamphlet cites anti-Christian slanders as examples of Jewish blasphemy, a serious offense that was punishable by death under imperial law. According to Pfefferkorn, Jews call Jesus "seducer of the people" (which works as a Hebrew pun on the name "Jesus of Nazareth").[89] Worse is a list of curses that Jews allegedly use for Jesus, Mary, and Christians: they are, respectively, "bastard," "whore," and "devils." In order to amplify the impact of these incendiary charges, Pfefferkorn gives all the abusive language in Hebrew, transliterated Hebrew, and German translation.[90] The "original" Hebrew bestows the aura of authenticity on the "exposé." Before this time, it was unusual to find Hebrew phrases or words printed in a text, especially in a German-language text. Despite the awkwardness of the printed Hebrew, this typographical achievement gives Pfefferkorn's invective a certain measure of rhetorical authority and, although this was not his intention, also offered Christians rare access to a few authentic Jewish prayers.

The Enemy of the Jews cites two prayers in the original Hebrew text along with transliteration and German translation. Pfefferkorn alleges that both prayers are really imprecations against Christians. One is a section called the *Birkat ha-Minim* ("Benediction concerning heretics"), the twelfth benediction in the *'Amidah*, the central prayer of both private and public worship in Judaism since the destruction of the second temple.[91] According to Pfefferkorn the benediction begins with the statement, "There is no hope for the baptized" (see Figure 5.1).[92] Most liturgical scholars would probably agree that Pfefferkorn's interpretation is basically defensible, even though the Hebrew literally says "There is no hope *for the apostates*" ("ve-la-meshummadim").[93] Pfefferkorn also cites some lines from the prayer *Avinu Malkenu* ("Our Father, Our King") in Hebrew and German, claiming that the words "May God destroy the thoughts and plans of our enemies with murder and the sword"[94] express Jewish hatred of Christians. In particular, he quotes lines that suggest disloyalty to the empire, a fearful issue as Christian Europe faced the threat of an expanding Ottoman Empire and was sometimes inclined to see Jewish residents as potential traitors within. Pfefferkorn also insists that, when Jews greet Christians, they use a German-Hebrew pun that means, in German, "Be welcome" and, in Hebrew, "Devil, welcome."[95] The original is "Seid Wilkommen," pretty ordinary German. Later (in his *Recommendation* of 1510), Reuchlin fumed over the philological weakness of the alleged pun, for the Hebrew word for devil is "Shed" not "seid."[96] Despite Reuchlin's sharp rebuke to Pfefferkorn's Hebrew vocalization, Martin Luther would later repeat Pfefferkorn's innuendo with even greater hostility.[97] Pfefferkorn also alleges

FIGURE 5.1. Johannes Pfefferkorn, *The Enemy of the Jews* (Augsburg 1509), fol. A3ʳ, showing an excerpt from a Jewish prayer ('*Amidah*) in Hebrew and German translations used as evidence against Jewish books. The Hebrew letters are to be read right to left, but the Hebrew words are arranged left to right. Bayerische Staatsbibliothek München, Res/4 Jud. 17 zp, fol. 3ʳ.

that the Jews call the sacrament "unclean bread" and the Latin language, the language of Christian worship, the "unclean language."[98]

The second section of *The Enemy of the Jews* presents allegations of the social harm caused by Jews: "The second part tells how the Jews corrupt the country and people. Although we encounter numerous sects and beliefs of different kinds in the world, none among them steals, swindles, and harms Christians more than the unclean and accursed Jews."[99] Most of this section unfolds as a fantastic calculation of compounded interest charged by Jewish usurers. After thirty years (and after Pfefferkorn's mathematical gymnastics), a debt of one gulden has grown into "106 tons of gold, 45, 810 Gulden, 28 Pfennige, and 11 Heller."[100] He reaches this figure by using an exorbitant, usually illegal, annual interest rate of more than 70 percent.[101]

The third part is a loosely connected rant on the ways Jews corrupt Christians. The following series of quotations will convey its gist:

> The Jews cause many Christians, learned and unlearned, to doubt
> their faith.... Thus there is much heresy where Jews live. Also one
> finds Christians commit unchaste acts with Jews and have children
> with them.[102]... Now God will no longer save them or hear their
> prayers because they have committed greater sins than their forefa-
> thers who killed the prophets. They have killed the son of God.[103]...
>
> They must do all kinds of menial work, such as cleaning the
> streets or sweeping chimneys or, likewise, emptying the cesspools
> of toilets and removing dog manure, etc. And, in the meantime, as
> I have often said, we must not allow them to keep the false books of
> the Talmud, and we should leave them nothing except the text of the
> Bible alone. If that is done, they undoubtedly will adopt a different
> mind and heart. And then they will abandon their false beliefs and
> follow the truth of our faith.[104]

The Book Pogrom

All of Pfefferkorn's writings of 1507–9 call for confiscation of Jewish books, but his pamphlets sound more like the rhetoric of a fanatic trying to stir deep emotions rather than the formulation of a realistic plan of action. It was apparently with Franciscan assistance that this outcry was turned into political policy. The Franciscans and Dominicans had long been at the forefront of anti-Jewish agitation throughout Europe. As one scholar concluded, "Dominican and Franciscan friars directed and oversaw virtually all the anti-Jewish activities of the Christian clergy in the West."[105] Everywhere in Europe, it was the Dominicans, the "dogs of the Lord" ("domini canes"), who led the inquisition, the judicial inquiries, under canon law, into heresy. Even the attacks against the Talmud and the claim that it is heretical derive from Dominican agitation, beginning with the deed of another Jewish convert, Nicholas Donin, who in 1242 organized a public burning of the Talmud in Paris.[106]

According to Pfefferkorn's account, Observant Franciscans in several houses, including Munich, urged him to approach Emperor Maximilian I with this plan and request imperial authorization to impound Jewish books.[107] Pfefferkorn also recorded that the Franciscans decided that a prudent first step would be to enlist the support of Duchess Kunigunde, Maximilian's widowed sister, for the mandate. Upon the death of her husband, Kunigunde became abbess of the Poor Clares convent in Munich and was therefore likely to look favorably on a Franciscan initiative. In July 1509, Pfefferkorn had an audience with her in Munich, apparently delivering one of his standard anti-Jewish sermons, which, as we have seen, had evolved into vitriolic philippics against any form of toleration of Jews.

Convinced by Pfefferkorn's portrayal of Jewish blasphemy and heresy, Kunigunde immediately "took to heart" his plan and became such a dedicated sponsor that she wrote out "in her own hand" a recommendation that Maximilian immediately order the confiscation of Jewish writings.[108] On 1 August 1509, Pfefferkorn presented that endorsement to Maximilian in Padua, Italy, where the emperor was mired in war with the Republic of Venice. Although Maximilian's military situation was urgent, he granted the prominent crusader an audience.

The result of their conference was a complete victory for the anti-Jewish campaign. Maximilian was so won over to this plan of action that he designated Pfefferkorn "Servant and Loyal Subject of the Empire" ("Diener und des Reiches Getruwen")[109] and gave him the legal instrument to proceed with a different war—this one against the Jews. On 19 August 1509, he signed the infamous mandate in Padua (which has survived in some five slightly different versions):[110]

> We are reliably informed that you [i.e., Jews in the Holy Roman
> Empire] have in the libraries in your synagogues or otherwise in
> your possession, several unfounded, worthless books and writings
> that not only are fabricated and designed to scorn, ridicule, and
> eradicate our Christian faith and its followers but that are also
> against the books and laws of Moses, which you claim to believe
> and uphold. These books not only turn you away from our Christian
> faith, but they also make errors in your Jewish faith, deceive you, and
> spur you to heresy.[111]

Furthermore, Maximilian explicitly bestowed on Johannes Pfefferkorn the power to determine the legality of all Jewish books:

> to inspect, assess, observe all your books and writings everywhere
> and if among them there should be any that are in contradiction
> to the books and laws of Moses and the prophets and, as is written
> above, should without reason ridicule and offend the Christian
> faith, all of those very books should be taken away from you and
> suppressed, though in every place this should be done with the
> knowledge of the council and in the presence of the priest and of two
> members of the council or government.[112]

The mandate is a page from Pfefferkorn's book, both metaphorically and literally, for Pfefferkorn soon printed the mandate in a major pamphlet of 1510, *In Praise and Honor of Emperor Maximilian*. The two most perilous accusations from Pfefferkorn's propaganda are embedded in the mandate—that the Jews blaspheme the Christian God and that the Jews are heretics within Judaism. These are grave charges, alleging capital offenses under imperial law, although the mandate does not explicitly threaten capital punishment but rather authorizes confiscation and destruction in the ostensible hope of fostering conversion, once the Jews are deprived of rabbinic literature.

The mandate places important limitations on the confiscation. Not all books may be taken, but only those that are injurious to Christianity or distort biblical Judaism. Moreover, the Jewish books are to undergo inspection in the presence of priests and two members of the council (i.e., the local city council). Although, as we will see, the confiscations would proceed under the supervision of local council members and priests, as required, Pfefferkorn and his allies would completely ignore the stipulation that the books' contents be evaluated, thereby placing no limit on the scope of the confiscation.

With the mandate in hand, Pfefferkorn returned to Munich to celebrate and consult with Kunigunde. She expressed "great joy" over her brother's bold decision and gave Pfefferkorn further letters of recommendation to encourage officials to help him implement the new policy.[113] As events unfolded, Kunigunde would remain committed to this cause and continue to press Maximilian to support eradication of German Jewry.

This is also the likely moment for a significant yet somewhat mysterious event: Pfefferkorn's personal conference with Reuchlin in Stuttgart. The meeting definitely occurred—both men would describe it, although neither mentioned its date. According to Reuchlin's account, Pfefferkorn visited him after securing the first imperial mandate in order to enlist the scholar's participation in the Rhineland campaign.[114] Therefore, the encounter took place between 19 August 1509 (date of the Padua mandate) and 20 September 1509 (beginning of the campaign in Frankfurt). Pfefferkorn obviously wanted the famous author of *Rudiments of Hebrew* to confer academic credibility on his implementation of the imperial mandate in Frankfurt. The blessing of such a prominent scholar and lawyer would have immediately seasoned his newfledged plan. But why did he see a potential ally in Reuchlin, of all people?

In 1505, Reuchlin had published *German Epistle: Why the Jews Have Been in Exile So Long*, a brief pamphlet of some eight pages that explained, in answer to an unnamed nobleman's question, why God inflicted the diaspora on Jews. Reuchlin contended that the continuous Jewish rejection of Jesus manifested itself as blasphemy, a sin worthy of God's wrath: "I conclude that the Jews have been punished for so long for no other sin than blasphemy of God, which their forbears committed against the true messiah, our lord Jesus, and their progeny have agreed to persist in that up to the present day."[115] Impressively, Reuchlin cited an array of biblical texts and a few Jewish authorities (in particular Rashi and Moses Maimonides) in the original Hebrew to document Jewish concepts of sinfulness, none of which, despite Reuchlin's suggestions to the contrary, pertained to the rejection of Jesus as the messiah. More important, he specifically identified three blasphemous Jewish writings and contended that contemporary Jews routinely disparaged Jesus and Mary. The most important specific allegation in this tract was that the *Birkat ha-Minim* (which he refers to as "ve-la-meshummadim") from the *'Amidah*, which would play such a prominent role in Pfefferkorn's agitation, was directed against Christians. In later writings (beginning in 1510), Reuchlin would argue vehemently against this interpretation. While Pfefferkorn would accuse Reuchlin of inconsistency and imply that bribery was the reason for his new understanding, the simple explanation is that Reuchlin's attitude toward Jews and understanding of Judaism evolved from this early expression of medieval anti-Judaism. Nevertheless, even in the 1505 pamphlet, he did not advocate coercive action against Jews and, in subsequent publications, would repudiate nearly all allegations of blasphemy and express increasingly favorable sentiments about Jews and Judaism.

While Reuchlin declined to join the Frankfurt campaign in person, the two men parted amicably, with Pfefferkorn convinced that Reuchlin was on his side: "Then he offered many flattering words to me, saying that he would help me in this matter not just with words and writing but also with deeds."[116] Even later, Reuchlin insisted that the mandate was proper "as far as it concerned (destruction or confiscation of) blasphemous books." In fact, Reuchlin seems to have left the impression that he was trying to help Pfefferkorn by pointing out some legal weaknesses in the wording of the mandate. Unfortunately, we do not know what those quibbles were, although Reuchlin later claimed that he carefully wrote them down for his visitor.[117] Pfefferkorn left Stuttgart no doubt with the assumption that Reuchlin shared his desire to end Judaism in Germany.

But before colliding so explosively with the scholar he had mistaken for an ally, Pfefferkorn hastened to Frankfurt, home of the most vibrant Jewish community in the empire, to bring his propaganda enterprise to political fruition, beginning, as it were, a new chapter in the history of anti-Semitism.

6

Who Saved the Jewish Books?

For it is to be feared that, God forbid, great disaster will arise from this.

> —Jonathan Kostheim, writing on 15 November 1509 to the Jewish community in Frankfurt on the confiscation of Hebrew books

Johannes Reuchlin's role in undermining the book pogrom has been incompletely and often erroneously construed. Historians, with few exceptions,[1] have been inclined to give him sole credit for saving the Jewish books,[2] an assumption that would seem to be justified in light of the bitter claims of his enemies that he was responsible for resolving the crisis. Reuchlin himself once boasted to Rabbi Bonet de Lattes that "after our lord, the emperor—exalted be his majesty—read my book and recommendation, he ordered the confiscated books be returned to their owners."[3] Nonetheless, the extensive archival records for the confiscations, in particular those from the free imperial city of Frankfurt am Main, indicate that factors other than Reuchlin's famous *Recommendation* influenced the outcome.[4] Moreover, among the surviving documents are petitions from the Frankfurt city council to Emperor Maximilian that prefigure several of the principal lines of argumentation that Reuchlin would later use against the confiscation. Thus, we are left with a question: what was Reuchlin's impact on the actual Jewish book crisis? Who, or what, saved the Jewish books?

As exemplified by such disparate historians as Heinrich Graetz and Salo Baron, most assessments portray the confiscation plot essentially as a reiteration of the Talmud controversies of the Middle Ages, the intermittent efforts, beginning in 1240 in France, to suppress the Talmud on grounds of alleged heresy and blasphemy.[5] Unquestionably, the Talmud pogroms (and, especially, the anti-Talmudic preaching campaigns in the Holy Roman Empire) were important backgrounds to Maximilian's mandates, but the distinctive element in the new policy was not only that it was the first imperial assault against the Talmud but also that it attempted to ban all Jewish books. The implementation of the mandate revealed its intention, for, as Reuchlin accurately stated, the anti-Jewish forces were trying to find "how they could take away from the Jews in the entire Roman empire all of their Hebrew books, large and small, whatever format they were, leaving them only the unglossed text of the Bible."[6] The Jewish community of Frankfurt immediately recognized the ultimate intention: "if our...books are taken from us without examination, as we hope will not be the case, then we would be unable to worship God the Almighty during our holy days and festivals according to our practices, as has been granted to us by earlier popes and emperors."[7] Thus, the confiscation would undermine the practice of Judaism, which had been officially tolerated in both ecclesiastical and imperial law since the beginning of the empire. Moreover, the aftermath suggests that the book controversy inspired the only other multi-territorial effort in the empire to end the practice of Judaism.

The Frankfurt Campaign

Johannes Pfefferkorn launched the ground campaign, so to speak, against Jewish books in Frankfurt am Main. A flourishing commercial emporium, Frankfurt was home to one of the few German Jewish communities that was thriving at the time.[8] In fact, the community would prosper throughout the sixteenth century, growing from around 250 inhabitants in 1500 to well over 2,000 (perhaps as many as 3,000) by the century's end.[9] Emperor Maximilian was probably right when, in August 1509, he characterized the synagogue of Frankfurt as the "most distinguished" in the realm.[10]

According to his own account, Pfefferkorn targeted Frankfurt because it was one of only three major centers of Jewish life in the empire (the other two being Regensburg and Worms),[11] and it had a Talmudic academy, which he even dignified with the title "hohe Schule" (i.e., university).[12] The venerable communities of Regensburg and Worms, once the most illustrious seats of Jewish learning in Germany, had already entered a steep decline, the ineluctable result of several persecutions over the previous half-century.[13] The anti-Jewish forces probably hoped that success in Frankfurt would create unstoppable momentum for purging the rest of the empire; that the first battle would decide the war.

But initially it proved hard to build momentum, for Pfefferkorn's attempt to implement the Padua Mandate soon failed. This did not happen for any lack of effort on his part. On 20 September 1509, he presented the mandate to the Frankfurt city council, which was initially prepared to cooperate with him. Already a known quantity from his publications and earlier missions,[14] Pfefferkorn had been in Frankfurt as recently as 29 March 1509 to debate Jews during an international commercial fair.[15] Moreover, the council was probably expecting his arrival in September because Maximilian had sent letters to several imperial cities, including Frankfurt, about the new policy.[16] The mandate required every jurisdiction to form a commission consisting of members of the local government and at least one member of clergy to supervise seizure of the books. Without delay, the Frankfurt council formed such a commission with members of its own body and three priests from the Collegiate Church of St. Bartholomew, the city's most powerful church. After informing the Jewish community on 25 September that all their books were about to be confiscated, Pfefferkorn was able on 28 September to impound 168 books, all the books then present in the synagogue library. The Jews claimed that they were unable to assemble all their personal books, to which the commission responded with a new deadline of three days hence. According to a Jewish source,[17] Pfefferkorn at this point also ordered the Jews not to use the synagogue for prayers, in essence to end Jewish religious observances in Frankfurt. There is no record of the community having complied with this order.

The Frankfurt community immediately appealed the mandate to every possible legal authority: the Imperial Chamber Court, the Frankfurt city council, the elector-archbishop of Mainz, and the emperor. The Frankfurt Jews also dispatched emissaries to other communities in the empire to request assistance, and tried, unsuccessfully, to convene a diet of Jewish communities to address this threat.[18]

The appeal to Archbishop Uriel von Gemmingen of Mainz bore fruit. On Saturday, 29 September (despite it being the Sabbath),[19] the Frankfurt community sent Gumprecht Weissenau, son of Simon Weissenau, perhaps the wealthiest Jew in Frankfurt,[20] to the archbishop's residence in Aschaffenburg. Archbishop Uriel was in debt to Simon (owing him the considerable sum of 1,500 gulden[21]), which may have given Gumprecht some leverage in his negotiations. While he did not have civil authority in Frankfurt, which as a free imperial city was a highly sovereign entity of the empire, the archbishop did control the operation of the church and administration of canon law there. All parties realized that the imperial mandate's allegations that the Jewish books were heretical and blasphemous would typically fall to an ecclesiastical court for adjudication.[22] Gumprecht Weissenau, thus, had fertile ground for a protest that Maximilian's action trampled ecclesiastical authority. Even the imperial mandate had stipulated the presence of clerics at the confiscations, which, arguably, amounted to tacit acknowledgment that the issues raised also belonged to the competency of an ecclesiastical court. Archbishop Uriel wrote at once to Maximilian in protest, insisting that no further mandates be issued without his approval.[23] He also instructed his envoy at the imperial court in Italy to assist Jewish emissaries who would be contesting the legality of the mandate.[24] Thus, insofar as the mandate impinged on his authority, the archbishop sided with the Jews.

Even more favorable for the Jewish community was the archbishop's decision to issue a decree directing the priests of St. Bartholomew to end further participation in the confiscation immediately or face harsh punishment.[25] With that move, he instantaneously blocked further action since the mandate explicitly required priestly cooperation. Weissenau arrived in Frankfurt with this decree on Tuesday just minutes before the large-scale confiscation, the seizure of books held privately in Jewish homes, was set to begin. The priests, apparently sorely disappointed by the intervention, requested that the city council appeal to the archbishop, but the council declined to do so.[26] Thus, as of 2 October, the Jewish community could rejoice that it had blocked implementation of the Padua Mandate. On the other hand, they had achieved this only on the basis of a technicality, and the fate of the 168 books from the synagogue library remained in limbo.[27]

The archbishop's actions temporarily saved the vast majority of books in Frankfurt and also set the stage for a confrontation between the anti-Jewish campaign and Jewish emissaries at the court of Maximilian I, then in northern Italy because of war with the Republic of Venice. Upon encountering the archbishop's roadblock, Pfefferkorn hurried to the emperor to seek a reformulation of the mandate in response to the archbishop's concerns. But Jonathan Kostheim,[28] a Jewish emissary from Frankfurt, had reached the court first, and was working feverishly to undermine the mandate. Several Italian Jews, Isaac of Trieste and Isaac's brother-in-law, helped him gain influence among the courtiers: "We gave a little here and promised a little there until we brought the matter before our lord, the emperor."[29] The Jews were able to speak directly to the emperor and also through the mediation of an unknown great lord among his courtiers, who confirmed their interpretation of the charters from earlier emperors and popes that Kostheim had brought as evidence.[30]

Obviously taking the Jewish appeal seriously, Maximilian promised an answer. While that was welcome news, Kostheim also disabused the Frankfurters of their hope that the emperor had little real interest in the confiscation scheme. There was much to fear, for the court was profoundly against the Jews, and they should not think of this as simply the case of a few lords creating a crisis to enable them to extort money from the community. Kostheim therefore urged the community to send more funds and "men who are much wiser and more understanding that I" to manage this imminent peril: "For it is to be feared that, God forbid, great disaster will arise from this."[31] In a postscript to a dispatch of 15 November,[32] Kostheim added a few ominous words: "If you had heard and seen what I have heard and seen, fear and terror would have seized you more than I am able to write down."[33]

Indeed, the anti-Jewish forces prevailed. On 10 November 1509, Maximilian issued the Roveredo Mandate (so named after Roveredo, Italy, where he signed the document), which established Elector-Archbishop Uriel as the prime agent in this action and empowered him to create an academic commission to review the Jewish books. The Roveredo Mandate explicitly reaffirmed Pfefferkorn's competence to serve as an arbiter and to destroy questionable books, which was ominous because every Hebrew book was dubious to Pfefferkorn. In addition to Pfefferkorn, the commission was to include the following entities: the elector-archbishop; (unspecified) professors from the Universities of Cologne, Mainz, Erfurt, and Heidelberg; Victor of Carben; Jacob Hoogstraeten; and Johannes Reuchlin. Only the confiscated books with unobjectionable contents were to be returned to the Jews.[34] This was an important development for henceforth the campaign against Jewish books would also be the concern of German universities.

According to Kostheim's dispatches, Pfefferkorn won over the emperor by arguing that the Jews of Frankfurt had arrogantly rejected the emperor's authority. In fact, the Frankfurt council had issued Pfefferkorn an affidavit that attested that the Frankfurt Jews rejected the imperial mandate, declaring that "the emperor has no power over us; we are only subjects under their [i.e., the council's] government."[35]

From this point on, Archbishop Uriel von Gemmingen was an effective proponent of confiscation. His passionate misgivings about the Padua Mandate had not stemmed from any concern to protect Jews but, rather, from the desire to defend his own prerogatives. When the second mandate designated his authority in the review of Jewish books, he felt free to manage the confiscation as he saw fit, paying relatively little regard to the emperor's stipulations. Contrary to the terms of Maximilian's mandate, Uriel actually appointed Pfefferkorn and Hermann Ortlieb, the latter a professor of theology and rector of the University of Mainz, as sole commissioners for censuring the Jewish books.[36] The move was significant, however, for it added academic and ecclesiastical authority to further implementation of the mandate.

In fact, the archbishop reissued the imperial mandate as part of his own authorization for confiscation. In a carefully formulated document, he quoted the Roveredo Mandate in its entirety, while adding his own significant stipulations. On the strength of this document, Pfefferkorn and Ortlieb were able to resume the book confiscations in December 1509. This time, though legally armed to the teeth, they did not strike the strongest target first. Instead, they swiftly conducted confiscations throughout the Rhineland, first in Worms,[37] then, Mainz, Bingen, Lorch, Lahnstein, and Deutz. Local records for these actions, with the exception of the Worms confiscation,[38] do not survive, although an account by Pfefferkorn indicates that he and Professor Ortlieb implemented the mandate successfully. Moreover, after the resumption of the campaign, the archbishop issued a glowing character reference for Pfefferkorn, which was sent to Maximilian I in order to urge continued support of the confiscation policy, when the issue was contested yet again in March 1510 at the Diet of Augsburg.[39]

With the archbishop of Mainz having emerged as an enthusiastic proponent of confiscation, the Jewish community now found its most resourceful ally in the Frankfurt city council. The council's actions in the fall of 1509 indicated a strong inclination to support the mandate, but it is also likely that the city council was narrowly divided on the issue of Jewish policy. In any event, local animosity toward Jews was rising. On 30 December 1507 and on 6 July 1508, the council had discussed the desirability of expelling the Jewish community. The question of banishment would be raised again in July 1511 and then repeatedly over the subsequent five years, that is, during the course of the Reuchlin Affair.

The Frankfurt city council had unusually broad power over its Jewish community. Most significantly, it still held the taxing authority over the Jewish community that it first acquired in 1372 from Emperor Charles IV.[40] Accordingly, as far as we know, the Jewish community did send its first appeal to the council on 27 September, and the community did, in fact, argue that the mandate was invalid because they were subject only to the authority of council (i.e., and not the emperor).[41] By this time, such a contention had become a fairly familiar response of both the Frankfurt Jewish community and the city council against any effort by the emperor to levy special taxes on the Jews. This case, however, was different because it was not prima facie an attempt to tax the Frankfurt Jews.

By the end of December 1509, the Frankfurt city council reached a major decision: it would embrace the Jewish side and contest the Roveredo Mandate, even though no attempt had yet been undertaken to implement it in its territory.[42] The council probably feared that a significant weakening of the Jewish community would diminish the Jewish tax base as well as Jewish contributions to commerce. Moreover, a jurisdictional principle was at stake: the council wanted to defend its authority over the Jewish community and it had begun to suspect that the book crisis would become a device to extort money from the Jews.[43]

Beginning in January 1510, the council sent a series of dispatches to its emissary in Augsburg (who was there awaiting the start of an important imperial diet) instructing him to act: "Whatever our Jews, through themselves or through their embassy, ask of you, be helpful and well disposed to them in so far as it may be justifiable."[44] This culminated in a demand of 16 March that the 168 confiscated books remain in Frankfurt pending resolution of the controversy; acting otherwise would be an imperial violation of Frankfurt's authority over its Jewish residents as originally granted in the charter from Charles IV.[45]

The anti-Jewish forces rallied at Augsburg as well. Pfefferkorn not only appeared at the diet in person but also published two inflammatory works to bolster support for the Roveredo Mandate. In *In Praise and Honor of Emperor Maximilian*, a pamphlet first printed in Augsburg in February 1510, he explicitly interpreted the mandate as authorizing confiscation of all books except the Hebrew Bible. The lengthy excoriation of Jewish practices leads to an "admonition to princes, lords, and other estates" to end toleration of "those errors that are from the worthless, false books of the Jews."[46] He also issued a broadside, *Announcement to All Ecclesiastical and Secular Lords*,[47] describing the book confiscations in the Rhineland as a success and urging Christians not to succumb, as he claims, to the bribes of desperate Jews.[48] His sense was that the end of Judaism was within grasp, if only Christian authorities would resist the corrosive force of Jewish money. Indeed, Pfefferkorn consistently argued, in quite daring formulations, that it was the financial interests of the princes that most threatened the goal of eradicating Judaism. Pfefferkorn's criticism of magisterial protection of Jews was so strong that Reuchlin was able to accuse him of inciting "a rebellion and insurrection against their rulers."[49]

At this point, the anti-Jewish campaign made a bold gambit. Ortlieb and Pfefferkorn suddenly left Augsburg to undertake a direct assault in Frankfurt without any further political reinforcement. The uneasy quiet, which Frankfurt had experienced since the first week of October 1509,[50] was shattered on 22 March 1510, when Ortlieb and Pfefferkorn demanded the right to enforce the Roveredo Mandate immediately.[51] The city council and the Jewish community, however, did not acquiesce at once. In consideration of the Easter season, the council managed to justify a delay of more than two weeks, scheduling implementation to begin on 9 April. On about 3 April, Frankfurt sent a

complex dispatch to its emissary in Augsburg, providing him with three petitions that supported the Frankfurt Jews but offered different resolutions that
were decreasingly advantageous (see Figure 6.1). The first proposed resolution
demanded an end to the confiscations and the immediate return of the 168
books; the second version, to be submitted if the first version failed, requested
that the books be returned to the Jews but that the Jews provide an accurate catalog of the books and agree to keep the books in Frankfurt pending a review;
the third petition requested that the matter be assigned to the jurisdiction of
the Imperial Chamber Court.[52] The Frankfurt Jewish community also provided some 200 gulden to help the emissary accomplish one of the objectives.

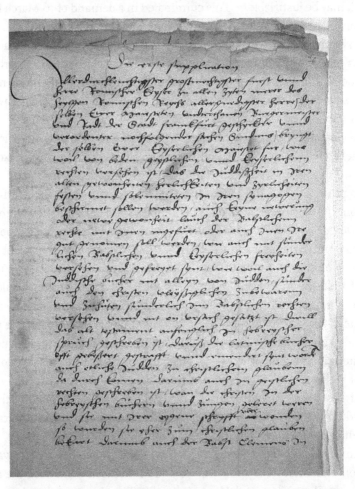

FIGURE 6.1. Petition of the Frankfurt City Council to Emperor Maximilian
("Die erste Supplication"). Institut für Stadtgeschichte Frankfurt am Main,
Juden Akten 779, fol. 36ʳ. Courtesy of Institut für Stadtgeschichte Frankfurt
am Main.Photograph: Dr. Michael Matthäus.

Each of the three petitions began forcefully, with the following preamble concerning Jewish legal rights:

> The council brings to the attention of your imperial majesty that, as is provided in both ecclesiastical and imperial law, the Jewish community should be protected in their old customs, authority and ornaments, holy days and liturgies in their synagogues; furthermore, according to papal law, no innovation or new custom should be imposed on them; or likewise that their property should not be taken from them, as is also provided in various papal and imperial charters; moreover that Jewish books are diligently to be preserved and protected not only by Jews but also by Christians, as is especially provided for in papal law, and it is so established for good reason since the Old Testament was originally written in the Hebrew language, from which the Latin books have frequently been improved, corrected, and emended; also some Jews have come to the Christian faith through this; therefore, it is also written in ecclesiastical law, if Christians would be knowledgeable in the Hebrew books and language, and overcame them [i.e., the Jews] with their own writing, thus would they be more likely to convert to the Christian faith. Therefore Pope Clement also mandated in ecclesiastical law that Hebrew books are to be read and studied in various academies and universities, in order that it will be understood, what benefit such Jewish books can bring to Christianity. Therefore the Jews keep their books in their synagogues in great honor, from which in their holy days and festivals, according to their customs and splendor, they worship God the Almighty, which they would not be able to accomplish without those very books.[53]

With receipt of this petition, Maximilian faced a legal challenge grounded in both civil and ecclesiastical law. The Frankfurt petition cogently insisted that the Jews' right to practice their faith implicitly included the right to possess their prayer books. With equal emphasis, the petition also advanced the argument that the Jewish books should not be destroyed because they were beneficial to Christianity. This last point, the council contended, agreed with well-established ecclesiastical principles. All told, this was a substantial challenge and all its points, moreover, would soon reappear in the argumentation that Reuchlin would develop in his famous *Recommendation*.

The council and the Jews waited for a reply from Maximilian by the deadline of 9 April, but it was not forthcoming. Ortlieb and Pfefferkorn were able to proceed with a complete confiscation of Jewish books—they impounded all the books and stored them in shipping barrels, obviously hoping to examine and destroy the books elsewhere, in a venue such as Cologne where Jews were not allowed and there would likely be no resistance to their action. By the end of the day on 11 April 1510, nearly 1,500 books had been taken, the entire scriptural fabric of Frankfurt Jewry, except the Bible.[54] By 13 April, an inventory of all the books had been prepared (see Figure 6.2).[55]

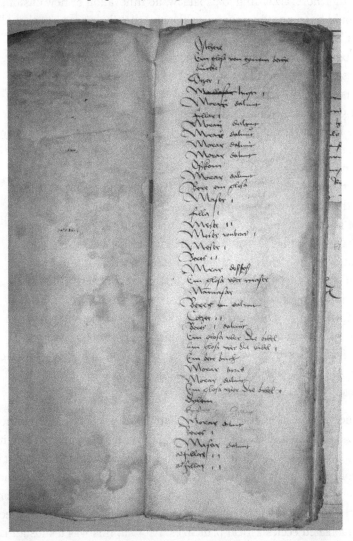

FIGURE 6.2. Inventory of Jewish books confiscated in Frankfurt in 1510. Institut für Stadtgeschichte Frankfurt am Main, Juden Akten 779, fol. 44ᵛ. Courtesy of Institut für Stadtgeschichte Frankfurt am Main. Photograph: Dr. Michael Matthäus.

Because of problems arising from the 28 September confiscation of the books in the synagogue library, the council did not permit seizure of Jewish books in Frankfurt that were owned by foreign (non-Frankfurt) Jews.[56] The Jews, however, were required to swear "that they would not use these [i.e., books of foreign ownership] in their synagogue and would not remove them from the city without permission of the council."[57] Moreover, fearing removal (and destruction) of the great treasures of Frankfurt's Jews, the council petitioned the emperor on 12 April for a mandate that the impounded books must remain in Frankfurt pending final review.[58]

Imperial Policy in Flux

Although never replying directly to the Frankfurt petition, Maximilian did offer a stunning response to events in Frankfurt and the Rhineland: in May 1510, he abruptly revoked authority for the confiscations. Several factors probably contributed to this reversal: (1) a decision to use the crisis for short-term fiscal advantage; (2) the emperor's growing confidence that he would be able to expand his taxing authority over the Jews of the empire, thus making the destruction of German Jewry counterproductive; and (3) the powerfully argued petitions from the Frankfurt council. Soon, the extensive legal analysis by Johannes Reuchlin cast profound doubt on the legitimacy of the action.

In the end, a fiscal consideration initially compelled the emperor to rescind the confiscation order. He agreed in May 1510 to return the books, if Jewish creditors in Frankfurt would renegotiate the terms of a major loan, then in default, to one of Maximilian's most important military allies, Duke Erich of Braunschweig. As early as 12 November 1508, Maximilian intervened, asking the Frankfurt city council to secure a three-month extension;[59] on 18 November 1509, Maximilian had to request another extension for Erich.[60] In April 1510, Frankfurt creditors, including Gumprecht Weissenau, Itzing Bopfingen, and Jonathan Kostheim, were attending the Augsburg Diet in order to compose a final settlement for the loan, including clearance to sell off the collateral (apparently including the Braunschweig crown jewels). According to the envoy of the Frankfurt city council, "Maximilian decreed that if the pledges [i.e., for the loan] are allowed to stand another year with the duke, then a favorable decision [i.e., on the Jewish books] will be issued,"[61] to which the creditors soon assented. It is not clear how great a monetary concession this was, or if the Jewish community compensated the creditors for the loss. A slightly later letter from Duke Erich to the Frankfurt Council (2 June 1511) implies that the obligation could have been as much as 5,400 gulden.[62] We can only assume that the loss was substantial and that it was a few business leaders who absorbed it. Individual Jewish merchants often accepted such burdens to benefit the larger Jewish community. (Official financial declarations of 13 August 1510 indicate that the personal wealth of Itzing Bopfingen and Jonathan Kostheim declined significantly at this time.[63])

Another factor in Maximilian's calculus was his successful expansion of imperial taxing authority over German Jewry. On 20 May, he issued a special tax levy, approved by the diet, on all the Jews in the empire, indicating explicitly his determination to collect this tax from the Frankfurt Jews as well, despite their long-standing claim to immunity from imperial levies. From this point forward, Maximilian probably began to weigh the possibility of generating more tax revenues over time from stable Jewish communities rather than from one-time revenues generated from settlements with local jurisdictions seeking to expel Jewish residents.

A fundamental question, one that cannot be definitively answered, is what Maximilian's Jewish policy was. Most historians have seen a record of indecisiveness and vacillation in Maximilian's actions regarding Jewish life in the empire. Nonetheless, much indicates that Maximilian had emerged during the first seventeen years of his reign (ca. 1493–1510) as a strong threat to German Jews. Unlike his father and predecessor, Friedrich III, he frequently conducted negotiations with local authorities in order to receive compensation in return for his agreement to allow a local expulsion. Between 1494 and 1510, he authorized at least thirteen expulsions in return for sizable fiscal settlements.[64] In the large-scale banishments from Styria and Carinthia (1496ff.), the expulsion mandate even stated that the Jews were perpetrating host desecration and ritual murder—two extremely dangerous innuendos that emperors and popes had always rejected previously.[65] In 1508, immediately prior to crowning himself emperor in a complex ceremony in Trent (necessary because the pope refused to do so), Maximilian prayed before the shrine of Simon of Trent,[66] the alleged victim of ritual murder in 1475, arguably the most prominent blood libel accusation in early modern anti-Jewish propaganda. Nonetheless, beginning in 1510 and in the aftermath of the book controversy, Maximilian's policy gradually turned in a new direction. Exploitation of Jews remained a constant goal but the mechanism of exploitation appears to have shifted, for, after 1510, Maximilian would authorize only one further expulsion. His resistance to a powerful campaign in the 1510s to expel the Jews of Regensburg was unusually resolute, although it had the unintended result of allowing so much pressure to mount that, immediately upon the emperor's death, anti-Jewish forces exploded in a brutal (and illegal) banishment in February 1519 during the interregnum.

In any event, as required by the settlement of the Braunschweig loan, Maximilian wrote on 23 May 1510 to the authorities in Frankfurt and Mainz revoking the Roveredo Mandate and directing them to return the confiscated books to the Jews. His instructions roughly corresponded to the second outcome proposed by the city of Frankfurt in its petitions of April. The Jews were to receive their books, but they had to provide an inventory of them and had to keep the books in Frankfurt pending a final review. Apparently, the confiscated books in the other Rhineland communities were also returned, probably with the same stipulations.

This decision, however, was in no way the end of the confiscation crisis, for Maximilian had not yet definitively decided if he could profit more from the assaults on the Jewish community or from expanding his ability to generate tax revenues from Jewish communities. On 6 July 1510, the emperor issued a new (third) mandate, the Füssen Mandate, addressed once again to the archbishop of Mainz, authorizing an immediate assessment of the desirability and legality of a confiscation of Jewish books. This move responded to the objections raised in the petitions from the city council of Frankfurt. Most tellingly, the new mandate sought clarification on the very issue the Frankfurt petition had contradicted: would destruction of Jewish writings benefit Christianity? The new decree was also designed to strengthen the campaign since it required four major university faculties (Cologne, Mainz, Heidelberg, and Erfurt) and three individual scholars (Victor of Carben, Jacob Hoogstraeten, and Johannes Reuchlin) to evaluate the proposed destruction of Jewish books. In light of the original legal protests from the Frankfurt city council, the imperial court realized that the campaign now needed academic confirmation of the specific allegations against Jewish writings. With such endorsements in place, the emperor would again be able to authorize seizure of the Jewish books.

Reuchlin himself offered this interpretation of the Füssen Mandate. According to the account he published in 1513, his first thought upon reading the mandate was that the emperor unfortunately was determined to destroy Jewish books, an unconscionable tyranny that no previous emperor had ever contemplated: these were books that no emperor, "from first to last," had ever burned.[67]

Maximilian arranged for the reevaluation to be conducted under the supervision of the elector-archbishop by a group of authorities who appeared certain to decide against the Jews. The situation was so ominous that the Frankfurt city council even warned the Jewish community that the confiscation was going to resume. After all, Maximilian now indicated that the returned books were not to be removed from Frankfurt pending his final decision.[68]

The university faculties and the three experts submitted their recommendations enthusiastically and, with the one exception of Reuchlin, in accord with expectations. The evaluations indicate that a driving force, in addition to the elector-archbishop of Mainz, was Cologne. Pfefferkorn was himself a resident of Cologne and no fewer than three of the seven recommendations originated there: those of the University of Cologne, the inquisitor Hoogstraeten, and the Jewish convert and priest Victor of Carben. These authorities agreed that all Jewish writings, not just the Talmud, should be impounded and subjected to stringent review; they also expressed confidence that the writings would be found to be objectionable and worthy of destruction, and that this action was absolutely necessary. The Cologne faculty concluded that "it is manifest that the book of the Jews which they call the Talmud contains not only such errors and falsities but also blasphemies and heresies against their own law."[69] The intent of this analysis was to subject Jews to laws governing heresy, one of the most aggressive elements of the strategy, for it promised to override all legal protection based on property rights or charters that permitted Jewish residency and worship.

The University of Mainz went even further, probably under the leadership of the rector of the theology faculty, Professor Ortlieb, who had already collaborated on the Rhineland campaign of spring 1510. The Mainz professors called for the destruction of all Jewish writing and even for the confiscation and review of Hebrew Bibles. According to them, the Jews had falsified their texts of the Tanakh by altering passages that prophesied Jesus as the messiah.[70] The University of Heidelberg composed a brief noncommittal statement, suggesting that a conference among all the authorities would be the best way to formulate a unified recommendation of this issue. The University of Erfurt, though unable to respond quickly because of other pressing matters, ultimately endorsed the burning of Jewish books, as did Victor of Carben.[71]

Jacob Hoogstraeten, professor and dean of the faculty of theology, participated in the recommendation submitted by the University of Cologne.[72] In accord with the emperor's mandate, he also submitted a separate recommendation in his capacity as the papal inquisitor. In this carefully written analysis, Hoogstraeten fulminated that the Jewish books must be burned, and that the Jews themselves be burned if they refuse to recant the abominations in their books. This condemnation, which he titled *The Consultation against the Filthy Jewish Books*,[73] pertained to all Jewish writings except the Hebrew Bible and commentaries on the Bible. To a greater extent than the other evaluators except Reuchlin, he cast his *Consultation* in legal terms, citing both ecclesiastical and civil law to support his proposal. Above all, he stressed that previous popes (specifically Gregory IX) had consigned the Talmud to the inquisition's fires and that imperial law provided explicitly for the immediate burning of books deemed heretical or blasphemous by an ecclesiastical inquisition.

In the *Consultation* Hoogstraeten announced a new direction for the campaign, writing that it would be a "most worthy work...if a formal inquisition were to be instituted against the Jews."[74] He proposed that a list of articles be drawn up against the Jews, including blasphemies and heresies in their books, and that these charges be turned over to the inquisition at once. Essentially, Hoogstraeten, as the papal inquisitor for the province of Teutonia, was indicating his readiness to assume leadership of the book confiscation pogrom. Eventually, Reuchlin would read the document this way, declaring that Hoogstraeten's *Consultation* had threatened "a formal inquisition against the Jews."[75]

Reuchlin's *Recommendation*

Reuchlin's *Recommendation* did not directly save the Jewish books in the first instance; they had already been returned and the confiscation had been suspended. Nor was he the first Christian authority to argue forcefully on behalf of the Jews; the Frankfurt city council had already done that. Nonetheless, his *Recommendation* would ultimately derail the concerted efforts to restart the campaign based on Maximilian's Füssen Mandate. Reuchlin's memorandum differed from the others: while theirs were brief and enthusiastic endorsements of the policy, his was an exhaustive analysis of the issue on the basis of the law and the evidence that would run to some forty-two pages in its first printed edition and deliver a resounding rejection of the strategy. Instead of having assembled a united academic front against the Jewish books, Hoogstraeten, Pfefferkorn, and Maximilian now faced a rebuttal that outweighed all the endorsements.

Reuchlin's strategy was lawyerly.[76] He vigorously attacked the mandate from as many perspectives as possible and with a full apparatus of references to law codes and standard commentaries. He appealed on the basis of the Bible, ecclesiastical law, civil law, and—a perspective that needs scrutiny—anti-Jewish ecclesiastical tracts of the fifteenth century.[77] He also scrupulously presented and refuted potential counterarguments. The nature of the charges—that is, that Jewish books were blasphemous and heretical—induced him to review the evidence in a sweeping presentation of Hebrew literature, a daunting task at this inchoate stage in the history of Jewish studies. In this undertaking, he pursued the ancillary goal of documenting a history in which Christianity acknowledged benefits from Jewish writings.

Reuchlin constructed much of his argument on the basis of civil law, as one might expect from someone with his legal background. In that regard, he grounded his position in the contention that Jews residing in the empire were not serfs or slaves but rather fellow citizens ("concives"): "We and they are fellow citizens of one and the same Roman Empire,"[78] a position Reuchlin probably derived from some late-medieval Italian legal commentaries.[79] Although he did not intend this as an assertion that, over all, Christians and Jews had equal legal rights, it did mean that, as fellow citizens, Jews were protected from state seizure of their property: "imperial and monarchical law and other princely law codes have established that no one should lose his property by force."[80]

Reuchlin's "concives" argument immediately encountered a torrent of academic non placets so fierce that he qualified it by the fall of 1511, though without retracting his position on Jewish property rights.[81] His theological opponents objected that he was contradicting the well-established principle of the servitude of the Jews. Indeed, a typical, but not universally held, assumption was that Jews fell under the category of slaves and were therefore excluded from many basic rights of citizens. The Christian theologian Duns Scotus supported that view, as did Ulrich Zasius, perhaps the most influential German legal scholar of the early sixteenth century.[82] Zasius even used the concept of Jewish servitude as a basis for arguing, in a notorious case, that Jewish children could legally be taken from their parents by force and baptized.[83] Reuchlin vehemently rejected the legality of coercive baptism in the *Recommendation* and elsewhere.

But even on these issues, it is important to observe a deeper reliance on ecclesiastical law.[84] Referring specifically to passages in the *Decretales* of Gregory IX,[85] Reuchlin wrote, "Therefore, we are ordered in ecclesiastical law, in *Sicut Judaeis*, not to take their belongings from the Jews, whether money or something of monetary value."[86] Indeed, basic property rights had been enshrined in the foundational medieval law governing Christian-Jewish relations: the *Sicut Judaeis*, often called the *Constitution for the Jews*, a papal bull first issued in the 1120s but harking back to policies formulated by Pope Gregory the Great (590–604).[87] When he composed the *Recommendation*, Reuchlin had not yet read Hoogstraeten's *Consultation* and was unaware of his plan to convene an inquisition against Jewish books in the empire. According to his own account, he was motivated by a desire to stop Maximilian, not the church, from an illegal and destructive blunder. Apparently, however, Reuchlin could already envision the campaign as a matter headed for ecclesiastical adjudication—after all, Maximilian had been moving in that direction ever since he entrusted implementation of the Roveredo Mandate to Archbishop

Uriel. Moreover, the terms and questions of the Füssen Mandate—such as, would destruction of the Jewish books benefit Christianity?—suggested that the ultimate legal authority would be ecclesiastical. Consequently, Reuchlin's *Recommendation* often sounds like a preemptive defense against putative inquisitional charges in addition to being a legal memorandum prepared for the Holy Roman emperor.[88]

Even if under both civil and ecclesiastical law the Jews enjoyed the right to own such things as religious books,[89] those books would still be subject to seizure and destruction by the state, if they were heretical, blasphemous, or libelous. Reuchlin addressed this as the most serious legal question. And, to his mind, the answer hinged on an accurate analysis of the evidence—the Jewish books themselves.

In the end, Reuchlin's assessment of Jewish literature was devastating to the campaign. This was the prime reason that Hoogstraeten, Pfefferkorn, and von Tongern, among others, would immediately attack him with such fury and resolve. After compressing a comprehensive review of Jewish writing to pamphlet size, Reuchlin authoritatively pronounced Jewish books innocent of all charges of blasphemy and heresy, with the exception of two minor books that, according to Reuchlin, were taboo among Jews anyway.[90]

In his pamphlets, Pfefferkorn had cited actual Jewish prayers as liturgical examples of Jewish hatred of Christianity. Understanding the importance of such an allegation—confiscation of liturgical and devotional books would end the normal practice of Jewish worship—Reuchlin focused on this aspect of Jewish writing: "As for their books of sermons and disputations, also the prayer book, song books, the guidelines ('order') for their services, customs, and devotions, what should I say other than what praiseworthy emperors and holy popes have said and legislated about it, that one should allow them in their synagogues to keep their ceremonies, rituals, practices, customs and devotions in peace."[91]

Reuchlin specifically addressed the accusation—one that both Schwarz and Pfefferkorn had emphasized—that "ve-la-meshummadim" ("for the apostates" there is no hope) was a prayer (from the 'Amidah) for the demise of Christianity as well as, specifically, the Holy Roman Empire. Characterizing German Jews as benevolent fellow citizens, Reuchlin asserted that Jews were not the enemies of Christians, and that they prayed for peace in the Holy Roman Empire.[92] Perhaps more impressive to Reuchlin's contemporaries was his philological critique. He argued that the roots for "meshummadim" (i.e., from the verb "שָׁמַד" [destroy]) could not designate baptism (i.e., those who had become Christians) but referred more generically to those who opposed Judaism, as Reuchlin translated: "whoever wants to destroy us" ("wer vns vertilcken wölte").[93] He also listed parallel usages from the Hebrew Bible, thus offering an early example of humanist biblical philology at work, in order to support his analysis of "meshummadim."

Reuchlin devoted the longest segment of the memorandum to defending the Talmud. On the one hand, he said that the Talmud was a valuable source of ancient learning about such subjects as medicine and agriculture.[94] He also acknowledged the centrality of the Talmud as a legal code and a compilation of Jewish theological authorities, comparing it specifically to such fundamental Christian works as Gratian's compilation of canon law (the *Decretales*), Peter Lombard's *Sentences* (the most influential digest of theology in the late Middle Ages), and Thomas Aquinas's *Golden Chain* (a handbook of ancient, authoritative Christian interpretations of the Bible).[95] He even erroneously claimed that the church had never condemned the Talmud, until in his own lifetime Schwarz and Pfefferkorn had done so in their tracts.[96] Reuchlin's point, though, was that the Talmud should not be used as evidence that Jews had become heretics within Judaism, that is, that they had departed from Old Testament standards and that such a deviation was actionable under heresy laws. Instead, Reuchlin insisted that historically the church had granted Jews immunity from charges of heresy as they were outside the Christian faith and had never fallen from it.[97] He quoted Gratian's compilation of canon law for unambiguous corroboration: "Jews are not heretics."[98] ... "They are not members of the Christian church and their faith is not our business."[99] This is a critically important component of the legal strategy, since Reuchlin knew that the outcome would be disastrous for the Jews, if they were subjected to Christian heresy laws.

A curious feature of Reuchlin's argument was the depth of his reliance on published anti-Jewish tracts. In the *Recommendation*, he favorably quoted an array of academic anti-Jewish tracts printed in the fifteenth century; the only notable exception was one by Peter Schwarz, which he also cited, but disapprovingly.[100] Clearly, Reuchlin had already become an expert on anti-Jewish writings and campaigns. Prior to the appearance of his *Recommendation*, he was actually known as an anti-Jewish apologist who had published his own anti-Jewish tract in 1505, one that advocated conversionary missions to German Jewry.[101] In the *Recommendation*, he disclosed that he had had discussions not only with Pfefferkorn but also, presumably long ago, with Schwarz.[102] Pfefferkorn left a personal meeting with Reuchlin in August 1509 convinced that the famous scholar and lawyer supported him as he began implementation of the Padua Mandate.

Why was the defender of Jewish literature quoting anti-Jewish zealots so liberally? Citing a host of authorities, Reuchlin contended that Jewish writings should be saved in part for their potential use in missions to convert the Jews: "the books are not the real reason they refuse to convert to Christianity.... Rather, their books could indeed be a reason for them to convert readily, if we had capable people, knowledgeable in that very language, who were able to converse with them rationally."[103] Learned anti-Jewish crusaders such as Paul of Burgos and Peter Schwarz had long argued for the training of such academic missions. Paul of Burgos and Schwarz had also produced comprehensive handbooks, replete with extensive quotations from Hebrew sources (from the Tanakh and the Talmud), to equip missions to debate with Jews. This very old method had been developed in the hope of increasing the effectiveness of missions to the Jews. In 1475 and 1477, Schwarz, an active Dominican missionary in southern Germany, published two massive tracts, one in Latin and one in German, "proving" such things as the trinity and the messiahship of Jesus on the basis of passages from the Tanakh, all of which he quoted in the original Hebrew (transliterated in the Roman alphabet) along with word-for-word translations into Latin or German.

Reuchlin's adversaries would soon pillory him for asserting that Jesus' statement in John 5:39, "Search the Scriptures because you think that in them you have eternal life; and it is they that bear witness to me," referred to the Talmud in addition to the Tanakh.[104] Reuchlin even said that this passage was "my foundation for this recommendation" ("Mein grundtfeste diß ratschlags"),[105] placing God behind the acknowledgment of the Talmud. Hoogstraeten, Pfefferkorn, and their allies professed horror at the thought of a Christian contending that the Talmud possessed religious value or that Jesus himself had endorsed its validity. Arnold van Tongern emphasized this in his set of heresy charges against Reuchlin from 1512, the first of several to be drawn up. In a way, however, Reuchlin was doing little more than citing the title and opening pages of Paul of Burgos's massive *Scrutinium scripturarum* (Searching of the Scriptures), a work, frequently printed in the fifteenth century, whose very title quoted Jesus' statement in John 5. Paul of Burgos, a leading Sephardic rabbi before conversion, made a distinguished career as a Christian theologian and leader, ultimately being named bishop of Burgos. His conversion occurred in the horrific context of the Spanish pogroms of 1391, though he would always characterize it as voluntary. According to Paul, when Christ spoke the words quoted in John 5:39, he was referring to "Talmudic authorities" and other writings that are authentic among the Jews "from which effective arguments can be taken against them."[106] Reuchlin summed up this backhanded tribute to the Talmud with an appeal to yet another anti-Jewish campaigner, Alfonso de Spina:

When they [i.e., Christian scholars who know Hebrew] want to
dispute with Jews, they take up the Talmud and combat them with
the Talmud, as, for example, the famous Franciscan theologian
Alfonso de Spina, who composed the *Fortalicium fidei* in Spain.... He

supported his ideas for us and himself with fine skill on the basis of the Talmud, as if he wanted to slay the Jews with their own dagger.[107]

Reuchlin's attempts, as exemplified by his use of John 5:39, to cite the Christian Bible in support of Jewish books would become particularly vulnerable points for heresy accusations. Several of his substantial references to the Christian Bible, such as this one, would be cast in Reuchlin's teeth as defective (and heretical) instances of humanist Bible philology.

Reuchlin was cleverly deploying the older anti-Jewish tactics of the Middle Ages—conversionary missions—in order to undermine the new anti-Jewish weapon—confiscation and destruction of their books. Anti-Jewish crusaders such as Paul of Burgos may have despised Judaism but their method, however strained and contorted, unmistakably asserted that Jewish books offered access to Christian truth. As Reuchlin saw it, that alone should vitiate any proposal to destroy them. I should add, however, that medieval controversialists also took a somewhat opposite approach, claiming that parts of the Talmud were so patently absurd that they, too, could abet conversion. Reuchlin used both of these arguments—that some Jewish books confirmed Christian truths and others, with their inanities, effectively undermined the credibility of Judaism—to insist that Jewish writings be preserved.

More significant than the links to recent anti-Jewish missions, however, is Reuchlin's determined revival of the protective elements of ecclesiastical law. Thus, Reuchlin cited canons verbatim that outlawed forced conversion and that granted property rights, two prominent issues protected by the armor of Sicut Judaeis. Reuchlin also quoted a canon that advocated that missionaries use kindness as well as Jewish books:

> Whosoever desires, with pure intentions, to bring to the true faith
> people who are standing outside, foreign to it, should undertake
> that effort with gentle language and not with harsh assertions, lest
> disgust drive them away whom reason might be able to turn from
> error. And those who do otherwise and, using a disguise want to
> turn them away from their customs, they, we should realize, are
> not doing God's business but their own. Thus we should treat them
> in such a way that they are moved more by reason and kindness
> and that they would rather follow us than flee from us, so that we
> can convert them manifestly with God's help to our Mother, the
> Christian church, on the basis of their own books.[108]

Obviously, Reuchlin's mentality falls well short of modern expectations for religious toleration. His implicit assumption everywhere is that Christianity offers the only path to salvation and that the only hope for Jews is conversion.

We could safely conclude that above all Reuchlin was offering an extensive elaboration of the *Sicut Judaeis* toleration of Judaism, a form of toleration that permitted the practice of Judaism but also subjected Jews to significant legal disabilities and humiliations.

Reuchlin's embrace of Jewish writing was also firmly rooted in the new humanist focus on biblical philology, portrayed by him as a realization of goals set long ago by the church hierarchy. The progress in Christian-Jewish relations that Reuchlin implicitly advocated was, thus, in several respects, a historical step backward—arguably a salutary step backward—to a pre-banishment mentality in the Holy Roman Empire. In some ways, this may sound like a modest proposal, but, given the circumstances of his time, it should be understood as a basis for significant improvement. Reuchlin was advocating a stabilization of the legal status of the Jews against the tidal wave of Jewish eradication engulfing the Holy Roman Empire.

Indeed, the ultimate point of Reuchlin's *Recommendation* was connected to the ideology of Renaissance humanism: Jewish books will benefit Christianity and Christian scholars need to turn to them in earnest. This applies to the Talmud, Bible commentaries, Kabbalistic works, and, above all, the Masoretic text of the Tanakh. Yet, even in this respect, Reuchlin tried to bolster his recommendations with references to standing ecclesiastical policy. For instance, he claimed that some Jewish writings, in particular Kabbalistic tracts, had already received explicit endorsement from various popes. Quoting a passage in Pico's *Apologia*, Reuchlin wrote that "Pope Sixtus IV ordered the same Kabbalistic books to be translated and interpreted into the Latin language, as a special benefit to our faith."[109] The conclusion to the *Recommendation* began on this note, urging Christian scholars not only to learn to read the Bible in the original Hebrew but also to mine Jewish literature for valuable material:

> With my slight understanding, my best advice is that His Imperial
> Majesty direct the universities of Germany—for the sake of God and
> our Christian faith—that each one hire two capable lecturers for a
> ten-year term who should teach and instruct our pupils and students
> in the Hebrew language, as the *Clementines* [i.e., a section of canon
> law] require under the title "de magistris prima." To this end, Jews
> living and residing in our land should help us, in a good-hearted and
> neighborly spirit, by lending us their books (assured against losses
> by an appropriate damage deposit).[110]

This passage refers to the famous canon from the Council of Vienne under Pope Clement V (1305–14) that mandated the study of Hebrew at European universities, a canon never really implemented but which, as Reuchlin presents it, implies appreciation of Jewish learning. According to Reuchlin (evoking the words of St. Jerome), Jews were the noble librarians of God's word,[111] the people who preserved the Hebrew original text, that, in Reuchlin's comparison to Bible translations, is "immaculate"[112] and therefore authoritative.

The Jews were not only the guardians of the original text—a duty in which the Christians had failed miserably—but they also preserved the philological knowledge necessary for understanding the text.

> Sacred, ecclesiastical law says, at Gratian I, 9, 6, that the faith of the old books [i.e., the Old Testament] must be preserved through the Hebrew text and if the words and statements of Rabbi Solomon [i.e., Rashi], who wrote about the Bible, were to be cancelled and removed from Nicholas of Lyra, who also wrote about the Bible, all that would remain that Nicholas of Lyra had written about the Bible from his own reflection I would be able to reduce and summarize in just a few pages.[113]

Thus Reuchlin argued—and modern scholars would agree[114]—that substantial elements in the most prominent Christian Bible commentary of the late Middle Ages were derived from one of the leading biblical scholars in the Jewish tradition. Reuchlin also contended that the Apostle Paul became the greatest theologian among the New Testament writers because he, alone among the apostles, had enjoyed a rabbinic education: "Our Apostle Paul learned all the arts of the Jews and went to school under the rabbis. What did he accomplish? More than all the other apostles."[115]

Reuchlin, moreover, raised an embarrassing question. What happens to Christian theology if it lacks an anchor in Jewish studies? His answer was bound to raise hackles among scholastic theologians:

> Such commentaries [i.e., Jewish research on Hebrew] the Christian church cannot and may not let go of, for they preserve the Hebrew language in its native usage, which the Holy Scriptures cannot be without, especially the Old Testament. Just as we could not manage without the Greek language, Greek grammars and commentaries in the New Testament, as the already mentioned canon "Ut veterum" directs. I'd like to take the liberty, as politely as possible, of saying that there are many theologians in our Christian faith who because of their ignorance of the two languages [Hebrew and Greek] cannot interpret the Holy Scriptures correctly and have often become ludicrous. Therefore we should not suppress the commentaries and glosses of men who have studied Hebrew thoroughly ever since

their youth; rather, wherever they [i.e., Jewish books] are, we should acquire them, establish them, and hold them in great esteem, as if they were fountains from which the real meaning of the language and understanding of the Holy Scriptures flowed. For that reason, canon law states "Many of our scholars have conflicting opinions. Therefore we are compelled and forced to take recourse to the Jews and to seek the truth of the art [i.e., skill at reading Scripture] from the source rather than downstream from rivulets."[116]

Given the fact that in 1510 virtually no professors of theology knew either Hebrew or Greek, these were caustic, though earnest, words that the academy had to take seriously.

It is in the area of representation, in his characterization of Judaism, that Reuchlin took the longest stride forward. To Reuchlin, Judaism still offered pristine sources for Christianity, and Jewish scholars offered Christians the only hope they had for gaining access to those sources.

Reuchlin even defended Jews against some hostile traditions of the Christian church. Most astonishingly, he delivered a scathing critique of the Good Friday liturgy, in which Christians notoriously prayed for the "perfidious Jews" (an issue that could reemerge in twenty-first-century Catholicism with revived interest in the Tridentine Mass). His point was to claim that Jews did not libel Christians; it was the other way around: Christians libeled Jews when doing such things as calling them "perfidious." "For so long as we publicly call them during our Good Friday services, year after year, 'perfidious Jews,' that is faithless Jews, which in good German means they have kept neither their word nor their faith; thus they may respond among themselves and in accord with the law: 'they are lying about us; we have never broken our faith.'"[117] According to Reuchlin, the devout Jews were anything but "perfidious," for they had stood the test of their faith countless times.

Indeed, Reuchlin sincerely urged Christians to embrace the value of Jewish studies without being unduly judgmental: "The Jew belongs to our Lord God as much as I do. If he stands, he stands before the Lord; if he falls, he falls before the Lord. Each person will have to give a reckoning. Why should we pass judgment on another soul, when God is so powerful that he can restore him?"[118] This passage, too, implies conversion as the ultimate result of God's grace. But it is also striking that in this formulation Reuchlin suggests removing Christian intervention from that process and that, despite their rejection of Jesus, he grants Jews equal standing, equal dignity, before God. These words, "The Jew belongs to our Lord God as much as I do," though derived from the Christian Bible (see Romans 14), were foreign to the discourse of Reuchlin's Christian culture.

Conclusion in Frankfurt

If anything, the six years following the return of the Jewish books saw a marked rise in anti-Jewish hostility in Frankfurt. Outrage greeted Johannes Reuchlin's publication of his defense of Jewish writings, with the city council (on 9 September 1511), the emperor (7 October 1512), and the elector-archbishop of Mainz (7 March 1513) forbidding distribution of Reuchlin's writings in Frankfurt.[119] At one point the city council discussed reports that an aroused populace was complaining that Jews had bribed council members; at another point, the council felt the need to issue a proclamation to the citizenry explaining that harm would befall the city if mobs murdered the Frankfurt Jews (6 July 1513; also 4 July 1513). Ominously, in 1515 a host desecration case flared in Frankfurt but apparently was not pursued.

Soon two realignments occurred. As of 1511, the city council began openly debating the desirability of banishing its Jewish residents and Maximilian gradually stepped forward as the protector of the Jews. In this stormy atmosphere in Frankfurt, the Jews turned to Maximilian with a request for a new imperial patent of protection. The patent was first issued on 30 July 1513. It explicitly protected them from banishment (thus from the new threats emanating from the council) and also from further harassment from Pfefferkorn. The council, which objected to the charter, was dismayed when the Jews accepted it nonetheless. Maximilian assessed the Jews no less than 2,000 gulden for the new charter, which, of course, qualifies as a major success in strengthening his authority over the Frankfurt Jewish community. As of 1514, Maximilian began writing letters in support of Reuchlin in his heresy trial brought by Hoogstraeten and the Cologne Dominicans. The most important of these was a direct appeal from the emperor to Pope Leo X, which Reuchlin published prominently.[120]

The peak of anti-Jewish agitation in Frankfurt was reached with an extraordinary attempt, initiated by Frankfurt in the spring of 1515 (24 April 1515), to organize a multi-territorial expulsion of Jews from the entire area of the archdiocese of Mainz (including the Palatinate, the Electorate of Mainz, the Landgraviate of Hesse, the Free Imperial City of Frankfurt, etc.).[121] Under the leadership of Albrecht of Brandenburg, the new archbishop of Mainz, a group of twenty to thirty territories met in Frankfurt in January 1516 to discuss this major initiative. The Frankfurt Jewish community, having gotten wind of the proposal, requested and received protection from Maximilian under the new charter. After Maximilian forbade further discussion of this unusual strategy, the effort ended in February 1516. Pfefferkorn, however, dedicated his 1516

Defense (*Beschyrmung*) to Archbishop Albrecht in an attempt to support the new campaign.[122]

Tensions remained high, even though the book controversy had ended. By 1514, Maximilian had become protector of the Frankfurt Jews and of Reuchlin. Reuchlin's relatively swift rehabilitation with the emperor was hardly surprising for he had maintained close ties with the imperial court throughout a lengthy legal-diplomatic career. The emperor had long been an active supporter of the humanist movement and Reuchlin was the most visible advocate of humanism in the empire. Reuchlin, moreover, had effectively championed humanist biblical philology, still highly controversial, in a way that made its aims appear consistent with those of the medieval church. More important, Reuchlin's views on Jews and Judaism were beginning to look compatible with the emperor's own policy, as it developed during the 1510s.

Reuchlin's famous report did not directly defuse the controversy and his argumentation is partially prefigured in petitions submitted by the city council of Frankfurt. Nonetheless, his report is a conscientious effort to strengthen the legal status of Jews in the Holy Roman Empire. Furthermore, though I would not cite it as a cause, it does stand at the beginning of a long-term development—one that lasted for about seventy-five years—during which the legal position of Jewish communities in the empire did in fact stabilize and the age of banishments gradually ended.

7

Inquisition

I favor the Jews so that they not suffer any wrong and not commit
any wrong...injustice is a monstrosity that is repugnant to all
humanity.

—Johannes Reuchlin, 1513, in his *Defense* against
the Cologne professors

The fallout from Reuchlin's *Recommendation* has been measured in
different ways. While his report unleashed widespread controversy
over Christian policies on the status of Judaism, many historians
have also argued that the burning issue was really the introduction
of humanism at German universities, especially the growing success
of humanists who, in the aftermath of Erasmus, were questioning
the foundations of scholasticism. Thus, the harsh response
to Reuchlin was an effort by scholastic theologians to stymie
Renaissance humanism. These were to be significant features of
the Reuchlin Affair over time and we will explore them (mostly in
chapter 8). But it is also important to observe that the impassioned
action against Reuchlin derived from a different source, one that
historians have overlooked: the determination to restart the anti-
Jewish campaign. Reuchlin's opponents did not see this as a mere
academic difference of opinion. They collided with Reuchlin as they
were arming for resumption of the campaign against Jewish books
and doing so with great confidence of success.

A key to understanding the beginnings of the Reuchlin Affair is the fact that in the immediate aftermath of Maximilian's Füssen Mandate the inquisition was preparing to assume responsibility for the confiscation of Jewish books. Inquisitor General Hoogstraeten had announced this intention in his formal evaluation to Maximilian, *The Consultation against the Filthy Jewish Books.*[1] Hoogstraeten's plan, which was still in an inchoate state as Reuchlin composed his *Recommendation*, had to be modified in response to Reuchlin's position. The conflict with Reuchlin became so obscenely bitter not because scholastics were defending their turf or intolerant ecclesiastics wanted to impose iron-clad orthodoxy on scholarship but rather because fervent anti-Jewish forces had become convinced that the ultimate victory—the end of Judaism in Germany—was within their reach. Their frustration over Reuchlin's interruption of their progress boils over on every page of their pamphlets.

Emperor Maximilian had suspended the anti-Jewish campaign in May 1510, but he had not decided to end it and no one was showing any signs of willingness to give up the fight. As we have seen in the continuation and attempted expansion of the Frankfurt campaign, the political attacks against Judaism intensified between 1510 and 1516. With the publication of Reuchlin's *Recommendation*, the scope of the effort widened to include a massive confrontation of the scholar and, by extension, any Christian authority that would support toleration, however limited, of Judaism. But the focus of Reuchlin's opponents, especially in the years 1510–14, remained eradication of the Jewish books and their owners. Every attack against Reuchlin was also an uncompromising insistence that Judaism be destroyed.

Reuchlin's evaluation, as we have seen, was a repudiation of nearly every aspect of Pfefferkorn's campaign and the emperor's mandate. It offered an extensive, multifaceted, and well-documented legal justification for its position, replete with lengthy rebuttals to potential counterarguments. The cursoriness of the other evaluations, along with their sweeping conclusions, were marks of overconfidence. Except for Hoogstraeten, no one even bothered to advance a legal rationale for the book burnings or even cite a law code or a legal commentary.[2] These evaluations were, to be sure, strongly worded, but their substance was breezy. Reuchlin, remarkably, was still the only lawyer involved at this stage. His dissent was not only a strong challenge to the campaign but also a lightning strike on a cloudless day. He had been included among the evaluators because Pfefferkorn was convinced, based on Reuchlin's 1505 *German Epistle: Why the Jews Have Been in Exile So Long* and conversations with Reuchlin about the Padua Mandate, that the Hebrew scholar shared his commitment to ending German Jewry. Thus, it is hard to fault Pfefferkorn, Uriel von Gemmingen, and Maximilian for assuming that the expert on anti-Jewish writings was an implacable foe of Jews in Germany. Reuchlin had given several indications that he could be counted on as a proponent of the anti-Jewish movement.

Reuchlin submitted his evaluation to Archbishop Uriel on 6 October 1510 and the archbishop scrupulously included it in the documents he forwarded to Maximilian on 29 October 1510.[3] In his summary evaluation to the emperor, however, the archbishop emphatically endorsed the recommendations of the University of Cologne and Hoogstraeten: the books, if not the Jews, should be burned.[4] That conclusion was also reached by a commission led by Gregor Reisch, prior of the Carthusian Charterhouse in Freiburg, that reviewed all of the evaluations for Maximilian in December 1510. Reisch, a highly respected scholar who also became the emperor's confessor, specifically condemned Reuchlin's opinion as "scandalous."[5]

From the moment Reuchlin submitted his *Recommendation*, Pfefferkorn had access to it, for the latter, as the official "solicitor" of the commission, was responsible for collecting the documents from all the evaluators. Pfefferkorn, thus, had every right to read Reuchlin's document, despite the author's later objections to the contrary. Soon, however, Pfefferkorn overstepped his authority egregiously by publishing a pamphlet against Reuchlin and the Jews in spring 1511, liberally quoting from Reuchlin's confidential memorandum.

This work, *Magnifying Glass* (*Handt Spiegel*), was more than a thunderous attack—ad hominem and ad rem—against Reuchlin; it was also a murderous escalation of the assault on Jewish culture. With *Magnifying Glass*, Pfefferkorn ignited a conflagration of anti-Semitic rhetoric, relinquishing any show of restraint. Now, Jews appear not only as corrosive usurers and despicable blasphemers but also as bloodthirsty murderers of Christians. This work also unleashed a new and dangerous wave of public anti-Jewish agitation, this one emanating from the theology faculty of the University of Cologne.

Pfefferkorn's *Magnifying Glass*: Against the Jews and Their Defender

Once Reuchlin's *Recommendation* had been submitted, the anti-Jewish forces realized that their hope for unanimous scholarly condemnation of Jewish literature (and Judaism) had not materialized. That Reuchlin was the one to express such serious misgivings was nearly incomprehensible to them. They had been blindsided.

Worse than that disappointment, everyone involved—Pfefferkorn, Archbishop Uriel, Inquisitor General Hoogstraeten, professors at the University

Cologne, and many others—knew that they were now dealing with a second serious challenge to their campaign (the first being the successful negotiations conducted by the Frankfurt Jewish community). Reuchlin ranked among the most respected constitutional lawyers in the Holy Roman Empire; many saw him as the founder of humanism in Germany; everyone recognized him as the pioneer of Christian Hebrew studies. He was even personally acquainted with the emperor. This universally admired man—a scholar, judge, and diplomat— had submitted a cogent argument against the confiscation policy. The path forward could not simply ignore his intervention.

Pfefferkorn reached for his usual weapon—pen and paper—and attempted to obliterate Reuchlin's objections in his new pamphlet, *Magnifying Glass*. According to the title page, *Magnifying Glass* opposed both the Jews and "several Christians" who defended them.[6] In a strict sense, this was the book—this challenge to Christian defenses of Jewish life—that gave rise to the Reuchlin Affair, for it was only in response to *Magnifying Glass*'s vitriolic portrayal of him and his scholarship that Reuchlin chose to publish the *Recommendation*.[7] This step, in turn, would result in nine long years of turmoil, but Reuchlin really had no other option. *Magnifying Glass* appeared in early spring 1511 (from the venerable publishing house of Peter Schoeffer in Mainz[8]) and immediately became the hottest item at the international Frankfurt book fair that April. Reuchlin managed to publish his rebuttal (*Augenspiegel*, or *Eye Glasses*)—which was also a massive counterattack—in time for distribution at the autumn book fair, September 1511, in Frankfurt. Thus began the new public debate.

Pfefferkorn pursued several goals in *Magnifying Glass*. One was a defense of his own integrity, for Reuchlin had included in the *Recommendation* some dismissive statements about Pfefferkorn's ability to assess Jewish writings. This part of the response gives some interesting biographical information about Pfefferkorn, including the fact that Pfefferkorn studied the Talmud in Moravia under an otherwise unknown uncle named Rabbi Meir Pfefferkorn. It was essential that the anti-Jewish forces be able to claim competence in their attack on the books.

With an impressive apparatus of legal and ecclesiastical authorities, Pfefferkorn assailed the argumentation of the *Recommendation*, thereby prefiguring the heresy charges that the inquisition would soon level. While Pfefferkorn does not explicitly allege that Reuchlin's views amount to actionable heterodoxy, his critique leaves the strong impression that preparations for a heresy trial were already underway. The pamphlet is dedicated to none other than Arnold van Tongern, the Cologne professor of theology who did, in fact, draw up the first formal set of charges against Reuchlin. But the primary issue is still the Jews, not the Christian scholar. According to Pfefferkorn's tribute to Tongern, the theologian had expressed astonishment that the campaign against Jewish books had been suspended.⁹ Inquisitor General Hoogstraeten is also cited as the source of a story about a Christian who tried to follow Jewish law.¹⁰ *Magnifying Glass* even features a fictional "inquisitor" who poses questions about charges against Jews.

Several of Pfefferkorn's condemnations would reemerge in the heresy trials. Pfefferkorn expresses his greatest contempt for Reuchlin's classification of Jews as "fellow citizens" under imperial law. It would be more appropriate "to find Christians who say that they [the Jews] are fellow citizens of the devil."¹¹ Pfefferkorn contends that Reuchlin's favorable view of Judaism generally contradicts the conclusions of authoritative Christian theologians and that his defense of the Talmud is specifically at odds with the medieval condemnations by Gregory IX and Innocent IV.¹² By implication, this is an allegation that Reuchlin has run afoul of ecclesiastical law.

The fierce attack on his personal integrity appears to have rankled Reuchlin. Pfefferkorn alleges that Reuchlin has a covert relationship with the Jews he is protecting; that he is receiving bribes in return for taking his position. Pfefferkorn also demonstrates—convincingly, we might add—that the *Recommendation* flatly contradicts specific views expressed in Reuchlin's *German Epistle: Why the Jews Have Been in Exile So Long*. Indeed, as Pfefferkorn correctly points out, Reuchlin's pamphlet featured a scathing attack on the *'Amidah*, claiming that it blasphemed Christianity, whereas the *Recommendation* offered a stout defense against Pfefferkorn's identical criticism of the very same prayer (which Pfefferkorn had published in his *Enemy of the Jews* in 1509).¹³ Did bribes change his mind? That was what Pfefferkorn suggested. In a slightly later work, Pfefferkorn openly contended that prior to 1510 Reuchlin expressed strong support for the book confiscation.¹⁴

Most insultingly, Pfefferkorn dismisses Reuchlin's knowledge of Hebrew as a fraud. He baldly states that Reuchlin may have published a Hebrew grammar, but he did not write one. That was the work of his Jewish friends.¹⁵ This would become a standard feature of anti-Reuchlin diatribes, especially after Pfefferkorn escalated the attack in his *Fire Glass (Brantspiegell)* of 1512.¹⁶ Pfefferkorn also excoriates Reuchlin for daring to defend the Talmud when the scholar admits that, as of 1510, he had not read any part of it.

The bulk of the poisonous rhetoric, however, is not intended for Reuchlin (his *Recommendation* had, of course, not even been published yet). Rather, as Pfefferkorn said in 1512, "I did not publish [*Magnifying Glass*] against him but against the Jews."¹⁷ The specific counterarguments to Reuchlin are something of a sideshow, sometimes merely an excuse to unleash another scorching diatribe against Judaism. Pfefferkorn portrays contemporary Jews as murderous enemies of Christians, as blasphemers, and as heretics. He characterizes the mere presence of Jews as a peril to Christian society. The destructiveness of Jewish money lending is mentioned several times,[18] but Pfefferkorn focuses most sharply on the theme of Jews undermining the faith of Christians. He and others will eventually contend that Reuchlin's *Eye Glasses* is designed specifically to weaken the faith of simple Christians, mainly because it was published in German.

Pfefferkorn narrates several vignettes about Jews converting Christians and the dire results. One case, which is so banal that it almost rings true, is of a Christian messenger ("Bote") from Deutz who was severely punished by the inquisition for wearing phylacteries, apparently trying to observe Jewish ritual. Jacob Hoogstraeten may be the source for this story.[19] Two other darker tales involve conversion and murder. One is of a Christian doctor named Thomas who secretly became Jewish, murdered some 600 Christian patients, and fled to Prague with a priest and two Christian youths he had seduced into conversion.[20] The other is a long story of an ardently anti-Jewish Franciscan preacher who was tricked into believing his biological father was Jewish, converted to Judaism, and married a Jewish woman. When he eventually sought to return to Christianity, his Jewish father-in-law ghoulishly murdered him and distributed parts of his corpse to Jewish communities around the empire.[21] These outlandish stories are presented as facts and also as earnest warnings about the hazard of tolerating Jews in Germany.

Most dangerously, Pfefferkorn conjures up the deadly specter of blood libel and host desecration cases. The pamphlet cites four recent cases of host desecration,[22] along with breaking news about a major new incident, the Berlin host desecration travesty of 1510.[23] The Berlin case resulted in the execution of thirty-eight Jewish victims as well as the banishment of all Jews from Brandenburg. Moreover, it invigorated anti-Jewish campaigning throughout the empire.[24] Pfefferkorn's endorsement of these terrible judicial hoaxes is unusual—other prominent converts who became anti-Jewish campaigners did not malign their former brethren with such deadly accusations. Every reasonable authority knew that these witch hunts were illegitimate. Popes and emperors routinely forbade their prosecution—often to little avail with local authorities. The Brandenburg convictions would even be rescinded in 1539 and Jews would be able to resettle there. But Pfefferkorn chose to exploit these myths in order to support his contention that Jews are dangerous and nefarious enemies of Christianity and to denounce Reuchlin for maintaining that the Jews could be a benign presence in Christian society. He wanted to associate his campaign with the notable success of the anti-Jewish movement in Brandenburg. As we will see, Inquisitor Hoogstraeten and the Cologne theology faculty would publicly back his embrace of the harsh Brandenburg actions.

Nonetheless, Jewish writings remained his theme and their destruction his aim. Therefore, much of the pamphlet is taken up with repeating the specific allegation used in his previous tracts. He offers a direct rebuttal to Reuchlin's philological defense of Jewish prayers, insisting, on the strength of further quotations from Hebrew writings, that Jews blaspheme Christianity. Now he presents twenty articles against the Talmud, contending that his sampling of Talmudic perversions of Judaism was sufficient to warrant eradication of the book.[25] The goal is to heighten hatred of Jews and the public resolve to destroy their literature.

Magnifying Glass reveals the close collaboration between Pfefferkorn and the Cologne theologians. The tract itself was dedicated to Professor Tongern, but even more significant are the similarities between Pfefferkorn's arguments and those that will follow in the writings of the faculty. There is no reason to doubt Pfefferkorn's authorship of his German pamphlets, although the Latin versions of them must have come from academic pens.[26] Yet, we should observe that, when Pfefferkorn cites canon law against Reuchlin in *Magnifying Glass*, he explicitly says that theologians provided him with all the references.[27]

University of Cologne: The Gathering Storm

As we have seen, Jacob Hoogstraeten had already announced a papal inquisition of Jewish writings in his response to Maximilian's Füssen Mandate. But the publication of Reuchlin's *Eye Glasses* forced Hoogstraeten to modify his strategy for resuming the confiscation campaign. He would now have to deal with the scholar, too, as he advanced the case against the Jews. Hoogstraeten, moreover, decided to seek a formal condemnation of Reuchlin from the theology faculty of Cologne before impaneling an inquisitional court.

Why did Hoogstraeten take the initial step against Reuchlin in his capacity as dean of the theology faculty rather than as papal inquisitor of Germany? For one thing, the faculty had the legal authority to censure books without further authorization, whereas a papal inquisition in Germany required formal authorization from the local archbishop.[28] More important, the faculty review promised to be a quick matter with a predetermined result, since, of course, the faculty had already issued a strong endorsement of Pfefferkorn's campaign in response to Maximilian's mandate. Above all, Hoogstraeten was aiming at the creation of a broad coalition of theologians at Cologne and other universities (Louvain, Paris, Erfurt, Heidelberg, Mainz) to become activists in the anti-Jewish push, building a firewall against any future academic attempt at defense and, most important, compelling Maximilian's court to resume the campaign. Only this approach had the potential to create the desired unanimous academic front against Jewish books. This time, however, Dr. Johannes Reuchlin would be excluded from academic consensus as a misguided heretic. Hoogstraeten was determined that Reuchlin would publicly retract his views.

Hoogstraeten's first action, technically the first action of the faculty, was to commission an assessment of Reuchlin's tract from Arnold van Tongern.

Tongern submitted his findings at once: Reuchlin's writings were "impermissibly favorable to Jews and Judaism"; they also contained some forty-three heretical or erroneous statements, which he duly listed. He compiled his findings in a document called the *Articles*, usually quoting the offending statements directly from Reuchlin's *Recommendation*. Tongern alleged misinterpretations of the Bible, insufficient respect for ecclesiastical authorities, and misuse of statutes in both civil and canon law. Reuchlin's classification of Jews as "fellow citizens" was a perilous contradiction of the ecclesiastical concept of the "servitude of the Jews" ("servitus Judaeorum").

As condemnatory as Tongern's *Articles* may have been of Reuchlin, the most significant aspect of their ultimate publication (at the end of 1512) is the professor's general assault against Judaism. He repeated all the insinuations against the Talmud and Jewish prayers. But he also insisted that Jews poisoned wells, desecrated the Christian Eucharist, and ritually murdered Christian children,[29] issues that had nothing to do with Reuchlin's defense. While these vile innuendos marred Christian-Jewish relations in the late Middle Ages, it was highly unusual for an academic authority to propagate them. The *Articles* would ultimately receive the imprimatur of the university when the faculty formally condemned Reuchlin on 16 August 1513. This chilling feature of the *Articles* is a strong indication that the Hoogstraeten group was aiming to crush Reuchlin only en route to achieving the greater task: the destruction of German Jewry. They would stop at nothing in their demagoguery or their strategic maneuvering to achieve this goal.

On 2 January 1512, and writing in the name of the entire faculty, Hoogstraeten informed Reuchlin that the university was going to censure his *Recommendation* because it was an unacceptable effort to subvert the confiscation of Jewish books, which had "laudably" begun at the behest of Emperor Maximilian.[30] Furthermore, Reuchlin's favorable treatment of Judaism was especially pernicious because it created the appearance—something abominable to the faculty—that the Jews had found a renowned Christian scholar to defend their faith. Hoogstraeten briefly reviewed some of the allegations of heresy expressed in the *Articles* (specifically, misinterpretation of Scripture and misapplication of civil and ecclesiastical statutes) with a certain amount of decorum, but he could not reign in his disgust as he reviled Reuchlin for allegedly empowering Jews to blaspheme Jesus and the Christian faith.[31] The letter concludes with a demand that Reuchlin accept the findings of Professor Tongern and formally retract his own defense of Jewish writings and Jewish legal rights.

On 4 January, a certain Professor Konrad Kollin, also a Dominican (and destined to be Hoogstraeten's successor as papal inquisitor), wrote to Reuchlin in a similar vein but with a kinder tone. Kollin was a friend of Reuchlin's, and Reuchlin had contacted him in 1511 in the hope of persuading the Cologne faculty to look benignly on his actions. Kollin's older brother Ulrich, also a member of the Dominican Order, had written to Reuchlin on 26 October 1511 to warn him that the Cologne theologians were either going to burn his *Eye Glasses* or initiate an inquisition against him.[32] Now, Konrad Kollin informed his friend that, if he wanted to preserve his honor, Reuchlin had little choice other than to recant the articles drawn up against him.[33] Kollin said there would be no shame in admitting error since Reuchlin was, after all, not a theologian but a jurist and lay scholar. Ominously, Kollin also stated that one could hope that such an admission on Reuchlin's part would be adequate to stop further heresy investigations against him. Thus, enormous pressure was being applied on Reuchlin to join the otherwise unanimous academic condemnation of Jewish books.

Reuchlin prudently adopted a compliant tone in his initial replies to the faculty and to Kollin. He said that he had already made a written reply to nearly all the issues raised in the *Articles* and that he had published those preemptive responses in the *Arguments* section of his *Eye Glasses*. Now, with the feigned goal of giving the faculty even more satisfaction, Reuchlin indicated that he would shortly publish a German translation of the *Arguments*, which he in fact did under the title of *A Clear Explanation*.[34] Taking up Kollin's suggestion, he pleaded special indulgence in the event he may have expressed something inappropriately on the grounds that he was a layperson, unschooled in the intricacies of theology; he disingenuously assured him of his eagerness to receive correction from the faculty.[35]

It is important to note that Reuchlin, here and elsewhere, consistently stated that he would accept the decision of the church should he have erred in any formulation whatsoever. This assurance of obedience to the church removed Reuchlin from the threat of a heresy trial against his person and is the reason that all of the cases pertained technically to the statements in his book and not to the author himself. That would change, of course, in the event that he should fail, contrary to his promises, to recant an officially condemned article.

His ruse of obedience was transparent to the faculty. In separate letters, both Kollin and the faculty informed Reuchlin that his reply was inadequate.[36] Kollin demanded a written retraction of the *Recommendation* to be published in time for distribution at the next Frankfurt book fair. He implied that the situation was becoming dangerous for Reuchlin as rumors were swirling around the Rhineland, including an allegation that Reuchlin believed Jews were justified in their execution of Jesus.[37] The faculty demanded that Reuchlin publish a notice, also in time for distribution at the next book fair, requesting that all copies of *Eye Glasses* be returned to the author and explicitly stating that he, Reuchlin, "opposes the perfidious Jews, and their blasphemous books, specifically the Talmud."[38] This letter features an unambiguous threat that, in the event Reuchlin refuses to recant now, the faculty will summon him before an ecclesiastical court. It is unclear if it meant a court convened by the papal inquisitor (Hoogstraeten) or an episcopal court, probably the former.

Reuchlin now replied in open and scornful defiance. To the faculty, he repeated that his only answer would be the German translation of the *Arguments*.[39] He expressed the same intention to Professor Kollin but also added boastful jibes. For example, as Reuchlin put it, it was a good thing that Hoogstraeten and the faculty had not yet initiated a heresy trial for such an affair would only heap disgrace and shame on their heads. According to Reuchlin, "The poets and historians—a great many of whom now living venerate me, as is right, as their teacher—would make a permanent record of this injustice perpetrated by my enemies, and they would portray me as an innocent victim to the ever-lasting disgrace of the University of Cologne."[40]

Reuchlin, thus, accurately predicted that German humanists would take up his cause, even if the tone of his prediction was unhelpfully provocative. From this point onward, Reuchlin found it advantageous to portray the Cologne effort as being directed against biblical humanism as much as it was against the Jews in the empire.

Now the faculty threw down the gauntlet. The result was incendiary. It published Tongern's *Articles* for distribution at the September 1512 Frankfurt international fair as an insult to Reuchlin and also as an escalation of the war on Judaism.

Reuchlin's Second Defense

Reuchlin responded with his own *Defense of Johannes Reuchlin against the Cologne Calumniators* (March 1513), partially an abusive polemic that, understandably, infuriated the faculty and, in fact, made peaceful resolution forever impossible. We can read Reuchlin's outrage and indignation on many pages, but also his confidence that he will triumph over the pamphleteers, no matter how august their positions of authority were. At this point, he opted for carpet bombing the faculty of theology: the Cologne professors "are not true theologians who should be trusted. These men are unworthy of the great and precious name of theology. For they are not theologians, but appear as the vilest scoundrels, wickedest babblers, and lowlife slanderers."[41] He says that the venerable faculty of theology at Cologne has, like an old man, lost its wits.[42] Combining the words *theologian* and *sophist*, he dubs the professors "theologists," an anti-scholastic epithet he may have derived from Erasmus. Occasionally, they are "devilogians."[43] He hurls his share of accusations, too, charging at one point that all they are trying to accomplish "in their inquisition, which they seem to desire, is to extort money from the Jews."[44] Reuchlin is most abusive in his characterizations of Arnold van Tongern, at one point even questioning his masculinity: "everything you find in Arnold is soft, effeminate, puerile."[45] Pfefferkorn is an "ignorant butcher," a "heretic," and a "half-Jew" intent on destroying Christianity. If Reuchlin was seeking to make lifelong enemies, his tract was a brilliant success.

The *Defense*, nonetheless, is also a serious work, one steeped in classical and Christian learning, and addressed to Emperor Maximilian as another carefully documented analysis of the legal status of Jews and Jewish books in the empire. Reuchlin even delivered the printed pamphlet personally to Maximilian on 10 June 1513 in Geislingen.[46] The emperor promised to arrange for the bishop of Augsburg to look into the attacks against Reuchlin. (Apparently pressed by the need to return rapidly to Italy, the emperor did not contact the bishop.)

Reuchlin now saw the need to argue copiously that the foundation of the Cologne-Pfefferkorn campaign was incompatible not only with standing laws of the church and empire but also with the history of Christian-Jewish relations. His gravest concern appeared to arise from the pernicious accusation that Jews were heretics: "With these pamphlets from Cologne they are propagating the contention everywhere that the Jews are no longer Jews, but rather heretics and our enemies."[47] Reuchlin also repeated at length his defenses of the Talmud and Jewish prayers, even adding at one point that Jews, far from praying for the demise of Christianity, actually pray for peace and harmony in the Holy Roman Empire.[48] Once again, Reuchlin argues that the basis of the inquisition's charge is flawed since Jews have no reason to undermine Christianity as a religion since they believe non-Jews find salvation through their own faiths.[49]

Reuchlin's rhetoric becomes passionate. He boldly addresses the charge of including Jews as fellow citizens, embracing and even strengthening the connection in the hope, he says, that it will cause his enemies in Cologne to explode with fury.

> I know my enemies have been vexed because I said the Jews are our
> fellow citizens ("concives"). Now I want them to rage even more in
> anger, and I hope their guts burst, because I am saying that the Jews
> are our brothers. Brothers of Arnold, brothers of all the Cologne
> "theologists," not only because we have one father, the creator of
> all things, in heaven, . . . but also because they were created with
> us on earth by the same father. Although not of our limb, they are
> nonetheless brothers with us.[50]

These are remarkable cases of purple prose in his oeuvre. He grounds his defiant proclamation that he is a true "favorer" of Israel on the foundations of such church authorities as St. Paul, St. Clement, St. Jerome, St. Thomas Aquinas, St. Gregory the Great, Pope Alexander III, Pope Clement III, and the emperors Valentinianus, Valens, Honorius, Theodosius, and Arcadius, giving an honor roll of Christians who had granted Judaism a legal or a theological basis for existence, often doing so in ecclesiastical and civil law codes.[51] Reuchlin's conclusions were an attempt to cloak his *Recommendation* in the protective mantle of tradition and justice:

> See what kind of favorer I am! I oppose their detestable disbelief
> but nonetheless I do not recommend that the Jews be wronged in
> this. . . . I am therefore a favorer, as I must be, as is appropriate, as
> St. Paul, as St. Jerome, as St. Thomas Aquinas, as the popes, as the
> emperors as all the learned and Christian jurists—not in opposition
> to the church but for the church because I have acted for justice and
> to the advantage of the church. . . . I am a favorer because I justly
> prevent perverse and harmful men from doing evil and intolerable
> things.[52]

The Response

What to do? How was Cologne to react to this scorching rebuke to the faculty, published for all the world to read? According to surviving records, Reuchlin's intemperate polemic in the *Defense* infuriated the theologians mightily. The Cologne professors initiated consultations with other theology faculties in Germany and at Louvain and also with the law faculty in Cologne.[53] Their initial inclination was to bring a libel case against him, though the Cologne faculty of law expressed uncertainty over how such a charge might play out in the courts. That approach posed significant complexities because it would have to be pursued in a civil court. The law faculty also expressed concern about the expenses such a case might incur.

Nonetheless, on the advice of Hoogstraeten, the theology faculty continued to contemplate bringing a libel case against Reuchlin. Hoogstraeten emerges in these documents as a careful legal strategist. He urged the faculty to document the insults suffered from the tract in the presence of a notary.

Hoogstraeten, however, also advised the faculty to request permission from the archbishop of Mainz to confiscate Reuchlin's book and to convene an inquisitional court, under the authority of the papal inquisitor (i.e., himself), to review Reuchlin's positions. This was a necessary step because a commission of the local bishop was required in Germany for a papal inquisition. Interestingly, Hoogstraeten also wanted the faculty specifically to request a determination from the archbishop that this case, once it started, would not be transferred to any jurisdiction other than Hoogstraeten's papal inquisition.[54]

Ultimately, the theology faculty did not bring a civil suit against Reuchlin in its own name. Instead, the faculty turned to the city council of Cologne with a request that it bring suit against Reuchlin for slandering the university. This was a good legal strategy because the city of Cologne was the legal patron of the university. The city council responded by writing to Emperor Maximilian with the request that Reuchlin's *Defense* be banned on the emperor's authority.[55] The emperor, moreover, responded favorably to that request with a writ of 9 July 1513.[56] This writ, as matters developed, would be the last time that Emperor Maximilian appeared to favor the anti-Jewish forces.

At this point, the university resumed its proceedings against Reuchlin's *Eye Glasses*. The faculty had requested an evaluation of Reuchlin's pamphlet from the University of Louvain. The Louvain decision, which was reached in July 1513, emphatically endorsed the burning of Reuchlin's pamphlet on the grounds that it favored the Jews and contained errors.[57]

The Cologne faculty issued its formal condemnation of Reuchlin's *Eye Glasses* on 16 August 1513:

> We have judged and concluded that this pamphlet [i.e., Reuchlin's
> *Eye Glasses*] gravely offends the pious ears of the Christian faithful,
> especially ordinary Christians; furthermore that it contains
> numerous and varied statements that are most dangerous to the
> faith and scandalous, even savoring of heresy, and, above all, in
> agreement with the perfidy of the Jews.[58]

On 2 September 1513, the theology faculty ordered Hoogstraeten to burn Reuchlin's book on the basis of the imperial mandate forbidding its distribution.[59] Hoogstraeten, however, did not do so, either feeling that it was not yet the right moment for that step or fearing that the imperial mandate did not explicitly authorize a public burning.[60]

Instead, Professor Hoogstraeten exchanged his academic for his judicial robes and convened a formal proceeding against Reuchlin. On 9 September 1513, he summoned Reuchlin to appear before an inquisitional court that would be impaneled in Mainz on 15 September.[61]

The Mainz Inquisition

Johannes Reuchlin faced many powerful opponents in the controversy over Jewish books and Jewish legal rights, including popes, kings, and eminent scholars, but none of his adversaries was as determined as Jacob Hoogstraeten. He would equal Pfefferkorn's venomous rhetoric in his pamphlets and, more significant, would devote himself entirely to the Reuchlin case for more than five years, putting aside all other matters that a professor of theology, prior of a Dominican convent, and papal inquisitor for Teutonia might have been expected to handle. Like Pfefferkorn, Hoogstraeten pursued Reuchlin out of the conviction that the destruction of Jewry was crucial for sustaining the health of the church. Now the prerequisite for restarting the anti-Jewish campaign was the difficult and unseemly task of staining Reuchlin's formidable reputation.

Hoogstraeten, as papal inquisitor for the archbishoprics of Trier, Mainz, and Cologne (collectively known as the ecclesiastical province of Teutonia), was the most significant inquisitorial power in Germany by far. In this capacity, he would eventually distinguish himself for Catholics as an early and effective polemicist against Martin Luther. His *Colloquy with St. Augustine* (1521) was a compelling demonstration that Luther was at odds with the teachings of the early church, even with those of St. Augustine, whom Luther still claimed as an authority.

After studying in Louvain and concluding his theological studies with a doctorate from Cologne (1504),[62] Hoogstraeten became an ambitious force in the German Dominican Order, the order that functioned in Europe increasingly as the guardian of orthodoxy and, moreover, as a force that actively sought to chanel Christian anti-Semitism into anti-Jewish policies. Hoogstraeten served as regent of the Dominican Studium (i.e., college) in Cologne from 1505 through 1507. His first known publication, a book of 1507, was a copious defense of the right of mendicant friars to hear confession in any parish despite the resulting tensions with local secular clergy.[63] Hoogstraeten's approach to this sensitive issue was not diplomatic. He openly antagonized the secular clergy by expressing harsh criticism of moral laxness among the parish priests.

Perhaps more than anything else, his first publication demonstrated his inquisitional temperament, especially his keenness for arguing points of doctrine. An inquisitional character emerged more clearly in his next project—a series of theological attacks against Pietro Tomasi (often called Peter of Ravenna), a professor of law at Cologne. Hoogstraeten would publish some three books against Tomasi for the jurist's claim that German magistrates were wrong (and thereby committing sin according to Christian practices) to allow the bodies of executed criminals to rot on the gallows as a horrifying warning against lawlessness. Instead, proper Christian burial should be accorded to any executed criminal who had received the sacrament of penance.

These tracts, one of which was dedicated to the papal legate to Germany, Bernardino López de Carvajal, soon to be a judge in the Reuchlin Affair, appear to have bolstered Hoogstraeten's career, for in 1510 he was elected prior of the Dominican house in Cologne. The convent in Cologne, historically the home of such luminaries as St. Albertus Magnus and St. Thomas Aquinas, was the most prestigious Dominican house in Germany and its prior was, ex officio, papal inquisitor. Hoogstraeten immediately, in 1510, addressed his new responsibility by publishing a merciless tract against witchcraft and magic with the explicit threat that he would burn at the stake anyone convicted of using magic of any kind.[64] But, as of October 1510, Hoogstraeten's waking concern shifted from witches and magic to Jews and Reuchlin. The newly elected inquisitor had decided to make his mark by leading the anti-Jewish campaign.

Hoogstraeten presented the formal case against Reuchlin in a document called the *Writ of Accusation* (*Libellus Accusatorius*). As was customary, this document was, for the most part, a lapidary list of questionable passages in Reuchlin's *Eye Glasses*. Despite its terseness, it is the most significant digest of the charges made against Reuchlin. It was the basis for the trials conducted in Mainz and Speyer and for Hoogstraeten's positions during the trials in Rome. Hoogstraeten did not prepare this document for publication but merely for submission to the court in Mainz, where he would provide necessary verbal amplifications and explanations. Nonetheless, it was published in 1518 as part of the *Acts of the Trials*,[65] a documentary account of the course of Reuchlin's trials, most likely assembled by Reuchlin himself.

The conclusion to the *Writ of Accusation* neatly expresses Hoogstraeten's general charges:

> We petition [the court] that, by your distinguished lord
> commissioners [i.e., judges] and your definitive judgment, the
> aforementioned pamphlet, *Eye Glasses* by Johannes Reuchlin, be
> pronounced, discerned, and declared to be full of heresies and
> errors, impermissibly favorable to the perfidious Jews, injurious

to the church of God, and disrespectful to the sacred doctors of the church; moreover, that this work, which has been printed and distributed throughout the archbishopric of Mainz, must be banned, condemned, suppressed, removed, and publicly burned.[66]

The specific charges, which are closely related to Tongern's *Articles*, are both a general case against Judaism and individual objections to Reuchlin's biblical exegesis. The very first charge emphatically denies the propriety of classifying Jews as "fellow citizens" in the empire on the grounds that this contradicts the church's teaching on the servitude of the Jews. Next, Hoogstraeten insists that Jews constantly blaspheme Jesus and Mary and that they utter imprecations against Christians every day. In this argument, Hoogstraeten claims that Reuchlin's defense of the *'Amidah* prayer is not only wrongheaded but also a contradiction of St. Jerome's teaching, as recorded in his Isaiah commentary,[67] on that same prayer; he bolsters this interpretation with references to Paul of Burgos, an authority that Reuchlin himself had used.[68] Hoogstraeten also raises the damaging observations of Pfefferkorn, namely that Reuchlin had himself charged that this prayer was anti-Christian in his earlier pamphlet, *German Epistle: Why the Jews Have Been in Exile So Long*. Moreover, Reuchlin's favorable treatment of Judaism was especially apparent in his rejection of the Christian Good Friday prayer "for the perfidious Jews."[69]

One way in which Reuchlin showed disrespect for Christian authorities was in his high estimation of Jewish biblical commentary, specifically the commentaries of Rashi. In the *Recommendation*, Reuchlin said that Rashi was the most important source for Nicholas of Lyra's commentary, the latter work having achieved canonical status among Christians, especially as a source for studying the literal meaning of the Old Testament Scriptures. Even though Nicholas of Lyra admitted this,[70] Hoogstraeten claimed that Reuchlin was asserting the superiority of Jewish over Christian exegesis.[71] Similarly, Hoogstraeten charged that Reuchlin held rabbinic teachings in much too high esteem, leading him to attribute Paul's preeminence among the apostles to rabbinic training.[72]

Hoogstraeten's legal case against Reuchlin was principally a case against Judaism, but it was also an assault on Reuchlin's philological approach to biblical exegesis. Reuchlin had taken the extreme liberty of pointing out to Maximilian that "in Christendom it is possible to find many theologians who cannot correctly interpret Holy Scriptures because of their ignorance of these two languages [Hebrew and Greek] and are therefore laughing stocks."[73] Reuchlin was even able to cite canons stipulating that theologians should know Greek and Hebrew. For his part, Hoogstraeten was also deeply concerned about the future directions of humanist biblical scholarship. In 1518, after Erasmus's New Testament appeared and after Luther had posted the *Ninety-five Theses*, Hoogstraeten would personally urge the University of Louvain to censure Erasmus's Bible. This is the subtext of Hoogstraeten's repeated complaints that Reuchlin showed insufficient respect for accepted authorities of the church—he also meant scholasticism and scholastic exegesis. Nonetheless, the specific objections are interesting—and, one might concede, not always specious, even if Hoogstraeten's goal is pernicious.

He pressed Reuchlin hard for implying that the Bible endorsed toleration of heresy. Reuchlin had cited 1 Corinthians 11:19 several times as part of an argument that good can arise from heresy or errors; therefore, even if the Talmud may be erroneous, it could be beneficial to Christianity. Reuchlin paraphrased Paul's statement as follows: "It is necessary that superstition and error exist because thereby those of true beliefs are confirmed."[74] What Reuchlin meant was that Christians could use the Talmud against Jews by exposing its faults. Hoogstraeten cleverly twisted this into an example of poor biblical exegesis, charging that Reuchlin had claimed that the Bible supports the existence of heresy.[75]

A major point was Reuchlin's interpretation of John 5:39, the "rock solid foundation of this recommendation."[76] "Thus I am basing my recommendation that the Talmud should not be burned on the Holy Gospel. For our Lord, Jesus Christ, said to the Jews in John 5, 'Ask, seek, search the Scriptures in which you suppose you have eternal life and those very Scriptures provide a witness of me.'"[77] Reuchlin insisted that these Scriptures referred to rabbinic writings, even to the Talmud itself (though Reuchlin acknowledged that the Talmud had not yet been compiled in its present form). Hoogstraeten emphatically rejected such an interpretation, arguing that the passage referred exclusively to the Jewish Bible.[78] Thus Hoogstraeten was endeavoring not only to ridicule Reuchlin's defense of the Talmud but also to undermine the credibility of the new humanist biblical philology. As far as Reuchlin's use of John 5:39 goes, Hoogstraeten would repeatedly express outrage over the scholar's temerity in misconstruing Jesus' words in order to privilege the Talmud.

Legal Wrangling

In addition to contesting the substantive issues, Reuchlin impugned the legitimacy of Hoogstraeten's court. His lawyer, the otherwise unknown Peter Staffel, challenged Hoogstraeten's standing as judge in such a case because he had demonstrated bias against the defendant's position in two ways: he had already issued a recommendation to Maximilian that was diametrically opposed to Reuchlin, and he was the driving force behind the book confiscations to begin with. Staffel and Reuchlin also alleged personal animosity, citing incivilities in Hoogstraeten's letters (including the use of the German informal "you" and inappropriate salutations) and claiming that Hoogstraeten was a leader of Reuchlin's detractors, feverishly working to destroy his honor. Most important, Reuchlin argued that the court in Mainz lacked proper standing for due process because Hoogstraeten was serving as both prosecutor and judge at the tribunal. Reuchlin also contended that the charges had no standing for a papal inquisition because they did not include an "explicitly expressed and condemned heresy."[79] This final accusation appears to have carried little weight. But the objection to Hoogstraeten's two roles as judge and prosecutor did serious damage to the inquisitor's case.

Nevertheless, although Reuchlin threatened an appeal to Rome from the outset,[80] the case went forward in Mainz under the auspices of the inquisition. Hoogstraeten appointed five other men as co-judges, four from Mainz and one from Cologne, all with the approval of Archbishop Uriel.[81] The co-judges were distinguished churchmen: three held doctorates in theology and two in canon law; and one was the suffragan bishop of Mainz.[82] Hoogstraeten also, wisely, decided to relinquish his role as judge, delegating that authority to the five scholars whom the archbishop had appointed to the bench. (Rome would not hear of that modification before issuing its response to Reuchlin's appeal.) The first session was held on 15 September 1513. Reuchlin, adamant about the illegitimacy of the tribunal, refused to appear, although Staffel did. Staffel submitted a formal challenge to the legitimacy of the newly formed court and requested permission to appeal to the Roman curia. When this request was denied, Staffel withdrew from the court, repudiating its authority.

Even the Mainz trial, with its bench stacked against Reuchlin, demonstrates that the scholar's confidence in his ability to garner support from powerful people was well founded. Immediately, the Cathedral Chapter at Mainz, the most elite ecclesiastical body of the archbishopric, attempted to arbitrate a settlement outside of court. Under the leadership of Lorenz Truchseß, the chapter was determined to spare Reuchlin the embarrassment of the inevitable conviction from Hoogstraeten's court. The details of the proposed settlement are not known. Accompanied by Jacob Lemp, professor of canon law at Tübingen, Reuchlin went to Mainz on 9 October, as invited by the chapter, to negotiate either directly with Hoogstraeten or indirectly through the Cathedral canons.[83] Hoogstraeten, however, released a mandate on 8 October (the day before Reuchlin's arrival in Mainz) requiring all Christians to destroy copies of *Eye Glasses* on pain of excommunication.[84] Therefore, upon his arrival in Mainz, Reuchlin immediately filed his appeal to the Roman curia.

With overweening confidence, Hoogstraeten invited his Cologne colleagues to hear the verdict of the court, to be announced on 12 October in Mainz. To be sure, a verdict had been reached but, as events unfolded, it would never be announced (nor are its terms known). As the court assembled on 12 October, a messenger from the archbishop of Mainz appeared in the courtroom and effectively silenced Hoogstraeten.[85] The archbishop demanded that the court go into immediate recess for an entire month. Should this demand be resisted, he ordered the four Mainz judges, all of whom were clerics subject to his authority, to resign from the court, thus making any action invalid. This was a veritable *deus ex machina* for Reuchlin's case. The archbishop had probably bowed to tremendous pressure from the distinguished canons of the Cathedral College to protect Germany's most famous scholar, at least for the time being, from the opprobrium of such a conviction.

Soon an even more dramatic intervention favored Reuchlin. Pope Leo X, apparently unaware of the efforts to find a compromise, acted expeditiously to support the famous humanist trapped in such an unpromising trial. In a breve of 21 November 1513,[86] Leo accepted Reuchlin's appeal of 9 October. He dissolved the papal inquisition in Mainz and entrusted a judicial review to the bishops of Speyer and Worms, intriguing choices because both dioceses still had important Jewish communities.

It is important to notice that with the suspension of the Mainz proceedings, the juridical focus in Germany would begin to expand beyond the goal of restarting the anti-Jewish campaign. At this point, preservation of the status quo of Jews in the empire was not the focus of Reuchlin's appeal to Rome nor of Rome's action. For the next six months, the proceedings would acknowledge the substantive issues of permissible attitudes toward Jews and Judaism, but both sides were also pursuing vindication at any cost. In all of this, one might conclude that Hoogstraeten was not quite Reuchlin's match, neither when it came to forming legal strategy nor when negotiation was involved. Reuchlin was also able to draw on a vast network of contacts in government and the academy. Nonetheless, Hoogstraeten did develop a credible strategy for responding to the great setback of the suspension of the Mainz inquisition.

Appellate Tribunal in Speyer

The pope's breve mandated a hearing of Reuchlin's appeal in Germany. Leo assigned the case to either the bishop of Speyer, the bishop of Worms, or a comparable authority able to conduct a summary proceeding. According to the papal instruction, the first task of the new court was to decide if the Mainz proceedings had legal standing. If they did not, the new court was empowered to issue a verdict on the charges of heresy brought against Reuchlin's book.

The new bishop-elect of Speyer, Georg of the Palatinate, assumed sole responsibility for the case.[87] Bishop Georg, who had been one of Reuchlin's charges at the electoral court in Heidelberg, proved to be well disposed to the scholar's interests from the start. He ruled that the court would not conduct an inquisitional trial, for which the court assumed responsibility for building a corpus of evidence. Rather, the litigation would be a contest between the two parties—Reuchlin and Hoogstraeten—in which the court's responsibility would be limited to evaluating the evidence adduced by each side and issuing a decision.

Bishop Georg immediately appointed two judges, Thomas Truchseß and Georg von Schwalbach, to convene the court. Three co-judges ("assessores") were also named and assigned the task of analyzing Reuchlin's *Eye Glasses* afresh. With the appointment of these men—Philipp von Flersheim, Jodocus Gallus, and Wolfgang Capito—Hoogstraeten's stars were crossed, for all had strongly humanist proclivities and some were firmly committed to humanist educational reforms. Moreover, all except Schwalbach were known as personal friends of Reuchlin. Capito, who had studied Hebrew under Reuchlin, was already emerging as a leading Christian Hebraist. Erasmus would soon praise him for surpassing Reuchlin in his knowledge of Hebrew.[88] Not only was the case doomed to failure but the court was also being shaped to guarantee an outcome that was likely to boost the prestige of humanist studies in Germany.

On 20 December 1513, Georg issued a formal summons to Reuchlin and Hoogstraeten to appear before the court at the end of January (either on 25 or 26 January 1514) on pain of excommunication.[89] Reuchlin appeared in person, accompanied by his trial lawyer, an otherwise unknown Johannes Greiff. Hoogstraeten apparently decided that it was now his turn to boycott court proceedings, though he did so with the excuse that his responsibilities as prior of the Dominican house in Cologne presently precluded his participation in Speyer. Although he harbored no illusions about Speyer, he arranged for legal representation from Johannes Host, a Dominican from Cologne. (Host would also continue to represent Hoogstraeten in Rome.)

On the first day of the court, however, Greiff successfully challenged Host's representation on numerous technical grounds. For this and all other legal maneuvers of the case, we can safely assume that the real strategist was Reuchlin himself, one of the greatest lawyers of Renaissance Germany.

In accepting Greiff's challenge to Host, the court adjourned the case until 20 February.[90]

Reuchlin undertook an aggressive strategy when the court reconvened. Greiff moved that Hoogstraeten be cited for contempt of court for failing to appear and that the court issue a summary judgment in Reuchlin's favor. Greiff concisely impugned the legal standing of the Mainz tribunal on several grounds, including Hoogstraeten's original dual role as judge and prosecutor and, subsequently, Hoogstraeten's delegation of judicial authority to the co-judges appointed by the archbishop of Mainz.[91] Greiff also included a cursory statement that the charges were invalid, a prefiguration of an argument he and Reuchlin would soon flesh out in detail.

Greiff moved that the Speyer court nullify the Mainz proceeding, affirm the orthodoxy of Reuchlin's *Eye Glasses*, and assess Hoogstraeten for the defendant's court costs. Naturally, the court was not yet prepared to rule on all of those issues, but it did respond with a preliminary decision. It affirmed that Reuchlin's appeal was justified and it nullified all actions of the Mainz tribunal. Now the court was ready to proceed at once to hear the arguments of both sides on the original issue: the orthodoxy of *Eye Glasses*. But before that could begin, a stunning event disrupted the proceedings.

On the very day of the hearing, no less a figure than Johannes Pfefferkorn posted a document at the entrance to the courtroom (in the bishop's palace) announcing that an inquisition had been convened in Cologne and that it had condemned Reuchlin's *Eye Glasses* on 10 February.[92]

What had caused this amazing turn of events? Apparently, Hoogstraeten had boycotted the Speyer proceedings in order to devote himself to a new strategy in Cologne. Building on the strength of the anti-Reuchlin fervor at the university, he managed to convince another inquisitor, a certain Johannes de Colle, to convene a court even without the necessary authorization of the archbishop.[93] Records for this maneuvering do not survive, nor for the court proceedings in Cologne. The result, however, was just as Pfefferkorn announced in the dire broadside he was distributing in Speyer—the book was now officially condemned by the inquisition: "we declare that the said pamphlet savors of heresy, contains many errors, is more favorable to the Jews than is appropriate, is harmful to the church of God and disrespectful to the holy theologians of the church...it must be burned publicly."[94] In fact, on 10 February Reuchlin's *Eye Glasses* had been burned in front of the Dominican church of St. Andreas in Cologne. Previously, no one in Speyer, not even Reuchlin, although he was technically the defendant for the Cologne proceedings, knew anything about this. Although this mysterious proceeding would appear to qualify as an early modern equivalent of a kangaroo court, the action—the burning of his book by church officials—was a painful embarrassment to the scholar and lawyer.

In all of this, Reuchlin was quite fortunate that the papal authorization for the appellate court in Germany had been so carefully formulated. Leo's breve had included the stipulation that no other court besides the one established pursuant to the breve was to consider any aspect of the case. On the strength of that explicit directive, the court in Speyer would be able to proceed with its review and rebuke the Cologne intervention. Greiff immediately challenged Pfefferkorn's action as contempt of court and even called for his excommunication. He also formally rejected the Cologne proceedings on several grounds, in particular because it showed contempt for the court convened in Speyer on papal authorization. Pfefferkorn was not excommunicated, though the court ordered the removal of his broadside. Apparently, despite these remarkable twists, the court went into an orderly recess until 13 March 1514.

The next session, as promised, addressed the question of the orthodoxy of Reuchlin's *Eye Glasses*. According to the *Acts of the Trials*, Greiff submitted Reuchlin's "Libellus excusatorius," a comprehensive rebuttal to Hoogstraeten's charges and actions, painstakingly going through the specifics of each point.[95] Mounting a novel defense against the heresy inquisition, Greiff and Reuchlin contended that Hoogstraeten had failed to produce an actionable charge and that, according to them, a heresy trial can only pertain to an alleged contradiction of an affirmed dogma of the church or to the embrace of a belief that the church had explicitly condemned. They further tried to constrain the scope of the inquisition by arguing that statements taken out of context could not be used as articles against a defendant. For Reuchlin's case, this was the insistence that, contrary to the procedures adopted in Mainz, Reuchlin's published explanations (i.e., the *Arguments* appended to his *Recommendation*) must be taken into consideration. These two requests ran counter to late-medieval practice for heresy prosecutions, for any statement held to be incompatible with the church's teaching or deemed in any way to be harmful to the church was actionable. Moreover, statements (i.e., charges listed as "articles") were to be assessed according to "how they sound," and not according to the intentions of their authors.[96] Thus, Reuchlin was advocating significant limitations on the scope of a heresy prosecution.

Greiff concluded with the formal petition that the court find Reuchlin's *Eye Glasses* free of any whiff of heresy and wholly benign to the church. Greiff adopted the specific formulations of Hoogstraeten's indictment (and the finding of the Cologne inquisition), demanding that they be overturned:

> (May the court) find and declare concerning the said pamphlet that it does not manifestly savor of, or contain, any heresy or error that has

been publicly condemned by the church, that it is not favorable to the perfidious Jews more than is appropriate or the laws permit, that it is neither harmful nor disrespectful to the church of God and the holy theologians of the same [i.e., church].[97]

Neither Hoogstraeten, who was in Cologne, nor his attorneys offered any evidence or arguments to the contrary. Therefore, the court went into recess to deliberate its verdict.

The court reached a decision by 29 March, when Bishop Georg signed it, but delayed formal announcement until 24 April. It handed down a nearly verbatim copy of Reuchlin's petition. The only significant difference was that the Speyer court specified that its finding was based on consideration of the explanations that Reuchlin had annexed to the publication of the *Recommendation*.

> We find and declare concerning the said pamphlet along with its declaration which is appended to it [i.e., the *Arguments*]...that it does not manifestly savor of, or contain, any heresy or error publicly condemned by the church, nor is it favorable to the Jews more than is appropriate or the laws permit, nor is it harmful or disrespectful to the church of God or the holy theologians of the same [i.e., church]. And *Eye Glasses* itself along with its appended declaration (which we want to be conjoined and considered with the pamphlet with its individual points) may be read and published.[98]

The court also assessed Hoogstraeten for the defendant's court costs of 111 gulden, a princely sum, that he was to pay Reuchlin on pain of excommunication. This was an unprecedented rebuke from a German ecclesiastical court to an inquisitor, and Reuchlin capitalized on the strong wording, publishing the text several times.[99] As soon as the Luther crisis emerged, many conservative churchmen in Germany would decry this humiliation of the Dominican inquisition as a factor that fomented the early Protestant disobedience.

The punishing terms of the verdict, however, did not weaken Hoogstraeten's resolve to proceed with his campaign. If anything, the result raised temperatures even higher in Cologne. The terms of the verdict must have been known to some extent before 24 April, for a faculty meeting of 21 April was devoted to the Speyer decision. At that meeting, the university pledged to support Hoogstraeten's appeal of Speyer. It apparently approved an initial outlay of some 200 florins (advanced as a loan to the theology faculty by the faculty of the arts) to cover Hoogstraeten's expenses.[100]

Hoogstraeten was determined to continue the campaign against Judaism, though now he had to contend with the issue of the new phenomenon of biblical humanism advocating Jewish studies. He also had to defend his own honor as professor of theology and prior of the Cologne Dominican convent. Nonetheless, he still hoped to forge a united academic consensus, blessed by a ruling of the papal curia, against the Jewish books.

He decided to embark on a two-pronged strategy against Reuchlin's *Recommendation* and the Speyer affirmation of it. Assisted by the theology faculty in Cologne, he petitioned other theology faculties, most important the Sorbonne, to condemn Reuchlin's pamphlet. Moreover, he resolved to appeal the Speyer ruling to the Roman curia, where he would rely on support from the Dominicans and inquisitional forces at the Fifth Lateran Council. Indeed, during that appeal, many church leaders from all corners of Europe would ardently urge Rome to confirm Hoogstraeten's condemnation of Reuchlin and the Jews. Hoogstraeten and his allies were prepared to strive diligently to enlarge their base of support, above all, by expanding their case against Reuchlin and the Jews.

8

Trial at Rome and the Christian Debates

It is not that Reuchlin has been saved by us but that we have been
saved by Reuchlin.

> —Cardinal Giles of Viterbo, Prior-General of the
> Augustinian Order, writing from Rome in 1516

When receiving the inquisitor's appeal of the Speyer ruling, Pope
Leo X and the Roman curia knew they were facing a complex and
impassioned controversy, one that would touch on such disparate
issues as Christian-Jewish relations, enforcement of orthodoxy, and
the future of the Renaissance humanist movement. The Reuchlin
Affair had exposed a significant rift in the northern church that
seemed likely to widen as the humanist movement progressed. What
Leo and the curia could not have foreseen was the vastly greater
cause of disunity, the "Luther Affair," that would soon erupt in the
context of adjudicating the Reuchlin case.

In the 1510s, the papacy faced an unprecedented series of
challenges. However much we now admire the cultural achievements
of Leo X, the rubric of "the Reformation" adds a scarlet accent,
indelibly, to every historical account of the first Medici pope. It is not
my intention to attempt yet another apology for, or diatribe against,
this unusually controversial pontiff; it is, I think, more illuminating
to use the Reuchlin Affair as a perspective for understanding

the complex circumstances of the Roman church at this historic crossroads. One of the important things to grasp about Renaissance Rome is that its reputation was simultaneously (sometimes dramatically) moving in opposite directions. The astonishing success of Luther's movement has made it seem appropriate for historians to emphasize a defiant mood among Europeans and to document tensions caused by insufficient discipline among the clergy, the secular lifestyles of some princes of the church, and, perhaps most significantly, the political-military policies enacted by the popes as they governed an ambitious Italian state. Corruption was rampant and systemic. Great resentment (and incompetence) arose from venality—the "selling" of church offices with benefices (i.e., incomes)—and indignation from the fiscal motivation for new practices of the church, such as Jubilee celebrations and, especially dispiriting to many Germans, the large-scale promotion of indulgences.

On the other hand, Rome was governing the European church more effectively, reemerging as a center for international diplomacy, and, not least, committed to supporting the arts on a truly grand scale. A large part of Rome's moral authority as of the 1510s accrued from promotion of humanist culture.[1] To cite just one example of a favorable portrayal, as a correspondent, Erasmus was prone to lapsing into wistful remembrances of Rome as a humanist utopia; in a letter from 1515, he wrote:

> A deep longing for Rome is inescapable, when I think of its large
> store of great advantages available together. First of all, the bright
> light, the noble setting of the most famous city in the world, the
> delightful freedom, the many richly furnished libraries, the sweet
> society of all those great scholars, all the literary conversations, all
> the monuments of antiquity, and so many leading lights of the world
> gathered in one place.[2]

Like many northerners, Erasmus was hopeful that, after the war-torn reign of Julius II, Leo X might support cultural change, even embody the humanist challenge to scholasticism: "That very fertile garden of your mind found by far the most elegant of men to cultivate it, that most polished scholar Poliziano. By his care you were initiated, not into the prickly and quarrelsome subjects of the schools [i.e., scholasticism] but into those genuine studies rightly called the humanities."[3] Fittingly, both Erasmus and Reuchlin would dedicate monuments of their scholarship—the Bible in Greek and the Christian Kabbalah—to an appreciative Leo X. In some ways, Reuchlin's controversy at Rome offers evidence that the papacy's cultural orientation was generating cautious optimism among northern intellectuals. A noticeable element in the publications by Reuchlin and his supporters is that they represent the papal court as a major source of patronage for humanist reforms. In particular, Rome was emerging as a relatively advanced (and growing) center of Christian Jewish studies. Rome of the 1510s was also showing at least some promise of becoming a force that might halt or at least slow the tragic downward spiral of Christian-Jewish relations in Europe, although that would soon change as the church responded harshly to the challenges posed by the Reformation.

Reuchlin and Rome

Long before his fate was hanging in the balance at the Roman curia, Johannes Reuchlin had meticulously cultivated close ties with the Vatican. He visited the holy city three times, in 1482, 1490, and 1498. His lifelong association with the Roman curia indirectly confirms two of the points I have been making. In the final quarter of the fifteenth century, Rome had reemerged as a significant European power and, moreover, was rapidly becoming a center for humanist scholarship. For these reasons, it is not at all surprising that Rome is a common address in Reuchlin's epistolary exchanges.

In a way, Reuchlin got his start in government because of Rome. Fresh out of law schools, with degrees from Orléans and Poitiers, but also with a distinctive ability to speak Latin eloquently, he was recruited for the entourage of Count Eberhard of Württemberg's pilgrimage to Sixtus IV's Rome. Eberhard, who had recently founded the University of Tübingen, was determined to enter the mainstream of international, Renaissance culture. In particular, Württemberg wanted to establish strong ties to the papacy as it undertook monastic reforms and sought ecclesiastical support for the University of Tübingen. During his second trip (1490), Reuchlin led a delegation from Württemberg to attend a congress that Innocent VIII had convened in a fruitless attempt to rally Christian princes against the expansion of Islam in eastern Europe. The third trip, the one of 1498, entailed a moment of crowning glory for the now famous Reuchlin: the privilege of delivering an oration before the pope (see chapter 3). As we saw in chapter 4, the third residency in Rome enabled Reuchlin to study intensively with Obadiah Sforno and acquire several crucial Hebrew books for his research.

In the last decade of the fifteenth century, Rome was an ideal place, perhaps the most congenial in all of Europe, for a Christian to study Jewish culture. Naturally, Reuchlin later took special pains to stress the Hebrew studies of churchmen in Rome. In the *Recommendation* itself, Reuchlin wrote that "Pope Sixtus IV had ordered that these very books of the Kabbalah be translated into Latin and thus be made accessible for study since they would be of particular importance for our Christian faith,"[4] and, similarly, that Pope Innocent VIII endorsed the Kabbalah as a valuable source for Christian research.[5] Reuchlin also celebrated Alexander VI as the pope who vindicated the Christian study of the Kabbalah specifically by ending the heresy proceeding against Pico della Mirandola.[6] To Reuchlin, Alexander VI was not the corrupt, nepotistic, worldly Borgia pope. Rather, he and his court embodied the ideals of his Christian Hebrew scholarship. The Renaissance papal tradition, which he knew first-hand from his three trips, validated his own Jewish studies, so he argued.

There may be a degree of exaggeration in Reuchlin's claims about the late fifteenth-century papacy's enthusiasm for Hebrew studies. Nonetheless, thereafter, in the final two decades of Reuchlin's life—and substantially under the influence of his own research—Rome did develop into a center of Christian-Jewish studies. The Roman cultivation of Jewish studies expanded initially under Julius II and, then, with great vigor during the papacy of Leo X. Leo established a chair for Hebrew at the University of Rome in 1514. He licensed a Hebrew printing press at Rome and also in Venice. Famously, Leo granted Daniel Bomberg a papal license for the printing of the Talmud (twelve volumes, printed in Venice), the primary target of the Pfefferkorn and Hoogstraeten campaign.[7] It was also Leo who sponsored the research of Santi Pagnini, whose new literal translation of the Hebrew Bible would exert enormous influence on nearly all the Protestant vernacular Bible translators of the Renaissance.[8] Under Leo, other high churchmen in Rome began supporting Hebrew studies: Cardinal Domenico Grimani, Cardinal Adriano Castellesi,[9] and especially Giles of Viterbo, prior general of the Augustinian Order (as of 1506) and cardinal (as of 1517).[10]

In fact, Reuchlin, a consummate legal strategist, had decided that his best hope for success against the inquisition lay in securing Rome as the venue for his trial. In a Hebrew letter, written probably by September 1513, Reuchlin asked Bonet de Lattes, a Roman Jew, to use his influence at the papal court to keep the jurisdiction for the case in Speyer or to have it transferred to Rome immediately.[11] An acquaintance of Reuchlin from his Roman pilgrimages, Lattes had been the head physician for the popes ever since Alexander VI and Reuchlin thought he was Leo's physician. However, Lattes may have died before the letter reached him (and, sure enough, no reply to this letter survives).[12] Lattes was also the *dayyan* of the Roman Jews and the major source of contact between the papacy and the Jewish community. He, too, probably smoothed over Reuchlin's entrée into the Jewish community in 1498. In 1514, on Reuchlin's instructions, one of his Roman attorneys filed a brief requesting that any appeal of the case be heard in Rome because it was the only jurisdiction with a sufficient number of scholars who studied the three holy languages that Reuchlin cited in his offending pamphlet, *Eye Glasses*.[13] Thus, in every sense of the word Rome commanded the greatest competence for judging Reuchlin's Christian Jewish studies properly.

The Roman Trial

After the Speyer ruling, Hoogstraeten appealed the case immediately to the Roman curia. The initial cause for the appeal was his contention that the original proceedings in Mainz had been valid and should never have been transferred to the jurisdiction of Speyer.[14] The appeal, however, meant that all Hoogstraeten's charges and all Reuchlin's defenses would be subject to a comprehensive review.

As soon as the appeal was filed, political maneuvering on all sides began in earnest, though initially with special urgency from Hoogstraeten's supporters. The University of Cologne backed Hoogstraeten energetically at this point. It had already declared Reuchlin's book heretical and arranged for Erfurt, Louvain, and Mainz to do the same. Now the theology faculty turned to the University of Paris to request a condemnation despite the ruling of the episcopal court in Speyer. This was an aggressive, though indirect, attempt to force the curia into Hoogstraeten's camp before hearing the appeal itself.

The University of Paris reacted with shock to Reuchlin's portrayal of Judaism. King Louis XII was sufficiently aroused by his confessor, the Dominican Guillaume Petit,[15] to write twice to the Parisian theology faculty, urging condemnation of Reuchlin's *Recommendation* as a heretical expression of support for Jews and Judaism.[16] The prospect of a formal censure from the most important theological faculty in Christendom was so alarming that Reuchlin wrote a conciliatory letter to the faculty and immediately began lobbying his humanist contacts there.[17] Reuchlin also induced Duke Ulrich of Württemberg to write to the University of Paris in support of his innocence.[18] These efforts were in vain, except that a small party of Reuchlin supporters, headed by the famous humanist Jacques Lefèvre d'Etaples, did form at the university.[19] On 2 August 1514, the theology faculty at the University of Paris issued a severe condemnation of Reuchlin's *Eye Glasses*, insisting that it was a heretical book and must be burned.[20] Going to the heart of the matter, Paris concluded, above all, that the Talmud should be burned as a heretical and blasphemous book. The assault on Jewish books, thus, received powerful new reinforcement. Pfefferkorn published a translation of the Paris decision in yet another scorching attack on Reuchlin and the Jews, the *Storm Alarm* of 1514.[21] The original Latin version was also published separately in 1514, virtually under the imprimatur of the University of Cologne, as *The Acts of the Parisian Doctors against the Eye Glasses.*[22]

The University of Cologne also contacted the Roman curia directly. On 25 April 1514, the theology faculty sent a letter to Cardinal Bernardino López de Carvajal requesting intervention on Hoogstraeten's behalf.[23] According to Reuchlin, Carvajal became an effective advocate for Hoogstraeten and he immediately succeeded in persuading Leo X to suspend the penalties that Speyer had imposed on Hoogstraeten, most important the payment of court costs on pain of excommunication.[24] Nonetheless, as we will see, other actions taken by the pope were beneficial to Reuchlin's cause.

Initially, Leo named two distinguished members of the College of Cardinals, Domenico Grimani[25] and Pietro Accolti, to serve as judges. Grimani, who would play the leading role in the trial, was appointed on the explicit recommendation of Reuchlin's side and was widely viewed as being well disposed to his case. Grimani's first ruling, sure enough, appeared to favor Reuchlin. He summoned Hoogstraeten to Rome to appear in person before the court, while Reuchlin, ostensibly in consideration of his age (he was then fifty-nine), was permitted to participate in absentia through his lawyers. This preferential treatment had an unintended side effect with benefits for historians: Reuchlin's participation from Germany created a substantial correspondence, some of which has survived. Reuchlin's lawyers in Rome were Caspar Wirt, Caspar Vaihingen, and Johann von der Wyck, who were frequently assisted by the canon Martin Gröning (who had a doctorate in law). Among other contributions, Gröning produced the Latin translation of the *Recommendation* that was used in the trials in lieu of the version prepared by Reuchlin's opponents in Cologne.[26] Moreover, a long report he sent Reuchlin in September 1516 is one of the most valuable sources for ascertaining the events of this phase of the trial.[27] Stephan Rosinus, the imperial ambassador to Rome,[28] and Michael Hummelberger, who studied canon law in Rome from 1514 through 1517, also strongly supported Reuchlin's defense at the Vatican. In several letters, Hummelberger repeatedly urged Reuchlin to provide more financial support for the case.[29]

Hoogstraeten, who arrived in Rome probably by the end of September 1514, protested the makeup of the bench. He proposed that Cardinal Carvajal be appointed as a third judge on the grounds that the judges would need assistance since the ongoing Fifth Lateran Council occupied so much of their attention.[30] Carvajal was a powerful cardinal who had just been restored to his offices by Leo X, after having been formally deposed by Julius as a result of participation in the schismatic Council of Pisa.[31] He would but narrowly lose the next papal election, in the hotly contested conclave of 1521–22, to Adrian of Utrecht.[32]

The petition to make Carvajal a judge was refused, as were several requests that the appeal be removed from Grimani and Accolti's jurisdiction and assigned to the Fifth Lateran Council. Charles of Burgundy (the future emperor Charles V) and his illustrious tutor-guardian Adrian of Utrecht (future pope Adrian VI), also weighed in to support the transfer of the case to the Fifth Lateran Council.[33] As rector of the University of Louvain, Adrian had already presided over the condemnation of *Eye Glasses*.

In the surviving records, Hoogstraeten and his supporters do not explain their reasoning for preferring adjudication by the ecumenical council. Clearly, though, they had assumed that the council, with its broad cross-section of the church's leadership,[34] would be certain to condemn Reuchlin's portrayal of Judaism. Indeed, while the "height of laxity"[35] in enforcing restrictions on Jews occurred under Leo and the other early sixteenth-century popes, the Fifth Lateran Council was of an entirely different frame of mind. Mounting anti-Jewish fervor was palpable in the council. The Fifth Lateran, arguably the first ecumenical council to address the issue of the worldwide mission of the church, would recommend legislation urging an aggressive approach to converting Jews and destroying Judaism. The most influential tract to emerge from the council, the *Libellus* (1513) by Paolo Giustiniani and Pietro Querini, focused in four of its six sections on the need to missionize the Jews (in addition to proposing sweeping reforms of the clergy, liturgy, hierarchy, and canon law). The *Libellus* advocated harsh enforcement of restrictions on Jews with the goal of compelling conversion:

> However, if so led [i.e., by blandishments] they do not wish to convert, on account of their stiff-necked perfidy, they should be handled with bitter and harsh measures: not because you wish to harm them, for no one should be forced to the faith; but, so that seeing those of them who did wish to convert being treated caressingly, and the others, who never acquiesced to do this [i.e., convert], being treated harshly, they will more easily be incited by those stimuli—as if by two spurs—to seize the way of truth.[36]

And, should all efforts at conversion fail, the *Libellus* insisted on complete expulsion: "Last of all, you must order them, as dead sheep, to be separated from the Christian flocks so completely that you do not allow them to remain in any place of Christian sovereignty or to pass through them."[37] Not surprisingly, Leo X rejected all of these harsh recommendations.[38]

In January 1515, Grimani and Accolti began to review the case, and, as far as we can determine, the decisions they reached favored Reuchlin. First, they ruled that the court would use Gröning's Latin translation of the

Recommendation rather than the one Hoogstraeten's supporters had prepared for the University of Paris. Moreover, they decided to base their review on the entire text of *Eye Glasses* (including Reuchlin's lengthy exculpatory notes), and not just on the *Recommendation*. This was highly advantageous to Reuchlin because *Eye Glasses* included a comprehensive defense that directly countered Pfefferkorn's *Magnifying Glass*, the original work to charge that Reuchlin favored Jews and undermined a legitimate attempt to promote and defend Christianity. Grimani also issued an official rebuke to Hoogstraeten for having solicited a formal ruling on Reuchlin's pamphlet from the theology faculty of the University of Paris at a time when Hoogstraeten knew that the Roman curia would have the case under review. As far as Rome was concerned, this effectively neutralized any legal impact that Paris's powerful condemnation of Reuchlin might have had.

Thereafter, as far as we know, not much happened for several months. Hoogstraeten may have been right with his contention that Grimani and Accolti had too much on their plates at the Fifth Lateran Council to handle the appeal expeditiously.

Much worse, on 14 September 1515, a disaster struck the papacy. This was the first in a series of crises—the final one being the stunning success of the early Reformation movement—that would alter the course of the trial. The papal army, constituted primarily of Swiss mercenaries, suffered catastrophic defeat at the hands of the French in the bloody battle of Marignano. (For a young priest who was serving as a chaplain—Ulrich Zwingli, soon to be the founder of the Reformed movement—Marignano was a life-changing experience.) All business in Rome ground to a halt between September 1515 and February 1516, for Leo X and leaders of the curia had to go to Bologna for intensive peace negotiations with King Francis I. This ultimately resulted in the Concordat of Bologna, which would give the French monarchs effective control over the high clergy in their domain.

Hoogstraeten, too, went to Bologna (and Florence) for he saw this as an opportunity to rally the French to his cause.[39] After all, France had long ago expelled the Jews, and Paris's condemnation of Reuchlin's *Recommendation* was by far the most significant endorsement Hoogstraeten's case had gotten to date. The strident Parisian call for the burning of the Talmud, backed by the previous French monarch Louis XII, had expressed enthusiasm for the Pfefferkorn-Hoogstraeten attack against Judaism in the empire. Now, Francis I also pressed Leo to issue a ruling in Hoogstraeten's favor, this being Francis's second known attempt to intervene in the case.[40] Thereafter, some records indicate that French theologians in Rome, the identities are unknown, would lobby the Vatican for vindication of the inquisitor. Guillaume Petit, now the

confessor of Francis I, is known to have journeyed to Rome during the negotiations in order to pressure Grimani in person on behalf of Hoogstraeten.[41]
The French humanist Jacques Lefèvre d'Etaples, however, would continue to
support Reuchlin, as would Guillaume Cop.[42]

There is no proof that Francis's intervention had a direct impact.
Nonetheless, upon returning to Rome in February 1516, Leo did take new measures to ensure that the appeal was heard by a broader spectrum of prelates
and brought to a conclusion. He now instructed Grimani and Accolti to form a
commission of distinguished "assessors" to decide the case. The sources vary
as to the exact number of commissioners. One claims twenty-six members;
another cites eighteen.[43] From February until July, many in the highest ech-
elon of the church were involved in some way with the case, including the pope
and his cousin, Cardinal Guilio de' Medici (future Pope Clement VII).

We do not have an official list of the members of the commission, although
various documents indicate or strongly suggest that the following men were
among them: Girolamo Aleandro (who, in his function as papal legate, would
soon draft the Edict of Worms, the first imperial condemnation of Luther);
Giorgio Benigno Salviati (archbishop of Nazareth); Thomas Cajetan de Vio
(General of the Dominican Order); Cardinal Bernardino López de Carvajal;
Cardinal Adriano Castellesi; Cardinal Niccolò Fieschi (also specifically
Cardinal Protector of the Dominican Order); Gargano of Siena (a Franciscan
professor of law, also chaplain to Cardinal Grimani); Pietro Griffo (Bishop of
Forlì);[44] Bernardino Prati (General of the Franciscan Order); Sylvester Prierias
(a Dominican who served as *magister sacri palatii*); Giovanni Battista Secchia
(General of the Carmelite Order); Giles of Viterbo (General of the Augustinian
Order); the bishop of Malfi (identity unknown); and, probably, Enrique de
Cardova (Bishop of Barcelona). Several of these men had recently acquired a sig-
nificant command of Hebrew, including Aleandro, Gargano, Giles of Viterbo,
as well as Pietro Galatino (a learned Franciscan then associated with Cardinal
Lorenzo Pucci) and would prove to be staunch advocates of Reuchlin's cause.[45]

The commission held four sessions between 19 June and 2 July 1516. The
first and second sessions, which convened in the Sistine Chapel, featured
robust diatribes against Reuchlin, delivered by Sylvester Prierias.[46] During
the second session, Gargano of Siena and Giles of Viterbo answered Prierias;
Giles apparently gave a lengthy dissertation on the value of the Talmud and the
Kabbalah, much to the consternation of Hoogstraeten and his supporters.[47]
During these two sessions, the commissioners covered the basic procedural
issues systematically and also reviewed Reuchlin's *Eye Glasses* carefully. The
secretary read aloud Gröning's Latin version of the *Recommendation* to all the
commissioners. At the end of the first and second sessions new members were

added to the commission, some from the circle of Cardinal Carvajal, and thus likely Hoogstraeten supporters.

The third session, which, like the final one, convened in the Church of Santa Maria della Pace, adjourned with the decision to bring deliberations to a conclusion at the next meeting. Each commissioner was to prepare a written evaluation of *Eye Glasses* for submission. New members of the commission who had not participated in the official reading of *Eye Glasses* in the Sistine Chapel were to undertake that task as a group in the palace of Bishop Enrique de Cardova (an ally of Carvajal) before the final session. We know that Reuchlin's legal team, Johann von der Wyck and Martin Gröning, participated in that reading. Gröning reported that this special session was highly favorable to Reuchlin for he and von der Wyck were able to argue persuasively that Reuchlin had answered all of Hoogstraeten's objections to the *Recommendation* in the commentary section (the *Arguments*) of the original publication of *Eye Glasses*. According to Gröning, Hoogstraeten left the session in a gloomy mood.[48]

None of the briefs submitted at the final session have survived. Nonetheless, several of Reuchlin's supporters on the commission, notably Giorgio Benigno and Giles of Viterbo, wrote tracts and letters in support of Reuchlin, thus making it possible to see the legal strategies of the Reuchlinists. Above all, they contended that Jewish writings were valuable for the study of Christianity. It is also probable that the Reuchlinists on the Roman commission were aware of German charges that the inquisition was attempting to undermine the progress of humanist studies. Erasmus, at any rate, pressed that issue in letters he sent to Grimani and the powerful Cardinal Raffaele Riario.[49] Erasmus urged both prelates to do their best for Reuchlin in order to bolster the humanist movement in the empire. Grimani should understand, Erasmus wrote, that the German humanists "have great hopes that with your assistance this excellent man [i.e., Reuchlin] may be restored to the world in general and to literature [i.e., humanist studies] in particular."[50] According to Erasmus's letter to Riario, Reuchlin "has all Germany in his debt, where he [i.e., Reuchlin] was the first to awaken the study of Greek and Hebrew."[51] Erasmus published both of these letters prominently in 1515. Neither of them, however, so much as mentions Reuchlin's defense of Jewish writings.

The outcome of the final session of 2 July 1516 is clear, even if the records give conflicting accounts for several significant details. Probably the most accurate account for this meeting is a long letter by Gröning (dated 12 September 1516); another valuable source is the *Acts of the Trials*, which Reuchlin partisans, possibly Reuchlin himself, published in 1518. All the accounts agree in the essential point that the commission voted overwhelmingly to sustain the Speyer verdict, that is, in favor of Reuchlin. *Acts of the Trials* states that seventeen of eighteen commissioners (Prierias was the exception) voted for Reuchlin.[52] Yet a third source, a letter addressed to Willibald Pirckheimer, claimed that there were twenty-six commissioners, nineteen of whom voted for Reuchlin. Gröning, moreover, wrote that only "three or four of the worst enemies" spoke out against Reuchlin's book, but not against Reuchlin him-self.[53] He also says that the Dominicans and the Parisian theologians were the dissenters.[54] Whatever the precise details may have been, all sources for the event and all subsequent actions clearly indicate that the vote was a triumph for Reuchlin.

But, in another breathtaking turnabout, on the day of the vote Leo X issued a *mandatum de supersedendo* (mandate of supersedure) that suspended the legal standing of the commission's findings pending the pope's final determi-nation of the case. This concession was extracted from Leo the very morning of 2 July, apparently by the Dominican Prierias, who dramatically presented the mandate at the final session. It is also possible that Cardinal Guilio de' Medici for unknown reasons helped Prierias get the mandate.[55] Gröning reports that the mandate was produced before the voting and in order to stop it; according to this account, Cardinal Castellesi immediately pressed Leo to allow the vot-ing to proceed. According to *Acts of the Trials*, the mandate was handed down after the voting. Whatever the sequence of events, this was a disappointment to Reuchlin's side for a definitive victory eluded them at the very last second and perhaps ominously, it seemed. Even if it was a tumultuous day with a mixed result, Reuchlin's supporters expressed confidence that the match really was all over except for the referee's final whistle. Indeed, the 1518 *Acts of the Trials* celebrated the conclusion as a victory, for it left the Speyer decision in force: "Finally, the above named inquisitor departed from the Roman curia, where he had personally labored for four years with various methods to invalidate the Speyer trial, and he returned to Cologne with empty hands. And the Speyer judgment still remains in force and honor and will remain so forever."[56]

The Christian Debates

Despite pressure from both sides for closure, it would be four more years before Leo X decided the case, more than ample time for a full-fledged debate to develop on two issues: the status of Judaism and Jewish writings and the conflict between scholasticism and Christian humanism. From the perspec-tive of the Roman hierarchy, such a drawn out controversy, waged openly in the print media, may have appeared to have some advantages. Since in one way or another the church would need to absorb the impulses that humanism and Jewish studies were generating, there was a certain convenience in letting scholars argue these issues in such a spontaneous way before the church reached any official decisions. There is, however, no evidence that the pope's extreme hesitancy arose from any carefully thought out strategy. It is probably most reasonable to suppose that a certain wariness over the intellectual flux of the moment, especially the worsening acrimony between scholastics and biblical humanists, made a quick resolution seem problematic. Many favored reining in the inquisition's authority as humanism expanded, but there is no evidence of any desire to impair the inquisition permanently. As it turned out, the four-year delay had important drawbacks. It provided opportunities for both sides to publish disrespectful, even slanderous, remarks about each other. The Vatican did crack down on a few truly scurrilous depictions of the Dominicans and others,[57] but to little avail. Even Hoogstraeten repeatedly ignored the gag orders issued by the Speyer court and the Roman curia. By autumn 1517, tensions had returned to several universities in the north; writing from the University of Louvain on 3 November 1517, Erasmus said: "The controversy, I see, is resuming, which, above all, I hoped had ended."[58] The delay also made the Reuchlin Affair a liability to the church because it created a context for a favorable reception of the early Reformation movement. As we will see in the next chapter, the controversy agitated several people who would be among Luther's first supporters, leaving some of them primed for action against the church just as Luther appeared on the scene. Although it is but one factor, the Reuchlin Affair also directly stirred Luther himself.

After the Speyer verdict and the enthusiastic vote of support from the Roman commission, northern humanists were emboldened to denounce the conflict as the inquisition's attempt to stifle the now surging humanist movement. One of the reasons for this emphasis in the north was that the sudden success of Erasmus's Bible was raising anxiety among some theologians and churchmen. From May 1515 until October 1519, Erasmus carefully avoided taking a public position in support of Reuchlin, but his launch of the new biblical studies movement during this time energized Reuchlin's supporters. In the aftermath of his publication of Praise of Folly (1511) and in the much hyped run-up to the appearance of the Bible in Greek (1516), a strong conviction formed in many quarters that an irreconcilable clash was occurring between the "poets"—that is, professors of the humanities who, inspired by Erasmus and Reuchlin, were advocating biblical philology—and the "theologians," the entrenched masters of late-medieval scholasticism.[59] Eventually, Erasmus would decry the old guard as being jealous of their power and unwilling to shoulder the preparatory studies that humanist biblicism required. In a published letter to Cardinal Thomas Wolsey, archbishop of Canterbury,

Erasmus expressed his fear and aggravation that "such men cannot be induced to believe that their authority need not utterly collapse if we read the Scriptures in a corrected text and seek out understanding of them from the source" (i.e., biblical texts in the original languages).[60] In an important letter to Albrecht of Brandenburg of 19 October 1519—a letter that was frequently printed— Erasmus wrote caustically of scholastic professors who had opposed Reuchlin and were now mustering forces against Luther:

> I cannot refrain from letting you in on one secret [i.e., about "both Reuchlin's case and Luther's"]—that those people [i.e., the opponents of Reuchlin and Luther] have very different objects in view from those that their words profess. They have long resented the new blossoming of the humanities and the ancient tongues, and the revival of the authors of antiquity, who up to now were worm-eaten and deep in dust, so that the world is now recalled to the source. They are afraid for their own shortcomings, they do not wish it to be thought that there is anything they do not know, and they fear their own prestige may suffer.[61]

Many a modern historical study has demonstrated that the worldviews of these two groups were not really diametrically opposed; that many a scholastic, Hoogstraeten being an excellent example, absorbed Erasmus's research on the Bible, and many a humanist continued to take instruction in dialectics (logic), the foundation for scholasticism, very seriously. Nonetheless, the two camps were antagonists and some among the old guard were expressing concern that Erasmus's new Bible, with its implicit rejection of the Vulgate, would wreck the foundations of Christianity as they knew it. Reuchlin's career, though it came first, was understood in the 1510s to be the vital Hebrew complement to the Erasmian movement.

As of around 1515, and specifically in the aftermath of the stunning rebuke that the Speyer court delivered to the Dominican inquisition, it is possible to detect swelling confidence among the humanists, a palpable expectation that a definitive victory over conservative theologians was within their reach. In this respect, we can see that Reuchlin's supporters had moved beyond the question of Jewish rights and Jewish scholarship and were deeply engaged in efforts to support biblical philology and church reform. Ulrich von Hutten composed a poetic celebration of the controversy whose title alone conveys their soaring spirits: *The Triumph of Reuchlin* (1518).[62] In 1517, Count Hermann von Neuenahr published an exquisite piece of purple prose in which he proclaimed that Apollo, the ancient god of poetry, would ensure that Reuchlin prevailed in this scholarly battle.[63] More prosaically, in a speech delivered at the

1519 election of Charles V in Frankfurt, Neuenahr urged the new emperor to extinguish the last embers of the inquisition's attempt to punish the humanist movement.[64] The eminent Nuremberg patrician Pirckheimer had interpreted the inquisition's action in much the same fashion in an important tract of 1517. He, too, portrayed the trial as an abysmal failure for the Dominicans, a sign of moral-intellectual decrepitude in the German church hierarchy. Although originally the scholastic-humanist debate was not a primary concern to him, Reuchlin also began inserting criticisms of scholastic methods into his own publications.[65] By 1519, Hoogstraeten would be compelled to undertake a lengthy defense of scholastic logic, especially the Aristotelian syllogism, in addition to sustaining the campaign against Judaism and Reuchlin.[66]

In their various publications, Hutten, Neuenahr, and Pirckheimer were forming a line of attack that had been used in *The Letters of Obscure Men*, perhaps the most successful, and unquestionably the most entertaining, defense of Reuchlin. This satire, which despite being banned would go through many editions in the sixteenth century, is routinely ranked among the classics of humoristic literature and nearly always cited as a barometer of how low the church's prestige had fallen "on the eve of the Reformation."[67] As the phrase "obscure men" signals, the book is a collection of bogus letters, all of which are addressed to Ortwin Gratius, professor of the arts at the University of Cologne, to express support for the campaigns to crush Reuchlin. Gratius probably earned the dubious honor of being the addressee of the letters because he, as a professor of the humanities and as the likely figure behind the Latin translations of Pfefferkorn's tracts, had raised the particular ire of Reuchlin's humanist supporters.[68] The "obscure men," some of whom are actual professors at Cologne and most of whom are fictitious academics, describe their various sexual escapades, drunken and gluttonous entertainments, absurd disputations on theological issues, and petty squabbles with humanist professors throughout the empire. Much of the satire is at the personal expense of Gratius, Hoogstraeten, Tongern, and, above all, Pfefferkorn, but the real issues are larger: clerical discipline, humanist studies, and scholastic theology, especially syllogistic logic and speculative philosophy. A favorite comic technique is the use of pseudo-logical analysis to assess the precise nature of a personal lapse on the part of an obscurantist, frequently one of a sexual nature.

Publication of such a work that so brazenly lampooned an inquisitor general carried extreme peril. Obviously, it was necessary to print it anonymously and to preserve strict secrecy about its authorship. We now know that it was the work of three men, Crotus Rubeanus, Ulrich von Hutten, and Hermann Busch,[69] all of whom had had firsthand experiences at the University of Cologne and, most important, were engaged in the advancement of humanist studies in Germany. Crotus Rubeanus, who was then a highly respected teacher (and monk) at the monastery of Fulda, was the primary author for the first edition of the letters. Many of the new letters, which appeared in the second and third editions of the work (1516 and 1517), came from Hutten's pen. Hutten, an imperial knight, was one of the most talented writers of his generation and also an active political force during the early years of Luther's movement.

In virtually every letter, the authors connect the Reuchlin trial to broad questions of church reform. They forge an especially strong link between the Reuchlin controversy and the mounting enthusiasm for Erasmus's biblical philology, as we can see in the final letter of the first edition (Hoogstraeten writing to Gratius):

> It is said that Erasmus of Rotterdam hath composed many treatises
> on theology; I cannot believe that he hath avoided error. He
> beginneth by writing a tract to vex theologians, and now he writeth
> theologically himself—so that it passeth! If I come back to Germany
> and read his scribblements, and find in them the smallest jot on
> which he hath gone astray—or which I do not understand—let him
> take heed to his skin![70]

The same letter also exudes the northern humanist conviction that Rome is supporting their cause; in reference to the situation in Rome, Hoogstraeten says, "All men deride me and plague me, and now Reuchlin hath more friends here [i.e., in Rome] than in Germany, and many more cardinals and bishops and prelates and curialists love him."[71]

Pirckheimer's *Apologetic Letter* of 1517 illustrates even more clearly that the defense of Reuchlin and the plea for a humanist foundation for church reform had substantially merged. Though ostensibly an unfettered defense of Reuchlin, the *Apologetic Letter* actually amounts to a succinct formulation of the goals of the humanist movement for reforming theology. In broad strokes, Pirckheimer depicts Reuchlin as nothing less than a martyr for Christian theology, the man who suffers the wrath of scholastic theologians because he prepared the way for the new methodology, a return to the ancient texts of the faith.

Thus, much of Pirckheimer's approach depends heavily on Erasmianism—and Erasmus wrote to Pirckheimer immediately to endorse the tract.[72] Like Erasmus, Pirckheimer insists that a moral lifestyle for all involved is a prerequisite for theological education and leadership in the church. He is taking another page from Erasmus's book when he rejects the complexity of scholastic theological speculation as an unnecessary obfuscation of the simple gospel message. "These men neglect the Old Testament and they scorn the

New Testament as a work written for ignorant people and they consider the teachings of the apostles scarcely worth reading. This comes from the fact that they scorn St. Jerome as a (mere) grammarian."[73] He includes many a caustic reference to the excessive dependence on Aristotle and speculative theology, the preoccupations that result, as nearly all humanists contended, in neglect of the textual study of the Bible and early Christian writers. In one memorable passage, he muses that St. Augustine, should he come back to life, would be utterly unable to comprehend the discourse of contemporary scholastics.[74]

Pirckheimer injects considerable emotion and fervor into his plea for biblical philology. "It is necessary to be expert in Latin, Greek, and Hebrew.... In Hebrew because all the mysteries of both the Old Testament and the New Testament are revealed."[75] Now that Erasmus had published the New Testament in Greek, it is natural to equate "Reuchlinists" and "Erasmists"; Pirckheimer proclaims himself both since each is essentially the same "praiseworthy" thing.[76] Over all, Pirckheimer advocates expanding the scope of theological authorities to include philology and legal studies (his own specialties) as well as Aristotle, Plato, Pythagoras, and Jewish theology, especially the Talmud and Kabbalah.[77] Aristotle, thus, hardly disappears from the apparatus of the theologian, though he becomes but one of several possible sources of authority.

Pirckheimer includes as well a long list of theologians who, according to him, were already engaged in an Erasmian-Reuchlinist reorientation of their discipline. This list is fascinating for it mingles under the one rubric of humanist theologian the names of leading figures about to separate into opposing armies over Luther's revolt: Johannes Cochlaeus, Erasmus, Johannes Eck, Hermann von Neuenahr, Johannes Oecolampadius, and Luther himself. Published during the momentous month of October 1517, no other book so effectively conveys the sense that humanism had firmly established the expectation of a paradigm shift among intellectuals before Luther posted the *Ninety-five Theses* on 31 October 1517. This crucial development, which humanists felt was finally beginning to happen with the appearance of Erasmus's new Bible in 1516, guaranteed a serious and attentive audience for Luther's radical protest.

While none of Reuchlin's supporters questioned the importance of Hebrew for biblical studies, the northerners were largely silent about the value of the Talmud and Kabbalah. Pirckheimer was exceptional with his assertion that Reuchlin's enemies could make better use of their time if "they would bring to light those things that still lie hidden in Kabbalistic and Talmudic works" and "enrich the church of God with them."[78] Pirckheimer specifically endorsed suppositions that the Kabbalah offered reliable research on the text of the Bible, the virgin birth of Jesus, and the transformation of the wine and bread of the Christian Eucharist into the body of Jesus, among other topics.[79] The dominant stance among Reuchlin's supporters was quite different; even for them, Jewish writings had value primarily as a potential weapon in their anti-Jewish arsenal. Renaissance biblical research, though it did constitute the definitive paradigm shift in the history of Christianity, was nonetheless a long way from the refinements of the nineteenth and twentieth centuries, when many biblical scholars turned to early Jewish traditions to find historical perspective for assessing Jewish elements of the Christian New Testament. Neuenahr typified northern attitudes when he went out of his way to stress that Reuchlin's Italian supporters, especially Pietro Galatino (see below), were strengthening the Christian mission to the Jews by "discovering" Christian revelations in Jewish works.[80] Hoogstraeten, however, would continue to fulminate that the Jewish books were so pestiferous and evil, so harmful to Christianity that they had to be destroyed.

Moreover, when Hoogstraeten argued that the Jewish works could not contribute to the advancement of Christian scholarship, he was espousing a view that was also held by two of Reuchlin's most famous supporters: Erasmus and Luther. Both of them expressed their scorn for the Talmud and the Kabbalah, though, as long as the conflict persisted, Luther did so only in private correspondence.[81] Eventually, as we will see, Luther's violent condemnations of Judaism and the Talmud would make Hoogstraeten's rhetoric seem mild. Erasmus, in fact, was diametrically opposed to Pirckheimer and Reuchlin's position on Jewish writings. He never lost a chance to scoff at Jewish writings. In a 1518 letter to Wolfgang Capito, one of the first scholars to profit from Reuchlin's Hebrew primer, Erasmus vented his anti-Semitic perspective on the birth of Christian Hebrew studies:

> I could wish you were more inclined to Greek than to that Hebrew of
> yours, with no desire to criticize it. I see them as a nation full of the
> most tedious fabrications, who spread a kind of fog over everything,
> Talmud, Kabbalah, tetragrammaton, *Gates of Light*, words, words,
> words. I would rather have Christ mixed up with Scotus [i.e., the
> scholastic theologian] than with that rubbish of theirs. Italy is full
> of Jews, in Spain there are hardly any Christians. I fear this may
> give that pestilence that was long ago suppressed a chance to rear
> its ugly head. If only the church of Christians did not attach so
> much importance to the Old Testament! It is a thing of shadows,
> given us for a time; and now it is almost preferred to the literature of
> Christianity.[82]

This passage comes from a private letter. In a missive to Thomas Wolsey, which Erasmus and others repeatedly published, he expresses his view more mildly: "Personally, I have never felt an attraction to Kabbalah or Talmud."[83]

Thus, those defenses of Reuchlin that arise from a strongly anti-scholastic bias, such as Erasmus's and Pirckheimer's, tend to exhibit profoundly anti-Semitic attitudes. Pirckheimer may have accepted Reuchlin's claims for the value of Jewish books but he also expresses blood-chilling scorn for Jews and their religion. He explicitly deems any effort by a Christian to form a friendship with a Jew a "crime," and insists that Reuchlin is innocent of such a despicable failing.[84] He doubts that a Jew could ever convert to Christianity, persists in labeling Pfefferkorn a "half-Jew," and even defends his own call, expressed in a published letter, that Pfefferkorn be executed.[85] It was Hoogstraeten, no less, who protested that the brutality of this rhetoric should discredit Pirckheimer altogether.

The Letters of Obscure Men displays a similar hatred for Jews despite the furious attack against Reuchlin's opponents. Pfefferkorn and his wife are the most common objects of anti-Jewish innuendos, a disquieting circumstance especially since neither one was still Jewish. In one letter, we read "Pfefferkorn was a reckless man, and, like all Jews, regarded not his own good repute so long as he could make money."[86] Another letter, one that first appeared in the third edition, offers the following attempt at humor: "the other day a fellow who had resided in Cologne ten years ago told me that he believed not that Pfefferkorn was yet a good Christian: for he declared that he met him a year back and that he still stank like any other Jew."[87] These innuendos are virtually ubiquitous. The strongest anti-Jewish leitmotif is actually that a Jew can never really become a Christian.[88] The final letter of the first edition ends on that very note: "I have heard that Johannes Pfefferkorn hath once more become a Jew."[89]

The second letter of the collection offers a paradigmatic portrayal of Christian-Jewish relations. A fictitious academic named Magister Pelzer writes to Gratius to ascertain what kind of absolution is necessary for having removed one's hat in a gesture of respect to Jews. Magister Pelzer had just committed this sin, unknowingly, to two Jews in Frankfurt: "if I had known them to be Jews, and had nevertheless done them reverence, then I should have been deserving of the stake, for it would have been heresy. But, heaven knoweth, neither from word or gesture did I gather that they were Jews, but I thought that they were Doctors (of Theology)."[90] This is intended as a mocking vitiation of the charges against Reuchlin of having been impermissibly favorable to Jews, but, of course, accomplishes that by depicting any display of respect for Jews as something utterly ludicrous, virtually unimaginable.

Rome and the Jewish Question

While Reuchlin's northern European supporters, many of whom were engaged in the effort to establish humanist curricula at universities and schools, often focused on the hegemony of scholasticism (and, generally, on the failings of the church hierarchy), the Reuchlinists at the Roman curia addressed more directly the questions of what constitutes proper and legal treatment of Jews and whether or not Jewish writings have any relevance to Christian theology.

Giorgio Benigno Salviati, titular archbishop of Nazareth at Rome ("Romae archiepiscopus Nazarenus") and formerly a well-respected humanist professor and a protégé of both the Medicis[91] and Cardinal Carvajal,[92] composed *Whether the Jewish Books, Which They Call the Talmud, Should be Suppressed or Kept and Preserved*, which Neuenahr published in Cologne in 1517 as the centerpiece of a pamphlet titled the *Defense of the Most Distinguished Man Johannes Reuchlin*.[93] The very title page of this work proclaims that Benigno had been the first member of the Roman commission to cast his vote in favor of Reuchlin.[94] Benigno paints Reuchlin, from Rome's perspective, as the premier humanist of the north, one of the very few to have had an impact in culturally advanced Italy: "Now I, living at Rome as the archbishop of Nazareth have written, among other things, this tract, or rather this commendation of Johannes Reuchlin of Germany, a man most eloquent in both languages [i.e., Latin and Greek] or rather in every language—he comprehends Hebrew and Aramaic—and most distinguished in both divine and human philosophy."[95] Benigno not only promotes Reuchlin as the ideal biblical humanist but also suggests that the pioneering scholar has received greater recognition in Rome than in Germany. And he scolds Germany for its reluctance: "Should not a man who brings honor, glory, and esteem to his country receive honor, glory, and esteem from his own country?"[96] These words are aimed at Emperor Maximilian, to whom the pamphlet is dedicated.

Benigno adopted the literary form of the dialogue for his defense, with himself and Reuchlin as the interlocutors. In most segments of the dialogue, the archbishop raises one of Hoogstraeten's actual heresy charges and discusses it with Reuchlin. The result has a surprisingly academic feeling, for the tract is not an endorsement of every statement Reuchlin made in the *Recommendation*. The colloquy begins with Reuchlin's repetition of the passage in 1 Corinthians 11:19 on the necessity of heresy (or error) as part of the process of establishing and recognizing the truth. Reuchlin had always claimed that Paul's statement could be applied to support the toleration of Jewish writings, and that it, moreover, is a key to the productive use of erroneous Jewish writings by Christian scholars. Benigno counters that this has definitely not been the position of every pope throughout history; that Gregory IX and Innocent IV had specifically condemned the Talmud and ordered its destruction in the thirteenth century. In counterargument, Reuchlin simply claims that other popes did not concur with this decision and, moreover, that Gregory and Innocent had been inappropriately influenced by advisors when they issued their—by implication, mistaken—decrees against the Talmud. To this, Benigno, apparently giving his tacit assent, replies nothing and moves on to another issue.[97]

Several other substantial issues are discussed. Could Jews be heretics? Should Jews be labeled "perfidious," as in the liturgy of Good Friday? Did Reuchlin claim that Paul was the most significant apostle on the grounds that he had the finest Jewish education? Is the Talmud a more efficacious witness to Jesus' messiahship for Jews than is the Old Testament?

Reuchlin, as interlocutor, offers qualification and clarification for all of these questions. Reuchlin's persona continues to argue that Jews should not be treated as heretics because they are outside the church. He states that Paul was well qualified to teach God's law because of his education but that it was God's will and grace that made him a vessel for the gospel. Significantly, Reuchlin insists that Jewish writings must be a source for Jewish conversion because they are the core of Jewish faith; the residual implication here is that Jewish writings, to a degree, contain elements of the Christian gospel. Reuchlin, in fact, appears to concede that the prophetic writings of the Old Testament will not serve effectively as a basis for Jewish proselytism.

On one issue, the Reuchlin of the dialogue accepts a slight modification from Benigno. Benigno rejects the interpretation of John 5:39, "Search the Scriptures," as referring explicitly both to the Hebrew Bible and to the Talmud. Reuchlin argues his position earnestly, claiming that Jews always read Scripture from the perspective of their exegesis; therefore, Jesus must have meant Scripture and tradition ("Scriptures and commentaries"), though, as Reuchlin now concedes, this is only by implication (and therefore "Scriptures" does not literally mean "Talmud").[98]

This tract, though a far cry from Enlightenment espousals of toleration, nevertheless has a few elements of potential benefit to Renaissance Jews. It rejected the history of papal suppression of the Talmud, finding no traces of anti-Christian blasphemy or slander. While it did stress the Christian goal of converting the Jews, the tract left Jews free to practice their faith with the guidance of their books, especially the Talmudic tractates.

The most massive publication that came out of Rome to support Reuchlin is a 1518 book of 622 folio-size pages by Pietro Galatino, *On the Hidden Elements of the Catholic Truth*.[99] It includes such extensive quotation from the Talmud and other sources in Aramaic and Hebrew that it was necessary to arrange for the great Jewish printer Gershom Soncino to do the presswork, even though the peripatetic Soncino was then in Ortona (on the central Adriatic coast of Italy). The work begins with a prefatory letter by Emperor Maximilian (dated 1 September 1515) encouraging Galatino to defend his "imperial councilor, Johannes Reuchlin"[100] but unfolds largely as a manual for anti-Jewish debating, in particular the use of the Talmud for proselytizing Jews. In fact, *On the Hidden Elements of the Catholic Truth* is heavily dependent on Ramón Martí's thirteenth-century *Dagger of the Faith* (*Pugio fidei*),[101] a work that elaborated the polemical thesis, perhaps first articulated by Pablo Christiani in 1263,[102] that the Talmud offers proof that Jesus was the true messiah. Reuchlin was deeply gratified that this work was dedicated to him and his cause. While Galatino's weighty book was published as a tribute to Reuchlin, its anti-Jewish stance epitomizes the direction that Reuchlin's supporters were taking.[103] It is important to recall that Reuchlin himself always expressed a traditional Christian view of the exclusivity of redemption through Christ, even if he and his supporters, for the most part, rejected violent persecution of Jews as well as confiscation of their books.

In 1519, Reuchlin published a new collection of letters: the *Letters of Illustrious Men*. An important feature of this book is the goal of projecting an image of unity between Reuchlin and the Roman curia. The second volume of this book (the first volume is a reprint of the letters Reuchlin published in 1514) begins with a reprint of Reuchlin's 1498 speech in the Sistine Chapel before Alexander VI[104] and, otherwise, includes many letters to and from the most distinguished churchmen of Rome. For example, one 1517 letter from Rome recounts a conversation between Francesco Poggio and Leo X: "Francesco Poggio of Florence recently beseeched the pope: 'Holy Father, I will take the side of Reuchlin, and I wish to stand in his place. I read all of his research, all that I was able to get. An injustice is happening to that man.' After a while, the pope responded to him: 'Poggio, don't worry. I will not allow that man to suffer any harm.'"[105]

Perhaps the most significant among the Roman correspondents in volume 2 of the *Letters of Illustrious Men* is Giles of Viterbo.[106] As we have seen, Giles was prior general of the Augustinian Order. (It was to negotiate with Giles that Luther journeyed to Rome in 1510–11.[107]) He was also one of the great humanist cardinals of Leo's Rome, well known for his determination to support reform of the church, especially to enforce high standards of discipline among the clergy. Inspired by Reuchlin's Hebrew grammar and by the speculations of Pico della Mirandola, Giles had completely immersed himself in Hebrew studies. Like Reuchlin, he was convinced that Kabbalistic mysticism must be applied to the Christian faith. He wrote a short study of the Kabbalah in 1517 and a larger one in 1532, neither of which was published until the twentieth century.[108] Under the mistaken impression that the *Zohar* originated in ancient Palestine, Giles expended great effort in 1514 to import a manuscript of this fundamental Kabbalistic work from Damascus.[109]

For years, Giles supported Elijah Levita, one of the greatest Jewish grammarians of the Renaissance. As Levita himself noted, "There was a great outcry against me"[110] among the Jews for teaching Christians the Torah and Hebrew. But Rome was emerging as the place where scholars like Sforno and Levita were willing to collaborate with increasingly benevolent Christians. Levita and his family lived for thirteen years as devout Jews in the Roman palace of Cardinal Giles of Viterbo. Levita dedicated a number of works to Giles—probably the first time in history that a Jew so honored a Christian. One was his great tract on biblical Hebrew, his *Sefer ha-Bahur* (1518), which was not only dedicated to Giles but also printed in Rome with the official approbation of Leo X.

Giles wrote several letters in support of Reuchlin, four of which appeared prominently in the *Letters of Illustrious Men*. One bestows the honor of affiliate membership in the Augustinian Order on Reuchlin, his brother, Dionysius, and his sister, Elisabeth.[111] Another expresses heartfelt thanks upon receiving a copy of Reuchlin's *Art of the Kabbalah*.[112] Most important, the volume prints a letter from 1516 in which Giles praises Reuchlin for nothing less than having "saved the Talmud from the fires," and concludes with these words: "in your trial, on which we have labored this summer in this dangerous heat, we understand that we have defended and preserved not you but the law and not the Talmud but the church. It is not that Reuchlin has been saved by us but that we have been saved by Reuchlin."[113] But these words referred to the Roman commission's exoneration of Reuchlin—there was still no final verdict from the pope.

What stands out in the publications of 1516–20 is that the Reuchlinists successfully portrayed the Roman curia, for the most part, as their allies in the effort to promote humanism generally and Hebrew studies specifically. During the nearly ten years of controversy, Reuchlin published several polemics and apologies to support his cause, but he also managed to devote himself to research. He used the final years of his life to make contributions to three areas of humanist studies: history of early Christianity, Hebrew philology, and the Kabbalah. The specific contributions include such items as a Latin translation of a Greek biography of Constantine, a translation of Athanasius's commentary on Psalms, a translation with his own commentary of a tract attributed to Athanasius, an important book on Hebrew grammar, an edition of the seven penitential Psalms in Hebrew and Latin, a translation of a medieval Hebrew wedding poem (by Joseph Ezobi), and a major study on the Jewish Kabbalah.[114] It was an ambitious scholarly program.

Reuchlin began packaging his publications to make them appear to be an integral component of a Roman network of scholarship. For example, he dedicated Athanasius's *Commentary on the Psalms* to the influential papal protonotary Jacob Questenberg (12 August 1515),[115] and his new tract on Hebrew grammar (1518) to Cardinal Adriano Castellesi, who sponsored humanist Hebrew studies, studied Hebrew himself, and served on the papal commission that exonerated Reuchlin's writing.[116] *Art of the Kabbalah* (1517), the work Reuchlin viewed as his most important accomplishment, was published in honor of Pope Leo X. In the dedication, Reuchlin unabashedly claimed that "nearly the entire city of Rome is defending my integrity."[117] The Vatican librarian, Philipp Beroaldus the Younger, conveyed the pope's gratitude for the homage in *Art of the Kabbalah*, adding, in a letter of 25 May 1517, a papal endorsement of the work: "The pope read your books on the Kabbalah avidly, as is his wont when reading good things."[118] In 1519, these words, too, became a prominent part of the public record when Reuchlin published them in his *Letters of Illustrious Men*.

Hoogstraeten's Appeal

Not contemplating defeat after the Roman commission delivered its near definitive rebuke, Hoogstraeten launched yet another offensive against Reuchlin. Whereas his early works show relatively little concern about humanist methodology,[119] in a tract written just after July 1516, the *Erroneous Assertions*, the inquisitor general did acknowledge that humanists were alleging his opposition to their movement. But through 1518, he continued to focus on dogmatic correctness and remained passionately committed to the anti-Jewish campaign. Therefore, he persisted in making many of the charges first compiled by Arnold van Tongern in 1512 for the University of Cologne, although by now he had condensed them to nineteen "erroneous assertions" occurring in Reuchlin's *Recommendation*. Hoogstraeten originally prepared this document in the hope that it could serve as a basis for disputations he wanted to hold in Rome in 1516 and 1517 in the presence of the Fifth Lateran Council. But despite the dogged efforts to have the case placed on the agenda, that venue was never granted to him. As he was finally returning to Germany in 1517, after three grueling years of pursuing the case in Rome, he allowed his lawyer, Johannes Host, to have the *Erroneous Assertions* printed. The articles show that Hoogstraeten was still arguing the technicalities of the case, vehemently asserting that the *Arguments* section of *Eye Glasses* should be excluded from consideration because those exculpatory notes were not really explanations but rather outright contradictions of Reuchlin's offending statements in the *Recommendation*.

Although Hoogstraeten framed the case above all as a debate on Christian theology and the ongoing efforts to eradicate Judaism, the conflict between scholasticism and humanism was gradually emerging as an issue for him too. One of his principal charges was simply that Reuchlin's scholarship was faulty; six of the nineteen articles in *Erroneous Assertions* attacked Reuchlin's interpretation of John 5:39.[120] On the surface, this might appear to be an ordinary disagreement, and that is precisely how Reuchlin's supporters sought to characterize it, but Hoogstraeten's subtext was to question the use of new biblical philology by humanists who lacked training in scholastic theology.

A new argument, moreover, was that Reuchlin's defense of the Talmud impugned papal authority because it ignored the papal condemnations of the Talmud from the thirteenth century. This history of papal opposition to the Talmud was a highly sensitive issue, especially since Leo would soon authorize Daniel Bomberg's publication of both the Babylonian and Palestinian Talmuds. Hoogstraeten, however, dropped his attack against the Jewish prayers. The claim that some were anti-Christian slanders—an allegation that had long been a source of acrimony between Christianity and Judaism—formed a major part of his case in the Mainz-Speyer trials. Possibly, he realized that the substance of these innuendos would appear weak, unlikely to make the desired impression on Roman jurors, several with some competence in Hebrew.

In addition to the *Erroneous Assertions* of 1517, the inquisitor issued a series of three substantial books against Reuchlin's position on Judaism and Jewish writings during the years 1518–19. Although he did not publish it until February 1518, Hoogstraeten wrote the *Apology*, a forceful articulation of his position, immediately upon his return to Cologne in 1517. The *Second Apology* was a thorough response to Neuenahr's publication of the *Letters of Three Illustrious Men*, a work that included the *New Defense*, an anonymous tract in support of Reuchlin that had been written in Rome in ca. 1516, most likely by someone on the Roman commission. Hoogstraeten's final publication in the Reuchlin Affair was his 1519 *Destruction of the Kabbalah*, an extensive work, also composed as a dialogue, that both rejected Reuchlin's Kabbalistic research (as published in the 1517 *Art of the Kabbalah*) and defended the methods of scholasticism.

The *Apology* was a new manifesto, written to counter a host of Reuchlinist books, specifically, Pirckheimer's *Apologetic Letter*, the anonymous *Letters of*

Obscure Men, and Neuenahr's *Defense of the Most Distinguished Man Johannes Reuchlin* (which featured Giorgio Benigno's dialogue). Hoogstraeten expressed horror over the irreligious mockery in *The Letters of Obscure Men*, in particular, a scornful squib against the Shrine of the Three Kings in Cologne, one of the most revered holy sites in all of Germany: "They do not shudder to say that the bodies of the Magi are farmers from Westphalia."[121] Raising a common objection to criticism from humanists (most of whom were professors of the arts faculty), Hoogstraeten scoffs several times at Pirckheimer's *Apologetic Letter* as the work of someone unqualified to address theological issues.[122] Pirckheimer's harsh rejection of theological method, especially his scorn for syllogistic (deductive) reasoning, elicited a spirited reply. In a later work, the *Destruction of the Kabbalah*, Hoogstraeten would assert more expansively that many elements of Christianity, including the primacy of the papacy, cannot be derived from the Bible without resorting to syllogistic logic. His basic point is that the humanist philological method is too narrow.[123]

Nevertheless, Hoogstraeten's main goal in the *Apology* is to strip the Talmud of any validity whatsoever—scholarly or religious—for both Jews and Christians and to prevail in the effort to destroy it. Therefore, he continues to use Reuchlin's notorious defense of Jewish writings as the point of departure for his attacks on Judaism.

According to Hoogstraeten, Jews in a Christian society are confined to a state of servitude (or slavery). In this regard, he goes well beyond the limitations that the "cameral servitude" of imperial law imposed on Jews. He asserts, with abundant evidence, that Jewish servitude is an explicit part of papal law and that it enjoys ubiquitous support in Christian theology, especially in the works of Thomas Aquinas, the Dominican "Doctor of the Church" who functions as Hoogstraeten's main authority on this issue.[124] Consequently, the church and the state have the fundamental authority to confiscate and destroy Jewish books: "But those perverse books—which are the exterior arms of their interior or their internal malignity and perfidy—are under the authority of the princes and the church."[125] Hoogstraeten also cites Aquinas to back the claim that "the Jews are the servants of the church. The church has the power to dispose the depraved books of the Jews."[126] Thus, it is abundantly clear that Hoogstraeten is not contemplating any retreat from the Dominican war against the Jews. He boldly claims that Reuchlin's failure to observe the "servitude" of the Jews and his unprecedented attempt to accord Jews the rights of "fellow citizens" are acts of extreme wickedness: "Wickedly you bend this to the favor of the Jews when you write that they are fellow citizens of the holy empire, whom canon law says are subject by the law to perpetual servitude and whom the sainted emperor Constantine (as administrator of this law) subjected to perpetual servitude."[127]

Once again, Hoogstraeten attempts to disqualify Reuchlin as a Bible exegete. In the *Apology*, the major issue remains Reuchlin's reading of John 5:39— "Search the Scriptures"—as a reference by Jesus to the Talmud. The heresy has ramifications, according to Hoogstraeten, that go well beyond a simple philological error. He stresses that Reuchlin is undermining the authority of papal law with his (faulty) biblical exegesis by pitting a commandment by Jesus to "search the Talmud" (according to Reuchlin) against the thirteenth-century papal laws to burn the Talmud. This, moreover, is impermissible favoring of the enslaved Jews. As Hoogstraeten writes on Reuchlin's reading of John 5:39, "What could Reuchlin have sung that was sweeter than this to the Jews or more vile to the papacy and Christianity?"[128] It strengthens Judaism and impugns the papal church. Because Reuchlin at one place expressed understanding for the inability of Jews to accept the divinity of Jesus (implying that the New Testament did not make Jesus' divinity as clear as did other texts), Hoogstraeten went so far as to characterize Reuchlin as Jewish—he even labels him the "archrabbi,"[129] on the grounds that he rejected Jesus' divinity: "what an insult to God, our savior, indeed, the greatest blasphemy."[130] Therefore, he alleges that Reuchlin was reviving the ancient heresy of Arianism: "For he said, alas, with his audacious mouth—in this he has been seen to have revived the Arian plague—that in the New Testament it is insufficiently and without evidence expressed that Jesus was the son of the extraordinarily blessed Mary, that he was the true God."[131]

Hoogstraeten departs in one fundamental way from the mainstream of the Dominican campaign against Judaism: he argues that Jewish writings will never help the mission. First of all, evoking Nicholas Donin's strategy, he insists that the Talmud constitutes a heretical perversion of Judaism, that it contains "many heresies against the law of Moses."[132] He cites Aquinas's commonplace objection that the Talmud alleges that God once sinned and needed to seek reconciliation (it is "a most wicked blasphemy"),[133] and more generally, also with references to Aquinas, concludes: "Also many things included in their teaching [i.e., the teachings of the Talmud] are false, erroneous, evil, and absurd, deeply repugnant not only to divine but also to natural law."[134] In fact, according to Hoogstraeten, Jesus even ordered the destruction of the Talmud, when he condemned the writings of the Pharisees: "The teachings of the Talmud arose from the sect of the scribes and Pharisees, and they were condemned by Christ and therefore they are truly heretical."[135] This novel argument is a pernicious reversal of Reuchlin's contention that Jesus had endorsed the study of the Talmud. Moreover, disputation on the basis of the Talmud will never be efficacious for the simple reason that the Talmud does not offer

Christian theology. It has more that is "against Christ than for him,"[136] for "the Talmud was published in order to resist our faith."[137]

While a basic lack of evidence makes it impossible to assess what impact Hoogstraeten's writings may have had in Rome, it is clear that he managed, under trying circumstances, to compose a truly comprehensive rebuttal to the Reuchlinists. Even though, as we will see in the next chapter, several political developments of 1519–20 would further erode Hoogstraeten's position, he had nonetheless delivered a rationale for condemning Reuchlin's *Eye Glasses* and resuming the offensive against Jewish books. He had vigorously responded to every Reuchlinist position. As a consequence, the situation remained volatile.

Erasmus's Response

In one respect, Hoogstraeten's *Destruction of the Kabbalah* had a result that must have gratified Reuchlin—it provoked Erasmus to end his four-year public silence on the controversy and rush two letters into print that expressed appreciation for Reuchlin's contributions to the humanities and castigated the fierceness of Hoogstraeten's prosecution. These letters, which were addressed to Cardinal Wolsey (composed 18 May 1519) and to Hoogstraeten himself (11 August 1519), appeared in print by the end of October 1519 in *A New Miscellany of Letters of Desiderius Erasmus of Rotterdam.*[138]

A specific reason for Erasmus's intervention is that Hoogstraeten had included in his *Destruction of the Kabbalah* an extensive harangue against some annotations in Erasmus's 1516 Bible. Although he did not mention Erasmus by name, Hoogstraeten pronounced Erasmus's defense of divorce, which he quoted verbatim, as heresy and appeared to be laying the groundwork for a legal action against the Greek Bible. This ominous development appeared to confirm what Erasmus had been privately contending all along, namely that a major motivation for the inquisition's prosecution of Reuchlin had been the hope of impeding the humanist Bible movement. Obviously, humanist biblical philology—and its heretical results—was the link Hoogstraeten was trying to forge between Erasmus and Reuchlin, but he also managed to connect Erasmus's Bible and Reuchlin's cause by condemning Erasmus's view of matrimony as an example of (humanist) "Judaizing." This expansion of Hoogstraeten's target was disturbing for, as Erasmus says, "heresy is a hateful word."[139]

Erasmus's reply is an excellent example of his ability to combine circumspection with withering criticism. He framed his letter as an attempt to assist Hoogstraeten—"it is your interests that I am trying to serve"[140]—but the theme of the letter is, unmistakably, a vindication of Reuchlin and an impeachment of Hoogstraeten's prosecution. In no uncertain terms, he states that Hoogstraeten should never have brought the case to begin with since Reuchlin's views pose no threat to Christian orthodoxy. His main goal is to defend humanism from any threat of heresy. Indeed, on the topic of humanism and Judaism, Erasmus wrote the following notorious words:

> Moreover, it behooved a man of sense like you to consider whether that piece of Reuchlin's [i.e., *Eye Glasses*] contained anything that might do serious harm to Christianity. But the only point of issue in it is that the Jews should not be unfairly treated. What was the object of such a vigorous campaign to make the Jews unpopular? Which of us does not sufficiently detest that sort of men? If to be a Christian is to hate Jews, then we are all thoroughly Christian here.[141]

Ultimately, Erasmus condemns Hoogstraeten for not embracing humanism as a valid contribution to theological study:

> You will find that you have done much, not only for the Dominican Order but also for the whole order of theologians, if you use your authority to suppress the brainless calumnies of some people...who pour out their poisonous attacks on knowledge of the ancient languages and the humanities, the fair name of which they blacken by prating of Antichrist and heresy and other histrionic stuff, though it is clear enough what the church owes to men skilled in those languages and in the art of writing. These studies do not obscure the dignity of theology, they set it in a clearer light; they are not its enemies but its servant.[142]

Erasmus may not have been a kindred spirit to Reuchlin but he was his colleague in the enterprise to harness the humanities as a source for theological renewal. As a gesture of respect, Erasmus personally sent Reuchlin the New Testament in Greek as soon as it came off Froben's presses,[143] also acknowledging the crucial role that Reuchlin's twelfth-century Greek manuscript had played in the preparation of the new biblical text, as well as Reuchlin's contributions to his other epochal work of 1516, the critical edition of St. Jerome.[144]

From the very outset of the trial in Rome, Erasmus expressed not so much concern for the Jews or the Christian exploitation of their writings as, rather, his dread that the controversy would undermine humanism and the Bible movement. In a bitter complaint to Neuenahr about *The Letters of Obscure Men*, Erasmus gave voice to this fear: "Why contrive such unpopularity for me?"[145] In fact, Erasmus wanted to distance himself from the substance of Reuchlin's controversy, the defense of Jewish writings, while identifying fully with the cause of the humanities as Reuchlin had come to embody it. In his famous letter to Albrecht of Brandenburg, elector-archbishop of Mainz, of 19 October 1519, Erasmus wrote: "And what do I have in common with Reuchlin or Luther? But they [i.e., the opponents of Reuchlin and Luther] have cunningly confused all these things in order to lay on all those who embrace the humanities a load of ill will which all share."[146]

Soon, however, after the dust of the early Reformation movement had settled with the papal condemnation of Luther in June 1520, Erasmus would move Reuchlin out of the Luther ledger and place him in his own. On 8 November 1520, Erasmus sent an unusually gracious letter to Reuchlin in which he composed the same theme, but with a significantly revised melody: "It has always been my aim to separate the question of Luther from your cause, which is also the cause of the humanities, because the confusion exposed us equally to the risk of sharing his [i.e., Luther's] unpopularity."[147] This position, however self-serving it may appear for November 1520, indicates clearly that Erasmus feared only for the humanities when he contemplated the Reuchlin Affair.

Erasmus's final analysis of the Reuchlin affair, with its combination of linkage to, and differentiation from, the Luther Affair, also brings us to the subject of the following chapter.

9

The Luther Affair

You may think that there is now so much to handle with Martin Luther that you will be forgotten. Reuchlin, I'm telling you—and believe it—you will never be forgotten.

—Johannes Pfefferkorn, 1521

As we have seen, the mere absence of a definitive papal ruling was provocative for both sides. At least as many polemics were published after the 1516 papal mandate of supersedure (setting aside the Roman commission's vindication of Reuchlin) as during the previous five years of bitter controversy. In addition to those impassioned debates, the final four years of conflict were also marked by rising turmoil in European politics, including several crises that impacted the outcome of the trial. Among them were a sordid attempt to assassinate Pope Leo X in 1517, the invasion and collapse of Reuchlin's homeland, the Duchy of Württemberg in 1519, the death of Emperor Maximilian, followed by the contentious election of his successor, Charles V, in 1519, and, above all, the sudden transformation of the reform movement, soon to be known as the Protestant Reformation, into a widespread political rebellion. The increased instability in the Holy Roman Empire also inflicted great harm on German Jewry. In February 1519, during the interregnum following Maximilian's death, the Jewish community of Regensburg was expelled from the city in a brazenly illicit act of hatred.

In retrospect, Leo X's failure to conclude the Reuchlin Affair decisively in summer 1516 looks like a political miscalculation, for it left the German academic world in a state of high agitation precisely at the moment another professor, Martin Luther, challenged the church's magisterium. Despite the fervid production of pamphlets on the controversy, the period from July 1516 until November 1518 witnessed no detectable activity on the task of adjudicating the inquisitor's appeal to Rome.[1] To their credit, even if they indulged themselves in harsh attacks, Reuchlin and Hoogstraeten did continue to focus their publications on the substantive issues of Jewish studies, Jewish legal rights, and the controversy between humanism and scholasticism. But why had the case stalled in the curia? Evidently, resolution of the Reuchlin trial was not an appealing prospect since a decision either way was certain to inflame resentment among ecclesiastical power brokers, and each side had advocates at the highest echelons of authority.

Leo X faced several political and military crises from 1516 through 1518 as well. One distraction was the discovery in April 1517 of a lurid plot: a conspiracy of cardinals, under the leadership of Alfonso Petrucci, to murder the pope. In the aftermath, Leo drastically reorganized the College of Cardinals, appointing some thirty-one new members, an action that both doubled the size of the college and also diminished the power of individual members. While the enlargement of the college was not motivated in any way by Reuchlin's case, it nonetheless created some serious disadvantages. For one, it marked the elevation to the purple for Tommaso Cajetan, the prior general of the Dominican Order and a fierce opponent of Reuchlin. Cajetan, who soon became famous as the ardent foe of Luther, would also play a leading role in the final hearing of Reuchlin's case. A cardinal's hat was also bestowed on Adrian of Utrecht, mentor of the soon-to-be Charles V and the prelate who would succeed Leo X as Adrian VI in 1521. Adrian, who in 1517 was already inquisitor general of Aragon and thus a successor to the infamous Tomás de Torquemada, was a determined agitator against Reuchlin—he had not only urged Leo to condemn Reuchlin's *Eye Glasses*, but had also arranged for Charles, then king of Spain and duke of Burgundy, to do the same.[2] Upon becoming cardinal, Adrian encouraged his fellow inquisitor Hoogstraeten to persevere at all costs in the increasingly unpopular struggle against Reuchlin, which Adrian portrayed as a noble stand for orthodoxy. Hoogstraeten published his unqualified endorsement as part of the introduction to his *Second Apology* (1519),[3] another list of carefully argued charges against Reuchlin.

As 1518 was drawing to a close, Reuchlin began betraying signs of discouragement over the lack of progress on the ground in Rome. Chaffing under the heavy psychological burden created by prolonged inaction, he wrote a pessimistic letter to the papal secretary Jacob Questenberg, his friend of some thirty years, lamenting that time had become his worst enemy. He feared that various incidental developments were depleting the ranks of his supporters at the curia while, to his unbearable frustration, the case was still hanging in the balance.[4] Philip Beroaldus, the Vatican librarian who had spoken so eloquently on Reuchlin's behalf to Leo, died on 30 August 1518. More inopportune were the departures of cardinals Domenico Grimani, Giles of Viterbo, and Adriano Castellesi, all prominent members of the Roman commission that had exonerated him and all scholars committed to the advancement of Hebrew studies. Castellesi had been forced into exile for an allegedly minor role in the Petrucci plot, a turn of events that did not deter Reuchlin from dedicating Accents and Orthography of the Hebrew Language to him in 1518. Johann von der Wyck, one of Reuchlin's lawyers at Rome, had fallen ill. Martin Gröning, the translator of the Eye Glasses into Latin for the Roman trial, had also left the city. Johannes Potken (another pioneer in Semitic languages, still remembered as editor of the first Ethiopic imprint, a 1515 printing of the Psalms) and Count Hermann von Neuenahr had returned to Cologne. Neuenahr, a canon in the cathedral chapter at Cologne, had been one of the most dedicated Reuchlinists in Rome. Although Reuchlin regretted the loss of Neuenahr's voice resonating in the Vatican, the count took the fight against the Dominicans and Hoogstraeten to their home base of Cologne.

As far as we can tell (the surviving records are somewhat sparse), Reuchlin persisted in pursuing his case energetically through his Roman connections in 1518. He composed a set of letters to Questenberg, Achilles de Crassis, Pietro Anconitano, Lorenzo Pucci, and Domenico de Giacobazzi, all cardinals except Questenberg, pleading for support and pressing for resolution. Reuchlin suspected that the appointment of Giacobazzi as a replacement judge for the retired Grimani was the machination of his enemies.[5] Nonetheless, he dispatched a most cordial letter to him feigning pleasure over his involvement and also enclosing a copy of the Acts of the Trials, an account of the trial, written in a factual tone, but highly favorable to his side.[6] Reuchlin had become so distressed that in May 1518 he aired his doubts about Leo X in a letter to Elector Friedrich the Wise of Saxony: "It is of no help to me that the emperor, elector-princes, princes, bishops, abbots, and cities have asked the pope that his Holiness quickly permit a decision in my favor. I pray to God that he grant us grace and that we subjects become worthy of better leaders."[7] By February 1519, Reuchlin told Questenberg: "Rather many of our supporters have begun to lose faith in Leo, and suspect that he is not the man that all the lovers of the humanities once thought he would be."[8]

A German Resolution

If the situation in Rome now appeared disconcertingly opaque, support for Reuchlin within Germany was growing steadily, reaching its highest levels ever by 1520. The inquisition's standing in Germany, despite the propaganda published by Hoogstraeten, Ortwin Gratius, and Pfefferkorn, had plunged to its nadir by 1519, so low that the German Dominicans appear to have contemplated forcing Hoogstraeten into a form of early retirement. The decisions of the Speyer court and the Roman commission inspired Reuchlin's supporters to adopt a triumphant tone, raising hopes that the controversy would end with a vindication of humanism.

The exuberant satire of *The Letters of Obscure Men* formulated the equation that a Reuchlin victory would amount to a conviction of scholastic theology on charges of intellectual irrelevance if not vacuity. So damaging was the impact of *The Letters of Obscure Men* that Gratius and Pfefferkorn had to devote major publications to rebuttals, but to little avail.[9] The University of Cologne's prestige had been tarnished so badly that enrollments plummeted to pitifully low levels by the early 1520s (while matriculations at Luther's University of Wittenberg were soaring).[10] New editions with additional material attacking the Dominicans and other supporters of Hoogstraeten continued to appear throughout 1516 and 1517. The third edition, published anonymously in summer 1516, had new letters by the gifted lampoonist Ulrich von Hutten and the fourth edition featured a new book of attacks, most of which were written by Hutten as well (all printed anonymously). The entire European world of letters took immense delight in the works, as Thomas More wrote to Erasmus: "It is rewarding to see how everyone loves *The Letters of Obscure Men*."[11] This brilliant literary success was also politically potent—to be a German humanist after 1516 meant to be a Reuchlin partisan. The ranks of rebel academic power only swelled when Hoogstraeten began threatening Erasmus's humanist Bible of 1516 with an inquisition trial, ostensibly because of Erasmus's notes on matrimony, but certainly also because of his many objections to scholastic theology.

Swaggering with confidence (despite Reuchlin's doubts), the Reuchlinist camp all but destroyed Hoogstraeten in a series of publications and actions between 1517 and 1520. Reuchlin himself issued a number of works on his own behalf, in many cases choosing to publish scholarship to promote his methodology rather than resorting to the rough attacks of earlier years (as in his vitriolic but tactically unwise *Defense against the Cologne Calumniators* of 1513). Most significant among his publications were the masterful *Art of the*

Kabbalah (1517) and *Accents and Orthography of Hebrew* (1518), two substantial works of scholarship that featured occasional, brief but effective, references to the Roman case. Similarly, Thomas Anshelm anonymously published *Acts of the Trials* in 1518, a work of basic importance for any reconstruction of the case for it provides not only an account of the various trials but also prints official trial documents that otherwise would have disappeared. *Acts of the Trials* portrays Hoogstraeten's legal efforts as a failure and concludes with the inquisitor's ignominious exodus from Rome. Perhaps the most impressive propaganda that Reuchlin issued was the second edition of *The Letters of Illustrious Men* (1519), a literary monument that celebrates the enthusiastic support Reuchlin had garnered from humanist luminaries, such figures as Giles of Viterbo, Willibald Pirckheimer, Luther, and Erasmus. Even Leo X makes a cameo appearance in *The Letters of Illustrious Men* as a Reuchlin partisan. After all, despite his susceptibility to the political pressures of the inquisition's supporters, Leo probably did agree with Reuchlin on issues of substance. In 1520, he authorized Daniel Bomberg to print the entire Babylonian Talmud with a papal imprimatur, in a significant way the ultimate vindication of what Reuchlin represented.[12]

By 1519 (as we saw in chapter 8), the three most prominent humanists in the Holy Roman Empire, aside from Reuchlin, had published works against the inquisition's case: Hutten, Pirckheimer, and Erasmus. Moreover, Neuenahr energized a large cell of Reuchlinists in Hoogstraeten's backyard of Cologne. Although unquestionably a fervid supporter of Reuchlin, Neuenahr was also determined to break the hegemony of scholastic theology, a goal he pursued vigorously in 1524 and 1525 when serving as chancellor of the University of Cologne. A relative and advisor of Hermann von Wied, the archbishop and prince elector of Cologne, Neuenahr had access to the highest levels of power in the empire. His circle of devoted Reuchlinists in Cologne included Johannes Caesarius, Gröning, Hermann Busch, and Hutten. In 1517, Neuenahr published in Cologne Giorgio Benigno's *Defense of Reuchlin*, the work that provoked Hoogstraeten to answer with his first book against the new concept of Christian Kabbalah. In May 1518, Neuenahr edited the caustically polemical *Letters of Three Men*.[13]

Neuenahr's campaign for Reuchlin reached its apogee with his activism at the Diet of Frankfurt (June 1519), where he served as Archbishop Hermann von Wied's plenipotentiary. He delivered two forceful speeches in support of Charles that were immediately published in Cologne in a volume titled *Vivat Rex Carolus* (*Long Live Charles, King of the Romans*). In the second of those speeches, Neuenahr proclaimed that of all the Germans celebrating Charles's election none were more fervent than the humanists. Neuenahr's theme was that humanist reform of education would usher in a new golden age, a goal that Charles's grandfather Maximilian had already been pursuing with his patronage of the new learning. The great opponents of culture in Germany were the scholastic professors (the "theologistae") and the Dominicans (the "fraterculi").[14] The lightning rod for his fulminations was Hoogstraeten, whom he named in bold print in the speech. Probably in an oblique reference to Luther as well as Reuchlin, Neuenahr said, "The one and only plague in Germany, believe me, is Jacob Hoogstraeten."[15] If his inquisition could be stopped and if he could be silenced, learned men would rejoice. Neuenahr promised Charles that if the emperor supported humanism against Hoogstraeten's inquisition, as Maximilian had, "soon you will see Athens reborn in Germany."[16]

There is no record of the emperor's reaction to Neuenahr's call to action against Hoogstraeten. It is, however, entirely possible that the powerful imperial knight Franz von Sickingen was responding to this call when he prepared in July 1519 literally to take up arms to settle the Reuchlin Affair once and for all. By this date, many people, including Sickingen and Hutten, had begun to associate the young Luther with Reuchlin's battle against the Dominican inquisition.

Sickingen was one of the most feared military figures of the time. He was an imperial knight with substantial holdings in the Palatinate and Alsace, which he had expanded through various military adventures, some of which were endorsed and others condemned by imperial authorities. In 1519, he enhanced his political standing in the empire by contributing needed support to the Swabian League's intervention against Duke Ulrich of Württemberg. Before his death in 1523 (in military campaign), Sickingen would also take up arms as a supporter of the Luther movement. He forcibly installed Lutheran clergy, led the highly disruptive Revolt of the Imperial Knights (1522), and even attempted, though unsuccessfully, to occupy and secularize the ancient electoral archbishopric of Trier under a banner of reform.

The Swabian League's invasion of Württemberg in 1519 inflicted grinding hardship on Reuchlin as he endured three occupations of Stuttgart, the collapse of law and order, and ultimately another voluntary exile. The military occupation was a rapid response to Duke Ulrich von Württemberg's illegal seizure of the free imperial city of Reutlingen in February 1519. Having already condemned Duke Ulrich for the brutal murder of Hans von Hutten (in May 1515), a cousin of Ulrich von Hutten, the league had no more patience for his tyranny. Fortuitously, however, the invasion brought Reuchlin into personal contact with Sickingen, who not only embraced Hutten's position on the Reuchlin-Hoogstraeten controversy but also felt a filial obligation as a former student, so he claimed, of the aging scholar.[17] Sickingen and Hutten, who were among the military leaders of the first occupation of Stuttgart on 7 April 1519, were able to take special precautions that no harm would befall Reuchlin or his property. Despite further protection from the two leaders, on 9 November Reuchlin fled the misery of Stuttgart to assume a professorship at the University of Ingolstadt in Bavaria. On 8 November, Reuchlin wrote to Pirckheimer:

> In the midst of horrors I stand, diligently thinking how I could devote myself to philosophy with more tranquility. Plague rules here, as does the vengeance of the victors, envy, oppression of good men, extortion. First there was famine then came the sword, and pestilence comes at last. And the worst problem is that nearly our entire country is struggling because of factions. Since there are more people being crushed by debt and poverty than who are wealthy, the commoners are eager to steal and to seize the property of the wealthy. They have lost their leader, endowed with the same sort of mind. Therefore they are planning how they might recover their prince of thieves [i.e., the deposed Duke Ulrich].[18]

In the meantime, on 26 July 1519, Sickingen published a pamphlet, *The Demand and Announcement to and against the Provincial, Priors and Convents of the Order of the Preachers in Germany, and Especially Friar Jacob von Hoogstraeten on Account of and in the Name of the Highly Learned and Famous Johannes Reuchlin,*[19] in which he announced his determination to enforce the Speyer verdict against the entire Dominican Order in Germany. The pamphlet demanded that all parties cease and desist from publishing any further books harmful to Reuchlin's reputation and that the Dominican Order pay Reuchlin the settlement of 111 florins mandated by the Speyer verdict.

Suddenly facing the urgent prospect of armed intervention from a man not known to bluff, the Dominicans immediately sought appeasement. On 26 December 1519, the prior general of the province of Teutonia, Eberhard of Cleves, met with Sickingen to assure him that the Dominican Order would no longer tolerate any harassment of Reuchlin, and that it would impose silence on Hoogstraeten and dispatch representatives to Reuchlin to negotiate a permanent settlement. Within weeks (by 18 January 1520), two representatives of the order, including the humanist friar Michael Vehe, met with Reuchlin, then a professor at the University of Ingolstadt, to offer terms. Reuchlin, who now had complete confidence in his champion, referred them to Sickingen directly for working out all the details.[20]

Before those negotiations could occur, Reuchlin and Sickingen became aware of a most unfavorable turn of events in Rome. Apparently, during the first weeks of January 1520, adversaries at the curia attempted to have the Speyer verdict declared null and void. Although the scant surviving records indicate little concerning the cause or the ramifications of this development, we have to assume that this new direction for Reuchlin's case was a consequence of Rome's decision to take a hardline position against the general ecclesiastical crisis engulfing Germany. Reuchlin himself saw this as a reaction to reports of the pressures Sickingen was applying to the German Dominicans.[21] It is also known that on 29 March 1520, Cardinal Adrian of Utrecht had written to the University of Cologne from Aragon, where he was inquisitor general, to pledge his commitment to stopping the Roman curia from approving any agreement that Sickingen could coerce from the Dominicans. He also claimed that he would arrange for Charles V to block Sickingen's plan.[22]

This complication notwithstanding, Sickingen and the German Dominicans were still determined to settle the matter on their own terms. An excellent opportunity for negotiations presented itself in the annual chapter assembly of the Dominican Order of Teutonia, which convened in Frankfurt on 6 May 1520. By 10 May, Eberhard of Cleves and Sickingen had hammered out an agreement,[23] based on the decisions of a panel of arbitrators they had appointed. The arbitrators were highly respected churchmen, but unquestionably predisposed to favor Reuchlin. One of them, Philipp von Flersheim, not only had served as a juror in the Speyer decision but also was Franz von Sickingen's brother-in-law. The other two arbiters, Johannes Wacker (Joannes Vigilius) and Simon Ribysen, were friends of Reuchlin as well.[24] The agreement exonerated Reuchlin, awarded him the III florins in court costs, and ordered all parties to desist from pursuing the conflict ever again. Although the formal agreement also declared that the matter was being settled without detriment to the reputation of either litigant, it was a harsh verdict against Hoogstraeten. It characterizes his appeal as frivolous and states that the resolution is necessary to restore the honor of the Dominican Order. Moreover, the Dominican Order agreed to withhold any form of assistance if Hoogstraeten pursued the case further. Eberhard of Cleves was required to petition Leo X immediately for ratification of the settlement; the agreement indicates that Ludwig, prince-elector of the Palatinate, would do the same. A roster of dignitaries of the Dominican chapter of Teutonia signed the document.

Eberhard of Cleves wrote to Leo X that very day to urge ratification of the settlement. According to his petition, the heresy trial against Reuchlin's *Eye Glasses* had tarnished the reputation of the German Dominicans, who had become objects of loathing and ridicule, and now the order's prestige could only be restored if this unpopular controversy were put to rest. Moreover, Eberhard attempted to distance the provincial chapter from Hoogstraeten by claiming that the case had been prosecuted entirely on Hoogstraeten's initiative and without the assistance or consent of the order as a whole. As for Reuchlin, Eberhard wrote that his "erudition, the honesty of his life, and the sincerity of his faith" [25] warrant this outcome and informed Leo that the entire provincial chapter had approved the settlement.[26] Eberhard, moreover, arranged for no fewer than five lawyers to work on his behalf in Rome to ensure papal confirmation.[27] On 20 May 1520, Elector Ludwig of the Palatinate wrote to Leo, also urging acceptance of the 10 May agreement.[28]

The Dominicans now turned against Hoogstraeten. He was stripped of his two offices as prior of the Cologne Dominican convent and as inquisitor general of the province of Teutonia.[29] Given all these developments, Reuchlin felt confident that the matter had finally been laid to rest and to his complete satisfaction. On 11 May 1520, he wrote to Questenberg at the Vatican, requesting that his friend supervise the formulation of all the curial documents that would enact this settlement and to be on the watch lest any statement creep into one that could be construed in any way as a criticism of his research or the positions he expressed in *Eye Glasses.*[30]

The Verdict

But no such documents were ever drawn up.

On 23 June 1520, just eight days after signing *Exsurge Domine*, the thundering condemnation of Luther,[31] Leo X issued a verdict against Reuchlin. He also ordered the German Dominicans to restore Hoogstraeten to his offices as prior of the Cologne convent and as papal inquisitor of the province of Teutonia.[32] The original version of the papal condemnation of Reuchlin does not seem to have survived, though its contents are indirectly quoted in several documents, including the minutes of a meeting of the faculty of theology at the University of Cologne. Those minutes record the reading of the papal decision in Cologne on 23 July 1520 as follows:

> The named book, *Eye Glasses*, was and is scandalous and offensive
> to the pious ears of Christians and is excessively favorable to the
> impious Jews and moreover it must be removed from circulation
> and from the hands of Christians and its use must be inhibited,
> etc., along with the imposition of perpetual silence on the same
> Johannes [Reuchlin] and a sentence laid on that same man [to pay]
> the expenses incurred in the same trial both in these parts and
> at the Roman curia, and that by the same decision the doctrinal

condemnation of the same book, *Eye Glasses*, by the theological faculty of our university stands as being justified, approved, and confirmed.[33]

The University of Cologne also received a letter from Cardinal Cajetan commending the faculty of theology for its unwavering opposition to both Luther and Reuchlin. This letter suggests that it had been Cajetan who urged papal action on the Reuchlin case immediately following the condemnation of Luther on 15 June 1520. Although Reuchlin felt no inclination to endorse Luther's movement, he was well aware that Luther's revolt created a new perspective for assessing the aggressive Reuchlinist attacks against the Dominican Order. At least since 1519, Hoogstraeten and his partisans had been arguing loudly that the papacy's indecision on the Reuchlin case had emboldened Luther and his adherents to even greater disobedience to the church.[34] In April 1521, at the beginning of the Diet of Worms, Pfefferkorn wrote: "Yes, Reuchlin, if the Pope had done this to you eight years ago, Martin Luther and your disciples of the *Obscure Men* would not have dared to wish or contemplate what they are now publicly pursuing to the detriment of the Christian faith. Of all this, you alone are the spark and the enabler, to drive the holy church into error and superstition."[35] As if to make this point, an anonymous pamphlet appeared in 1521 ridiculing the Dominican Order and Hoogstraeten for the persecution of both Reuchlin and Luther.[36] The title page woodcut, which features Reuchlin, Luther, and Hutten as "patrons of liberty," may be the only authentic likeness of Reuchlin that has survived (see Figure 9.1).[37]

Reuchlin never acknowledged a direct connection between his case and Luther's. According to his longest account, which appeared in an unpublished letter to Elector Friedrich of Saxony, it was Hoogstraeten's skulduggery that turned things around:

> The said friar Jacob is, however, duplicitous and broke his vow to his order and superiors and disregarded his obligation to obedience and during the absence of my procurators and lawyers in Rome during the time of recess, when customarily no courts are convened, he produced a decision from Rome, as often happens there, that everything was null and void that had been decided before by my gracious Lord of Speyer and that my pamphlet and *Recommendation*, given to his imperial majesty, should be voided, suppressed, and forbidden to be read, for which they dared to present no other reason than that it was a nuisance and favorable to the Jews and they dropped the charges of heresy and heterodoxy.[38]

FIGURE 9.1. Title page woodcut showing, on the left, Johannes Reuchlin, Ulrich von Hutten, and Martin Luther as "Patrons of Liberty" against members of the Dominican and Franciscan orders in the center, including Jacob Hoogstraeten. From Thomas Murner, *History of the Four Heretics of the Dominican Order* (Strasbourg, 1521). Bayerische Staatsbibliothek München, Res/4 P.o.germ. 145 ap, fol. 1r.

Since Hoogstraeten was not even in Rome at this time, Reuchlin was clearly ignoring one certain reason for the reversal, the growing force of a conservative backlash in the curia.

The purpose of the letter to Elector Friedrich is important. Reuchlin was soliciting his support for an effort to persuade Charles V to hear an appeal of the papal decision, an extraordinary legal gambit that, as far as we can tell, was unsuccessful. As early as November 1520, it was known that Reuchlin was planning to pursue the case further, as Hutten explained in an enthusiastic letter

to Martin Bucer: "Reuchlin has appealed, which Franz [Sickingen] is supporting in every possible way."[39] Ludwig Geiger, aware of this passage, caustically
commented "to whom?"[40] The surprising answer lies in the letter to Friedrich
of Saxony, where Reuchlin tries to persuade the elector to endorse the legality
of such an appeal. His legal rationale is that since the curia dropped charges
of heresy (an assertion that is debatable) the other matters on which the curia
ruled—that is, that the book was a scandal and favorable to the Jews—are
within the competence of a civil court and therefore appropriate for imperial
adjudication: "I am of the opinion, insofar as I am a layman and not under
holy orders and the affair does not touch on questions of the faith but as their
judgment says only scandal, nuisance, and favor to Jewry, therefore this affair,
as a secular and not a religious one, belongs to the competence of the Roman
emperor."[41] But, unlike Luther, Reuchlin would not get a hearing at the Diet of
Worms (nor would he be condemned there).

Remarkably, at the conclusion of an extensive pamphlet of 1521, *An
Impassioned Protest*, Pfefferkorn challenged Reuchlin to a debate at the Diet
of Worms. Pfefferkorn was well aware of Reuchlin's appeal to Charles V (he
mockingly referred to it as commuting death by hanging to death on the
wheel[42]) and cleverly embraced it after a fashion. Pfefferkorn now called for an
imperial trial against Reuchlin on charges of libel and blasphemy, obviously
evoking the strategy for dealing with Luther, who after his final papal condemnation (3 January 1521) was then awaiting trial on capital charges to take place
in the emperor's presence at the Diet of Worms (April 1521).

To this end, Pfefferkorn composed yet another comprehensive review
of Reuchlin's *Eye Glasses* but now with the new purpose of persuading civil
authorities to burn Reuchlin—the man in addition to his book—at the stake.
As Pfefferkorn states at the beginning of the tract, Reuchlin deserves death
because he is "a blasphemer of the holy church, a counterfeiter of Holy Scripture,
a murderer of souls, a swindler and a seducer of the Christian people, a traitor of
the Roman imperial throne, a traitor to me, and an advocate and patron for the
perfidious Jews."[43] After the lengthy rebuttal of *Eye Glasses*, Pfefferkorn dramatically listed eighteen authorities that had already condemned Reuchlin, beginning with Gregor Reisch's initial 1510 condemnation of the *Recommendation* to
Emperor Maximilian, including Maximilian, Charles (at the time of his intervention, duke of Burgundy), the universities of Cologne, Erfurt, Mainz, Louvain,
and Paris,[44] and concluding with the king of France, Francis I, and Pope Leo X.[45]
All that remained to be accomplished was a final conviction by imperial authority, followed by the execution of Reuchlin, a prospect gruesomely depicted on
the last page of the book, where Reuchlin's body is quartered and displayed on
four posts with a copy of *Eye Glasses* on the ground (see Figure 9.2).[46] In a most

FIGURE 9.2. Woodcut illustration from Johannes Pfefferkorn, *An Impassioned Protest* (Cologne, 1521), final leaf, depicting Pfefferkorn and the execution of Johannes Reuchlin. A copy of Reuchlin's *Eye Glasses*, now officially condemned by Pope Leo X, lies on the ground. Bayerische Staatsbibliothek München, Res/4 Polem. 2328 p, fol. [H6ʳ].

unseemly turn of phrase, Pfefferkorn gleefully anticipated Reuchlin's burning at the stake: "I can smell the bratwurst."[47]

The pamphlet is yet another example of the effectiveness of Pfefferkorn's printed propaganda—it is caustic and pungent, but also offers a clear argument, supported with copious evidence, for the condemnation of Reuchlin. Some of the charges, to be sure, fall flat: Reuchlin had accepted Jewish bribes and his expertise in Hebrew was elementary, as Pfefferkorn puts it, "childish."[48] But Pfefferkorn undertook an extensive review of the specific charges

of blasphemy in the Jewish books and accused Reuchlin of knowingly allowing the Jews to continue in their godlessness, making him complicit in their
crimes. With copious direct quotations, he effectively proved his accusation
that Reuchlin's *German Epistle: Why the Jews Have Been in Exile So Long* (1505)
and *Recommendation* were blatantly contradictory,[49] with the former accusing
the Jews of deicide and blasphemy and the latter offering a sweeping vindication of Jewish books and customs, an incongruity that Pfefferkorn scornfully
depicts in a crude woodcut showing Reuchlin with a forked tongue.[50]

The attack on Reuchlin is as severe as one could imagine but we should
also notice that Judaism continuously suffers collateral damage. Pfefferkorn is
still hoping to restart the anti-Jewish campaign. In order to restoke Christian
animosity, Pfefferkorn rehearses all of his familiar innuendos, dwelling in particular on Jewish hatred of Christians and the use of prayers that blaspheme
Jesus and the Virgin Mary (especially the old charge that the *'Amidah* includes
prayers for the demise of Christianity). He repeats the dangerous accusation
that Jews should be treated as heretics since they rely on the Talmud, a perversion of biblical Judaism. We also encounter the poisonous accusations that
Jews murder Christian children for their rituals and torment the consecrated
host as a reenactment of their deicide.[51]

In response to a rhetorical question—"Pfefferkorn, tell us the reason, what
did you write concerning the Jews that so outraged Reuchlin and made him
work against you so feverishly?"[52]—Pfefferkorn enumerated six proposals that
were at the heart of his campaign to eradicate German Jewry:[53]

1. Jews must not be allowed to charge interest.
2. They must be required to attend Christian sermons.
3. "All their blasphemous books should be taken away and suppressed,
   as Emperor Maximilian of blessed memory ordered."[54]
4. Jews must be restricted to "menial labor to stave off starvation."[55]
5. Jews are "heretics . . . for they observe neither the Old nor the New
   Testament, neither one, nor the other, and, moreover, they are not
   much concerned about their messiah, whether or not he will arrive or
   has arrived because money and wealth are their only God and faith."[56]
6. The major synagogues of the German Jews, those in Regensburg,
   Frankfurt, and Worms, must be destroyed to promote conversion:
   "thus they [i.e., Jews] would soon disappear on their own and they
   would profess the Christian faith."[57]

From this perspective, Pfefferkorn launched a direct appeal to German magistrates to destroy the synagogues (and thereby the Jewish communities) of
Frankfurt and Worms. According to Pfefferkorn, "God heard my prayer with

the synagogue at Regensburg," which "pious Christians" have in the meantime razed, a reference to the sudden destruction of Jewish Regensburg in
February 1519.[58] Now, at the conclusion of the pamphlet, just before he issued
the final challenge to debate Reuchlin at the Diet of Worms, Pfefferkorn calls
on the city councils of Frankfurt and Worms to expel their Jewish communities, which constitute the only "Ertz Sinagogen" (arch-synagogues) remaining
in the empire, in order to weaken German Jewry fatally: "The Regensburger
have taken care of it in short order. Lords of Worms and Frankfurt, thus you
should also deal with the Jews—raze, level, knock and tear down their devilish
synagogues and erect a chapel or a convent in honor of our beloved Lady, as
other imperial cities have done in this situation."[59] He expressed confidence
as well that Charles V will endorse the banishment.[60] Of course, we cannot
measure the impact of this tract, but it was prepared for circulation at the
Diet of Worms, where, in fact, Jewish efforts to reestablish the community of
Regensburg were definitively quashed by the emperor and the estates.[61]

Despite requests from both Reuchlin and Pfefferkorn, an appeal, or new
trial, was not heard at the Diet of Worms. Moreover, in the aftermath of Luther's
"Here I Stand," everyone's attention was riveted on the vastly larger crisis, and
many who had opposed the inquisition of Reuchlin now attacked the church's
condemnation of Luther and his reforms. As of 1521, Hoogstraeten, still an
energetic papal inquisitor, began publishing tracts against Luther, never again
returning to the anti-Jewish campaign or the Reuchlin trials that had consumed a full decade of his life. Only in this one respect were Pfefferkorn's
taunting words, quoted as the epigraph to this chapter, mistaken.

Reuchlin and Luther

The national memorial to the Protestant Reformation in Germany, Ernst
Rietschel's complex *Luther Monument* (1868) in Worms, casts Johannes
Reuchlin in life-size bronze, across from Philipp Melanchthon and grouped
with Friedrich of Saxony and Philipp of Hesse, as one of four patrons of the
Reformation (see Figure 9.3). Reuchlin was elevated to this high honor after having been slated initially for a place among four precursors of the Reformation,
Peter Waldes, John Wycliffe, Jan Hus, and Girolamo Savonarola. It is somewhat
ironic that Savonarola was assigned Reuchlin's original place, for Reuchlin
cited the execution of the Dominican Savonarola for flouting papal authority as an admonitory precedent for the recalcitrant Hoogstraeten (who kept
on publishing tracts against Reuchlin in violation of a papal gag order).[62] But
Reuchlin's inclusion among Luther's leading patrons is more than ironic; it is

FIGURE 9.3. Ernst Rietschel, *Johannes Reuchlin* (1868), statue in bronze for the *Luther Monument*, in Worms, Germany.

hard to resist calling it a brazen distortion of history, even if it misrepresents history in a way that Luther himself initially fostered.

By pairing Reuchlin and Melanchthon (and removing Reuchlin from the group of medieval heretics), Rietschel portrayed biblical philology as a foundation for Luther's revolution, rather than suggesting that the church's condemnation of Reuchlin prefigured its reaction to the reformer's theology. Although the historical fact of Reuchlin's rejection of Protestantism remains an embarrassment for the monument, the connection it forges between Luther's movement and humanism is historically meaningful, for his success was partly dependent on the foregoing innovations of Erasmus and Reuchlin. Luther, after all, found himself teaching at a university that by 1516 was already experiencing the curricular success of biblical philology and plunging enrollments in courses on scholastic theology, a shift that had everything to do with the achievements of Erasmus and Reuchlin and, at that date, little to do with his own.[63] It is unlikely that Luther could have conceptualized his *Against Scholastic Theology*, the most important prelude to the *Ninety-five Theses*, if Erasmus and Reuchlin's supporters had not impugned scholasticism so vehemently. Thus, his claim, in the *Ninety-five Theses*, that "all of Aristotle is to Christianity as darkness is to light" would have sounded polemical but hardly revolutionary in a Wittenberg classroom. It was a compelling formulation, but Reuchlin and Erasmus had nurtured a generation of students eager to applaud it; they created an academic culture primed for theological controversy and turmoil before Luther's career ignited.[64] Yet Erasmus and Reuchlin remained steadfastly Catholic, a reminder that humanism should not be construed as a factor in an equation that leads to the Reformation as its only possible solution.

As the Reuchlin Affair waned, Reuchlin's enemies turned their sights on the new threat. The Dominican Order, and the universities of Paris, Louvain, and Cologne, all of which had censured Reuchlin's *Eye Glasses*, now rapidly attacked Luther. Cajetan, Adrian of Utrecht, and Hoogstraeten were among the early advocates of cracking down hard on Luther. Similarly, Reuchlin's humanist partisans tended overwhelmingly to hear Luther's manifestos with receptive ears. It surely helped the young Luther that Reuchlin had already attracted support from such important Saxons as Elector Friedrich the Wise and his Privy Councilor Georg Spalatin. Many humanist acolytes of Reuchlin—such as Willibald Pirckheimer, Hermann Busch, Eobanus Hessus, Conrad Pellican, Nicholas Gerbellius, Johannes Cellarius, Wolfgang Capito, Sebastian Münster, Martin Bucer, Johannes Oecolampadius, Philipp Melanchthon, and Ulrich von Hutten—were among Luther's early promoters. Above all, Ulrich von Hutten and Franz von Sickingen immediately cast Luther's case as a German political-cultural campaign against Rome. Sickingen even mustered an army in an early effort to break the power of the Roman church by force (so violently that Luther had to repudiate him). Although he would ultimately remain Catholic, Pirckheimer was at first a "good Lutheran" and, after the Leipzig Debate, published *Eccius Dedolatus*, a hilarious but brutal character assassination of Johannes Eck.[65] In a broadside printed after the Leipzig Debate, Luther himself attacked Hoogstraeten (who in an anti-Reuchlin tract had labeled one of Luther's theses for Leipzig as heretical[66]), claiming "the sun has not seen a more pestiferous and shameless heretic than Jacob Hoogstraeten."[67] Many things motivated Reuchlin's supporters—commitment to church reform, embrace of humanism and biblical philology, rejection of scholasticism—but it is important to stress that they were also already in a high state of agitation, disdainful of the inquisition and disappointed by the Roman curia and the pope because of the lengthy prosecution. They were predisposed to dismiss another inquisition against a German intellectual as one more instance of ecclesiastical tyranny.

Reuchlin stood in the minority among his partisans with his own rejection of Luther. At first, he felt no inclination to express an opinion one way or the other regarding Luther's theology. It seems meaningful that not a single description of Luther's ideas occurs in the surviving corpus of Reuchlin writings. Until some point in 1519, Reuchlin probably viewed the Luther phenomenon benignly. In July 1518, after all, he personally arranged for Melanchthon to accept a professorship at Wittenberg, where he would be a colleague of the infamous crusader against indulgences. Although, as far as we know, he never wrote to Luther, he did send greetings via Melanchthon[68] and, most significantly, included a letter from Luther in his 1519 publication of the *Letters of Illustrious Men*. As of 1521, however, Reuchlin was sufficiently disturbed by the spreading and now officially heterodox Lutheran movement that he broke off communication with his dear protégé Melanchthon, asking him to cease corresponding with him.[69] A letter from Hutten, dated 22 February 1521, also indicates that Reuchlin sent a blunt condemnation (now lost) of Luther to the dukes of Bavaria, in which, according to Hutten, "you [i.e. Reuchlin] added that you were always opposed to Luther's case and you resented it when your name appeared in his writings and that you tried to turn away those of us who would support him." Hutten continued, "You dislike the Luther Affair, you oppose it, you wish it could be extinguished.... In me you will have a determined opponent, not only if you ever oppose Luther's case but also if you submit to the authority of the Roman pope."[70]

The position of Johannes Eck offers a good indication of the intricacy of Reuchlin's political chessboard newly arranged by the Luther Affair. Eck was a well-regarded professor of theology at the University of Ingolstadt. Luther expressed admiration for his scholarship even after Eck began counterattacking him on indulgences. Pirckheimer had singled out Eck in October 1517 as one of the few German intellectuals with sufficient background in humanist studies to participate in the new biblical philology he was advocating.[71] Deservedly so, for when Reuchlin offered Hebrew instruction at the University of Ingolstadt in spring 1520, one of his most avid students was none other than the august professor. Eck even continued his studies in Rome under the Jewish scholar Elijah Levita. Nonetheless, in the aftermath of the Leipzig Debate (June–July 1519) Eck had become a center of opposition to Luther, so much so that he was entrusted with the publication of the papal condemnation of Luther in Germany. The very fact that Reuchlin boarded at Eck's household during his residency in Ingolstadt (beginning in November 1519) suggests an alignment against the revolt, although not necessarily complete agreement with Eck's theology or tactics. For example, when in 1520 professors at Ingolstadt consulted with Reuchlin to see if Eck should be permitted to burn two of Luther's books in a public ceremony, Reuchlin advised against it, "lest they bring themselves or the entire university into disrepute,"[72] but without taking a position on the substance of Luther's or Eck's theology. (Interestingly, in a 1520 letter to Spalatin, the artist Albrecht Dürer linked Eck's plan to burn Luther's tracts to the burning of "Dr. Reuchlin's little book."[73]) Reuchlin even appears to have mediated a temporary—probably very brief—reconciliation between Eck and Melanchthon after the Leipzig Debate.[74] Nonetheless, despite their association, we cannot rule out the possibility of Eck's involvement in the papal condemnation of Reuchlin. Eck was in Rome during June 1520 to lead the German effort against Luther, and it is unlikely that he was not also consulted about the Reuchlin decision.

At the beginning of his academic career (in two of the ten earliest surviving letters in his corpus), Luther expressed unequivocal support for Reuchlin, but did so without endorsing any of Reuchlin's specific positions on Judaism or Jewish studies. In a 1514 letter to Spalatin, both court chaplain and privy councilor to Friedrich the Wise, Luther wrote, "You know, my worthy master, that I also hold this man in the highest esteem and affection, and my judgment is perhaps suspect, because, as they say, I am not unbiased or unpartisan. But because you desire it, I'll tell you what my opinion is: that I encounter nothing in his written recommendation that could be threatening" (i.e., to Christian orthodoxy).[75] He expressed himself in a similar vein to Spalatin in August 1514, when he defended the "most innocent Reuchlin,"[76] and castigated Gratius's *Apology against Johannes Reuchlin*, a work that had just appeared in February: "May the Lord grant that it [i.e., Reuchlin's case] end soon. But I am very happy that the case has gone to Rome and the apostolic seat rather than that the right of adjudication be given in other parts to these mean-spirited Cologne professors...for Rome has highly learned men among the cardinals" who will be likely to show Reuchlin "more favor." "Let us pray for our Reuchlin."[77] The assumption that the papal court would be a favorable venue was not only a tribute to Roman humanist culture of the 1510s but also a reflection of Reuchlin's actual legal strategy.

Encouraged by Melanchthon to initiate a correspondence, Luther sent a rather overblown tribute to the embattled scholar on 14 December 1518. Although a reply does not survive, Reuchlin apparently responded favorably for he included the letter prominently in the publication of *Letters of Illustrious Men* of 1519. One of the several remarkable features of this letter is that Luther stakes a claim to being Reuchlin's successor as defender of humanist learning against attacks from scholastic theologians and the inquisition:

> The Lord be with you, you most courageous man! I congratulate you on the mercifulness of God, which is with you, most learned humanist, through which you have succeeded in shutting the mouth of those defamers. You have certainly been an instrument of divine council, which, although unbeknownst to you, was much hoped for by the scholars of pure theology. Indeed, things quite different from what they appeared to you have now happened through God. I was among those who wanted to be with you but no occasion presented itself for that. Therefore in my prayers and wishes I have always been with you.
>
> But what was then denied to your ally has now been richly granted to your successor. The monsters are now attacking me with teeth, in the hope that in some way or other they might be able to repair their vile reputations (which they received from their battle with you). I, too, am fighting against them, though armed with less genius and erudition than you had when you met them and prevailed. But I have been fighting with no less spirit....
>
> Your steadfastness has broken many of their horns. For the Lord acted through you so that the tyranny of those sophists [i.e., scholastics] finally learned to oppose the true study of theology [i.e., biblical humanism] more warily and with less force, and Germany has begun to breathe with the true doctrine of the Scripture, which has not only been suppressed but also extinguished, alas, for centuries! It was necessary for this beginning of the new learning to be granted through a man of no small grace. But rather just as God—please allow this comparison—obliterated the greatest mountain, Christ, into the dust of death, and from this dust afterwards so many great mountains rose up, so you would have brought forth little fruit, if you had not been humbled [mortified] and reduced to dust, from which now distinguished biblical scholars are arising. And the prayer of the groaning church has been heard, "Redeem me, Lord, for no saint is present and the faithful are dwindling among the children of men" [Psalm 12:2], for the vilest among the children of men have been exalted to the height of God.[78]

It was not uncommon for Luther's early supporters to associate his theological innovations with the new biblical philology and, thus, with Reuchlin. In his introduction to Luther's 1519 *Commentary on Psalms*, Philipp Melanchthon explained that Luther the exegete was following the path blazed by Erasmus and Reuchlin in their efforts to recover the "genuine theology."[79] In 1521, Johannes Eberlin portrayed Reuchlin and Erasmus as Luther's supporters and as the scholars who had "laid the cornerstone of all salvation."[80] Andreas Osiander, the leading reformer of Nuremberg, claimed that the Reformation did not have its roots in the efforts of evangelical preachers (like himself) but rather sprang into existence "through the honorable and highly learned Johannes Reuchlin, doctor of law, and Erasmus, doctor of Holy Scripture, and other courageous and famous men" who were the first to recover the "three main languages of Latin, Greek, and Hebrew" and thereby expose the errors of the contemporary church.[81]

By 1509 at the latest, Luther, an aspiring Old Testament scholar, had acquired *Rudiments of Hebrew* and was using it extensively in his research.[82] In general, he could sound positively Reuchlinian in his encomiums to the Hebrew language—"Hebrew is the best language of all...and the purest"[83]— and, although he never became a specialist in Hebrew philology, Luther achieved a solid working command of biblical Hebrew. The specialized research of Siegfried Raeder has proved that Luther completely absorbed Reuchlin's *Rudiments* before undertaking his first commentaries on the Psalms and that the *Rudiments* remained a direct source for the 1519 Psalms commentary and several other works,[84] even though in future years Luther would prefer to consult Reuchlin's successors in Hebrew philology. Luther also studied Reuchlin's *Art of the Kabbalah* with great care but chose to comment not on its primary theme—the relevance of Jewish theology for Christianity—but rather on a minor issue in the tract (albeit a central one to Luther): the rejection of scholasticism.[85] An excellent illustration of the impact of Reuchlin's Hebrew research was Luther's 1517 *Seven Penitential Psalms*, which was a rendering of Reuchlin's 1512 Hebrew-Latin edition of those Psalms. This pamphlet marks the first time that Luther translated any part of Scripture from the original text into German, an important milestone in the history of producing reliable Bibles for lay readers. All told, Luther was one of Reuchlin's most industrious students during the 1510s.

When it came to the specific question of how to treat the great corpus of Jewish scholarship on the Bible, Luther shared little of Reuchlin's spirit or approach. Luther repeatedly rejected the sages and rabbis as a group of foolish liars who distorted the meaning of the Bible in their exegesis. If anything, the fierceness of his opposition to using rabbinic teachings exceeded that of Hoogstraeten. Despite keen interest in humanist study of the text of the Bible, Luther was a traditional Christian exegete, especially in his primary approach to Hebrew Scriptures as a source for the Christian gospel and as a prophecy of Jesus' messiahship.[86] In this respect, he differed little from the ancient methodology of St. Jerome (though Luther claimed that Jewish scholars had sometimes even deceived Jerome). But one of the salient features of Luther's major exegetical works, especially evident in his magisterial *Commentary on Genesis* (1534–45), was his continuous dialogue with Jewish philological exegesis.[87] Luther did accept the study of Jewish grammar books, specifically those of David and Moses Kimhi. But the grammatical or literal sense—the *peshat* approach initiated by Rashi—was abhorrent to him. Luther was so intent on finding allegories for Christ in Hebrew Scriptures that he freely elucidated what he called the "literal prophetic sense" of Scripture.[88] Therefore he sharply attacked Christians who followed the plain literal approach of Jewish commentaries and failed to see Christological allegories or allusions. He denounced them as "Judaizers," a group that included such distinguished scholars as Sebastian Münster and Santi Pagnini, both of whose brilliant Bible translations Luther nonetheless drew upon.[89] (In the 1520s, Pagnini also translated the philological works of David and Moses Kimhi into Latin, and Münster made the works of the contemporary Jewish scholar Elijah Levita available in Latin.) Likewise, claims that Jewish Kabbalah revealed Christian truths had no validity for Luther, though he objected to Christian Kabbalah and rabbinic exegesis without ever citing Reuchlin as the initiator of such defective methods.[90] He repeatedly rejected both Jewish and Christian concepts of the tetragrammaton as sheer nonsense. Similarly, beginning in 1532, Melanchthon included a harsh condemnation of Kabbalah in his influential handbook on rhetoric: "No less absurd are the Jewish Kabbalists, who, having discovered new words, promise wondrous mysteries, although they teach pure nonsense."[91]

Nonetheless, in the early 1520s, Luther momentarily adopted a strikingly benevolent attitude in a pamphlet about contemporary Jews. His first tract devoted to Judaism—*That Jesus Christ Was Born a Jew* (1523)—has always presented a conundrum to scholars because its kindly tone is so incompatible with the animosity and the hatred of his other pronouncements against Judaism. Were it not for this tract, the brutal anti-Semitism of the late Luther would seem to have developed in a continuous escalation from the foundational position of his Psalm lectures of 1513–16, wherein he characterized contemporary Jews as blasphemers suffering under God's wrath with no hope of improvement. The most common solution to this conundrum has been the contention that Luther's attitude did not really change that much for the underlying conviction in *That Jesus Christ Was Born a Jew* is that contemporary Jews must convert to Christianity. This approach seems justified, but not entirely satisfying for it ignores the difference between the rhetoric of anti-Jewish theology and proposals for actual violence. It is one thing to believe that all Jews are consigned to hell, as Luther fervidly did in his early tracts, but quite another to advocate destruction of Jews and their communities as the necessary response to their alleged godlessness and corruption, as occurs in Luther's late works.

When writing the tract of 1523, Luther was excited by a new hypothesis he had formulated, namely, that the recovery of the true gospel message, an achievement of his movement, would abet the conversion of Jews.[92] Medieval Christianity had been so defective that Jews acted wisely in resisting conversion: "If I had been a Jew and had seen such dolts and blockheads govern and teach the Christian faith, I would sooner have become a hog than a Christian."[93] The tract actually unifies the goals of proselytizing Catholic Christians and Jews and approaches the prospect of Jewish conversion with cautious optimism.

In a few respects, however, the work also evokes Reuchlin's defense of Judaism. Echoing Reuchlin (and unlike the violent tracts of 1543), Luther objects to illegal seizure of Jewish property, expresses regret over the cruel treatment of Jews as social outsiders, and appears to ridicule the baleful innuendo of ritual murder. He even implies that the trades should be opened to Jewish participation so that Jews won't be forced to pursue the odious profession of money lending:

> Therefore, I would request and advise that one deal gently with
> them and instruct them from Scripture. Then some of them may
> come along. Instead of this we are trying only to drive them by
> force, slandering them, accusing them of having Christian blood if
> they don't stink, and I know not what other foolishness. So long as
> we thus treat them like dogs, how can we expect to work any good
> among them? Again, when we forbid them to labor, do business,
> and have human fellowship with us, thereby forcing them into
> usury, how is that supposed to do them any good? If we really want
> to help them, we must be guided in our dealings with them not by
> papal law but by the law of Christian love.... If some of them should
> prove stiff-necked, what of it? After all, we ourselves are not all good
> Christians either.[94]

Even more reminiscent of Reuchlin's attitude is Luther's admiration of Jews for their preservation and study of the biblical texts: "God entrusted Holy Scripture...to no other people except the Jews."[95] Moreover, while the Jews assiduously study the text of the Bible with devotion, Christianity has devolved into "a mere babble without reliance on Scripture."[96] Like Reuchlin, Luther stressed that the Christian apostles were Jewish and that they drew upon

Jewish theological knowledge. In a forceful formulation, Luther called on his detractors to go ahead and denounce him as a Jew, if they tire of calling him a heretic.[97]

Nonetheless, *That Jesus Christ Was Born a Jew* does not express any inclination to acknowledge value in postbiblical Jewish theology or scholarship. It also adopts one important anti-Jewish stance of the Cologne inquisition that Reuchlin had rejected, that Talmudic Judaism should be considered a heretical divergence from biblical Judaism. Luther conveyed this idea vividly by labeling contemporary Jews "bad Christians," meaning that they had departed from the "Christianity" of Hebrew Scriptures. The alleged Christianity of Old Testament Judaism was deeply ingrained in Luther's exegetical makeup. For him, a Christological exegesis of Hebrew Scriptures not only locates prophesies of Jesus as the messiah but also perceives the gospel message—salvation through Christ—articulated in Hebrew Scriptures. It was on that basis that Luther was able to identify the first occurrence of the Christian gospel in Genesis 3:15 (the crushing of the serpent's head) and three subsequent gospel passages in the Old Testament.[98]

Thus we might look at *That Jesus Christ Was Born a Jew* as an attempt to create a new anti-Jewish program that eschewed the incitement and brutality of the Hoogstraeten-Pfefferkorn discourse (which was actually designed to arouse Christians anyway) but preserved the goal of ending Judaism. As indicated explicitly by Justus Jonas's dedication of a Latin translation, the work was to be used as a missionary pamphlet. Apparently, it captured the imagination of Christian activists for it went through some nine printings in 1523[99] and was even translated into Latin on two separate occasions.[100] Remarkably, it spawned creation of several other missionary pamphlets that rejected the brutality of early modern missions to the Jews.[101] At the conclusion of the pamphlet, Luther expressed his cautious optimism as follows: "For now, I will stop at this point, until I see what I have accomplished."[102] What Luther soon saw was that his outlook may have found resonance among Christians but not among Jews.

There was no way that the young Luther could have followed the legal controversies of the Reuchlin Affair so carefully and absorbed the Hebrew scholarship of Reuchlin so thoroughly without also being aware of Reuchlin's defenses of Judaism and favorable portrayal of Jews. Nonetheless, without ever polemicizing against Reuchlin by name, Luther managed over time to contradict every favorable attitude Reuchlin had expressed about Judaism. The Reuchlin Affair was, in fact, the context for one of Luther's earliest surviving condemnations of Judaism. In his letter of 7 February 1514, as we have seen, he explicitly sided with Reuchlin and maligned Hoogstraeten for prosecuting

the respectable scholar. Nonetheless, in this context, Luther was clearly react-
ing to the general issue of humanism facing a threat from the inquisition
rather than to any specific statements in defense of Jews in the Holy Roman
Empire. The letter as a whole is a curious contradiction for while it condemns
Hoogstraeten's prosecution (and even his anti-Jewish mission), it also rejects
key elements of Reuchlin's defense of contemporary Jews, as we can see in the
closing statement:

> Finally, this is my conclusion for this has been prophesied by all
> the prophets, namely, that the Jews will curse and blaspheme
> their king Christ. And I admit that whoever has not read this or
> does not understand this has not perceived the true theology. And
> therefore I assume that the Cologne professors cannot interpret
> Scripture because it has to happen in this way and Scripture has
> to be fulfilled. And if they would attempt to free the Jews from
> committing blasphemy, they would turn Scripture and God into
> liars. But be confident that God will be truthful, even if a thousand,
> thousand Cologne professors are laboring to the contrary in vain.
> For it will be God's work alone, working from within, and not the
> work of men working, or rather, playing from without. If those
> blasphemies are taken from them, they will compose even worse
> books. For God's anger has consigned them to their sinfulness so
> that, as Ecclesiastes says, they are irredeemable and everything that
> is irredeemable only gets worse from being corrected and never
> improves.[103]

Thus, in the midst of his endorsement of Reuchlin, Luther insists that the
Jews "blaspheme and curse God," precisely the contentions of Pfefferkorn,
Hoogstraeten, Tongern, and others whom Reuchlin opposed. Luther's quib-
ble with the Cologne professors is merely that they refuse to see Jewish blasphemy as an inalterable part of God's plan. This was the general perspective
on Judaism that Luther repeatedly expressed in his lectures on Psalms from
1513–16.[104] This anti-Semitism of the early Luther, which is conventional, if
emphatic, also serves as a reminder of the intense hatred of Jews common
among Reuchlin's humanist supporters, a phenomenon clearly visible in *The
Letters of Obscure Men*. One of the contributors to *The Letters of Obscure Men*,
Hermann Busch, in fact, became a strong supporter of Reuchlin only after he
came to see the controversy as a conflict between scholasticism and humanism. But earlier, when he perceived the case as a question of Jewish rights,
Busch composed a scathing poem, written in humanist Latin, "Against the

Jews and the Preposterous Lovers of the Jews," which was printed on the title page of Tongern's *Articles* against Reuchlin.[105]

The dimensions of Luther's anti-Jewish polemic are immense. Opposition to Judaism and hatred of Jews are ubiquitous elements in his commentaries, sermons, tracts, letters, and table talk. The last sermon of his ambitious ministry, delivered on 14 February 1546 in Eisleben, Saxony (his hometown), ended in an impassioned but ineffectual cry to mobilize support for expulsion of the local Jewish community. In the sermon (or in an addendum to the sermon[106]), he aroused his listeners by rehearsing the worst charges of the Renaissance campaigns: the Jews blaspheme Mary and Jesus, calling her a whore and him a whore's child; they are eager to kill Christians ("If they could kill us all, they would do it gladly, and they do it often, especially the Jews who pose as doctors").[107] His concluding sentence was that if Jews refuse to accept conversion, "we should neither tolerate nor endure their presence among us."[108]

Luther's most notorious anti-Jewish tracts are two books he published in 1543—*On the Jews and Their Lies* and *On the Tetragrammaton and the Genealogy of Christ*—in order to encourage political action against the remaining Jewish communities in the empire. When Heinrich Bullinger, Zwingli's successor in Zurich, read one of them, he justifiably observed: "If today that famous hero Reuchlin were to return to life, he would declare that Tongern, Hoogstraeten, and Pfefferkorn had returned to life in this one person, Luther."[109] The sources Luther names include Nicholas of Lyra, Paul of Burgos, the fourteenth-century Dominican Porchetus (author of *Victory against Judaism*[110]), and Antonius Margaritha (author of *The Entire Jewish Faith*, 1530), but many of the specific allegations and proposals were prominent in the Hoogstraeten-Pfefferkorn campaigns. According to Luther, Jews are guilty of corrupting Christian society with their usury, blaspheming and cursing Jesus, committing ritual murder on Christian children, poisoning wells, willfully distorting the meaning of Scriptures, departing from orthodox norms of Old Testament Judaism, and so on. On the allegation of well poisoning, Luther even argued in an unusually convoluted analysis that in the New Testament Jesus indicated that future Jews would commit this crime.[111]

In these tracts Luther insisted that coercive action—"sharp mercy"[112]—was necessary because the vast majority of Jews would never convert.[113] Moreover, because Christians are aware of Jewish crimes, they are obligated to take action or risk becoming complicit in the Jewish abominations: "We dare not tolerate their conduct....If we do, we become sharers in their lies, cursing, and blasphemy."[114] Christians must "set fire to their synagogues...so that God might see that we are Christians,"[115] destroy the Talmud and other Jewish books, even confiscate Jewish Bibles, outlaw Jewish banking and trading, and destroy Jewish homes. In one passage, Luther advocates murdering Jews on the open highways of the empire. He appears to accept the implication that his book, *On the Jews and Their Lies*, will encourage people to murder Jews.[116]

Luther claimed that under current conditions it was the duty of Christian pastors to agitate for expulsion. As we know from other contexts, Luther was appalled by rulers who tolerated Jewish residency. Good evidence indicates that his 1543 tracts were distributed among German princes and that Luther's efforts to change policies may have had some success. Justus Jonas (a Wittenberg colleague and confidant) and Philipp Melanchthon expended considerable effort on this campaign.[117] Jonas translated the tracts, dedicating the Latin translation of *On the Jews and Their Lies* to Duke Moritz of Saxony.[118] In particular, Melanchthon focused on the presentation of the tracts to Landgrave Philipp of Hesse, dispatching them with strong letters of endorsement. The Hessian effort may well have contributed to the issuance of a harsh decree for Hessian Jews in 1543, which imposed restrictions on commerce and required censuring of Hebrew books as well as compulsory attendance at Christian sermons. On 6 May 1543, John Friedrich of Saxony authorized the Torgau Mandate that, for a few years, outlawed Jewish travel, commerce, and residency in Electoral Saxony. In 1545, Luther wrote directly to Elector Joachim II of Brandenburg, urging adoption of an anti-Jewish policy, though in this instance without any apparent success.

His hostility extending well beyond the realm of exegesis,[119] Luther was committed to abetting a Christian transformation of society by combating an array of demonic forces—which he perceived among Muslims, Catholics, sectarians, and Jews—against the revival of the gospel. Even if an occasional historian might allow Luther to take cover under a veil of conventionality, it would still be necessary to observe that his animosity lies on the extreme edge of the spectrum of Christian anti-Semitism. This is significant for the obvious reason that Luther's cultural impact has been immense and his hatred of Jews has been a dangerous source available ever after to anti-Semites seeking to give their views credibility. The first comprehensive history of Luther's writings on Jews, though published well before the Holocaust, closes with this ominous observation: "Luther's hatred of the Jews has not disappeared without a trace, but continues to have an impact through the centuries. Whoever for whatever reason writes against the Jews believes he has the right to refer triumphantly to Luther."[120]

The case of Luther illustrates how Christian anti-Semitism often intensified in the context of the Renaissance appropriation of Jewish studies. Reuchlin and some of his followers came to admire not only Hebrew philology but also Jewish theology and piety. While Reuchlin, of course, never questioned Christian soteriology, the more he studied Judaism the more he came to respect the Jewish people for the depth of their devotion to God. This was a gradual development, but one that we can detect as Reuchlin expressed successively higher levels of empathy as he wrote *Rudiments of Hebrew* (1506), the *Recommendation* (1510), and *Art of the Kabbalah* (1517). Many of Reuchlin's own supporters, Luther preeminent among them, did not undergo such a development but rather found ways to absorb Jewish learning while developing even stronger strains of anti-Semitism. It would be easy to say that Luther was not a genuine supporter of Reuchlin and that Bullinger got it right, he was just the embodiment of the three-headed monster of Pfefferkorn, Hoogstraeten, and Tongern. One reason for this conundrum lies in the mechanism of defending against charges of favoring Jews, which suggested the need to oppose expressing sympathy for Jews (a phenomenon clearly discernible in defenses of Reuchlin). Another part of the answer stemmed from the primary interest of many Reuchlin supporters in defending humanism and biblical philology as well as countering the power of the inquisition. It is, moreover, evident that aspects of the anti-Jewish campaigns of Reuchlin's opponents were compelling to many people, including Reuchlin's own supporters. Pietro Galatino defended Reuchlin but did so in the context of publishing a manual for disproving the validity of Judaism (albeit without advocating violence, coercion, or expulsion). More threateningly, academics such as Luther, Bucer, Eck, and even Melanchthon—all of them, paradoxically, Reuchlin supporters who were nonetheless essentially in agreement with the Cologne campaign against Jews—moved beyond theology and portrayed Judaism as a political and social plague that had to be eradicated by political means, however cruel or harsh.

If we return to the conclusion of the Reuchlin case at the Roman curia, we can see another impact of the Reformation. The verdict against Reuchlin indicates the emergence of a new dynamic that inflamed Christian hatred of Jews, for the new pressures exerted by the need for counterreform were inimical to the maintenance of papal toleration of Judaism. The Reuchlin Affair suggests that, in many ways, Rome of the 1510s, with its unusually progressive embrace of humanist biblical research, was poised to nurture a scholarly reexamination of Christian-Jewish relations. Under the impact of humanism, Leo X, and then his cousin Clement VII, generally improved relations between the papacy and Jews. But the recovery of Hebrew and the emergence of the Christian study of Judaism soon lost any potential it might have had at Rome for strengthening Christian-Jewish relations. This happened as the battles over the Protestant

schism hardened doctrinal lines and diminished the intellectual pluralism
of Renaissance Rome. Leo's stunning verdict against Reuchlin's defense of
Jews was perhaps the first instance of collateral damage arising from the
Reformation. Of course, the verdict did not end Hebrew studies in Rome. But
it did prefigure the harsh paradigm of the Catholic-Protestant-Jewish dynamic
that would soon emerge.

As counterreformation policies were implemented, tolerance of Jewish life
plummeted to a new low point in the Papal States. As of the 1550s, Jews in the
Papal States were subject to the inquisition; some were burned at the stake; a
strict system of ghettos was imposed in 1555, and in 1569 Jews were expelled
from all parts of the Papal States except the ghettos of Rome and Ancona. This
aggressive anti-Jewish policy was consolidated by legislation of Clement VIII
in 1593 (*Caeca et obdurata*) and remained in place until the Napoleonic era
and beyond.[121] The emblematic figure for crushing all types of heresy, Paul
IV issued the punitive *Cum nimis absurdum* (1555), a stark repudiation of the
medieval *Sicut Judaeis*, the legal foundation for papal toleration of Jews in a
Christian society. On 4 September 1553, which in the Jewish calendar was
Rosh Hashanah, the future Paul IV (then, Cardinal Giovanni Pietro Carafa)
restarted the inquisitional fires in Rome to incinerate the Talmud, the foundation of rabbinic Judaism that Pope Leo X had explicitly licensed in 1520 and
Reuchlin had repeatedly defended against Christian attacks.

10

"As If the First Martyr of Hebrew Letters"

I would seem ungrateful and uncivilized, if I did not do all in my
power to make your name immortal.

—Daniel Bomberg, dedicating his edition of the
Psalms in Hebrew to Johannes Reuchlin,
26 September 1521

Reuchlin died on 30 June 1522 in Stuttgart, probably in his house
next to the Stiftskirche. The cause and other circumstances of
his death are not known,[1] except that his devoted student Conrad
Pellican visited him during his last weeks as he tried to convalesce
in the spa village of Liebenzell.[2] During the previous semester,
he had been well enough to offer Hebrew and Greek seminars in
Tübingen. A placard survives that announced Professor Reuchlin
"will begin...Ecclesiastes tomorrow [i.e., 21 February 1522] at
the hour of twelve and will lecture on that book to his listeners,
explaining Hebrew grammar."[3] In correspondence with the printers
Thomas Anshelm and Daniel Bomberg, he was diligently ordering
textbooks for his Tübingen students and also continuing the battle
for Christian Hebrew studies, defiantly describing himself in a letter
of January 1522 to Anshelm "as if the first martyr of Hebrew letters."[4]

He was buried in St. Leonhard's Church in Stuttgart next to his
second wife, although a memorial tablet for him had already been set

up on the other side of town in the Dominican Hospital Church, the site of his first wife's burial.[5] After World War II, the stone plaque was removed from the rubble and relocated to Leonhard's, closer to Reuchlin's (now lost) grave (see Figure 10.1). The plaque is inscribed in the three holy languages of Christianity he had studied with such devotion: the Latin inscription offers a concise, humanist sounding "greetings to Capnion's posterity"; the isolated word "resurrection" ("Ἀνάστασις") appears in Greek; and the Hebrew simply states "the world of the living" ("עלם החיים"),[6] a striking phrase for eternal life in the divine language that, according to Reuchlin, mediated salvation. After his death, several humanists wrote tributes to him (most important, Erasmus

FIGURE 10.1. Memorial plaque for Johannes Reuchlin (1501), now in the Leonhardskirche, Stuttgart, Germany. Courtesy of Evangelische Leonhardskirche, Stuttgart.

and Melanchthon), a gesture that many a German celebrity of later generations would eloquently emulate (Wieland, Goethe, Herder, Scholem, etc.).[7]

In the final two years of his life, Reuchlin was the dedicatee of two Hebrew Bible imprints by Daniel Bomberg, a Christian as well as the most accomplished printer of Hebraica in the Renaissance.[8] Obviously, this was a meaningful tribute to the founder of Christian Hebrew studies, but Bomberg's dedications to the scholar recently condemned for favoring Judaism also served as a kind of proclamation that the papal censure of Reuchlin would not stymie Christian Jewish studies or even hamper the distribution of Jewish writings among Jews. Despite the papal ruling, Bomberg not only affirmed Reuchlin as the inspiration for Hebrew studies for both Jews and Christians but also made it clear that Leo X had endorsed his 1520 printing of the Talmud (the *editio princeps*), "a work of great labor and expense that the pope entrusted to me."[9]

During Reuchlin's lifetime Jewish communities in Germany probably reached the lowest point of their historical decline prior to the Holocaust, the perilous result of "the Jewish tragedy of the fifteenth century."[10] At the beginning of the sixteenth century, the survival of every single Jewish community in Germany was uncertain. According to Marcus Wenninger's compilation only about one-eighth of the urban Jewish communities of 1400 still existed in 1520.[11] With the dissolution of the Nuremberg (1498) and Regensburg (1519) communities, along with the increasing number of expulsions from princely territories, German Jewish life was contracting ever closer to the point of extinction. With the communities holding on to existence by such a fraying thread, Reuchlin's defense of Jewish books was an important event in part because it thwarted an ambitious, well-supported action against German Jews and in part because it provoked such a major controversy over the status of Judaism and the Christian humanist movement. To be sure, Jewish communities had received political protection from many Christian entities for a variety of reasons in the past, but Reuchlin's support was of a new type: as his enemies pointed out, it was the first time that a Christian scholar defended the substance of Jewish religious culture and had done so at a moment of crisis. It is, therefore, understandable that Rabbi Josel of Rosheim expressed astonishment that Reuchlin's view actually prevailed on the legal question of the Jewish books, claiming that God had sent a "miracle within a miracle" in the form of a learned gentile who defended Jewish writings, even if, as we have seen, factors other than Reuchlin's defense were also involved in the resolution.

Reuchlin contributed to a stabilization of the legal status of Jews by formulating strong arguments in favor of preserving the statutory guarantees for toleration of Jews, as enshrined in both the imperial and ecclesiastical law codes.[12] While he contended that the confiscation of Jewish books abrogated ecclesiastical and imperial law, especially insofar as property rights or the standing of heresy allegations were concerned, he also took up a new scholarly task, one that was long overdue, of assessing the merits of the accusations that Christian polemicists—and now an imperial mandate—had leveled against Jewish writings and practices. The overall result was his firm insistence that no finding, legal or theological, warranted destruction of Jewish writings generally (with the exception of only two well-known examples of anti-Christian polemic). His *Recommendation* was destined to touch off great controversy not only because it undermined a potent campaign that had united popular, academic, ecclesiastical, and imperial interests against German Judaism but also because his academic judgment, formed through independent reconsideration of the evidence, challenged some established anti-Jewish verities of early modern Christianity. In some instances, he pressed the case harder than even his supporters would accept. For example, no Christian authority seconded his contention—one of the most stunning rebukes he hurled at the anti-Jewish campaign—that it was Christians who were prone to slandering Judaism in some of their practices (and not the other way around), as when they called the Jews (whom he characterized as a tenaciously faithful people) "perfidious" in their Good Friday services.[13]

Despite Josel of Rosheim's pious tribute, Reuchlin is fully comprehensible in terms of his own cultural experience. The earliest sources of his interest in Hebrew and Judaism were the humanist biblical movement, the Kabbalistic research of Pico della Mirandola, and the medieval anti-Jewish polemicists who used Hebrew texts in their works. Over time, he augmented those sources through extensive study of Jewish scholarship from the Middle Ages and his own day, much of it gained through private tutorials with Jacob ben Jehiel Loans and Obadiah Sforno. As he achieved the ability to form independent judgments on Jewish writings, Reuchlin began to question the substance of anti-Jewish innuendos and, through his readings, ultimately came to the conclusion that specific Christian allegations of blasphemy and heresy within the Jewish tradition were either baseless or trivial. He also took the further important step of repudiating the portrayal of postbiblical Judaism as the enemy of Christianity. That Jews and Judaism were not anti-Christian (and not antagonistic forces in a Christian society) was a foundational principle of his *Recommendation*, and a cause for the threatening and unrelenting attacks he would endure.

Reuchlin's research strongly suggested a need to reexamine the foundations of Christian theology, which, coupled with his benign portrayal of the Jewish tradition, made him a polarizing figure. A full decade before Erasmus's Bible, his *Rudiments of Hebrew* documented, albeit respectfully, the

insufficiency of the Vulgate text of the Bible and advocated Christian acceptance of the *veritas Hebraica* as their scriptural authority, proposing rather
ominously that "the ancient dignity of the Holy Scriptures must be restored
to a new appearance which is unknown to the Latin world."[14] More important,
and as was only feasible in the new world of printing technology, Reuchlin
and Thomas Anshelm gave Christian theologians a handbook that equipped
them to return to that original text. His success as a Christian humanist in
tapping previously inaccessible sources for biblical exegesis and theological
inquiry energized a European-wide defense of his scholarship, for his supporters, including many of the most powerful prelates at Rome, enthusiastically
welcomed his contributions to Hebrew philology, even if they were divided or
uncertain about his adaptation of Kabbalah for Christianity. Nonetheless, his
academic judgments on the theological value of Jewish writings and his political defense of Jewish books and Jewish ownership of those books also energized his opponents. It is important to acknowledge that, while anti-Semitism
was the major motivation, his opponents also had substantive disagreements
with his scholarly methods and conclusions. Before Reuchlin, Europe had a
long history of theological disputation between Christians and Jews but never
before had Christian scholars engaged each other in such bitter controversy
over the merits of Judaism, Jewish writings, and the acceptable Christian attitude toward Judaism.

Any evaluation of Reuchlin's favorable representation of Judaism needs
to acknowledge significant qualifications. Most important, he never departed
from the then orthodox principle that Christianity was the one true form of
religion. His historical interest in ancient religions and philosophies and his
assumption that elements of an original, true theology (*prisca theologia*) could
be discovered in ancient, especially Jewish, texts predisposed him to a favorable
reception of historical Judaism, but that did not really change his understanding
of redemption occurring exclusively through Christ's agency. To him, Judaism
had part of the truth, perhaps even a large part of the truth, but, without Jesus,
not the full truth. Such an exclusivist position vitiates Christianity's acceptance
of the integrity of any other religion and certainly separates Reuchlin from any
modern form of theological toleration and acceptance. This is what Ludwig
Geiger meant when observing that some of Reuchlin's perspectives were "not
in harmony with the demands of complete religious equality."[15] Moreover,
Reuchlin's early publications, *Miracle-Making Word* (1494) and *German Epistle:
Why the Jews Have Been in Exile So Long* (1505), show that he originally shared
many of the attitudes and expressed some of the anti-Jewish innuendos that
he found in medieval Christian polemicists, even if in these early books he
never advocated opposing Judaism through coercion, expulsion, or violence. It

is important to recognize that Reuchlin began his study of Judaism, at least in part, as a reader of anti-Jewish writers such as Peter Schwarz, Paul of Burgos, and Alfonso de Spina.[16] His outlook transformed over time: as he learned more, he steadily expanded the number of Jewish writers that he portrayed to his Christian readers as authoritative, often eloquently expressing admiration (and occasionally empathy) for Jews and Judaism in his publications from 1506 until 1519.

Reuchlin did not formulate a theology or philosophy of toleration, but he did defend Jewish life in two effective ways: he meticulously asserted the legal rights of Jews and the legality of Jewish writings, and, more distinctively, he created a new Christian discourse that represented Jews and Judaism favorably, thereby not only invoking a concept of justice for Jews (in accord with his general principle that "injustice is a monstrosity"[17]) but also encouraging Christians to develop respect for the beleaguered minority and its religious heritage. In 1517, a Christian proclaims a Jewish savant "our glory" as the climax to a work Reuchlin dedicated to the pope.[18] In a work of 1519, albeit without such an honorific epithet, Maimonides appears along with St. Athanasius as the most significant theological authority on such fundamental topics as the nature of God and the relationship of the soul to God.[19] To a degree, his commitment to philology, on the one hand, and his assumptions about Kabbalah, on the other, conditioned him to find validity in Jewish writings, but it was, above all, the Jewish tradition itself that prevailed over Reuchlin's early anti-Judaism. We can assume that he was not the only Christian of his generation who admired his Jewish books and acquaintances, but he was the first to represent Jewish theology and Jews themselves with admiration, sometimes even unqualified admiration, in public discourse. When it came to a few Jewish thinkers, his opponents' accusations, though bitterly formulated, that he valued Jewish authorities more than the doctors of the church were not entirely specious.[20] Major Jewish scholars such as David Kimhi, Rashi, Joseph Gikatilla, and, above all, Maimonides impressed him at a very deep level. It is not astonishing that he acknowledged the importance of Talmudic and medieval Jewish scholarship—even Luther consulted Jewish scholarship for his Old Testament exegesis—but it is striking that he so openly registered agreement with the wisdom and piety of the Jewish authors he studied. Yet, once again, Reuchlin would have considered his attitude nothing more (and nothing less) than a reasonable academic judgment of the works themselves.

Obviously, Reuchlin would not be the only Christian scholar to defend Jews and Judaism against injustice. One of his students, Andreas Osiander, the leading reformer of Nuremberg, diligently continued his studies of Hebrew and Jewish writings as part of his ministry and, in 1529, emulated Reuchlin's academic approach by arguing (albeit anonymously) that the Jewish tradition, contrary to Christian slanders, had no ritualistic purposes for human blood whatsoever.[21] But this theological refutation of the blood libel innuendo, grounded in knowledge of Jewish practices,[22] provoked an unusually strident objection from another of Reuchlin's students, the Catholic theologian Johannes Eck.[23] In this clash between two Reuchlin followers, we can plainly see that Christian Hebraists in the aftermath of Reuchlin would not by any means develop a uniformly favorable attitude toward Judaism, even if by the beginning of the seventeenth century a detectable "philosemitism" existed among some Christian scholars.[24] As we saw in the conclusion to chapter 9, several of Reuchlin's supporters, including a few of the most influential theologians on all sides of the confessional divides, would advocate using political force and, in the case of Luther, violence to end the practice of Judaism in Germany. Like Pfefferkorn and Hoogstraeten, they assailed Judaism not only as a defective faith but also as a menace to Christian society that had to be eliminated by political means, no matter how inhumane.

The bitterness of the controversy and the fear that it could undermine humanism prompted some Reuchlinists to profess their deep-seated antipathy for Judaism openly. This aspect of the Reuchlin Affair has nearly always been ignored or glossed over, but it was so prominent that we need to ponder the possibility that the Reuchlin Affair also gave scholars a historically significant context for accommodating Christian Hebrew studies to Christian anti-Judaism, even if, it is important to emphasize, they did so with varying degrees of hostility. In some respects a highly pressurized process of self-definition for Christian humanists, the Reuchlin controversy abetted the formulation of yet another new Christian discourse: many of his supporters defended the academic integrity of Jewish research—a major innovation of the Renaissance— while continuing to repudiate Judaism and, in some cases, perpetuate hatred of Jews. This phenomenon, which is significant for understanding the history of Christian-Jewish relations in modern times, raises a fundamental question about religious toleration: did Europe have to move well beyond the ideological hegemony of Christian dogma before Jewish emancipation could begin? Erasmus's exuberant tribute to Reuchlin, as the founder of humanist biblical studies, may seem inconsistent with his public statements against Judaism. In a published letter to Hoogstraeten that emphatically endorsed Reuchlin, Erasmus wrote, "If to be a Christian is to hate Jews, then we are all thoroughly Christian here,"[25] an astonishing admission of ambivalence toward the underlying issues of the controversy. Without taking recourse to his drastic solution, as expressed in the epigraph to chapter 1, of destroying the Jewish three-fourths of the Christian Bible,[26] Erasmus was ultimately able to persist in his anti-Semitism while promoting humanist biblical philology. Indeed, by the time the Reuchlin Affair had ended, Erasmus could comfortably hate Jews and Judaism while canonizing Johannes Reuchlin—without concern about contradiction.

Reuchlin was neither saint nor heretic, martyr nor miracle, but rather the first Christian to read ancient and medieval Jewish texts with primarily scholarly rather than polemical interests. Jewish books and Jewish teachers equipped him with the knowledge, and ultimately inspired him with the conviction, to explain and defend the validity of much of the Jewish tradition to his Christian world.

Notes

ABBREVIATIONS

CWE   Erasmus 1974–, *Collected Works of Erasmus.*
EE   Erasmus 1906–58, the correspondence of Erasmus.
LW   *Luther's Works: The American Edition* (St. Louis and Philadelphia: Concordia and Fortress, 1955–86).
WA   *Luthers Werke: Kritische Gesamtausgabe* (Weimar: Böhlau, 1883–).

CHAPTER 1

Epigraph source: *EE* 3:127, ll. 35–36 (no. 701, 3 November 1517): "Malim ego…totum Vetus aboleri quam Christianorum pacem ob Iudeorum libros rescindi" (*CWE: Correspondence* 5:181 [translation slightly modified]).

1. See chapters 5 and 6. Pfefferkorn had strong support from the Franciscans and the Dominicans definitely as of 1509 and almost certainly from the very beginning of his campaigns (ca. 1504–7). By the end of 1509, the book pogrom was being supported by the archbishop of Mainz, the University of Mainz, as well as the University of Cologne and the Dominican convent in Cologne. By 1510, the faculty of theology at Cologne and the Dominican convent at Cologne, both under the leadership of Jacob Hoogstraeten, were directing the anti-Jewish campaign.

2. See the mandate, as printed in Pfefferkorn 1516, *Streydt puechlyn*, fol. A3ᵛ-A4ᵛ.

3. A circular letter sent to rally support from other Jewish communities states that Maximilian had authorized seizure of "all prayer books and devotional books, including the holiday liturgies (Mahzorim) and the prayer

books for penance (Selihot) ("כל ספר׳ תפילת [sic] ותחנונים מחזורים וסליחות") as well as
Talmudic writings. See Bibliotheca Rosenthaliana MS 388, fol. 9ʳ; and Kracauer
1900a, 122–23 (item 2).

4. See Maimon 1978 for a discussion of an unusual attempt at a regional
(multi-territorial) expulsion of Jews under Elector-Archbishop Albrecht of
Brandenburg. See chapter 6.

5. For a good general account of the Spanish expulsion, see Gerber 1992, 115ff.;
for an extensive analysis, see Baer 1961–66. On the Portuguese forced conversion,
see Gerber 1992, 141ff.

6. There is still no comprehensive history of the Jewish expulsions in the Holy
Roman Empire. See Wenninger 1981 on the expulsions from the free imperial cities,
and Herzig 1993 for an assessment of the dire situation of German Jews during
Reuchlin's lifetime.

7. See Foa [1992] 2000, 122; and Bonfil [1991] 1994.

8. See Wirszubski 1989, on Pico della Mirandola's pathbreaking studies of
Kabbalah in the 1480s.

9. Among this small but influential group were, in rough chronological order,
Pico della Mirandola, Johannes Reuchlin, Giles of Viterbo, Daniel Bomberg, Santi
Pagnini, Sebastian Münster.

10. Conrad Pellican, a student and colleague of Reuchlin, had published a
primitive description of the Hebrew alphabet and some morphology in 1504 (De modo
legendi et intelligendi Hebraea). See L. Geiger 1870, 19ff.

11. Scholem 1969, 7. The entire passage is fascinating, for Scholem expresses
a profound identification with Reuchlin. "Wenn ich an Seelenwanderung glaubte,
würde ich wohl manchmal denken können, unter den neuen Bedingungen der
Forschung eine Art Reinkarnation Johannes Reuchlins, des ersten Erforschers des
Judentums, seiner Sprache und seiner Welt, und speziell der Kabbala, zu sein, des
Mannes, der vor fast fünfhundert Jahren die Wissenschaft vom Judentum in Europa
ins Leben gerufen hat." See Idel 2008, 54–55, for a critical assessment of Scholem's
identification with Reuchlin.

12. On Christian Hebrew studies in sixteenth-century Germany, see L. Geiger
1870; see also Walde 1916, for a valuable study of knowledge of Hebrew among
Christians in fifteenth-century Germany.

13. One other authority, namely the University of Heidelberg, expressed
uncertainty and, instead of responding to the question, called for a meeting of the
various authorities that the emperor had petitioned. See chapter 7.

14. A good source for the actual charges against Reuchlin is Jacob
Hoogstraeten's Libellus accusatorius, which was printed in several of the controversial
pamphlets including Neuenahr 1518, ed., Epistolae trium illustrium virorum and in
Acta iudiciorum 1518. Hoogstraeten stressed the basic accusation of being "excessively
favorable to the perfidious Jews" at both the beginning and conclusion of his work.
See Neuenahr 1518, ed., Epistolae trium illustrium virorum, fol. e2ʳ: "Dictum libellum
[i.e., Eye Glasses] in iudaicae perfidiae favorem" and fol. e4ᵛ: "libellum Speculum
Oculare Ioanni Reuchlin inscriptum, haeresibus et erroribus refertum, perfidis

iudaeis nimis fauorabilem, ecclesiae dei iniuriosum, ac sacris ecclesiae doctoribus irreuerentialem."

15. Tongern 1512, *Articuli*.

16. Beginning with the research of Ludwig Geiger, there has been frequent disagreement among scholars as to whether the Reuchlin Affair was more concerned with opposition to humanism or to Judaism. For instance, Overfield 1971 and Overfield 1984, 247–97, argued strenuously, and as a rebuke to Geiger's (admittedly one-sided) interpretation, that the Reuchlin Affair was not a "showdown between scholasticism and humanism" (with the one exception of Ulrich von Hutten's involvement). It will be clear in chapter 8 that the evidence does not support Overfield's interpretation and that both issues (opposition to Judaism and anxieties about the humanist biblical movement) were central. See also Peterse 1995, for a balanced assessment.

17. See Meyer 1969, 68, and the epigraph to this chapter.

18. For assessments of Erasmus's attitudes toward Judaism and Jews, see Augustijn 1980; Oberman 1983; and Markish 1986. It is probably fair to say that Erasmus's worst anti-Semitic remarks were provoked by Pfefferkorn's publication of the *Streydt puechlyn* in 1516. On that issue, see Augustijn 1980, 28ff.; and chapter 8.

19. *CWE* 38:244–55. Erasmus got the work into print with astonishing speed; it first appeared in an edition of the *Colloquies* from July–August 1522, just weeks after Reuchlin's death on 30 June.

20. On Jerome as the patron saint of Renaissance humanism, see Rice 1985; and Price 2003, 194–224.

21. Johann Wolfgang von Goethe, *Zahme Xenien*, Fünfter Abteil.

22. See chapter 8.

23. On Josel of Rosheim, see Feilchenfeld 1898; Stern 1959; and Fraenkel-Goldschmidt 2006. Opitz 1993 is a sensitive reading of Josel's life from the perspective of Reuchlin's.

24. See Feilchenfeld 1898, 22. Quotes are from Josel of Rosheim's *Memoirs*, as edited by Kracauer 1885, 88 (section 5). Translated into English by Fraenkel-Goldschmidt 2006, 312.

25. See discussion in chapter 9.

26. Weislinger 1730 is an early (and well-informed) Catholic rebuttal to Protestant historiography, though it had virtually no impact.

27. This tendency is strong even in recent work, such as Seebaß 2006, a valuable but unconvincing attempt to justify Reuchlin's prominent inclusion in the iconic *Luther Monument* in Worms. See chapter 9.

28. See Price 2008; and chapter 8.

29. Leutner 1957.

30. See Schäfer 2005 for an analysis of the depth of Heinrich Graetz's antipathy for Kabbalah within the Jewish tradition and Graetz's tendency to look benignly on Reuchlin's appropriation of Kabbalah for Christianity.

31. Graetz 1853–76, 9:63–156; in the English edition the analysis occurs in 1891–99, 4:422ff.

32. L. Geiger 1871, 233–34: "Manches mag noch darin sein, was mit den Anforderungen völliger religiöser Gleichberechtigung nicht ganz harmonirt, aber im Ganzen zeigt es reine und tolerante Grundsätze und schöne Auffassung."

33. See especially Kracauer 1887; Kracauer 1900a; and also chapter 6.

34. See Herrmann 2005, 219.

35. Scholem 1988, 27.

36. On Max Brod and Reuchlin, see Pazi 1993.

37. Scholars primarily interested in Reuchlin's contributions to Kabbalah have sometimes offered narrow assessments of his general accomplishments and historical significance. For example, Levi 2002, 214–16, an excellent book on early humanism, stresses Reuchlin's Kabbalistic research to the exclusion of his contributions to Hebrew philology and his legal defense of Judaism.

38. Oberman [1981] 1984, 27.

CHAPTER 2

Epigraph source: From the dedication of *De arte cabalistica* (1517) to Leo X. See Reuchlin, *Briefwechsel* 3:427, ll. 164ff. (no. 309, before 27 March 1517): "ego primus omnium Graeca in Germaniam reduxi et primus omnium ecclesiae universali artem et studia sermonis Hebraici condonavi atque tradidi."

1. As in the title of Schwab 1998, *Johannes Reuchlin Deutschlands erster Humanist: Ein biographisches Lesebuch*.

2. For a general description of the *studia humanitatis*, see Kristeller 1961.

3. See Wels 2000 for a description and analysis of the humanist reform of the medieval system of Latin grammar.

4. Spitz 1957, 23. Text is from Celtis's announcement of courses he was offering at the University of Ingolstadt.

5. Reuchlin was also steeped in the language of law, including canon law, which may account in part for his flexible use of post-classical Latinity in some instances.

6. Reuchlin 1506, *De rudimentis hebraicis*, 621.

7. See chapter 3 and chapter 8.

8. See Reuchlin 1504, *De arte praedicandi*; Evans 1985; and Peterse 1998, 149–51. In 1540 and 1570, Reuchlin's handbook was reprinted with tracts by Melanchthon on Christian rhetoric (see Benzing 1955, 23–24).

9. See Reuchlin, *Briefwechsel* 1:379–81 (no. 121, 1 January 1503).

10. See Landfester 1972 on the importance of moral philosophy for humanist historiography.

11. Johannes Nauclerus (in German, Vergenhans) was the first rector of the University of Tübingen and, apparently, a mentor of the young Reuchlin. Reuchlin's preface has been edited in Reuchlin, *Briefwechsel* 3:490–507 (appendix 3, ca. March or April 1516).

12. Reuchlin, *Briefwechsel* 3:495, ll. 80–81 (appendix 3, ca. March or April 1516): "scientiam antiquitatis ab Hebraeis petendam esse."

13. On Valla's contributions to biblical philology, see Bentley 1983, esp. 32–69.

14. See, for example, *CWE* 61:47: "I find it distasteful to say anything at all about his miracles." Reuchlin also offered crucial assistance for the completion of Erasmus's monumental edition of St. Jerome. See *CWE: Correspondence* 3:63, ll. 27–33 (no. 324) and 3:108, ll. 311ff. (no. 335), where Erasmus acknowledges Reuchlin as a contributor. Erasmus's letter 324 is also in Reuchlin, *Briefwechsel* 3:185–89 (no. 264, 1 March 1515). See also Reuchlin, *Briefwechsel* 2:134–35 n. 7 (no. 163, 26 March 1510), on his collaboration with the Amerbachs on the Jerome project.

15. On the crisis of late-medieval scholasticism, see Levi 2002.

16. Reuchlin's translation of Cicero's *Tusculan Disputations* survives in a manuscript in the library of the University of Heidelberg (Cod. Pal. Germ. 482), ed. Hartfelder 1883–84. See Reuchlin, *Briefwechsel* 1:356–58 (no. 112, 23 June 1501), for Reuchlin's dedication of the work to Elector Philipp of the Palatinate.

17. See note 119.

18. As, for example, in the introduction to his 1516 edition of the Bible; see Olin 1975, 100–101.

19. See Nauert 1973, on the humanist view of Aristotle, and also Nauert 1990, on early infiltration of humanism into northern European universities.

20. For example, see Reuchlin 1513, *Defensio*, in *Sämtliche Werke* 4/1:372, ll. 22ff. For Reuchlin's keen interest in Aldo Manuzio's spectacular edition of Aristotle in Greek (the *editio princeps* in Greek), see Reuchlin, *Briefwechsel* 1:313–17 (no. 97, 23 April 1499), a request for the supplement to volume 5.

21. *EE* 3:143, l. 1 (no. 713, 15 November 1517): "Germaniae nostrae decus." *CWE: Correspondence* 5:203. For a similar evaluation from 1514, see *EE* 2:3–4 (no. 300, ca. August 1514) and *CWE: Correspondence* 3:8, Erasmus writing to Reuchlin: "All of Germany can show nothing like you—you are the brightest ornament Germany has."

22. The most extensive study of Reuchlin's family background remains Decker-Hauff [1955] 1994.

23. See Reuchlin 1519, ed., *Illustrium virorum epistolae*, fol. p1ʳff.

24. Reuchlin, *Briefwechsel* 1:130ff. (no. 43, 5 June 1491) and 1:134ff. (no. 44, 16 June 1491).

25. See Reuchlin, *Briefwechsel* 1:325 (no. 100, 2 November 1499), ll. 56ff., for an effort to extend Dionysius's teaching appointment.

26. Rhein 1995, 63–71.

27. See Reuchlin, *Briefwechsel* 1:205 n. 2 (no. 65, 30 June 1494).

28. Reuchlin, *Briefwechsel* 1:204–6 (no. 65, 30 June 1494); see Rhein 1994c, 307–9.

29. Her father was Hänslin Müller, whose family was originally from the nearby village of Ditzingen, where he still owned property. Hänslin's son (and Reuchlin's brother-in-law), Hans Müller, was a municipal judge in Stuttgart. See Decker-Hauff [1955] 1994, 89; and Rhein 1994b, 286.

30. Rudolf Agricola mentions the marriage in a letter of 4 February 1485, suggesting that the marriage was recent. See Reuchlin, *Briefwechsel* 1:51, l. 10 (no. 14).

31. Ackermann 1999, 73 n. 254.

32. See Reuchlin, *Briefwechsel* 1:365 n. 4 (no. 115, 27 June 1502), on the probable fallacy of earlier claims that Reuchlin contemplated divorcing his first wife.

33. Decker-Hauff [1955] 1994, 94–95.

34. Decker-Hauff [1955] 1994, 91.

35. Bietenholz 1985, 46; and Rödel 2002, 27.

36. Reuchlin published the patent of nobility twice (in *Clarorum virorum epistolae* 1514 and *Illustrium virorum epistolae* 1519). See Reuchlin, *Briefwechsel* 1:429–35 (appendix 3, 24 October 1492), for the text.

37. Keen 1988, 9.

38. Scheible 1989, 24.

39. See Scheible 1989, 23. The sixteenth-century historian David Chrytaeus identified Melanchthon as Reuchlin's "ex sorore nepos."

40. See Scheible 1997, 15. Elaborating on Decker-Hauff [1955] 1994, Scheible 1989, 25ff., also postulated that Reuchlin's sister Elisabeth, the resident of Pforzheim, was a younger sister and not the sister who was a widow of Johannes Reuter. One problem with Scheible's proposal of two sisters is that Giles of Viterbo was aware of only two siblings, Dionysius and Elisabeth. See Reuchlin, *Briefwechsel* 3:369–73 (no. 297, 20 October 1516).

41. See Reuchlin, *Briefwechsel* 3:35–40 (no. 237, 20 April 1514), for a request to Jacob Questenberg to present a copy of *Clarorum virorum epistolae* personally to Pope Leo X.

42. The renaming of Melanchthon probably occurred in Pforzheim on 15 March 1509. See Scheible 1989, 30.

43. Reuchlin 1494, *De verbo mirifico*, in *Sämtliche Werke* 1/1:20–24. In Reuchlin's revision, Phorcys escaped with Aeneas, but somehow separated from Anchises' son, and ended up wandering around the Hercynian forest (i.e., Black Forest). When he came to the confluence of the Nagold and the Würm, he asked some natives the name of the river that flowed so beautifully from the double convergence of streams. The answer was the "Aeneas," which is supposed to suggest the actual German name of the river, "Enz." Phorcys took this as a sign that his culture would flourish there and named the new settlement after himself.

44. See Reuchlin 1513, trans., *Constantinus magnus*, reprinted in Reuchlin, *Briefwechsel* 2:379–96 (no. 220, 13 August 1513).

45. Older scholarship often gives Reuchlin's birth date, incorrectly, as 22 February 1455.

46. For a general essay on Pforzheim during Reuchlin's age, see Sexauer [1955] 1994.

47. Reuchlin, *Briefwechsel*, ed. L. Geiger, 320 (no. 286, 21 December 1519): "dimidium animae."

48. See Christ 1924; Preisendanz [1955] 1994; and Abel and Leicht 2005. According to Reuchlin's will, St. Michael's Church was supposed to make the library available for general use but was not to lend any books or allow them to be removed from the premises. This last condition was not respected, which is one of the reasons some of the books have survived into the twenty-first century.

49. Melanchthon [1552] 1843, 1009: "non voluit dissipari libros ab haeredibus."

50. Preisendanz [1955] 1994, 49; and Horawitz 1877, 176.

51. See Melanchthon [1552] 1843, 1009: "Cum ita accensa essent hominum studia, Tecelius [i.e., Johann Tetzel] aliud incendium maius excitat, irritat Lutherum,…"

52. Zier 1982, fig. 122.

53. Brod 1965, 38.

54. Holstein 1888, 54ff.

55. See Zier 1982, 43–46, on the Battle of Seckenheim, and 46–48, on the attempt to found a university.

56. On Thomas Anshelm as printer, see Alberts [1955] 1994.

57. He also created images in the words by using red for some of the letters and by superimposing outlines printed with woodcuts on the text printed with type.

58. According to Münster 1523, fol. Aa3ʳ–Aa3ᵛ, Anshelm had cut the Hebrew letters (i.e., the punches for them) himself, though a little roughly: "hebraicis formulis…quas ipse primus sculpserat, sed infelicius paulo."

59. Reuchlin, *Briefwechsel* 2:332–42 (no. 207, 31 August 1512).

60. Dates are according to Alberts [1955] 1994, 206.

61. Alberts [1955] 1994, 224.

62. See chapter 4 for an explanation of Reuchlin's alteration of the tetragrammaton.

63. See Pflüger [1862] 1989, 97.

64. On the general phenomenon of blood libel cases, see Hsia 1988. The earliest known blood libel case was that of the English boy William of Norwich in 1144.

65. Pflüger [1862] 1989, 88.

66. Oberman 1993, 57.

67. Fraenkel-Goldschmidt 2006, 57–67, 302–3.

68. Reuchlin, *Briefwechsel* 1:68, l. 6 (no. 20, 1 March 1488): "nusquam inveni libros Graecos, Graecorum vero liberos multos."

69. The following are the German universities in chronological order: Prague (1348), Vienna (1365), Erfurt (1379), Heidelberg (1385), Cologne (1388), Leipzig (1409), Rostock (1419), Freiburg (1456), Basel (1460), Greifswald (1460), Tübingen (1477). See Overfield 1984, 3–12, on the foundation of German universities in general. Overfield (9) is unaware of the failed attempt to found a university in Pforzheim. See Zier 1982, 46–48.

70. According to Scheible 1989, 11, it is plausible that Heynlin von Stein went to grammar school at Reuchlin's alma mater in Pforzheim.

71. Reuchlin, *Briefwechsel* 1:199, ll. 14–18 (no. 64, after 21 April 1494). The tribute is in the dedication of Reuchlin's *Miracle-Making Word* to Johannes von Dalberg.

72. Reuchlin, *Briefwechsel* 3:72, ll. 84ff. (no. 242, 19 June 1514), stated this in his letter to the faculty of theology at the University of Paris. See Preisendanz [1955] 1994, 35–36.

73. Anshelm printed Gaguin's *De arte metrificandi* in 1505 and 1506.

74. Gaguin's *Compendium de origine et gestis Francorum* was first printed in 1495.

75. See Levi 2002, 128.

76. On the early history of the University of Basel, see Bonjour 1960.

77. Reuchlin, *Briefwechsel*, ed. L. Geiger, 283 (no. 250, February 1518), the dedicatory letter of Reuchlin 1518, *De accentibus et orthographia linguae hebraicae*, to Cardinal Adriano Castellesi.

78. See Reuchlin, *Briefwechsel* 1:9–11 (no. 1, before 1 May 1477).

79. Reeves 1984.

80. Rudolf Agricola mentioned this in a letter to Reuchlin. See Reuchlin, *Briefwechsel* 1:39–47, esp. ll. 62ff. (no. 12, 9 November 1484).

81. Benzing 1955, 1–5.

82. Ackermann 1999, 212ff. Ackermann relies on the older but still valuable research of Stintzing 1880 and Seckel 1898.

83. See L. Geiger 1871, 68–77.

84. See Hieronymus 1979.

85. Melanchthon [1552] 1843, 1005, speaking of Reuchlin: "hic narrat se Germanum esse, et non omnino rudem Graecae linguae."

86. Melanchthon [1552] 1843, 1005: "Graecia nostro exsilio transvolavit Alpes." See Reuchlin, *Briefwechsel*, ed. L. Geiger 1875, no. 94 (p. 96 n. 3) on Melanchthon's first reference to the story in a work from 1533.

87. See Reuchlin, *Briefwechsel* 2:421–22, ll. 29–32 (no. 227, ca. 31 August 1513), a letter to the French humanist Jacques Lefèvre d'Etaples.

88. See Sicherl 1978, 25–26.

89. This was contrary to the terms of Ragusa's will, but something that Reuchlin carefully negotiated in 1488 with the Basel Carthusians, who had the legal right to claim Ragusa's library, if the Dominicans did not follow the terms of the will. See Reuchlin, *Briefwechsel* 1:78–91 (nos. 25, 26, and 27). For a list of other Greek manuscripts that Reuchlin borrowed from the Basel Dominican convent, see Reuchlin, *Briefwechsel* 1:90–91 n. 2 (no. 27).

90. Reuchlin, *Briefwechsel* 2:42, ll. 200ff. (no. 138, 7 March 1506): "frustillatim" (l. 205). See also Dibbelt 1938, 18.

91. Förstel 1999, 51. See Reuchlin, *Briefwechsel* 1:360 n. 1.

92. See Förstel 1999, 53.

93. Reuchlin 1519, trans., *Liber S. Athanasii de variis quaestionibus*, fol. K3^{r}ff., acknowledged Valla's objections to the apostolicity of the Dionysian corpus.

94. See chapter 4.

95. Reuchlin, *Briefwechsel* 1:13–15 (no. 3, 1477).

96. See Dibbelt 1938, 19.

97. Reuchlin, *Briefwechsel* 1:134–42 (no. 44, 16 June 1491). Reuchlin published the letter in *Clarorum virorum epistolae* 1514 and in *Illustrium virorum epistolae* 1519.

98. See L. Geiger 1868, 23.

99. See Reuchlin, *Briefwechsel* 1:239–42 (no. 76, before 28 August 1495).

100. See Poland 1899. The manuscript was copied by a Saxon who altered the original to accord with his own dialect.

101. See Mertens 1998, 237, and discussion in chapter 3. It is also possible that Reuchlin's purpose was to foster discussion among those opposing the French King Charles VIII's 1494 invasion of Italy.

102. See Bleicher 1972.

103. See Reuchlin 1510, trans., *Batrachomiomachia*. Reuchlin had completed the translation by 1491 and dedicated it to Erhard von Pappenheim, who, however, died (1497) before the publication. Pappenheim, one of the few Germans of his day who knew some Greek, was confessor at the Dominican convent of Altenhohenau am Inn (Bavaria). He translated the trial documents of the 1475 Trent blood libel case for Count Eberhard the Bearded of Württemberg and may have been a student of the anti-Jewish crusader Peter Schwarz. See Reuchlin, *Briefwechsel* 2:7–10 (no. 73a, before 8 August 1495), esp. 9–10, n. 5.

104. Reuchlin 1512, trans., *De praeparatione hominis*. See Reuchlin, *Briefwechsel* 2:247–60 (no. 192, after 17 February 1512).

105. Reuchlin, *Briefwechsel* 1:83 (no. 26, 22 July 1488).

106. See Reuchlin, *Briefwechsel* 3:90–95 (no. 246, August 1514), and *CWE: Correspondence* 3:5–8 (no. 300). The manuscript is Basel MS AN IV 2, from the twelfth century.

107. See Reuchlin 1529, trans., *Sermo Procli*, and Reuchlin, *Briefwechsel* 1:78–81 (no. 25, 22 July 1488), a letter to Jacob Lauber that accompanies the translation of Proclus. Lauber had been rector at Basel during the time of Reuchlin's studies. The work also survives in a manuscript in the Basel University Library, Codex E III 15. The manuscript includes a translation of Maximus of Tyre's *Cur deus autor sit bonorum*, which Reuchlin had prepared for Johannes Heynlin von Stein, who had recently joined the Basel Carthusians. See Reuchlin, *Briefwechsel* 1:80 n. 3.

108. The manuscript is in Paris, Bibliothèque Nationale, Codex suppl. Gr. 212. See Sicherl 1963.

109. On Athanasius in Reuchlin's library, see Hommel 1938.

110. Reuchlin 1515, trans., *S. Athanasius in librum psalmorum*.

111. Reuchlin even published the Speyer Verdict of 1514 as part of the dedication to Questenberg. See Reuchlin, *Briefwechsel* 3:248, ll. 162–202 (no. 273, 12 August 1515).

112. Reuchlin 1519, trans., *Liber S. Athanasii de variis quaestionibus*.

113. The dedication to Albrecht, which asserts yet again the orthodoxy of his position on Jewish writings, celebrates the archbishop hyperbolically as the strongest supporter of the humanities among the German princes: "te caeteris Germaniae principibus literarum amantiorem" (Reuchlin 1519, trans., *Liber S. Athanasii de variis quaestionibus*, fol. A4ᵛ).

114. The correspondence between Manuzio and Reuchlin suggests personal warmth between the men but also includes quibbling over the prices of Manuzio's books. See Reuchlin, *Briefwechsel* 1: nos. 97, 116, 118, and 119.

115. Christ 1924, 16–18.

116. See Lowry 1979, 180–216.

117. Reuchlin, *Briefwechsel* 1:314, ll. 13–14 (no. 97, 23 April 1499): "nosti Germaniam: Nunquam desiit esse rudis…non sumus te digni."

118. Reuchlin 1520, ed., Ἀπολογία Σωκράτους.

119. In 1477, while an advanced student at Basel, Reuchlin sent Jacob Hugonis, rector of the University of Basel in 1477/78, a Latin translation of Xenophon's *Apology of Socrates*. His translation survives in a manuscript at the

Badische Landesbibliothek in Karlsruhe, Codex Aug. 127, fol. 45–51. See Reuchlin, *Briefwechsel* 1:15–18 (no. 4, 1477).

120. Reuchlin 1522, ed., *Graeciae excellentium oratorum Aeschines et Demosthenis orationes adversariae*. The book is dedicated to Thomas Anshelm.

121. Reuchlin, *Briefwechsel* 2:421, ll. 29ff. (no. 227, ca. 31 August 1513); see Sicherl 1993, 533, who grants that Reuchlin's boasts are essentially justified. He had precious few predecessors who knew Greek—Nicholas of Cusa (1401–64) and Johannes Regiomontanus (1436–76)—and those few precursors did not strive to disseminate knowledge of the language.

CHAPTER 3

Epigraph source: Reuchlin, *Briefwechsel* 1:243, ll. 32–33 (no. 77, 1 October 1495): "literarum et patriae nostrae decus."

1. For a comprehensive history of the Reichsreform movement, see Angermeier 1984.

2. See Bock 1927; and Hesslinger 1970 on the formation of the Swabian League.

3. Herzig 1993, 13.

4. On the foundation of the University of Tübingen, see Haller 1927–29; on Duke Eberhard the Bearded, see Ernst [1933] 1970; Mertens 1994, 1998; and Angermeier 1994.

5. A great regret in Eberhard's life was that he had not learned Latin. His father, Count Ludwig I, had forced his ministers to swear an oath that they would stop the boy Eberhard from wasting his time on such a pursuit.

6. Worstbrock 1970, 53–56.

7. In *Eye Glasses*, Reuchlin asserted that displaying his Hebrew knowledge would have diminished his own status in Württemberg. See Reuchlin 1511, *Augenspiegel*, in *Sämtliche Werke* 4/1:157, ll. 27ff.: "dann es hett mir vil mer zü verclainerung gediennt." See Mertens 1998, 242.

8. From the beginning, Eberhard also relied on professors at Tübingen to serve as his advisors, which they typically did without receiving extra pay. See Reuchlin, *Briefwechsel* 1:93–94 (no. 29, 26 September 1488), and Mertens 1998, 233.

9. See Reuchlin, *Briefwechsel* 1:34–39 (no. 11, 2 October 1484) for a letter from the humanist Bernhard Adelmann von Adelmannsfelden, who scornfully included a letter written in the name of Princess Barbara in barbaric Latin.

10. Mertens 1998, 233 n. 32, quoting Trithemius, *Annales Hirsaugenses*: "Inter omnes Germaniae principes nostra, quos novimus, tempestate nullus fuit, qui curiam suam tot viris omnifariam eruditis promotisque in aliqua facultate doctoribus manuteneret ornatam, ut comiti Wirtenbergensium aliquo modo videatur comparandus."

11. See Mertens 1998, 234–35. Of the twenty-six princely retinues (both secular and ecclesiastical) surveyed, ten had no councilors with a doctorate and ten others had only one with a doctorate. Eberhard's retinue, with seven doctorates (out of forty-eight councilors) had the most academic distinction by far.

12. Frey 1989, 228, describes the court of Württemberg during Reuchlin's tenure as "one of the most advanced of its time." The procedural code of 1475 is no longer extant.

13. Lorenz 2009, 152ff.

14. Melanchthon [1552] 1843, 1003: "Ac ut in aulam citius vocaretur, occasio haec fuit, Princeps optimus Eberardus eo tempore Romam proficisci decreverat, quo cum senes Nauclerum, Petrum Arlunensem et Gabrielem [i.e., Biel] duceret, hi monuerunt, ut adiungeretur ipsis Capnio, qui et exteras nationes antea vidisset, et usum haberet latine dicendi et scribendi, et sonum pronunciationis minus horridum."

15. On Biel, see Oberman 1963.

16. See Nägele 1935.

17. Melanchthon [1552] 1843, 1003, reported that Reuchlin's hard work in Rome pleased the prince especially "because he noticed that the great men preferred to listen to Reuchlin speak rather than his other (councilors) who retained their native (i.e., Swabian) accent" ("quia animadvertit libentius audiri Capnionis orationem a summis viris, quam aliorum, qui retinebant patrium sonum").

18. Stinger [1985] 1998, 282–91.

19. See chapter 2.

20. Stievermann 1998, 38–39.

21. Stievermann 1998 and, above all, Ackermann 1999 are important studies of Reuchlin's service as a jurist.

22. See Stievermann 1998, 40, for a longer list of business trips.

23. Ackermann 1999, 104.

24. Ackermann 1999, 69–70.

25. Ackermann 1999, 66.

26. See Ackermann 1999, 66–68.

27. Reuchlin, *Briefwechsel* 1:99–102 (no. 32, 24 December 1489).

28. See Reuchlin, *Briefwechsel* 1:102 n. 8; and Ackermann 1999, 61.

29. Stievermann 1998, 44, implies that Reuchlin might have mounted an ineffective defense in order to make Heinrich's crime more notorious, but there is no clear evidence for this.

30. Reuchlin, *Briefwechsel* 1:114–16 (no. 36, ca. 2 April 1490). See also Ernst [1933] 1970, 42.

31. See Reuchlin, *Briefwechsel* 1:110–13 (no. 35, 2 April 1490), esp. 112 n. 5.

32. Reuchlin, *Briefwechsel* 1:115–16 n. 4.

33. Holzinger was in Mainz on a legal matter, while Eberhard the Bearded and Reuchlin were arbitrating a dispute between Trier and the Palatinate there.

34. See Ackermann 1999, 52–54, on the conflicts between Trier and Cologne and between Trier and the Palatinate. Records survive for one other imperial case in which Reuchlin served as associate justice under Eberhard's arbitration, a dispute in the bishopric of Worms in 1489–90. The bishop was at odds with a consortium holding the minting privileges for the realm. This case was settled out of court in 1491.

35. Reuchlin occasionally used this term himself, as in the dedication of the *Miracle-Making Word* to Bishop Johannes von Dalberg. See Reuchlin, *Briefwechsel* 1:199, l. 22 (no. 64, after 21 April 1494), referring to Johannes Amerbach and

Sebastian Brant as members of the *res publica literaria*. Michael Hummelberger, in Reuchlin, *Briefwechsel* 3:258, ll. 14–19 (no. 275, 28 August 1515), wrote that a Reuchlin defeat in Rome would be a great loss for the "res publica literaria."

36. Peter Jacobi had previously supervised Ludwig's education, especially his studies in Orléans.

37. The Latin dictionary Reuchlin helped assemble in 1478 was never published under his name.

38. On Questenberg's remarkable career and the extensive correspondence with Reuchlin, see Dörner 1999a.

39. Reuchlin, *Briefwechsel* 1:117, l. 4 (no. 37, 1 August 1490). Questenberg was also a protégé of Bishop Dalberg, who was Reuchlin's Heidelberg patron from 1496 through 1499.

40. Incidentally, it is known from Reuchlin's own statement that he was present at Friedrich's death. See Reuchlin 1513, *Defensio*, in *Sämtliche Werke* 4/1:328, ll. 24ff.; and Geiger 1868, 28.

41. See Carl 1998, 69ff., on the political negotiations.

42. Reuchlin's surviving correspondence with the leaders of the army of the Swabian League, Count Haug von Werdenberg and Wilhelm Besserer, and with Margrave Friedrich of Brandenburg, in charge of the imperial army, indicate his intense involvement in this crisis. See Reuchlin, *Briefwechsel* 1:158–61 (no. 51, 3 February 1492); 1:166–69 (no. 54, 28 March 1492); and 1:169–75 (no. 55, 21 April 1492).

43. See chapter 4.

44. See Abel and Leicht 2003, 89–96, on the manuscript, now known as the "Reuchlin-Bible," or as "Codex Reuchlin 1," which is currently in the Badische Landesbibliothek in Karlsruhe. The Bible also contains the Targum Onkelos as well as the Small Masorah and the Large Masorah.

45. Melanchthon [1552] 1843, 1003: "Delectatus est senex et sapiens Imperator studio hominis germani, et ad caetera dona hunc pulcherrimum codicem, qui non potuisset emi trecentis aureis, adiunxit."

46. The text of the patent of nobility is in Reuchlin, *Briefwechsel* 1:429–35 (appendix 3). Reuchlin printed the patent in both *Clarorum virorum epistolae* 1514, fol. k2^v–k5^r, and *Illustrium virorum epistolae* 1519, fol. m4^v–n3^r.

47. On the constitutional irregularities of the Diet of Frankfurt, see Angermeier 1994, 383.

48. Wiesflecker 1971–86, 1:191.

49. At this time, two men claimed to be king of Bohemia. Friedrich invited neither.

50. For an account of the political subtleties in Reuchlin's dispatches, see Angermeier 1994, esp. 384ff., on Württemberg's alignment with Austria at the Diet of Frankfurt.

51. *Deutsche Reichstagsakten* 1989, vol. 1/2, nos. 873–82. One of Reuchlin's dispatches has survived in finished form, whereas only the notes for several others are still extant. See also Reuchlin, *Briefwechsel* 1:53–58 (no. 15, 9 April 1486), for his report on the coronation in Aachen.

52. Angermeyer 1994, 383; and *Deutsche Reichstagsakten* 1989, vol. 1/2, no. 876 (p. 825).

53. Angermeyer 1994, 382; and *Deutsche Reichstagsakten* 1989, vol. 1/2, no. 874 (p. 813).

54. Wiesflecker 1971–86, 1:199. Angermeier 1994, 384, confirms that Eberhard would have been keenly interested in the accounts of the jousting tournaments.

55. See Laufs 1995.

56. For details on the tax, called the "Common Penny," see Laufs 1995, 670.

57. As Mertens 1998, 237, has noted, Cardinal Bessarion and Guillaume Fichet had already used a Latin translation of the *First Olynthian* speech in 1470/71 as anti-Turkish propaganda. Reuchlin was probably aware of that earlier effort.

58. A councilor to the archbishop of Magdeburg, Hermansgrün became an intellectual touchstone for the diet after he circulated a tract, called the *Dream*, in which Charlemagne, Otto the Great, and Friedrich Barbarossa called on the estates to unite behind the emperor in order to face foreign enemies. Even late in the diet, after all the compromises had been settled, Hermansgrün expressed bitterness over the princes' wrangling. See Reuchlin, *Briefwechsel* 1:239–42 (no. 76, before 28 August 1495).

59. Reuchlin, *Briefwechsel* 1:240, ll. 5–6 (no. 76, before 28 August 1495): "Utinam principio huius congregationis unicuique principum istas tuas translationes misisses."

60. Possibly, Reuchlin expressed this confidence in Maximilian's position after having heard overly rosy reports about the Battle of Fornovo di Taro (6 July 1495), which was claimed, erroneously, as a victory for the Holy League.

61. Reuchlin, *Briefwechsel* 1:229, l. 13 (no. 72, 25 July 1495): "an forte semper belligerandum est?" Hermansgrün had forcefully advocated increasing Maximilian's military resources.

62. Reuchlin's translation of Lucian survives in manuscript (Dresden, Staatsarchiv, H 184b). See Worstbrock 1976, 103; and, for the text, Distel 1895.

63. Mertens 1998, 236.

64. According to an inscription, Reuchlin received a manuscript of Joseph Gikatilla's *Ginnat Egoz* (*Nut Garden*) in Worms from Bishop Dalberg on 3 April 1495, just before the diet began. See Abel and Leicht 2005, 147.

65. See Reuchlin, *Briefwechsel* 1:246 n. 3 (no. 78, 5 October 1495), on the extreme likelihood that Reuchlin returned to Worms in October. Graf 1998, 223, questioned his return.

66. See Amelung 1986 on the circumstances of Eberhard's death.

67. See Reuchlin, *Briefwechsel* 1:260–63 (no. 81, 29 February 1496), an astute letter from Bernhard Schöfferlin (ca. 1436/38–1501), an important minister in the Württemberg court who was then an assessor for the Imperial Chamber Court. Schöfferlin would later be Reuchlin's precursor on the court of the Swabian League. See also Reuchlin, *Briefwechsel* 1:263–65 (no. 82, 21 April 1496), a letter from Pietro Bonomo (1458–1546), then a leading figure in the humanist circle at Maximilian's court, offering to help Reuchlin in every possible way during the crisis.

68. For a comprehensive (and critical) assessment of Philipp's patronage of the arts, see Backes 1992, 136–71; and Cohn 1971.

69. Reuchlin, *Briefwechsel* 1:39–47 (no. 12, 9 November 1484), esp. ll. 56ff.

70. See Backes 1992, 151.

71. Reuchlin, *Briefwechsel* 1:102–6 (no. 33, 1489). Reuchlin's tract, *De quattuor Graecae linguae differentiis*, was never printed. It survives in a manuscript in the University of Basel (F IV 54), copied by Johannes Drach (who had contacts with some of Reuchlin's former Greek students), and in another manuscript in the Württembergische Landesbibliothek (Codex poet. et phil. 4° 76), copied by Reuchlin's acquaintance Nikolaus Basellius.

72. Reuchlin, *Briefwechsel* 1:107–10 (no. 34, 1489). The text survives in the same manuscripts that have Reuchlin's *De quattuor Graecae linguae differentiis* (see previous note). See Wyss 1970; and Sicherl 1985.

73. See Reuchlin, *Briefwechsel* 1:153–57, ll. 11ff. (no. 50, 12 December 1491). Incidentally, as far as I can determine, no German-language poetry by Reuchlin has survived.

74. See Reuchlin, *Briefwechsel* 1:153–57, ll. 36ff. (no. 50, 12 December 1491).

75. See Abel and Leicht 2005, 145–49, esp. 147.

76. See Abel and Leicht 2005, 207–14, for evidence that Reuchlin's manuscript, which was destroyed in 1942, was actually of the *Nizzahon Vetus* and not of Lipmann's diatribe. For a discussion of Lipmann's *Sefer ha-Nizzahon*, see Limor and Yuval 2004.

77. This presentation copy survives in a deluxe manuscript in Heidelberg, Codex Pal. Germ. 482. See Reuchlin, *Briefwechsel* 1:356–58 (no. 112, 23 June 1501).

78. See Celtis 1934, 185, ll. 13–18 (no. 110, 13 May 1496). The entire passage, written by Heinrich Spieß, indicates that Reuchlin focused sharply on translating Greek texts: "Officium Joannis Reuchlin est transferre e Graeco in Latinum nostrum sermonem, quae volet Episcopus. Ipse vero rem iam pridem aggressus nonnulla egregia opera transtulit et inter alia vitam Constantini Magni et nonnullorum aliorum imperatorum, quae antea in toto Latio nusquam visa sunt; item transtulit aliquos libellos ex Homero."

79. Friedrich 1998, 164. Thomas Truchseß would serve as Reuchlin's judge in the Speyer phase of his trial (in 1514). See chapter 7.

80. Before leaving Heidelberg, he wrote a letter in Greek to Jodocus Gallus and Thomas Truchseß encouraging them to continue their Greek studies, presumably under the direction of Johannes Cuno. See Reuchlin, *Briefwechsel* 1:311–13 (no. 96, 12 March 1499).

81. For discussions of his surviving corpus of poems, see Holstein 1890 and, especially, Rhein 1989. Rhein 1989, 55, was aware of twenty-four poems (not counting translations or plays) by Reuchlin.

82. In 1496, the humanist poet and Tübingen professor Heinrich Bebel published two panegyrics on Eberhard's elevation to duke in his *Carmina*. In the same work, fol. B6ʳ–C1ᵛ, he also published two extravagant poetic tributes to Reuchlin, celebrating him as a scholar and humanist writer and also for "guiding the arduous deeds of the princes with your great skill" ("Ardua et magna moderaris arte | Principum…facta"). In the conclusion of his elegy to Reuchlin, Bebel expressed a wish that most German humanists of his generation shared: "I want to be counted

among your students so that your learned Minerva may give her erudition to me" ("Atque tuos inter famulos numerarier opto, | Ut nos erudiat docta Minerva tua"). See Reuchlin, *Briefwechsel* 1:247–58 (no. 79, after 25 February 1496), for Bebel's letter accompanying the presentation of the poems to Reuchlin. Reuchlin reprinted the poetic letters in *Clarorum virorum epistolae* 1514 and *Illustrium virorum epistolae* 1519.

83. Ironically, he used the elegy form to express his poetic insufficiency. See Reuchlin, *Briefwechsel* 1:236–39, ll. 27–28 (no. 75, August 1495): "Semper enim fugiunt Musas Nicer atque Bacenae, | Et nequit in Suevis vatibus esse locus." The term "Bacenae" is unclear. It seems to refer generally to an ancient forest in Germany, although Reuchlin appears to use it in other places to designate the Black Forest and here, perhaps, in reference to the Swabian Alb. See Reuchlin, *Briefwechsel* 1:239 n. 10.

84. Reuchlin 1498, *Scenica progymnasmata*, in Holstein 1888, 32, Jacob Dracontius writing: "primus et solus inter Germanos comoediae sit auctor." The original title of *Henno* was *Scenica progymnasmata*, that is, *Theatrical Exercises*.

85. See Roloff 1998, 187.

86. Benzing 1955, 7–10. Benzing also records six further printings of *Sergius* in imprints of *Henno* (see 20–23).

87. The music for Reuchlin's *Henno* was composed by the otherwise unknown Daniel Megel.

88. Melanchthon [1552] 1843, 1005: "Dalburgius lecta illi monachi insectatione [i.e., the play *Sergius*], dissuasit editionem et actionem, quod eodem tempore et apud Philippum Palatinum Franciscanus erat Castellus, propter potentiam et malas artes invisus nobilibus et sapientibus viris in aula. Intellexit periculum Capnio, et hanc comoediam occultavit."

89. Reuchlin 1504, *Sergius*, in Holstein 1888, 116–17, esp. ll. 242–67. The quote is from ll. 243–44: "Ausis poetarum sacrata munera | Temere profanare."

90. Reuchlin 1498, *Scenica progymnasmata*, in Holstein 1888, 30–31, addressing Dalberg: "Tu enim et primus et solus es, qui humanitatis studia et litteras politiores in hoc Heidelbergense lyceum, in hanc stoam…sed in hanc inquam scholam quasi humeris ipse tuis intulisti et ab indoctis incultis et invidis veteratoribus quotidie defensitas, adeo ut nullae sint litterarum deliciae, nulla Germaniae musa, quae non in tuas laudes merito aspiret, te tuamque illam nobilem familiam non in caelum usque summis efferat praeconiis."

91. Roloff 1998, 194.

92. Reuchlin 1498, *Scenica progymnasmata*, in Holstein 1888, 22, l. 245: "Nam auro est opus non aliter atque vita."

93. The letter is to Wenzeslaus Link, an Augustinian preacher in Nuremberg, who had been Luther's colleague in Wittenberg. *WA: Briefe* 1:185, ll. 29–31 (no. 83, 10 July 1518): "Canto cum Iohanne Reuchlin: 'Qui pauper est, nihil timet, nihil perdere potest, sed spe bona laetus sedet, nam sperat acquirere.'" Reuchlin added the line "discitque virtute deum colere" ("and he learns piously to worship god"). See the original passage in Reuchlin 1498, *Scenica progymnasmata*, in Holstein 1888, 18, ll. 150–53.

94. Humanist poetry, the theme of the choruses after acts 2, 3, and 4, is portrayed as a medium of divine illumination. See Reuchlin 1498, *Scenica*

progymnasmata, in Holstein 1888, 21, ll. 229–32: "Digna sunt Apolline | Quae concinunt poetae, | Quo coruscant numine | Divinitus prophetae" ("The songs the poets sing are worthy of Apollo; with the spirit of his divinity, the prophets are gleaming"). For an analysis of the choruses, see Ehrstine 1998.

95. Reuchlin, *Briefwechsel* 1:436–39 (appendix 4), for Reuchlin's appointment as a councilor to Elector Philipp.

96. Reuchlin, *Briefwechsel* 1:436–37, ll. 8ff. (appendix 4, 31 December 1497): "Wir, Philips etc., bekennen etc., das wir den ersamen, unsern lieben getruwen Johann Reuchlin, doctor, zu unserm rate, diener und hoffgesind und in sunder zu eynem obersten zuchtmeister unser lieben söne uffgenommen haben...auch unnser sachen ime bevohlen, in und ußwendig hoffs zu betrachten und zu handeln mit hochstem flyß."

97. See Backes 1992, 136–37; Friedrich 1998, 171ff.; and Ackermann 1999, 91ff.

98. Reuchlin 1519, ed., *Illustrium virorum epistolae*, fol. n3ᵛ: "qui [refers to 'Christus'] tuis istis clauibus spiritualibus, atque caelestibus, non solum aliquantulam terrae glebam, uerum et uniuersum hoc orbis terrarum spacium contulit." Excerpts from the speech were translated into German by Adalbert Weh in Schwab 1998, 105–10.

99. See *Acta iudiciorum* 1518, fol. F8ʳ: "S. V. Orator Ioan. Reuchlin," i.e., "Sanctitatis Vestrae Orator."

100. See Ackermann 1999, 94–95; and Reuchlin, *Briefwechsel* 1:363–65 (no. 115, 27 June 1502).

101. Reuchlin also conferred with Manuzio about plans to create a trilingual college (Latin, Greek, Hebrew) in the Holy Roman Empire. See chapter 2 and Reuchlin, *Briefwechsel* 1:313–17 (no. 97, 23 April 1499).

102. Reuchlin's correspondence shows that his colleagues in Heidelberg tried hard to retain him there. See Reuchlin, *Briefwechsel* 1:322–27 (no. 100, 2 November 1499).

103. For example, Reuchlin participated in hosting guests for Duke Ulrich's wedding in 1511. More important, he appears to have been involved in the enforcement of the 1514 Treaty of Tübingen, which ended the Poor Conrad revolt against Duke Ulrich, and in the 1517 dissolution of the Brethren of the Common Life houses in Württemberg. See Ackermann 1999, 97, 99; and Stievermann 1989, 288. Without any elaboration or explanation, the sources for these events only briefly mention or imply Reuchlin's involvement. Nonetheless, at least once, Reuchlin referred to himself as Ulrich's "Rat." See Reuchlin, *Briefwechsel* 3:27–28, ll. 27–29 (no. 235, 6 April 1514).

104. Reuchlin, *Briefwechsel* 1:329, ll. 2ff. (no. 102, 13 January 1500): "Gratulator...in primis, quoniam ab illa erumnosa te liberatum extractumque esse curiali molestia accepi."

105. See Frey 1979, 235–36 n. 29; and Ackermann 1999, 129–39, for the details of the complicated case history.

106. His salary was not always paid on time. When he resigned, Reuchlin had to retain possession of the court records for at least several weeks in order to compel

the Swabian League to pay his outstanding salary. See Ackermann 1999, 147; and Reuchlin, *Briefwechsel* 3:485–86 (appendix 1).

107. Ackermann 1999, 110.

108. The letter of dedication is in Reuchlin, *Briefwechsel* 2:13–32 (no. 137, 3 March 1506).

109. See Reuchlin, *Briefwechsel* 2:362–64 (no. 213, 4 January 1513), for Reuchlin's admiration of Adriani's scholarship. Adriani also translated the *Ave Maria, Salve Regina*, the *Magnificat*, the *Lord's Prayer*, and the *Apostles' Creed* in Adriani 1513, *Libellus hora faciendi pro domino*. Adriani included a critique of the Hebrew translations that Pfefferkorn had published in 1508. See Adriani 1513, *Libellus hora faciendi pro domino*, fol. D1ʳff. Reuchlin mentions Adriani's critique of Pfefferkorn in his letter to the faculty of theology at the University of Paris. See Reuchlin, *Briefwechsel*, 3:70, ll. 30–33 (no. 242, 19 June 1514).

110. As in the emperor's letter of 23 October 1514 to Leo X. See Reuchlin, *Briefwechsel* 3:487, l. 5 (appendix 2): "consiliarium nostrum."

111. Reuchlin 1518, *De accentibus et orthographia linguae hebraicae*, fol. a2ᵛ: "Potentissimorum Germaniae principum consiliis intereram."

CHAPTER 4

Epigraph source: Reuchlin 1494, *De verbo mirifico*, in *Sämtliche Werke* 1/1:162–64: "Simplex autem sermo, purus, incorruptus, sanctus, brevis et constans Hebraeorum est, quo deus cum homine, et homines cum angelis locuti perhibentur coram et non per interpretem, facie ad faciem ... sicut solet amicus loqui cum amico."

1. L. Geiger 1870, 24.

2. See Walde 1916, 70–151, for a valuable study of the most important Christian Hebrew scholar of the fifteenth century, Peter Schwarz (Petrus Nigri). Schwarz's goal was to combat Judaism.

3. On Nicholas of Lyra's anti-Judaism, see Klepper 2007.

4. See the introduction to Dan 1997 for a formulation of this question. In part, my discussion expands Dan's question, which he raised specifically about the history of Christian Kabbalah, to all of Reuchlin's Jewish scholarship, both theological and philological.

5. The mandate is decree 24 of the Council of Vienne, as edited by Tanner and Alberigo 1990 1:379–80. Though unmentioned by Reuchlin, the Council's stated goal was to create "catholic scholars acquainted with the languages most in use by unbelievers" ... to propagate "the saving faith among the heathen peoples" (1:379).

6. Reuchlin, *Briefwechsel* 2:37, ll. 94–96 (no. 138, 7 March 1506): "mecum ipse constitui ad tradendam Christianis Hebraici sermonis peritiam hoc libro prima fundamenta iacere pro Clementis papae quinti sacra constitutione de magistris lata."

7. Reuchlin 1511, *Augenspiegel*, in *Sämtliche Werke* 4/1:64, ll. 3–11 (the concluding point in Reuchlin's *Recommendation*).

8. Reuchlin, *Briefwechsel* 2:37, ll. 89–94 (no. 138, 7 March 1506): "Sane recordatus miseros nostra aetate Iudaeorum casus, qui non tam ex Hispaniae quam etiam Germaniae nostrae finibus pulsi coguntur alias sibi sedes quaerere atque ad Agarenos divertere, quo futurum est, ut tandem Hebraica lingua cum sacrarum literarum magna pernicie penes nos posset desinere atque evanescere."

9. Reuchlin, *Briefwechsel* 2:36, l. 40 (no. 138, 7 March 1506): "offerre me latratibus mordacium."

10. Reuchlin 1506, *De rudimentis hebraicis*, 1; and Reuchlin, *Briefwechsel* 2:35, ll. 12–14 (no. 138, 7 March 1506): "erit necesse veterem sanctarum literarum dignitatem in novam faciem Latinis hominibus hactenus incognitam reverti."

11. Reuchlin, *Briefwechsel* 2:43, ll. 250–51 (no. 138, 7 March 1506): "Quanquam enim Hieronymum sanctum veneror ut angelum et Lyram colo ut magistrum, tamen adoro veritatem ut deum."

12. Reuchlin, *Briefwechsel* 1:338 (no. 105, 1 November 1500): "domine mi magister Iacobe, dux meus et notus meus ... qui desydero et concupisco cernere vultum tuum suavissimum ad delectandum de splendore vultus tui lucentis, audiendo doctrinam tuam purissimam."

13. Pfefferkorn 1516, *Defensio*, fol. O3^v.

14. The letter was reprinted in Latin and Hebrew in Reuchlin 1519 ed., *Illustrium virorum epistolae*, fol. m1^r.

15. For the date of the letter, see Reuchlin, *Briefwechsel* 1:48 n. 1 (no. 13, between December 1484 and April 1485).

16. The manuscript, probably an autograph, survives in Sélestat, France. See Reuchlin, *Briefwechsel* 1:47–50 (no. 13, between December 1484 and April 1485).

17. Darlow and Moule 1903–11, 2/2: no. 5071.

18. Reuchlin mentions this more than thirty years after the fact in a mysterious passage in Reuchlin 1518, *De accentibus et orthographia*, fol. v4^v: "Audivimus sane olim Raimundum Mithridaten Romanum, quo tempore Galliarum et Germaniae universitates gymnasticas perlustraverat qui esset hebraice, graece, arabice ac latine peritus." See Zambelli 1969, 280.

19. On Flavius Mithridates' journey through Germany in 1484–85, see Bauch 1904, 79ff.

20. See Reuchlin, *Briefwechsel* 1:49 (no. 13, between December 1484 and April 1485), n. 5; and Raeder 1977, 77.

21. Reuchlin, *Briefwechsel* 2:45, ll. 275–80 (no. 138, 7 March 1506): "cui gravissimus astipulatur testis ille imperii Romani nobilis et generosus comes Ioannes Picus Mirandulanus philosophus in suis Conclusionibus, cum ait: Qui ordinem Hebraicae linguae profunde et radicaliter tenuerit atque illum proporcionabiliter in scientiis servare noverit, cuiuscumque scibilis perfecte inveniendi normam et regulam habebit."

22. See Reuchlin, *Briefwechsel* 2:45, ll. 294ff. (no. 138, 7 March 1506). Passage is quoted in the discussion of *Rudiments of Hebrew*.

23. See *Germania Judaica* 3/3:2075–78. In the fifteenth century, the counts of Württemberg had the power to authorize the existence or expulsion of a Jewish

community. Very few places in the County of Württemberg had Jewish communities in the second half of the fifteenth century. Eberhard the Bearded mandated the complete expulsion of Jews in his will, and although complete expulsion was not immediately carried out, by the first decade of the sixteenth century the duchy had no remaining Jewish communities.

24. Reuchlin 1512, *Ain clare verstentnus*, in *Sämtliche Werke* 4/1:175, ll. 4ff. See also Reuchlin 1518, *De accentibus et orthographia linguae hebraicae*, fol. s3ʳ.

25. Abel and Leicht 2005, 177ff.; and Christ 1924, 23. See Campanini 1999, 75: "Calman Iudaeus, Elementarius praeceptor Ioannis Reuchlin Phorcensis in alphabetho Hebraico, haec Vocabula scripsit eidem suo discipulo mercede conductus. Anno 1486."

26. This is in a letter from the humanist Johannes Streler, who had accompanied Reuchlin's brother, Dionysius, on a study trip to Italy and had been trying to acquire books for Reuchlin. See Reuchlin, *Briefwechsel* 1:175 (no. 56, 29 June 1492). The Bible in question would have been the second edition of the Hebrew Bible, which Joshua Solomon Soncino printed in Naples in 1491.

27. See Preisendanz [1955] 1994, 71; and Reuchlin, *Briefwechsel* 1:176 n. 6 (no. 56, 29 June 1492): "Hanc Bibliam Hebraicam emit Joannes Reuchlin Phorcensis LL. Doctor sex aureis. Et eam sibi iussit afferri ex civitate Pisana Italie, ubi ei empta est Anno domini Millesimo quadringentesimo nonagesimo secundo."

28. Reuchlin 1506, *De rudimentis hebraicis*, 249, 619. See L. Geiger 1871, 106; and Brod 1965, 81.

29. Reuchlin 1506, *De rudimentis hebraicis*, 619: "misericordia dei ueniat super eum."

30. See Fraenkel-Goldschmidt 2006, 312.

31. See chapter 3.

32. Brod 1965, 84.

33. See chapter 3.

34. See Reuchlin, *Briefwechsel* 1:192–95 (no. 62, ca. 1493–96), for a Hebrew letter from Rabbi Jacob Margolioth of Regensburg, indicating that Kabbalistic books Reuchlin was seeking were not available in Regensburg.

35. See Darlow and Moule 1903–11, 2/2:703.

36. See Campanini 1999, 79, for a list of the books acquired in Rome.

37. Kimhi's *Diqduq*, the grammar section of his *Sefer Mikhlol*, would have an immense impact on Christian Hebrew studies, but it would not be printed until 1525. Reuchlin's manuscript of the work, dated to 1282, was destroyed in a 1942 bombardment of Karlsruhe. See L. Geiger 1871, 112, for speculation that Reuchlin could have acquired Kimhi's lexicon (which had been available in print since 1480) during his first trip to Italy.

38. Abel and Leicht 2005, 230–31.

39. Abel and Leicht 2005, 203–6.

40. Abel and Leicht 2005, 115–20. The commentary is now attributed to Joseph ibn Nahmias (fourteenth century).

41. Abel and Leicht 2005, 227–29. This book was destroyed in the 1942 bombardment of Karlsruhe.

42. Abel and Leicht 2005, 97–103. The manuscript includes the Targum Jonathan.

43. See Preisendanz [1955] 1994, 75–76; and Dall'Asta 1999, 28.

44. See Reuchlin 1519, ed., *Illustrium virorum epistolae*, fol. C1ᵛ–C2ᵛ; and Reuchlin, *Briefwechsel* 3:236–41 (no. 272, 20 July 1515).

45. See Sforno 1987.

46. For a study of Sforno's Torah exegesis, see Pelcovitz in Sforno 1987, 1:xi–xxiv.

47. Reuchlin, *Briefwechsel* 2:37, ll. 82–84 (no. 138, 7 March 1506): "qui [i.e., Sforno] me quotidie toto legationis tempore perquam humaniter in Hebraicis erudivit non sine insignis mercedis impendio." I translate "humaniter" as "in the manner of a professor of the humanities." It also has a hint of the English "humanely."

48. Campanini 1999, 79.

49. See Campanini 1999, 81–82.

50. See Reuchlin 1511, *Augenspiegel*, in *Sämtliche Werke* 4/1:54; and Tosefta, Sanhedrin XIII 2.

51. For instance, John of Capistrano railed against a "terrible idea" that the Jews teach, namely, that "everyone can be saved in his own faith" in one of his anti-Jewish sermons delivered in the Holy Roman Empire. See Ben-Sasson 1966, 377–78.

52. See Sforno 1987, 1:339, a note to Exodus 19:5, "The righteous of all people are without a doubt dear to me." See also Campanini 1999, 82ff.

53. Melanchthon [1552] 1843, 1005: "Abdiam illum Iudaeum studiose audivit, deditque δίδακτρα, pro singulis horis, singulos aureos." The fee is unlikely for an hourly lesson. Nonetheless, the fact that Sforno's services were costly may indicate that he did more than provide lessons for Reuchlin, perhaps that he worked on Latin translations of Kimhi entries.

54. Reuchlin 1506, *De rudimentis hebraicis*, 3, and Reuchlin, *Briefwechsel* 2:37, ll. 82–84 (no. 138, 7 March 1506); see note 47 above.

55. Bayerische Staatsbibliothek, Codex hebr. 401.

56. Pellican 1877, 21ff.; Greive 1978, 402: "Annuit Capnion, et me vicissim exaudivit, petentem ab eo exemplar manuscriptum grammaticae R. Mosse Kimhi, quod ab eodem Judaeo germanice translatum habebat, qui Ulmensi sacredoti alia fragmenta transtulerat."

57. See Greive 1978, 397–400, for a valuable attempt to document the basic influence of Priscian's structure on Reuchlin.

58. Reuchlin, *Briefwechsel* 2:204, ll. 29–31 (no. 184, 28 October 1511): "Hebraeorum linguam in Latinas regulas, opus antea inauditum, redegerim eiusque dictionarium construxerim labore meo plenissimum."

59. A good source that documents the impact of David and Moses Kimhi is L. Geiger 1871.

60. Reuchlin 1506, *De rudimentis hebraicis*, 558ff.

61. Reuchlin 1506, *De rudimentis hebraicis*, 585.

62. For instance, for some paradigms Reuchlin uses פָּעַל, the verb from which the Hebrew nomenclature for stems is derived.

63. Reuchlin 1506, *De rudimentis hebraicis*, 591ff.

64. Reuchlin 1506, *De rudimentis hebraicis*, 593–94.

65. Reuchlin 1506, *De rudimentis hebraicis*, 595.

66. Sebastian Münster, Reuchlin's most important student by far, even added the Hebrew terminology to his 1537 revision of *Rudiments of Hebrew*, the only reprint of the work to appear during the Renaissance.

67. See Greive 1978, 405, for the analysis of Reuchlin's dependence on Moses Kimhi's presentation of weak verbs.

68. Reuchlin 1506, *De rudimentis hebraicis*, 615–20, for the section on "consignification."

69. Reuchlin 1506, *De rudimentis hebraicis*, 618.

70. Reuchlin 1506, *De rudimentis hebraicis*, 572–73.

71. Reuchlin 1506, *De rudimentis hebraicis*, 619: "Cum enim vau per seua notatum praeponitur uerbo praeteriti temporis quod transfert accentum suum in ultimam, tunc idem uerbum mutatur in tempus futurum."

72. An eye-catching feature of this genealogy is that, unlike its apparent source in Luke, it traces Jesus' lineage through Mary's line and not through Joseph. John Fisher, bishop of Rochester, wrote to Erasmus, requesting that he find out what Reuchlin's source was for this novel genealogy. See Reuchlin, *Briefwechsel* 3:185–89 (no. 264, 1 March 1515), esp. n. 7 (187–88) for an explanation of the genealogy's sources.

73. L. Geiger 1871, 113.

74. L. Geiger 1871, 112ff., on the dictionary is still definitive. Reuchlin did rearrange (and abbreviate) the material he found in Kimhi's *Book of Roots*. For instance, he mixed the quadraliteral roots in with the triliterals (as is done today in biblical Hebrew dictionaries), whereas David Kimhi listed all the quadraliterals after the triliterals.

75. Reuchlin 1506, *De rudimentis hebraicis*; and Reuchlin, *Briefwechsel* 2:37, l. 88 (no. 138, 7 March 1506): "Dictionarium enim Hebraicum multo et acri studio solus confeci."

76. Reuchlin, *Briefwechsel* 2:37–38, ll. 106–9 (no. 138, 7 March 1506): "Recte vero speraverim quoslibet religionis Christianae studiosos non tam libenter a Iudaeis quam abs te sacerdote et a memet ipso, quanquam uxorio, ista suscipere rudimenta Hebraica."

77. Reuchlin, *Briefwechsel* 2:45, ll. 294ff. (no. 138, 7 March 1506): "nostrates Iudaei vel invidia vel impericia ducti Christianum neminem in eorum lingua erudire velint idque recusant cuiusdam rabi Ami authoritate, qui in Thalmud...non explanantur verba legis cuidam gentili eo, quod scriptum est: Qui adnunciat verba sua Iacob, praecepta sua et iudicia sua Israel, non fecit similiter omni genti. Nobis autem in statu graciae aliter mandatur Matthaei decimo: Quod in aurem auditis, praedicate super tecta, quod et ego facio."

78. Reuchlin, *De rudimentis hebraicis*, 545: "Habetur optimo iure gratia regi nostro Messiae maximo. cuius nomini excellentissimo quod est Iesu hunc tantum et tam negociosum laborem in conquirendis hebraicorum uocabulorum primitiuis

noctu et interdiu uigili studio adhibitum dedicamus. orantes piis supliciis ac iugi uoto, ut post completos hactenus duos libros manum meam ad tertium opus instituat. quod cum suo foelici afflatu perfectum fuerit."

79. When Greive 1978, 203, says that Reuchlin only referred "four times to the work of David Kimhi," he means, I think, to the grammar section of Kimhi's *Sefer Mikhlol*. Reuchlin included numerous—perhaps nearly 100—explicit references to David Kimhi's *Book of Roots* (the lexicon section of *Sefer Mikhlol*).

80. See L. Geiger 1871, 111.

81. See L. Geiger 1871, 116.

82. This history book is often wrongly attributed to Joseph ben Gorion, ha-Cohen. Reuchlin made this common misattribution.

83. On David Kimhi's scholarship and especially on his Bible commentaries, see Talmage 1975.

84. See Reuchlin 1506, *De rudimentis hebraicis*, 290, 462; and L. Geiger 1871, 118.

85. Maimonides' *Guide for the Perplexed* apparently became a favorite book. Reuchlin also cited Maimonides frequently in his extensive annotations to Reuchlin 1519, trans., *Liber S. Athanasii de variis quaestionibus*.

86. Reuchlin 1506, *De rudimentis hebraicis*, 619–20.

87. See L. Geiger 1871, 122–23, for a list of Reuchlin's more than 200 challenges to the Vulgate.

88. Reuchlin 1506, *De rudimentis hebraicis*, 547; and Reuchlin, *Briefwechsel* 2:42, ll. 187–89 (no. 138, 7 March 1506): "insignem magistrum illum Paulum, episcopum Burgensem, Iudaeorum olim doctissimum, cuius ad nos sera conversio plurimis fuit hominibus saluti et cui me posthabitis reliquis herbam dare nihil pudet."

89. Reuchlin had to help Anshelm handle the storage and sales of the *Rudiments of Hebrew*. Apparently, several hundred copies were stored in his sister's home in Pforzheim. Most important, Reuchlin arranged for Johannes Amerbach to buy 600 copies of the book. See Reuchlin, *Briefwechsel* 2:132ff. (no. 163, 26 March 1510) and 2:332ff. (no. 207, 31 August 1512). The book appeared in a large print run of 1,500 copies, as Reuchlin indicated in his letter of 26 March 1510 to Amerbach.

90. Reuchlin, *Briefwechsel* 2:324, ll. 97–99 (no. 206, 1 August 1512): "Qui liber Rudimentorum meorum cum fere integrum Hebraice intelligendi artificium contineat, non potest derepente tanto usui esse, nisi et adhibeantur aliqua volumina bibliae, qua quidem ipsa tota lingua constat."

91. Reuchlin, *Briefwechsel* 2:324, ll. 99–105 (no. 206, 1 August 1512): "Sperabamus autem indubitata fide multas ad nos ex Italia biblias Hebraicis Soncini Pisaurive aut aliis in locis impressas cum caeteris Iudaeorum libris quotidie venturas. Quae cum obsistente grandi bello, quod Augustus Imperator Max. Aemilianus iam diu in Italia foeliciter gerit, emporio nostro non afferunter, tentanda nihilominus via est, ne nos ipsi nobis deesse videamur, in quo fateor tarditatem meam discendi cupidis onerosam." ("I was hoping, with complete confidence, that many Bibles printed in Soncino or Pisaro or other places and even other Hebrew books would come to us from Italy. Since the great war, which the august Emperor

Maximilian has been successfully waging for a long time in Italy, has hampered this, they are not being brought to our market. It is therefore necessary that I try another way so that I not fail myself, in which I admit that my own slowness has been a burden to those desirous of instruction.")

92. In Reuchlin 1519, trans., *Liber S. Athanasii de variis quaestionibus*, fol. 01ʳ, Reuchlin said that he had gained much of his theological knowledge from Jacob Lemp: "eximius in Theologia praeceptor et eruditor meus, uir egregius, Sacrarum literarum et Iuris Doctor IACOBVS Lempus, Generalis studii Tubingensis Gymnasiarcha, et Cathedrae Magistratum gerens, a quo mihi Theologicarum cognitionum maior pars contigit." Professor Lemp also represented Reuchlin at his legal negotiations in Mainz in 1513 (see chapter 7).

93. Reuchlin, *Briefwechsel* 2:324, ll. 114–325, esp. ll. 125ff. (no. 206, 1 August 1512): "Ut igitur institutio mea in rudimentis Hebraicis multo ante impressis habeat materiam,...posthabitis adversariis exposui iam omnibus in Hebraica scriptura erudiendis septem psalmos poenitentiales totis viribus ediscendos, quod tanto fiet facilius, quanto magis solemus eos in quotidianis precibus habere. Quae res mihi et pluribus mecum iisque literatissimis hominibus visa est omnium maxime utilis ad capessendam et legendi et pronunciandi et intelligendi facultatem. Erit autem sic: Primo ponuntur psalmorum verba Hebraica, deinde interpretatio mea iuxta verbum e verbo, postremum grammaticalis explanatio sermone usitato et quotidiano tritoque, ut scholastici facilius, quae velim, intelligant, semper ad libros Rudimentorum meorum ablegata."

94. The Psalms are numbered differently in the Tanakh and, because of the impact of the Septuagint, the typical Christian Bible. Since the concept of seven penitential psalms is Christian, I have used Christian numbering here. The numbering in the Tanakh is 6, 32, 38, 51, 102, 130, and 143.

95. L. Geiger 1870, 81. This statement is in Münster's 1525 edition of the Song of Songs (in Hebrew and Latin), which adopted Reuchlin's method of providing a basic explanation of every Hebrew word in the text.

96. For a still valuable study of biblical accents, see Wickes 1970, with an important preface by Aron Dotan.

97. Book 1 is the most extensive section, running from fol. a2ʳ to fol. p3ʳ; book 2 covers fol. p3ʳ to fol. s2ʳ; book 3 is fol. s2ᵛ to fol. x1ʳ. An appendix to book 3 (fol. x1ᵛ–v5ᵛ) gives musical notation for the cantillation accents.

98. Reuchlin 1518, *De accentibus et orthographia linguae hebraicae*, fol. r4ʳ–s2ʳ.

99. See Reuchlin 1518, *De accentibus et orthographia linguae hebraicae*, fol. x1ʳ, where Reuchlin indicates that a certain "Bossosthenius," probably Johannes Böschenstein, explained the melodies and that an otherwise unknown Christopherus Sillingus of Lucerne provided the four-part harmonies: "Diatonium autem modulamen nobis attulit Bossosthenius sacerdos. Harmoniam fecit Christopherus Sillingus Lucernensis." Johannes Böschenstein (1472–after 1540) taught Hebrew in many places in the Holy Roman Empire, including briefly at the University of Wittenberg (where he quarreled with Luther). In Reuchlin, *Briefwechsel* 3:58, l. 58 (no. 241, 2 June 1514), he addressed Reuchlin as "most humanist (cultivated) teacher" ("humanissime praeceptor").

100. Reuchlin 1518, *De accentibus et orthographia linguae hebraicae*, fol. v4ᵛ: "Universa haec iuxta Hebraeorum doctrinam scripsimus eo modo quo illi in suis libris tam grammaticis quam musicis sparsim de hac materia tractavere." See L. Geiger 1871, 144.

101. Reuchlin 1518, *De accentibus et orthographia linguae hebraicae*, fol. a3ʳ–a3ᵛ: "Nulla me fames auri (id ipsum enim liberaliter prodigebam in horum studiorum sumptus) adegit, ad hebraica mysteria discenda. Nulla inanis gloriae sitis, ea enim studia tum celanda vulgo erant, ut quae in tanta dignitate constituto viderentur indecentia." On fol. a3ᵛ, Reuchlin states that he has undertaken the project "amore pietatis."

102. Reuchlin, *Briefwechsel*, ed. L. Geiger, 289ff. (no. 252, 30 March 1518).

103. See Roling 2007, 362–71, on Ricci's support of Reuchlin. Ricci's son, Girolamo, sent Reuchlin a copy of the translation of Gikatilla, along with an extravagant tribute to Reuchlin, which was published in *Illustrium virorum epistolae*. See Reuchlin, *Briefwechsel* 3:298–303 (no. 288, 20 August 1516).

104. Reuchlin, *Briefwechsel*, ed. L. Geiger (no. 256, 7 May 1518), 296: "Man fände vielleicht sonst getaufte Juden, wer dess gute erfahrung hätte; aber, führwahr, wenn sie nicht in lateinischer zunge gelehrt sind, so könnten sie uns künstlicher weise in regeln nicht lehren, denn in teutschen landen empfahen die Juden ihre sprache allein aus gewöhnlichem brauch…wir müssen das hebräische erstlich durch regeln, und darnach durch viel lesen der bücher, gleichwie die lateinischen und griechischen zungen überkommen."

105. See L.Geiger 1870, 41–48. After expressing initial enthusiasm for Adriani, Luther became a bitter critic and drove him out of the university by 1521. He was succeeded by Matthäus Aurogallus, who would work congenially with Luther on the new German Bible translation.

106. Although Erasmus never learned much Hebrew, he also acquired Reuchlin's *Rudiments of Hebrew*. See *Graecogermania* 1989, 314–16, for a description of the copy Erasmus owned.

107. See Friedman 1983, esp. 165ff.

108. See L. Geiger 1870, 7: "non ex Rabinorum commentis." On Forster, see Friedman 1983, 169–75. In the dictionary, first printed in 1557, Forster also published a letter Reuchlin wrote in 1521, as he left the University of Ingolstadt, encouraging the student in his humanist studies and embracing him as a worthy successor in Hebrew; see Reuchlin, *Briefwechsel*, ed. L. Geiger (no. 300, 11 April 1521), 329–30.

109. Greive 1978, 401; and Christ 1924, 41.

110. Blau [1944] 1965, 16. Schmidt-Biggemann 2007, 265, on the other hand, claims that "die christliche Kabbala [gehört] in allen ihren Ausformungen zum Kern des europäischen Denkens."

111. Reuchlin may have wanted to keep his philological and Kabbalistic studies separate, although it is hard to decide this with any certainty. Nonetheless, he did not present Kabbalistic ideas or sources in his publications on Hebrew philology.

112. See, for example, Reuchlin 1494, *De verbo mirifico*, in *Sämtliche Werke* 1/1:190, ll. 28ff., for a lengthy correction of the Vulgate translation.

113. Dalberg's library was also distinctive for its inclusion of some Hebrew material. Dalberg gave Reuchlin manuscripts of the anti-Christian work *Sefer ha-Nizzahon* and Joseph Gikatilla's standard Kabbalistic tract *Ginnat Egoz*. Reuchlin also received a 1482 imprint of the Pentateuch with Rashi's commentary through a trade with Dalberg (apparently giving the bishop a manuscript of the Pentateuch). See Abel and Leicht 2005, 24–25.

114. See Idel 2008, for a discussion of Reuchlin's interest in Pythagoreanism.

115. See Idel 2008, 54.

116. Even Joseph Blau, although his focus was on the history of Christian Kabbalah, expressed the typical view that Reuchlin's historical impact came from his Hebrew philology and the controversy over Jewish books: "In our view his two cabalistic dialogues seem of less importance than his professorship of Hebrew, the Hebrew grammar, and the prolonged contest for the preservation of the Talmud" (Blau [1944] 1965, 41).

117. Zika 1998, 29: "*De verbo mirifico* ist kein mystischer Traktat, sondern legt dar, durch welche Kräfte der Mensch wundertätig wirken und die Natur beherrschen kann." See Schmidt-Biggemann 2007, 266ff., for some cautionary words against associating Christian Kabbalah with magic.

118. Magic was a component of the Kabbalistic theosophy of Heinrich Cornelius Agrippa von Nettesheim, who was strongly inspired by Reuchlin's pioneering work, as described in Zambelli 1969, 2007.

119. See Schäfer 2005, for a compelling analysis of Heinrich Graetz's aversion to Kabbalah, especially Graetz's association of Kabbalah with his understanding of the origin of Christian thought among the Essenes.

120. Reuchlin 1494, *De verbo mirifico*, in *Sämtliche Werke* 1/1:144, ll. 22–26: "Omne hominis miraculum, cuius vera et non imaginaria deprehenditur substantia, tum grande, tum mediocre, tum minimum, si ordo sacrorum praescriptus observetur, referendum est semper in deum gloriosum, cuius nomen sit benedictum in sempiterna saecula."

121. Reuchlin 1517, *De arte cabalistica*, fol. O6^v: "idonei Cabalistae…affirmant operationes miraculosas ex solo deo, et ab hominis fide pendere."

122. See Grözinger 1993, 179: "So fehlt bei Reuchlin fast völlig auch die mit diesem sefirotischen System verbundene Theurgie, das heißt die Möglichkeit, durch jüdische Riten auf die göttliche Welt der Sefirot einzuwirken."

123. See Blau [1944] 1965, 2ff., for an excellent exposition of these themes.

124. See Grözinger 1993 for an invaluable overview of the different types of Kabbalah that Reuchlin absorbed.

125. Grözinger 1993, 178ff.

126. Reuchlin 1517, *De arte cabalistica*, fol. B6^r: "Mose kibel. i. Moyses audiuit et accepit legem de Sinai. Vnde Kabala dicitur ab auditu acceptio."

127. See L. Geiger 1871, 169; 1498 edition of Pico della Mirandola's works, fol. I 2^v–K1^r.

128. See Schmidt-Biggemann 1999, 85ff.

129. Reuchlin 1494, *De verbo mirifico*, in *Sämtliche Werke* 1/1:208, ll. 16ff.

130. Vergil, *Aeneid*, 10:112: "Rex Iuppiter omnibus idem." See Reuchlin 1494, *De verbo mirifico*, in *Sämtliche Werke* 1/1:214, ll. 12–22.

131. Reuchlin 1494, *De verbo mirifico*, in *Sämtliche Werke* 1/1:218, ll. 11–12. Reuchlin also mentions here that Aristotle, an ungrateful student, opposed Plato's view of God as a fiery essence.

132. Reuchlin 1494, *De verbo mirifico*, in *Sämtliche Werke* 1/1:214–16.

133. Reuchlin 1494, *De verbo mirifico*, in *Sämtliche Werke* 1/1:220, ll. 9–20.

134. In his search for common theological and philosophical perspectives across various religions, as well as in his general understanding of a transcendent God, there are some similarities between his thought and that of Nicholas of Cusa. He knew some of Nicholas's writings well (and even quoted him in *Art of the Kabbalah*). In 1509, he also provided manuscripts of a few of Nicholas's works to Jacques Lefèvre d'Etaples, who was then preparing a critical edition of Nicholas (which appeared in 1514). For a discussion of connections between Reuchlin and Nicholas of Cusa, see Nagel 1976. See also Reuchlin, *Briefwechsel*, 2:117–25 (no. 159, 10 November 1509), and 2:419–27 (no. 227, ca. 31 August 1513).

135. Reuchlin 1494, *De verbo mirifico*, in *Sämtliche Werke* 1/1:222–32.

136. See Blau [1944] 1965, 46–47.

137. See Reuchlin 1517, *De arte cabalistica*, fol. M1^v–M2^r.

138. Reuchlin 1494, *De verbo mirifico*, in *Sämtliche Werke* 1/1:156, ll. 13–17: "Hebraeos nonnihil facultati nostrae contulisse, quos et imitamur saepe rectius quam caeteras gentes, quorum quidem religionem constat patrum memoria plurimam divinitatem habuisse deumque rite coluisse."

139. Reuchlin 1494, *De verbo mirifico*, in *Sämtliche Werke* 1/1:160, ll. 29–31: "Convenit vero utrique parti hoc vinculum verborum: deus enim spiritus, verbum spiratio, homo spirans."

140. Reuchlin 1494, *De verbo mirifico*, in *Sämtliche Werke* 1/1:102, l. 36–104, l. 2: "Quod vero istis tuis Iudaicis cessavere (ut ais) obsequi verba mirifica, non minutam obesse mihi crede causam oportet."

141. Reuchlin 1494, *De verbo mirifico*, in *Sämtliche Werke* 1/1:106, ll. 25–34: "Salubris ista potestas verborum, quae vos deseruit, nos elegit, nos comitatur, nobis ad nutum obedire cernitur. Ea non humano consilio, sed divinitus data et oblata perfectae religionis virtus, non fortuitu, verum diligentia et industria sua mutavit locum, quia vos legitima sacra mutastis. Ideoque frustra murmuratis, frustra deum invocatis, quem non, ut ipse vult, colitis, sed inventionibus vestris blandientes. Etiam nos dei cultores livore immortali oditis."

142. Reuchlin 1494, *De verbo mirifico*, in *Sämtliche Werke* 1/1:402, l. 31–404, l. 1: "Iungite universa haec, et cognoscetis facile omnium potentissimam usquequaque apparuisse virtutem et operationem semper efficacissimam, per nomen avorum Trigrammaton, et patrum Tetragrammaton, et filiorum Pentagrammaton, id est, in natura SDI, in lege ADNI, in charitate IHSUH. Nunc enim filii dei sumus: iccirco quinque litteris utimur propter eum, in quem credimus et quem invocamus mediatorem dei et hominis eundemque deum et hominem."

143. Reuchlin 1494, *De verbo mirifico*, in *Sämtliche Werke* 1/1:384, ll. 11ff.: "An vobis parum videtur cum tanto fructu evadere voti compotes? Hoc est illud verbum

mirificum, quod iam pridem expectatis, verbum portentificum, verbum deificum, immo deus verbum et verbum deus, et nomen verbi Ihsuh, et verbum nominis Ihsuh, et idem Ihsuh verbum et nomen, qui est dominus dominantium."

144. Reuchlin 1494, *De verbo mirifico*, in *Sämtliche Werke* 1/1:386, ll. 23–35: "et nitamur deo, inque dei filium, quo vivimus, movemur et sumus, inconcussam, sinceram et simplicem habeamus fiduciam, qui de suo veritatis ore nobis infallibiliter pollicendo promisit dicens: 'Amen, amen dico vobis, qui credit in me, opera, quae ego facio, et ipse faciet, et maiora horum faciet, quia ego ad patrem vado, et quodcunque petieritis patrem in nomine meo, hoc faciam, ut glorificetur pater in filio. Si quid petieritis in nomine meo, hoc faciam.' Haec sunt divina testimonia, haec sacrorum nostrorum monumenta, haec sacerdotia memoracula, haec purissima signa, hae nostrae cerimoniae paucis contentae, facile usu, vili apparatu."

145. Reuchlin 1494, *De verbo mirifico*, in *Sämtliche Werke* 1/1:388ff

146. Reuchlin 1494, *De verbo mirifico*, in *Sämtliche Werke* 1/1:106, l. 37.

147. Reuchlin is aware that many religions have purification rites that are similar to Christian baptism; see Reuchlin 1494, *De verbo mirifico*, in *Sämtliche Werke* 1/1:112.

148. Reuchlin 1494, *De verbo mirifico*, in *Sämtliche Werke* 1/1:108, ll. 36–38: "Resipiscentia vestra haec esto. A Thalmudim, Baruchia, tuque, Sidoni, ab Epicuro atque Lucretio receditote. 'Lavamini, mundi estote.'"

149. See Reuchlin 1494, *De verbo mirifico*, in *Sämtliche Werke* 1/1:120, ll. 20ff., for Baruch's touching description of the Talmud along with his sudden agreement to reject it.

150. Reuchlin 1517, *De arte cabalistica*, fol. D1ᵛ: "Cabalistae innumerabiles." .

151. For an orientation to the *Zohar*, see Scholem [1941] 1995, 156ff., and the English translation by Sperling and Simon, *The Zohar* 1931–34. Interestingly, Reuchlin did not quote directly from the *Zohar* in *Art of the Kabbalah* (see Grözinger 1993, 176).

152. See Scholem [1941] 1995, 194ff. Scholem speculates that Gikatilla may have also assisted his acquaintance Moses de León in the compilation of the *Zohar*.

153. On the *Sefer Yetsirah*, see Dan 1993, and the English translation by Knut Stenring, *Sefer Yetzirah* [1923] 1970.

154. Campanini 1999, 74, ascertained that Reuchlin did not quote Gikatilla according to Ricci's translation.

155. Idel 1993, xvi–xix, argued that Reuchlin probably had a manuscript that was similar to Jewish Theological Seminary, MS Halberstam 444. In Reuchlin [1517] 1995, *L'Arte Cabbalistica*, Saverio Campanini fully documented the correspondence between Halberstam 444 and Reuchlin's quotations from Kabbalistic works.

156. See Reuchlin 1517, *De arte cabalistica*, fol. D1ᵛ–D2ᵛ, for his catalog of sources for Kabbalah (expressed by Simon). Campanini compiled a list of Reuchlin's sources (both those mentioned and those used), in Reuchlin [1517] 1995, *L'Arte Cabbalistica*, LV–LXX.

157. Reuchlin 1517, *De arte cabalistica*, fol. D2ᵛ: "at mea tamen sententia nemo unquam de ista scripsit arte usque dudum artificiosius, nemo distinctius, nemo lucidius quam Rabi Ioseph Bar Abraham Castiliensis ciuis Salemitanus, tria huius

facultatis uolumina studiose molitus, quibus omnem Cabalistarum institutionem fecit clariorem, primum de dictionibus, secundum de literis, et tertium uolumen de punctis. Eius libri titulus extat גנת אגוז id est Hortus nucis, iuxta Salomonis cantica, 'In hortum nucis descendi, ut uiderem amoena uirgulta.'"

158. Reuchlin probably knew of Cusa's use of the Quran in some of his writings.

159. Reuchlin quotes the Quran several times in the work; see Reuchlin 1517, *De arte cabalistica*, fol. G6ᵛ and H5ᵛ. He would quote more extensively from the Quran in Reuchlin 1519, trans., *Liber S. Athanasii de variis quaestionibus*.

160. See Reuchlin 1517, *De arte cabalistica*, fol. B1ᵛ: "ex antiqua Iochaicorum prosapia." Reuchlin does not explicitly explain the significance of this lineage.

161. Reuchlin 1517, *De arte cabalistica*, fol. K1ᵛff.

162. Reuchlin 1517, *De arte cabalistica*, fol. K3ʳff.

163. Reuchlin 1517, *De arte cabalistica*, fol. K4ʳff.

164. Reuchlin 1517, *De arte cabalistica*, fol. K6ʳff.

165. Reuchlin 1517, *De arte cabalistica*, fol. L1ᵛff.

166. Reuchlin 1517, *De arte cabalistica*, fol. M1ᵛff.

167. Reuchlin 1517, *De arte cabalistica*, fol. M4ᵛff.

168. At some points, Reuchlin reviews the sequence of topics he has covered; see Reuchlin 1517, *De arte cabalistica*, fol. M1ᵛ.

169. Reuchlin 1517, *De arte cabalistica*, fol. B1ᵛ: "Nam esse Pythagoram omnia ferme dogmata istinc expiscatum aiunt."

170. See Zika 1998, 103; and Spitz 1963.

171. See Reuchlin 1517, *De arte cabalistica*, fol. K1ʳ (the entire passage): "Ego uero…ab iis quae mihi ordine recensuisti plane in eam mouecor opinionemque flumen illud suum, Pythagoras ex infinito Cabalistarum pelago cuius foelicem nobis Simon nauigationem pollicetur in agros graecorum limitauit, unde nostra tandem studia irrigare queamus, Ita pares mihi uidentur esse inter se Simonis de Cabalistis et tui de Pythagoricis tam sermones quam sententiae. Nam quod aliud intendit uel Cabalaeus uel Pythagoras, nisi animos hominum in deos referre, hoc est ad perfectam beatitudinem promouere. Quae autem alia uia qua similis utriusque tradendi modus et ambobus aequa exercitatio per symbola et notas adagia et paroemias, per numeros et figuras, per literas syllabas et uerba."

172. Reuchlin 1517, *De arte cabalistica*, fol. E5ᵛ: "Iudaeorum quaeque tam recepta quam inuenta exponi alienis furtis hinc graecorum inde latinorum, nihilque nostrum esse in philosophia quod non ante Iudaeorum fuerit, quantumuis hoc seculo adimatur eis merita gloria, et nunc uniuersa eorum contemnantur."

173. Brod 1965, 288.

174. Reuchlin 1517, *De arte cabalistica*, fol. B6ᵛ: "Est enim Cabala diuinae reuelationis, ad salutiferam dei et formarum separatarum contemplationem traditae, symbolica receptio."

175. Reuchlin 1517, *De arte cabalistica*, fol. B4ʳ: "non paucis oportet artibus, non ualde minutis humanorum studiorum scientiis…ut in ipsa ferme dei penetralia irrepat."

176. Reuchlin 1517, *De arte cabalistica*, fol. L3ᵛ: "amorem intensum et ardentem erga diuinitatem concipiamus."

177. Reuchlin 1517, *De arte cabalistica*, fol. M3ᵛ: "Sed is tandem qui cogitationes in corde suo illuc cogit, ut dimissis carnalibus, spiritualia legis meditetur, is inquam is beatus est, cum corde mundo deum uidebit."

178. See Reuchlin 1517, *De arte cabalistica*, fol. D2ᵛ.

179. Reuchlin 1517, *De arte cabalistica*, fol. D3ʳ. See also Idel 1993, xxi–xxiii.

180. See Reuchlin 1517, *De arte cabalistica*, fol. M3ʳ, for Simon's sudden introduction—"Let us proceed to the art" ("procedamus ad artem").

181. Reuchlin 1517, *De arte cabalistica*, fol. E2ʳ: "nihil...aliud etiam quod uel fingi posset animum nostrum arctius deo perinde...quam illam ipsam...sacram scripturam, quae nos primo in diuinorum admirationem ducit, tum in eorum pro humano captu agnitionem, deinde in illum ardentissimum qualitercunque cognitae diuinitatis amorem....Hic est solus uerae contemplationis campus, cuius singula uerba, singula sunt sacramenta, et singuli sermones, syllabae, apices, punctaque eius plena sunt arcanis sensibus."

182. Reuchlin 1517, *De arte cabalistica*, fol. M5ʳ: "ut Rabi Joseph Minor Salemitanus libros de hac arte a se conscriptos Hortum nominauerit, id est גנת propter ternas huius dictionis literas, quarum singulae singulas portiones artis Cabalisticae designant. Nam gimel significat גימטריא Nun נוטריקון Thau תמורה ."

183. Gematria is found, albeit rarely, in early rabbinic exegesis. It does not occur in the *Zohar*, but became common among Kabbalists in the aftermath of Joseph Gikatilla.

184. Reuchlin 1517, *De arte cabalistica*, fol. N1ᵛ–N2ʳ.

185. See a similar numerical analysis of "*Ehyeh*" ("I am," i.e., one of the names of God) in Reuchlin 1517, *De arte cabalistica*, fol. M2ʳ.

186. Reuchlin 1517, *De arte cabalistica*, fol. M4ᵛ: "Legite Isaiam capite lxv. Benedicetur in deo Amen. Ecquis est iste deus? Cabalistae respondebunt quod est אדני מלך נאמן. i. Dominus rex fidelis, tris enim has dictiones per capita, tres litterae אמן notabunt."

187. Reuchlin 1517, *De arte cabalistica*, fol. N6ʳ: "Multo forte occultiora inquit ostendam uobis in hac tertia cabalae parte quae תמורה nominatur."

188. Reuchlin 1517, *De arte cabalistica*, fol. N6ʳ–N5ᵛ, for Reuchlin's printing of a commonly used *tsiruf*.

189. For example, see Reuchlin 1517, *De arte cabalistica*, fol. C1ʳ–C1ᵛ, for a defense against Christian allegations that Jews taught that Adam had practiced bestiality.

190. See A. Geiger 1870, 14.

191. Reuchlin 1517, *De arte cabalistica*, fol. B6ᵛ: "Nestorea eloquentia." See especially the long tribute to his eloquence on fol. E4ᵛ.

192. Reuchlin 1517, *De arte cabalistica*, fol. E4ᵛ.

193. Reuchlin 1517, *De arte cabalistica*, fol. O7ᵛ. The farewells orchestrate a remarkable tolerance on both sides: "Tum Simon de more gentilicio inquit, Pax uobis. Ad quod ambo isti. Vale aiunt, I decus, I nostrum."

194. Reuchlin 1517, *De arte cabalistica*, fol. D6ᵛ: "Qui docebit populos ambulare in uiis tetragrammati, ut scribit Rabi Dauid Kimhi super eundem prophetam capite LI in versu, quia lex a me exibit, quam scilicet qui fecerit saluabitur, qui contempserit peribit."

195. See Reuchlin 1517, *De arte cabalistica*, fol. C 3^{r}ff.

196. Reuchlin 1517, *De arte cabalistica*, fol. O3^r: "respondit Rab Hakados quod ex tetragrammato fluit nomen xii literarum הקדש ורוח בן אב, i. pater filius et spiritus sanctus. Ex quo deriuatur nomen quadraginta duarum literarum quod ita pronunciatur בשלשה אחד אחד באחד שלשה אלהים הקדש רוח אלהים בן אלהים אב, i. Pater deus, filius deus, spiritus sanctus deus, tres in uno et unus in tribus."

197. Reuchlin 1517, *De arte cabalistica*, fol. O7^r. See Reuchlin [1517] 1995, 221, for the reference to the passage in midrash and, more important, the observation that the passage is quoted in MS Halberstam 444, the probable source for Reuchlin's knowledge of Kabbalah.

198. For the gematria analysis of cross, see Reuchlin 1517, *De arte cabalistica*, fol O7^r.

199. Brod 1965, 271: "ein Werk, in dem er mehr und Wesentlicheres zugunsten der verfolgten Juden und ihrer mißachteten und mißverstandenen Geisteshelden zu sagen wagte als in all seinen früheren Schriften zusammengenommen." See also 292 for Brod's statement that one of the main goals of his Reuchlin biography was to take Reuchlin's Kabbalistic writings (and Kabbalistic material in general) more seriously than had previous scholars.

200. Reuchlin 1517, *De arte cabalistica*, fol. O8^r: "mundi lumina."

CHAPTER 5

Epigraph sources: Pfefferkorn [1507] 1508, *Der Juden Spiegel* (Cologne), fol. d1^r: "Darumb, nemet in den weg der bucher, verbernet sy, so syn sie dan dester lichtlicher zo bewegen auf den weg der warheit." *Mirror of the Jews* is cited according to the Cologne edition of 1508, as reprinted in Kirn 1989, 205–30. The 1508 text, however, is a significant revision of the 1507 printings in Cologne and Nuremberg.

EE 3:117, l. 37 (no. 694, 2 November 1517): "cui [i.e., Pfefferkorn] non esset impingendum semiiudaei vocabulum, nisi factis sese declararet sesquiiudaeum."

1. See *CWE: Correspondence* 5:170, ll. 109ff. (no. 694, 2 November 1517) and *CWE: Correspondence* 5:203–4 (no. 713, 15 November 1517). Reuchlin published Erasmus's letter (no. 713) in *Illustrium virorum epistolae* of 1519.

2. Reuchlin himself frequently referred to Pfefferkorn's Jewish heritage in derogatory terms, often labeling him a "Taufjude." The introduction to Reuchlin 1512, trans., Hippocrates, *De praeparatione hominis*, which is a dedicatory letter to Dr. Johannes Stocker in Ulm, contains a fierce outburst against an allegedly corrupt physician in Ulm who had converted from Judaism to Christianity. The letter, moreover, clearly casts aspersions generally on Jews who convert insincerely to Christianity. The doctor under attack, whose identity cannot be traced, apparently clashed with Stocker, which was reason enough for Reuchlin to suggest an analogy between Stocker's experience and his own with Johannes Pfefferkorn. Reuchlin describes Pfefferkorn in this context as "Iudaeus baptizatus, sub nomine Christiano

persecutor Christianorum audacissimus" (Reuchlin, *Briefwechsel* 2:252, l. 120 [no. 192, after 17 February 1512]). Nonetheless, the same letter attributes the origin of medicine to the Jews, which was then passed down to the Greeks and Romans, as Reuchlin wrote: "Nos igitur Latini paludem bibimus, Graeci rivos, Iudaei fontes" (2:250, ll. 69–70). Campanini 1999, 74–75, suggested that Reuchlin preferred to associate with Jews who remained Jewish rather than with conversos. Nonetheless, in other contexts, Reuchlin expressed great admiration for the scholars Paolo Ricci and Matthäus Adriani, both of whom converted to Christianity.

3. See Bonfil [1991] 1994, 265, on the sincerity of many conversions; and Carlebach 2001, 35, on Christian suspicions about Jews who converted.

4. Weislinger 1730.

5. Oberman [1981] 1984, 70.

6. Pfefferkorn 1508 (Nuremberg), *Der iuden peicht*, fol. D2^r–D2^v. See W. Frey 1985, 160.

7. Pfefferkorn 1516, *Beschyrmung*, fol. M2^v. See W. Frey 1985, 163.

8. See Carlebach 2001, 52ff.

9. On Victor of Carben, see Carlebach 2001, 177.

10. Pfefferkorn 1516, *Streydt puechlyn*, fol. E2^r, says that he started the campaign "shortly after my conversion" ("kurtz nach meyner bekorung").

11. Pfefferkorn 1516, *Streydt puechlyn*, fol. E2^r–E2^v: "Ich han ouch den handell auß myr selbst nit vurghegenomen uoch [i.e., noch] bestanden. Dan die erwerdige andechtigen geistlichen Vetter vnd Herren. Obseruanten des ordens sant Francisci. haben mich darzů gereytzt. vnd in der beicht gelert vnd vnderwysen. ich moecht vff erden nichts bessers schaffen. das Gott beheglicher wer vnd myr dienstbarlicher zů dem ewigen leben gesein mocht Das ich vff die bane moecht brengen. vnd in fleißlicher arbayt seyn. das men den jůden yre falschen laster puecher in solcher masse (wie oben angezeigt) nemen vnd abthet Ouch jnen den schentlich wůcher nit mer zů gestatten. vnd das sy yr brott vnder den Christen mit vnlustiger arbait erschwingen můsten. Vnd dar zů das wort Gots zů geboerlichen zeitten von vnsern Predicanten zů hoeren gehalten wurden. Solche vnderrichtung vnd wegweiß. hab ich mit Rat vnd forderneß der selbigen vetter Obseruants vß etlichen Cloistern Als zů Mentz. Oppenheym Heydelburg. Vlm vnd Moenchem. die mich an die durchluchtigistin hochgeboren Furstin hertzochgin kay. ma. Schwester promouyrt hetten. Ouch etliche der selbigen vetter in gegenwertigkeyt des kay. vnd der Furstyn mit myr in der sache erfordert."

12. Pfefferkorn 1516, *Streydt puechlyn*, fol. E3^r: "so han ich yr boeßheit. vntrew. vnd gots laster an den tagh ghebracht. das vor meynen zeitten keyner so clair vnd so verstendich gedan hat." The continuation of the passage is also interesting: "Byn ich dan so vngeschickt. vnd soe vnueruaren Als mich die juden vnd Johan Reůchlin yr Patroen dargeben. so sagen sy wa kompt myr die kunst her."

13. On the history of the expulsion from Nuremberg, see Wenninger 1981, 135–54; and Price 2003, 169–93.

14. Pfefferkorn 1509 (Cologne), *Wie die blinden Juden yr Ostern halten*, fol. D2^r.

15. A strange aspect of Pfefferkorn's life was that he either had a historical doppelganger or his enemies created one. According to several printed broadsides,

a certain Johannes Pfefferkorn, a convert to Christianity, was burned at the stake in the Jewish cemetery of Halle on 9 April 1514 for various crimes, including desecrating the eucharistic wafer, posing as the messiah, and even ritualistically murdering a Christian child. With such a doppelganger (or such a hyperbolic innuendo), Pfefferkorn lived his new life as a Christian with awareness of persistent and potentially dangerous suspicions in the Christian world. See *Die geschicht vnnd bekantnüß des getaufften Juden genannt Johannes Pfefferkorn*, 1514.

16. Kracauer 1887, 161, adduced 1476 as the year of birth, whereas L. Geiger argued for 1469 or 1470.

17. Pfefferkorn 1510, *Zu lob vnd Ere*, fol. a3ᵛ.

18. Pfefferkorn 1521, *Ajn mitleydliche claeg*. See discussion in chapter 9. Pfefferkorn apparently suffered a debilitating illness in 1516. See Pfefferkorn 1516, *Streydt puechlyn*, fol. G4ʳ: "In schwerer kranckheit hab ich dyß puechlin beschryben in welcher kranckheit ich noch vmbfangen byn."

19. Pfefferkorn 1516, *Streydt puechlyn*, fol. F1ᵛ: "er sich dan by vns vormals Erlichen Zimlich Wesens gehalten hat."

20. See Brod 1965, 181–82, who places Rabbi Pfefferkorn in Prague but without strong evidence. *The Letters of Obscure Men* indicates that Pfefferkorn lived for a while in Moravia.

21. Pfefferkorn 1516, *Streydt puechlyn*, fol. F1ʳ. The letter is dated 21 January 1510.

22. On Lawrence as student of poetry and the liberal arts, see Pfefferkorn 1516, *Defensio*, in Hutten 1859–70, supplement volume 1:145: "Habeo filium Laurentium nomine, ingenuum profecto adolescentem et liberalibus disciplinis studiisque poeticis anxie impallescentem."

23. Pfefferkorn 1521, *Ajn mitleydliche claeg*, fol. E8ʳ–E8ᵛ. See Kirn 1989, 188.

24. Pfefferkorn 1516, *Defensio*, fol. N2ʳ. See also L. Geiger 1869a, 298.

25. Pfefferkorn does betray some familiarity with Jewish practices for slaughtering animals. See Pfefferkorn 1510 (Augsburg), *Zu lob vnd Ere*, fol. A8ᵛ–B1ʳ, where he argues that Jewish slaughtering of animals does not conform to the Bible and is therefore heresy. In particular, Heinrich Graetz and Isidor Kracauer were insistent that Pfefferkorn really was an uneducated butcher. They based their views on stridently anti-Pfefferkorn sources, the most important of which is a 1509 letter from the Count of Gutenstein that accused Johannes Pfefferkorn of having been both a butcher and a thief. See E. Martin 1994, 21ff., esp. n. 65. The letter was secured by the Jewish community of Regensburg in an effort to help the Frankfurt community discredit Pfefferkorn.

26. Even Kirn 1989, 11, makes dismissive remarks about his competence: "Die Gelehrsamkeit des Rabbi Meier kann nicht besonders groß gewesen sein, mißt man sie an dem, was sein Schüler [i.e., Johannes Pfefferkorn] von ihm gelernt hat."

27. Pfefferkorn 1510 (Augsburg), *Zu lob vnd Ere*, fol. A5ᵛ: "als ainem wolgelertnn/ vnnd erfarn euwers glaubens." The wording is different in other printings. For example, Pfefferkorn 1516, *Streydt puechlyn*, fol. A4ʳ: "als aynen wolgegründten. vnd erfarn Eûrs glaubens."

28. Reuchlin 1511, *Augenspiegel*, in *Sämtliche Werke* 4/1:166–67.

29. See the German excipit to his *Defensio* 1516, fol. O4ʳ.

30. Pfefferkorn probably knew at least some of Hans Folz's anti-Jewish publications. See E. Martin 1994, 118ff. On Folz, see Huey 2000.

31. Pfefferkorn 1516, *Streydt puechlyn*, fol. F1ᵛ: "dick vnd menchmol haben mich die judischeit in yre geschefften zů kůnigen vnd an fursten vnd heren vor eynen legaten vß geschickt."

32. Pfefferkorn published this letter in Pfefferkorn 1516, *Streydt puechlyn*, fol. F2ʳ–F2ᵛ. The letter is signed on "Tuesday after St. Bartholomew's Day" (i.e., Tuesday after 24 August).

33. Pfefferkorn 1516, *Streydt puechlyn*, fol. F2ʳ, where he claims fifteen souls were saved. In other places he claims fourteen. Pfefferkorn 1516, *Defensio*, fol. O3ʳ, says that Reuchlin undermined him. See also Hutten 1859–70, supplement volume 1:172.

34. Pfefferkorn 1521, *Ajn mitleydliche claeg*, final (unnumbered) leaf: "Pefferkoren wont an dem Rhein/ Zů Cöllen meyster im Spital."

35. It is also possible that Pfefferkorn had some knowledge of medicine. The Latin translation of *Enemy of the Jews* has a long addition that harangues Jewish physicians but also displays a certain familiarity with medicine. See Pfefferkorn 1509, *Hostis iudeorum*, fol. B3ʳ–B3ᵛ.

36. See chapter 6. Good evidence that Jews feared disputations with Pfefferkorn is in Jonathan Kostheim's 1509 dispatches to the Jewish community in Frankfurt from the court of Maximilian, then in Italy, for Kostheim clearly indicated that he was trying to avoid a direct debate with Pfefferkorn under any circumstances.

37. It appears that the pamphlets in the Cologne dialect, which were also printed in Cologne, were the first editions. A second, slightly abbreviated version of Pfefferkorn's first pamphlet, *Mirror of the Jews*, was published in both dialects as well.

38. See the bibliography in Kirn 1989, 201–4.

39. See Pfefferkorn 1510, *In laudem et honorem*, fol. D2ᵛ.

40. Pfefferkorn 1509, *In hoc libello*, fol. A1ʳ: "Et Jouis eterni gaudia mater habet.... Sed recutita suo concidit ense cohors."

41. Pfefferkorn 1509, *Hostis iudeorum*, fol. A1ʳ: "Ortwini Gratii Daventriensis liberalium disciplinarum professoris de pertinacia iudeorum epigramma politum."

42. See chapter 7.

43. Pfefferkorn 1509, *In hoc libello*, fol. A1ᵛ: "Tu bonarum artium profundissimus interpres.... Quo fit vt ad tuum collegium tanquam ad delphicum quodam Apollonis oraculum bonarum artium studiosi copiosius accurrant."

44. Victor of Carben 1509, *Opus aureum ac novum*.

45. Gerschmann 1969 argues that Pfefferkorn's translations were likely in German written with Hebrew letters.

46. See E. Martin 1994, 24; and Pfefferkorn [1507] 1508, *Der Juden Spiegel*, fol. A2ʳ: "Deßhalb ich aus Bruderlicher menschlicher trwe in barmhertzickeyt bewegt byn, vur mich zo nemen die bewerung der heylgen euangelia auß latinschen sprach in hebraische."

47. Kirn 1989, 20ff., 202 (imprint no. 3). Adriani 1513, *Libellus hora faciendi pro domino* (which was printed by Reuchlin's publisher Anshelm), offers competing Hebrew versions as well as a critique of Pfefferkorn's renderings.

48. Pfefferkorn [1507] 1508, *Der Juden Spiegel*, fol. C1ᵛ.

49. Pfefferkorn [1507] 1508, *Der Juden Spiegel*, fol. A3ʳ, states that Jewish rejection of the gospel induced him to translate the gospel into Hebrew: "deßhalb sie aus der latynschen spraich in hebraische gesatzt hab."

50. Pfefferkorn's approach to confirming the doctrine of the trinity is to list passages in the Old Testament that, according to him, express allegories of the trinity. See, for example, Pfefferkorn [1507] 1508, *Der Juden Spiegel*, fol. B2ᵛ, for his discussion of Isaiah 6:3.

51. Pfefferkorn argues that Christians ("we") invoke Mary and the saints in the same manner that Jews ("you") invoke Abraham, Isaac, and Jacob. See Pfefferkorn [1507] 1508, *Der Juden Spiegel*, fol. B3ʳ.

52. Pfefferkorn [1507] 1508, *Der Juden Spiegel*, fol. C1ᵛ. On Asher ben Rav Meier, see Kirn 1989, 30–32. Some of Asher ben Rav Meier's efforts may have been aimed against the practices of Sephardic Jews, who were then settling in Italy in flight from Spain and Portugal.

53. Pfefferkorn [1507] 1508, *Der Juden Spiegel*, fol. B2ᵛff.

54. See E. Martin 1994, 79, on a record from 1508 that Pfefferkorn had permission in Frankfurt to preach.

55. Pfefferkorn 1516, *Defensio*, fol. O3ʳ–O3ᵛ, in Hutten 1859–70, supplement volume 1:172.

56. Pfefferkorn [1507] 1508, *Der Juden Spiegel*, fol. C3ᵛ.

57. Pfefferkorn [1507] 1508, *Der Juden Spiegel*, fol. C4ʳ.

58. See the epigraph to this chapter.

59. Pfefferkorn [1507] 1508, *Der Juden Spiegel*, fol. C4ᵛ–D1ʳ: "der heßlich innehalt yrer bucher, so mit vnwarheit weder Cristum, Marie."

60. Pfefferkorn [1507] 1508, *Der Juden Spiegel*, fol. D1ʳ: "deßhalb yr, so habt den gewelt, nemet die van ynnen vnd laist in nit mer dan den text der heilgen geschrifft, das ist die Bibel."

61. Pfefferkorn [1507] 1508, *Der Juden Spiegel*, fol. D1ᵛ. While Pfefferkorn continued to express doubt about accusations of ritual murder, in his later tracts he emphatically condemned Jews for desecrating the eucharistic host (another innuendo that was used as a pretext for executing Jews and sometimes for expelling Jewish communities). See Pfefferkorn 1516, *Defensio*, fol. A2ᵛ.

62. Pfefferkorn [1507] 1508, *Der Juden Spiegel*, fol. C2ᵛ. The entire passage is: "O yr Cristenlichen fursten, Fursten und heren, stet vnd ander, hinder denen sy [i.e., the Jews] beschawrt, behawst vnd behoft werden vmb des sundigen, blutigen guts wegen, das ir van ynnen entfangt! Bedenckt, wie solichs van dem sweys vnd blut ewr vntersaissen so jemerlich gesogen wirt."

63. See Browe 1942, 186; and E. Martin 1994, 57.

64. Oberman [1981] 1984, 32–35, 68–70. Quote is from 33.

65. Pfefferkorn 1508 (Nuremberg), *Der iuden peicht*, fol. A1ʳ: "Doch das ich [i.e., the pamphlet, which is speaking] den iuden nit werde zu tayl."

66. Pfefferkorn 1508 (Nuremberg), *Der iuden peicht*, fol. B3^r: "han ich der iuden vngegrunte böse gewonhait geöffnet…darumb das solchs in gespötz weyse ynn fur gehalten werde."

67. Pfefferkorn 1508 (Nuremberg), *Der iuden peicht*, fol. A3^v–A4^r: "Sölcher yetz gehorter fluch wirt vber vns christen vnd nyemantz anders besunder gethon/ warumb wer mein getrewer rat nach meinen cleynen verstant sulch bücher der flüche von ynnen zunemen."

68. As L. Geiger 1871, 212, observes, Pfefferkorn took pleasure in making the rituals sound as absurd as possible, as in his description of *Kapparot*, in which a man or woman symbolically transfers sins to a rooster or hen.

69. Pfefferkorn 1508 (Nuremberg), *Der iuden peicht*, fol. B4^r: "Wo iuden in der christenheit wonnen sein sy schedlicher den menschen dan der teufel."

70. Like *Mirror of the Jews*, *Confession of the Jews* excoriates the princes for "sucking the blood out of their subjects" by allowing Jewish money lending. See Pfefferkorn 1508 (Nuremberg), *Der iuden peicht*, fol. C1^r.

71. Pfefferkorn 1508 (Nuremberg), *Der iuden peicht*, fol. C1^r–C1^v: "Treybt sy auß ewrnn landen ader verpitt yn wucher zunemen/ last sy arbeyten als wir christen müssen thun vnd halt sy/ sy thun eß gernn ader nit zu horen das wort gotz…seint nit in vil enden stetten vnd lande als Franckreich. Hyspanien. Denmarck vnd mer ander noch kurtzlich auch zu Nurmberg. Vlm. Nörlingen [i.e., Nördlingen] etc. juden gewest vnd gewonet habenn die nun mit einander vertryben sein. Ich frag was ist den schad vnwill ader nachrede dar auß erwachsen/ haben sy wol gehandelt in den sachen billich solt yr in nachuolgen bey ewer seel heyl."

72. Pfefferkorn 1508 (Nuremberg), *Der iuden peicht*, fol. B3^v–B4^r: "noch furter wer vngezweyfelt ein nutzlich erlich vnd gotlich werck das der talmut vnd ander yrer falschen Rabi pucher mit yren bede bucheren in welchen yr böse ordenung vnd gewonhait geschrieben ist von in genomen vnd gantz außgediliget wurden."

73. Pfefferkorn 1509 (Augsburg), *Wie die blinden Juden yr Ostern halten*, fol. A1^v: "Dan der Juden ostern ist anderst nit dan ein figur vnd anzaygung vnser ostern."

74. E. Martin 1994, 105; and Blumenkranz 1946, 154–55, on Augustine's allegorical interpretation of Jewish holy days.

75. Pfefferkorn 1509 (Augsburg), *Wie die blinden Juden yr Ostern halten*, fol. B3^r: "vnd alle die sitzen schrien mit lauter stim die wort des spalmistan [i.e., psalmisten] am acht vnd sibenzigsten psalmen [i.e., Psalm 79] also lautentd O herr gaüß deinenn zorn über die fölcker die dich nye recht erkant habenn da bye wyer Cristenn gemaint werden etc."

76. Pfefferkorn 1509 (Augsburg), *Wie die blinden Juden yr Ostern halten*, fol. B3^v: "Das gesatz Moysi…nit halten als yn gebotten ist." See Pfefferkorn 1508 (Nuremberg), *Der iuden peicht*, fol. B1^v, for a similar contention of Jewish heresy.

77. Pfefferkorn 1509 (Augsburg), *Wie die blinden Juden yr Ostern halten*, fol. A1^r: "Weiter würdt außgetruckt das die Juden ketzer seyn des alten vnd newenn testaments/ Deßhalb sye schůldig seyn des gerichts nach dem gesatz Moysi."

78. Among other things, he claims that Jews were wrong to extend the Passover Seder to a second day (an accepted practice still common among Jews living outside of Israel) and that they do not properly dispose of the sacrificial lamb at Passover.

79. Pfefferkorn 1509 (Augsburg), W*ie die blinden Juden yr Ostern halten*, fol. D1ᵛ: "So sind ir ritter cristi."

80. Pfefferkorn 1509 (Augsburg), W*ie die blinden Juden yr Ostern halten*, fol. C4ᵛ: "vnd verer solt yr biten das man von in auffheb alle bůcher vnd ynen allain laß den blossen tex der biblen/ dan die andren faltzen bucher so sy haben sein ain můter aller boßhait."

81. See Pfefferkorn 1509 (Augsburg), W*ie die blinden Juden yr Ostern halten*, fol. D1ʳ, where he seems to suggest forced baptism: "vnnd wenden yr iůng kinder zum cristen glauben auffzüsehen."

82. Pfefferkorn 1509 (Augsburg), W*ie die blinden Juden yr Ostern halten*, fol. D1ʳ-D1ᵛ: "der des nit thun völte [i.e., whoever doesn't want to embrace Christianity] den lassen gen als ain altenn schelmigenn hundt."

83. Reuchlin 1511, *Augenspiegel*, in *Sämtliche Werke* 4/1:155, ll. 18ff.: "Pfefferkorn hat inn ainem andern büchlin das sich anfahet: Jnn dißem büchlin findet ir ain entlichen fürtrag/ inn das gantz reich/ den vndertanen ainen sübtilen anschlag verkünt vnd sie gelert/ wie sie sollen ain vffrür vnd vfflauff wider ire aigen oberkait machen."

84. Pfefferkorn 1509 (Augsburg), *Wie die blinden Juden yr Ostern halten*, fol. D1ʳ: "Wurden aber die herren euch fur halten vnnd sagen wyr müssen iuden leiden vnnd zů lassen dan die recht lassen die zů. Dar auff miegt ir antwurten Es ist war die recht lassen Juden zů Sye verbiten aber schwerlich denn wůcher vnd blasfemirung gotes Vnd deßhalb ist vnser bith vnd beger dem rechten gantz gemes dan wir biten nit sye zůuerdiligen, sunder das der wůcher vnd schmach gots abgestelt vnnd die falchen bucher von ynen genomen werdenn."

85. On the effort to ridicule Jewish rituals, see Deutsch 2004, 204ff.

86. See Murner 1512, *Ritus et celebratio phase iudeorum*, which is probably the first Haggadah ever printed in Latin. It ends with the familiar: "Anno futuro omnes in iherusalem det sanctus deus vt ibi pasce celebramus et respondent omnes amen" (fol. c4ᵛ).

87. See Diemling 2006, esp. 328ff.

88. Pfefferkorn 1509, *Hostis iudeorum*, fol. A1ᵛ: "Est profecto maledictum hominum genus quod nec verbis. nec precibus. nec ratione. nec inductione commoueri potest. vt…Ortwinus Gratius…in suo epigrammate doctissime disseruit."

89. See Pfefferkorn 1509 (Augsburg), *Der Juden veindt*, fol. A2ʳ: "Der erste [i.e., the first derisive name for Jesus] wirt genent Jescheynozere יֵשׁ צֹרִי‎Ist gesprochen als ain verfürer des volks." I should point out that when Pfefferkorn quotes Hebrew in this and most other texts the words are to be read from left to right, even though the letters are to be read in the usual right to left direction. The Latin translation of *The Enemy of the Jews*, however, does print the Hebrew words from right to left.

90. See Pfefferkorn 1509 (Augsburg), *Der Juden veindt*, fol. A2ʳff. Illustration is of fol. A2ʳ.

91. Also called the *Eighteen Benedictions*. See Schwaab 1913.

92. Pfefferkorn 1509 (Augsburg), *Der Juden veindt*, fol. A3ʳ: "Zů den getaufften ist kain hoffnung."

93. Jewish converts had been pointing to this prayer to arouse Christian hatred at least since Nicholas Donin in the thirteenth century. See Carlebach 2001, 26. Peter Schwarz cited it in his *Stern des Meschiah*, which he published in Esslingen in 1477. (He also published a preliminary Latin version in Esslingen in 1475.) This was a major source for Martin Luther's anti-Jewish tracts, perhaps also for Pfefferkorn. Reuchlin once claimed that Pfefferkorn derived his quotes from Schwarz. Schwarz, however, cited Hebrew texts in transliterated Hebrew with interlinear German translations. Unlike Pfefferkorn, he did not use a Hebrew font for his many quotes.

94. Pfefferkorn 1509 (Augsburg), *Der Juden veindt*, fol. A3^v: "Gott soll zerstören die gedancken vnd Rat vnserer veind mit dem mord vnd schwert."

95. Pfefferkorn 1509 (Augsburg), *Der Juden veindt*, fol. A4^r: "So ain Crist zů ainem Juden kumbt so entphecht in der vnnd spricht Seind wilkum. das ist als vill gesprochen/ teufel bis wilkum/ dan seth ist ain teüffel."

96. Reuchlin 1511, *Augenspiegel*, in *Sämtliche Werke* 4/1:35, ll. 23ff.

97. See *WA* 53:514; and *LW* 47:257.

98. Pfefferkorn 1509 (Augsburg), *Der Juden veindt*, fol. A2^v.

99. Pfefferkorn 1509 (Augsburg), *Der Juden veindt*, fol. A4^r: "Das ander tail sagt wie die Juden landt vnd leuth verderbenn. Wie wol vil vnd mangerlai Seckten vnnd glauben in der welt gefunden werdenn/ So ist doch vnter allen kain diebischer dückischer vnnd der Cristenhait schedlicher volck dan die vnrainen vnd verflüchten Juden."

100. E. Martin 1994, 124.

101. See Kirn 1989, 80–81. Pfefferkorn claims that this is a rate used in Deutz, a suburb of Cologne where Jewish residency was permitted after Cologne banished Jewish inhabitants.

102. Pfefferkorn 1509 (Augsburg), *Der Juden veindt*, fol. B3^r: "Weiter Raytzen die Juden manichen Cristen menschenn gelert vnd vngelert zů vnglauben... Auch so geschicht wo Judenn wonen vil ketzerey dann man vindt vil Cristen die mit den iuden vnkeuschait treyben vnd so dan also von den selben kinder gemacht werden."

103. Pfefferkorn 1509 (Augsburg), *Der Juden veindt*, fol. C2^r: "Aber ytzund will sy got nit mer erledigen noch yr gebet erhören warumb si haben grössere sünd dan yr vorvordern (die propheten getödt heten) gethan vnd getöt den Sunn gotes."

104. Pfefferkorn 1509 (Augsburg), *Der Juden veindt*, fol. C2^v: "Sunder sy müsten alle verworffne arbait thuun/ als die gassen sauber halten oder dye Camin keren deßgelichen [i.e., deßgleichen] die scheüssheuser fegen vnd huns dreck klaubenn etc. Doch das nit vnnderwegen lassenn als ich manig mal erzelt hab/ von yn zů nemen die falschen Bücher des Talmut. vnnd ynen nichts weiters zů lassen dann allain denn Text der Biblen. vngezweyfelt nach solcher handlung wurden sy ain andernn sin vnnd gemüt an sich nemen. vnnd also bekant werden zůuerlassenn yr falschhait vnnd nachuolgen der warhidt vnnsers glaubens."

105. Cohen 1982, 13.

106. Cohen 1982, 63.

107. Pfefferkorn 1516, *Streydt puechlyn*, fol. E2^r–E2^v.

108. Pfefferkorn 1510 (Augsburg), *Zu lob vnd Ere*, fol. A5^r: "als der selb Pfefferkorn der gedachten fürstin söliche sach vnd handel der iuden halb furtragen

lassen/ hat/ sie die angenomen vnd zů hertzen gefast/ vnd yn mit yrn aignen handschrifften an irer fürstlichen gnaden Brůder die römischen k. m. gefertigt." According to a letter Reuchlin wrote to Bonet de Lattes, Kunigunde appeared personally before the emperor to plea for the mandate. See Reuchlin, *Briefwechsel*, 2:427–45 (no. 228, before September 1513).

109. Pfefferkorn 1510 (Augsburg), *Zu lob vnd Ere*, fol. A5^v.

110. It is found in Pfefferkorn 1510 (Augsburg), *Zu lob vnd Ere*, fol. A5^v–A6^v; Pfefferkorn 1516, *Streydt puechlyn*, fol. A3^v–A4^v; a manuscript copy in the Frankfurt City Archive; and a manuscript copy, written in Hebrew characters in Bibliotheca Rosenthaliana MS 388. This last named source derives from the Frankfurt Jewish community. A fifth version is part of a special mandate sent by the emperor to the city of Worms. See Freudenthal 1931, 231–32. Pfefferkorn's printings of the mandate were also translated into Latin in Pfefferkorn 1510, *In laudem et honorem*; and Pfefferkorn 1516, *Defensio*.

111. Pfefferkorn 1510 (Augsburg), *Zu lob vnd Ere*, fol. A5^v: "wyr glaubwirdig bericht seind/ wie yr in euwern Synagogen lybereien oder sunst bey üch haben solt/ etliche vngegruntde vnnutze bücher vnd schrifften/ die nit alain vnsern hailigen Cristen glauben vnd des selben nach folgen zů schmach spot vertilgung vnd übel. sunder auch wider die bücher vnd gesetz Moysi vnd der propheten die doch ir selbs zů glauben vnd zů halten bekennet."

112. Pfefferkorn 1510 (Augsburg), *Zu lob vnd Ere*, fol. A5^v: "Alle euwer bůcher vnd schrifften überal zů uisitieren zů erfaren vnd besehnn vnd was darunder befunden die wider die bůcher vnd gesatz moisi. auch der prophetn wernn vnd wie obstet vngegrunt/ vnser hailignn cristnn glauben zů schmach vnd übel richten/ die selben alle/ doch an ieden ort mit wissen ains raths vnd in gegnnwurtigkait des pastors/ auch zwaier von rathe oder der oberkait von üch zůnemen die awegzethon. vnd zů vnderrucknn."

113. See Pfefferkorn 1510 (Augsburg), *Zu lob vnd Ere*, fol. A6^v; and Pfefferkorn 1510 (Cologne), *In laudem et honorem*, fol. B2^r. The Latin version is more lucid than the German.

114. Reuchlin 1511, *Augenspiegel*, in *Sämtliche Werke*, 4/1:19, ll. 4–6: "Dem selben nach er by kayßerlicher maiestat durch vil übung vnnd mit treffenlicher grosser fürdernus am ersten ain gebott vnd mandat erlangt."

115. Reuchlin 1505, *Tütsch missiue*, in *Sämtliche Werke*, 4/1:9, ll. 26–30: "so beschlüs ich das die Juden vmb kein andere sünd so lang zyt von got gestrafft werden dan alein vmb gots lesterung die ire vordern an dem rechten Messiah vnserm hern Jhesuh begangen haben vnd ire nachkommenden daryn verwilligt auch söllichs biß vff disen hütigen tag steet vnd angenem halten vnd haben." See also 10, ll. 13–14: "Wie wol ich nün nit wölte das sye in nit hetten getödt, noch dan ist mir leid das sye inn der gotts lesterung verharren." ("Although I now would not wish that they had not killed him, nonetheless it pains me that they persist in their blasphemy.")

116. This is according to Pfefferkorn, as recorded in Pfefferkorn 1516, *Defensio*, fol. A4^r, in Hutten 1859–70, supplement volume 1:87–88: "Tunc multa blandissima mihi dedit verba, inquiens, se mihi in hoc negocio venturum auxilio non solum verbis et scriptis, sed etiam factis velle ostendere." See also L. Geiger 1871, 217, for

a rejection of Pfefferkorn's account. Reuchlin's description of the meeting suggests there was tension between the men, although Reuchlin clearly states that he gave Pfefferkorn written legal advice. See Reuchlin 1511, *Augenspiegel*, in *Sämtliche Werke*, 4/1:19. See also 165, ll. 4–5: "so hab ich in dannocht inn meinem huß gütlich gewarnet/ zü lügen das er selbs ain güter crist sei."

117. Pfefferkorn confirmed that he had the note written in Reuchlin's hand. See Pfefferkorn 1516, *Defensio*, in Hutten 1859–70, supplement volume 1:114.

CHAPTER 6

Epigraph source: Bibliotheca Rosenthaliana MS 388, fol. 13ʳ; Kracauer 1900a, 168, 172 (item 4): "כי יש לחוש דתיפוק ח"ו חורבה מני'." I used Kracauer's German translations as a guide to the documents in Rosenthaliana MS 388 and also relied on the expertise of Dr. David Gilner, who clarified several difficult passages.

1. The major exception to this is Isidor Kracauer, best known for his history of the Frankfurt Jews, who published several valuable articles on Jewish resistance to the confiscation decree (see Kracauer 1887, 1900a, 1900b).

2. This is endemic in Renaissance scholarship. For a typical example, see Friedman 1983, 26, where he mistakenly writes that "as a result of this presentation [i.e., Reuchlin's defense], the emperor rescinded his order on 23 May 1510." Similarly, Rummel 2002, 11, erroneously claims that Maximilian both negotiated with the Frankfurt Jews and returned their books after receiving assessments of the confiscation policy from Reuchlin and others.

3. Reuchlin, *Briefwechsel* 2:427–45 (no. 228, before September 1513). Reuchlin repeated this claim empathically in the dedication of his translation and commentary of a pseudo-Athanasius tract to Archbishop Albrecht of Brandenburg. See Reuchlin 1519, trans., *Liber S. Athanasii de variis questionibus*, fol. B3ᵛ: "Post autem quam prudentissimus Imperator Maxaemilianus, mei consilii audiens, hebraicorum librorum combustioni supersedisset."

4. I have reviewed the relevant material in the Institut für Stadtgeschichte Frankfurt am Main (abbreviated hereinafter as ISG-Frankfurt) and quote directly from those documents. Kracauer 1887 and 1900b have transcriptions of excerpts from the documents.

5. I do not intend to imply strong disagreement with Graetz's or Baron's treatment of the Reuchlin Affair (i.e., the controversy among Christians over Reuchlin's defense of Jewish rights and books), although I do feel that they exemplify the tendency to underestimate the significance of the threat posed by the book confiscation pogrom. See Graetz 1891–98, 4:422ff. ("Reuchlin and the Talmud"). Baron 1969, 13:186, compressed the anti-Jewish campaign to just a few sentences, although he retained a substantial discussion of the Reuchlin Affair (labeling it a "literary battle royal") on 182–91.

6. Reuchlin 1511, *Augenspiegel*, in *Sämtliche Werke* 4/1:18–19: "das man allen iuden in dem gantzen römischen reich alle ire hebraische bücher klain und groß inn was gestalt die wern nemen möcht/ allain den blossen text der bibel hindann

gesetzt." In this section, Reuchlin also says that the confiscation in Worms proves this was the goal.

7. ISG-Frankfurt, Juden Akten 779 (Judenschaft Ugb E 56 B), fol. 43^r: "Vnnd so vns gemelte vnsre bucher on besichtigung abhendig wurden, als wir nit furhoffen, konten wir an vnsren festzitten vnd vesten noch vnsren sitten got den almechtigen, als vns dan von alten Bebsten vnd Keysern zugelassen worden ist, nit loben." I wish to thank Dr. Michael Matthäus, Institut für Stadtgeschichte Frankfurt am Main, for his generous and expert assistance during my visit to the archive.

8. The Frankfurt community was reorganized as a separate ghetto on the edge of town in 1462.

9. Breuer 1972, 7:85; and Toch 1997, 25ff. Toch concludes that by 1610 2,700–3,000 Jews resided in Frankfurt, making up some 15 percent of the total population.

10. ISG-Frankfurt, Juden Akten 779 (Judenschaft Ugb E 56 B), fol. 2^r, a letter of 19 August 1509 from Maximilian to the city council, announcing Pfefferkorn's imminent arrival: "die Juden Ire hochste Sinagog in vnnser vnnd des Reichs Stadt bey Euch [i.e., in Frankfurt] haben." In his special mandate for Worms, Maximilian also said that the Worms synagogue was the most distinguished in the realm; see Freudenthal 1931, 227.

11. Pfefferkorn 1512, *Brantspiegell*, fol. D4^r–D4^v: "sey haben nit meer noch dan drij haubt synagogen in dem gantzen romischen reich Als nemlich Regenspurg. Wormes vnd Franckfort."

12. Pfefferkorn 1510 (Augsburg), *Zu lob vnd Ere*, fol. A6^v.

13. See Straus 1939; and Hsia 1988, 66–85, on the decline of the Regensburg community.

14. See ISG-Frankfurt, "Bürgermeisterbuch," 1508, fol. 118^r (*Regesten-Frankfurt*, no. 3581), an entry of 29 March 1509, for Pfefferkorn's challenge of the Frankfurt Jews to a disputation. The council granted permission for the debate, but it is not known if it took place. An undated, handwritten placard is preserved in ISG-Frankfurt, Juden Akten 441 (Judenschaft Ugb E 46 A3), item 5.

15. ISG-Frankfurt, "Bürgermeisterbuch," 1508, fol. 118^r, and *Regesten-Frankfurt*, no. 3581.

16. The letter to Worms survives. See Kirn 1989, 103.

17. Bibliotheca Rosenthaliana MS 388, fol. 6^v, ed. Kracauer 1900a, 119 (item 1). The Bibliotheca Rosenthaliana is located in the library of the University of Amsterdam. MS 388 is a sixteenth-century copy of documents from the Jewish community of Frankfurt.

18. See Kracauer 1887, 170ff.; and Kracauer 1900a, 120ff.

19. All the emissaries from Frankfurt received a dispensation permitting them, in this urgent matter, to travel and conduct business on the sabbath and holy days.

20. As of 1512, Gumprecht was severely estranged from his father (and was even accused of plotting the murder of his father's new stepchildren). See *Regesten-Frankfurt*, no. 3795.

21. See *Regesten-Frankfurt*, no. 3568, the record of the archbishop's debt to Simon Weissenau as of 17 November 1508.

22. In a letter of 1 October, Uriel of Gemmingen specifically stated that investigations into questions of heresy must be conducted under his auspices. ISG-Frankfurt, Juden Akten 779 (Judenschaft Ugb E 56 B), fol. 20 and 22. See *Regesten-Frankfurt*, no. 3607.

23. Bibliotheca Rosenthaliana MS 388, fol. 9ᵛ–10ʳ; Kracauer 1900a, 232–33 (item 9). MS 388 gives a transcription of the German letter in the Hebrew alphabet.

24. Bibliotheca Rosenthaliana MS 388, fol. 10ʳ; Kracauer 1900a, 233–34 (item 10).

25. See Uriel of Gemmingen's letter of 1 October 1509 in ISG-Frankfurt, Juden Akten 779 (Judenschaft Ugb E 56 B), fol. 20 and 22. See *Regesten-Frankfurt*, no. 3607.

26. ISG-Frankfurt, "Bürgermeisterbuch," 1509, fol. 57ʳ. See *Regesten-Frankfurt*, no. 3607.

27. Moreover, the community knew that it had so far failed to get a stay of execution for the mandate from the Imperial Chamber Court, located in nearby Worms. On Friday, 28 September, the Frankfurt community dispatched Jonathan Kostheim (also known as Jonathan Levi Zion) to Worms to file the appeal, but the court declined to consider the case. See the description by the Frankfurt community in Bibliotheca Rosenthaliana MS 388, fol. 6ᵛ–7ʳ; Kracauer 1900a, 119–20 (item 1).

28. Not much is known about the Frankfurt envoy Jonathan Kostheim apart from his efforts in this affair. In August 1510, he asked the council to acknowledge that his net worth (for purposes of taxation) had fallen to 1,420 gulden, which would have placed him, roughly speaking, in a second tier of elite Jewish bankers and merchants. Simon Weissenau, Itzing Bopfingen, and perhaps Rabbi Salman of Nuremberg would have formed the core of a super elite class in Frankfurt. See ISG-Frankfurt, Gesetzbuch der Judenschaft, Juden Akten 438 (Ugb 46 WW), fol. 23ᵛ (*Regesten-Frankfurt*, no. 3687).

29. Bibliotheca Rosenthaliana MS 388, fol. 13ʳ; Kracauer 1900a, 168 and 171 (item 4): "ונתננו קצת ונדרנו קצת עד שהבאנו הדבר לפני אדונינו הקיסר."

30. Bibliotheca Rosenthaliana MS 388, fol. 13ʳ; Kracauer 1900a, 171–72 (item 4).

31. See the epigraph to this chapter.

32. It appears that Kostheim began writing this letter perhaps as early as 19 October. It narrates events from 19 October until 15 November and does so in tones so different as to suggest he added to the letter a few times in the course of those days.

33. Bibliotheca Rosenthaliana MS 388, fol. 15ᵛ; Kracauer 1900a, 170–71, 176–77 (item 4): "אם שמעתם וראיתם את אשר שמעתי וראיתי חיל ורעדה אחזתכם יותר משאוכל לכתוב."

34. Copies with slight variations survive in ISG-Frankfurt, Juden Akten 779 (Judenschaft Ugb E 56 B), fol. 24–fol. 29 (*Regesten-Frankfurt*, no. 3617), Bibliotheca Rosenthaliana MS 388, and Reuchlin 1513, *Defensio*, fol. A4ᵛ–B1ᵛ.

35. Bibliotheca Rosenthaliana MS 388, fol. 14ʳ; Kracauer 1900a, 170, 175 (item 4): "שאין לקיסר כח עלינו רק אנו רובצים תחת ממשלותם."

36. See ISG-Frankfurt, Juden Akten 779 (Judenschaft Ugb E 56 B), fol. 35 (*Regesten-Frankfurt*, no. 3627).

37. The Worms confiscation is known to have occurred on 18 December 1509; see Freudenthal 1931, 231.

38. These are reprinted by Freudenthal 1931, 227–32.

39. This was printed in Pfefferkorn 1516, *Streydt puechlyn*, fol. F2ᵛ. See Kracauer 1900a, 238.

40. Emperor Maximilian formally recognized the validity of the 1372 charter on 27 May 1495. See *Regesten-Frankfurt*, no. 2791.

41. ISG-Frankfurt, Juden Akten 655 (Judenschaft Ugb E 55 B 10); see *Regesten-Frankfurt*, no. 3605.

42. The Padua Mandate, however, was still an active legal issue because the 168 books confiscated under its terms were being held pursuant to instructions Maximilian appended to the Roveredo Mandate.

43. The most explicit statement of this occurs in a letter of 12 April 1510 from the Frankfurt city council to its emissary in Augsburg, Karl von Hynsberg. See *Regesten-Frankfurt*, no. 3661.

44. ISG-Frankfurt, Reichstagsakten 25/8 (*Regesten-Frankfurt*, no. 3630): "so dich vnser Juden durch sich oder ire botschafft ansuchen werden du wollest ine so viel fuglich sin mag geraten vnd behelffen sin." See Kracauer 1900a, 233.

45. ISG-Frankfurt, Juden Akten 779 (Judenschaft Ugb E 56 B), fol. 34ʳ (marginal note): "auch vnser oberkeit, so wir inn die Juden haben, abbruchlich." See Kracauer 1900a, 238 n. 2.

46. Pfefferkorn 1510 (Augsburg), *Zu lob vnd Ere*, fol. b6ᵛ: "Das xiii capitel vermant Fürsten heren vnd anderen stenden fleiß an zů keren solliche yrthumb/ so auß der iuden vnnutzen valschen bůchern erwest abzůstellen."

47. *Allen und ieglichen geistlich oder weltlich*, in Spanier 1934, 581–87.

48. Pfefferkorn later boasted that he had resisted bribes offered by the Frankfurt Jews; see Pfefferkorn 1516, *Defensio*, fol. B1ᵛ.

49. Reuchlin 1511, *Augenspiegel*, in *Sämtliche Werke* 4/1:24, ll. 29–30: "wie die vndertanen imm reich ain vffrür vnd vfflauff gegen irer aigen oberkait machen sollen."

50. ISG-Frankfurt, "Bürgermeisterbuch," 1509, fol. 87ʳ (*Regesten-Frankfurt*, no. 3618), indicates a decision to wait until Pfefferkorn should return to Frankfurt.

51. ISG-Frankfurt, "Bürgermeisterbuch," 1509, fol. 117ᵛ (*Regesten-Frankfurt*, no. 3648). According to the "Bürgermeisterbuch," it was Professor Ortlieb who presented the documents.

52. At this point, the city council was apparently prepared to join the Jewish community as plaintiff in such a case. The attempt by the Jewish community to bring a case to the Imperial Chamber Court, the supreme court of the empire, in September 1509 was refused by the court, perhaps because the city was not a party to that petition.

53. ISG-Frankfurt, Juden Akten 779 (Judenschaft Ugb E 56 B), fol. 36ʳ–36ᵛ: [Radt der Stadt Franckfurt] "bryngt der selben Ewer Keyserlichen Maiestet fur/ wie woil von beden geystlichen vnnd Keyserlichenn rechten versehen ist/ das die Juddißheit in Iren alten gewonheiten herlichkeiten vnd Zyrlicheiten festen vnnd solemniteten In Iren synagogen beschirmet sollen werden/ auch keyne newerung

oder newe gewonheit lauth der Babstlichenn rechte mit Inen ingefurt oder auch
Inen Ire gut genomen soll werden, wie auch mit sunderlichen Babstlichen vnnd
Keyserlichen freyheiten versehen vnd gefreyet synt/ wie woil auch die Juddische
bucher nit alleyn von Judden/ sunder auch den christen vleyßiglichen zu bewarenn
vnd zuhüten sunderlich Inn Babstlichen rechten versehen vnnd nit on vrsach gesatzt
ist, dwill das alt testament anfenglich In hebreyscher spruch geschreben ist, daruß
die latinische bucher offt gebeßert gestrafft vnnd emendirt synt worden auch etliche
Judden zu christlichem glaubenn da durch komen darumb auch In geistlichen
rechten geschreben ist/ wan die christen In der hebreyschen buchern vnnd zungen
geleret weren vnd sie mit Irer eygene schryfft vberwonden so wurden sie eher zum
christlichen glauben bekart Darumb auch der Bapst Clemens In geistlichen rechten
der hebreyschen bucher in etlichen hohenschulen vnnd vniuersiteten zulesen
vnnd zuleren verordnet hait/ da mit verstandenn wirt/ was nutze soliche Juddische
bucher der christenheit bringen mogen/ darumb auch die Judden Ire bucher In Iren
synagogen In großen eren behalten/ daruß in Iren hochtzyten vnd festen nach Iren
sytten vnnd herlichkeiten got den almechtigen loben/ das sie sunst on die selben
bucher nit volnbringen mochten." I wish to thank Dr. Michael Matthäus for his
expert advice on transcribing the Frankfurt document.

54. See Kracauer 1887, 244ff., on the attempts by the city and the Jewish
community to stall the proceedings on 9–10 April.

55. ISG-Frankfurt, Juden Akten 779 (Judenschaft Ugb E 56 B), fol. 44–56
(Regesten-Frankfurt, no. 3663). Diplomatic transcription in Kracauer 1900b.

56. A few territorial princes had demanded that the Frankfurt city council
return books owned by Jews under their protection. See Kracauer 1887, 232ff.

57. This was recorded on folio 13ʳ of the inventory: "das sie dieselben [i.e.,
'die frembden bucher'] nit gebruchen sollen in irer synagogen, auch sunder d [?]
bescheidt des rats nit vsz der stat lassen" (Kracauer 1900b, 430). This is fol. 56ʳ of the
entire document.

58. Kracauer 1887, 244. See ISG-Frankfurt, Juden Akten 779 (Judenschaft Ugb
E 56 B), fol. 34ʳ (Regesten-Frankfurt, no. 3646).

59. See ISG-Frankfurt, RS II, nr. 250, item 12, and Regesten-Frankfurt, no. 3567.
Maximilian wrote to the council on 12 November 1508 to request arrangement of a
three-month extension for Duke Erich's loan. Duke Erich wrote to the council on 10
January 1509 to express his gratitude for the council's successful intervention with
the Jewish creditors on his behalf.

60. ISG-Frankfurt, RS II, nr. 250, 1a–e, 2–5, 8, and Regesten-Frankfurt, no. 3621.

61. ISG-Frankfurt, Reichstagsakten 25, fol. 61, and Regesten-Frankfurt, no. 3665;
Kracauer 1887, 246 n. 3: "hat er [i.e., Maximilian] gefuget, daß man die pande mit
dem herczogen [i.e., Duke Erich] laß an sthen ein jar lang, so wille man ein guten
bescheit geben."

62. ISG-Frankfurt, RS III, nr. 530, Regesten-Frankfurt, no. 3728.

63. In a letter of 27 May 1511, Maximilian reported that Itzing Bopfingen agreed
to a suspension of interest on Erich's loan for three further years. See ISG-Frankfurt,
RS II, nr. 294, and Regesten-Frankfurt, no. 3727.

64. See Tschech 1971, 80ff.

65. Tschech 1971, 67ff. See Hsia 1988, on the general phenomena of host desecration and ritual murder, though Hsia does not mention these innuendos.

66. Wiesflecker 1971–86, 4:10.

67. Reuchlin 1513, *Defensio*, in *Sämtliche Werke* 4/1:206, ll. 17–22: "Lectis tabulis et diplomate sacro, fateor, derepente primo aspectu obmutui, nescius, quid struere his coeptis, quid moliri, quid conari velles nisi forte libros comburere, quos neque historiis indubitatis neque annalibus approbatis aut aliis fide dignis monumentis constaret ab aliquo unquam imperatore Romanorum de primo ad ultimum connumerando fuisse combustos."

68. The Füssen Mandate of 1510, as quoted in Reuchlin 1511, *Augenspiegel*, in *Sämtliche Werke* 4/1:20, ll. 7–9: "Nun haben wir in verschiner zeit den iuden ire bücher wider zu geben verschaffen/ der gestalt das die also beschriben vnd vnuerruckt biß vff vnsern wytern beuelch behalten werden."

69. Pfefferkorn published these evaluations in Pfefferkorn 1516, *Defensio*, fol. B4ʳ, in Hutten 1859–70, supplement volume 1:94: "Manifestum est librum Iudaeorum quem Thalmut vocant tantos continere nedum errores et falsitates, verum etiam blasphemias et haereses contra legem propriam."

70. See Pfefferkorn 1516, *Defensio*, fol. C1ʳff.

71. The evaluations by Erfurt and Victor of Carben have not survived, though other records indicate that both advocated burning Jewish books. See Hutten 1859–70, supplement volume 1:99, 101.

72. Lotter 1993, 67, does not mention the extreme position of the University of Cologne or the threatening proposals of Hoogstraeten.

73. See Pfefferkorn 1516, *Defensio*, fol. C3ʳ–C4ᵛ, in Hutten 1859–70, supplement volume 1:99–101, for the memorandum. The full title is: "Consultatio venerandi ac benedocti Iacobi Hochstraten haereticae pravitatis magistri contra immundos libros Iudaeorum."

74. Pfefferkorn 1516, *Defensio*, fol. C4ʳ, in Hutten 1859–70, supplement volume 1:100, the key passage: "foret praeterea imperiali celsitudini opus dignissimum, si in praefata librorum examinatione per eos qui Iudaicam intelligunt scripturam extraherentur inibi contenti articuli erronei, impii et blasphemi contra propriam legem, et institueretur contra Iudaeos solemnis inquisitio, et super articulis extractis mature examinarentur."

75. Reuchlin 1513, *Defensio*, in *Sämtliche Werke* 4/1:250, l. 1: "contra Iudaeos solennis inquisitio." See the entire passage, 248ff.

76. As Ackermann 1999, 162ff., illustrates, Reuchlin's approach is not atypical for legal briefs from this period.

77. See Lotter 1993, 69, for valuable statistics on Reuchlin's use of civil and ecclesiastical law as well as the Bible. Like other scholars, Lotter overlooked Reuchlin's use of earlier anti-Jewish publications in his defense of Jewish books.

78. Reuchlin 1511, *Augenspiegel*, in *Sämtliche Werke* 4/1:35, ll. 5–6: "wir vnd sie ains ainigen römischen reichs mitburger synd."

79. See Ackermann 1999, 164–65. Reuchlin explicitly cited Bartolus a Saxoferrato for other aspects of Jewish legal status, though not on the question of citizenship (a status Bartolus had endorsed).

80. Reuchlin 1511, *Augenspiegel*, in *Sämtliche Werke* 4/1:28, ll. 7–8: "kaißerliche vnd künigkliche recht auch andere furstliche satzungen habent es fürkommen das nieman das syn verliere durch gewalt." In granting Jews the status of citizens, Reuchlin was relying on older statutes in the imperial code and also on some influential commentaries on Roman law by Italian jurists of the fourteenth century, especially Bartolus and Baldus de Ubaldis.

81. Reuchlin did this in the lengthy Latin commentary he published with the first edition of the *Augenspiegel*, a section he titled *Arguments* (*Argumenta*). These notes were an attempt to qualify some of the more favorable portrayals of Judaism in response to Pfefferkorn's abusive attack in Pfefferkorn 1511, *Handt Spiegel*. For the qualification of the "concives" argument, see Reuchlin 1511, *Augenspiegel*, in *Sämtliche Werke* 4/1:72ff.

82. See Kisch 1961.

83. Kisch 1961, 1ff.

84. Reuchlin's reliance on the Bible and canon law is so pervasive that Lotter 1993 proposed that Reuchlin generated a theological rather than a legal argument. Ackermann 1999, 160ff., objected strongly to Lotter's approach, but on narrow grounds, missing the value of Lotter's general observation.

85. The reference is to *Decretales Gregori* IX, 5, 6, 9. In *Corpus iuris canonici* 1879–81, 2:773–74.

86. Reuchlin 1511, *Augenspiegel*, in *Sämtliche Werke* 4/1:62, ll. 13–15: "Darumb ist vns gebotten inn den gaistlichen rechten. c. sicut iude. extra de iu. Das wir den iuden das ir nit sollen nemen/ es sei gelt oder gelts werdt."

87. For a convenient edition and translation of *Sicut Judaeis*, see Synan 1965, 229–32.

88. I state this despite the insistence in Ackermann 1999 that the amount of theological argumentation is not out of the ordinary for a legal memorandum of this period.

89. The right to own books is not mentioned in papal privileges with the exception of one issued by Martin V on 12 February 1418 (to protect Jews in Germany, Savoy, and Bresse). See Simonsohn 1988–91, 2:670–71: "Item, quod in eorum synagogis, festivitatibus, domibus, libris, cimiteriis, rebus et bonis…a nemine valeant gravari." See Kracauer 1911–27, 1:155ff., for a description of how Emperor Sigismund used this privilege to tax Jewish communities.

90. He condemned an infamous biography of Jesus (called the *Toledot Yeshu*) as well as Yom-Tov Lipmann's anti-Christian diatribe *Sefer ha-Nizzahon* (*Victory*) of ca. 1400. Nonetheless, Reuchlin 1511, *Augenspiegel*, in *Sämtliche Werke* 4/1:29, ll. 12–14, wrote: "I heard from them [i.e., Jews at the court of Friedrich III] that such books had been done away with, destroyed by them, and that all of their people were forbidden to write or to say anything like that ever again" ("solliche bücher von inen abgethon vertillckt vnnd allen den iren verbotten sy/ der gleichen nymmer mer zeschreiben oder zeredenn").

91. Reuchlin 1511, *Augenspiegel*, in *Sämtliche Werke* 4/1:51–52.

92. Reuchlin 1511, *Augenspiegel*, in *Sämtliche Werke* 4/1:34, ll. 28–30, where Reuchlin denies that this could possibly refer to Christians: "How could this [i.e.,

"meshummadim"] refer to Christians, since indeed there is no people on earth that grants them [i.e., Jews] such liberties and accepts them as do the Christians, as is apparent in canon and civil law" ("Wie kan aber das bedeütten die cristenn/ so doch kain volck vff erdenn ist das sie mit grössern fryhaitten handthabt vnd vnderschleufft dann die cristen/ als man inn gaistlichen vnd weltlichen rechten erfindt").

93. Reuchlin 1511, *Augenspiegel*, in *Sämtliche Werke* 4/1:34.

94. Reuchlin 1511, *Augenspiegel*, in *Sämtliche Werke* 4/1:31.

95. Reuchlin 1511, *Augenspiegel*, in *Sämtliche Werke* 4/1:31, ll. 3–4 (referring to the compilation of the Talmud): "als by vns das decret oder das büch Sententiarum/ oder catena aurea. "

96. Reuchlin 1511, *Augenspiegel*, in *Sämtliche Werke* 4/1:37. This was such a blunder that L. Geiger 1871, 249, called it a "white lie," suggesting that Reuchlin was being disingenuous to advance his argument.

97. Reuchlin 1511, *Augenspiegel*, in *Sämtliche Werke* 4/1:33.

98. Reuchlin 1511, *Augenspiegel*, in *Sämtliche Werke* 4/1:33, ll. 6–7: "die iuden nit seien heretici" (quoting Gratian II, 24, 3, 27).

99. Reuchlin 1511, *Augenspiegel*, in *Sämtliche Werke* 4/1:48, ll. 34–35: "Dan sie sind kain glid der christenlichen kirchen vnd gat vns ir glaub nichtz an" (with reference to a gloss on Clementines 5, 5,1, which is *Liber Septimus* of the *Corpus iuris canonici* and not included in Friedberg's edition).

100. Among the sources Reuchlin quoted are Paul of Burgos, Peter Schwarz, Alfonso de Spina, Ramón Martí, Nicholas of Lyra (his small tract *Contra Judaeos* and his famous biblical commentaries), the anonymous author of *Obiectiones in dicta Thalmut seductoris Judaeorum*, and, of course, Johannes Pfefferkorn.

101. See Reuchlin 1505, *Tütsch missiue*, in Reuchlin, *Sämtliche Werke* 4/1:3–12.

102. Reuchlin 1511, *Augenspiegel*, in *Sämtliche Werke* 4/1:37. Reuchlin also dedicated his translation of *Batrachomiomachia* to Erhard von Pappenheim, who was probably a student of Schwarz. See Reuchlin, *Briefwechsel* 2:9–10 n. 5.

103. Reuchlin 1511, *Augenspiegel*, in *Sämtliche Werke* 4/1:59, ll. 4–8: "die bücher kain wircklich vrsach seien darumb die iuden nit zü cristem glauben kommen. Luce xvi. Habent Moysen et prophetas/ sunder die bücher seien wol vrsach das sie leichtlich glaubig werden/ wa wir der selben sprach gelert vnd wolgeschickt leüt hetten/ die do vernünfftigklich mit inen kündten vmb gon."

104. Reuchlin 1511, *Augenspiegel*, in *Sämtliche Werke* 4/1:38.

105. Reuchlin 1511, *Augenspiegel*, in *Sämtliche Werke* 4/1:38.

106. The *Scrutinium scripturarum* was printed at least five separate times in the fifteenth century. Paul of Burgos's strategy for his conversionary guide was to supplement the traditional use of Hebrew Scriptures with material from other authentic Jewish writings, above all, the Talmud. See Paul of Burgos (Pablo de Santa Maria) 1475, *Scrutinium scripturarum*, fol. 1^r–1^v: "vero quod in predicto verbo notatur est. quod non solum ex scripturis sacri canonis s. veteris testa. sunt accipienda testimonia Christi. sed etiam ab aliis scripturis apud ipsos hebreos autenticis. Et ideo dixit. In quibus putatis vitam habere. quasi dicat. Non solum scrutemini scripturas in quibus vere vitam eternam haberetis. que in sacro canone veteris test. continentur.

sed etiam illas in quibus putatis vitam habere. scilicet que apud vos sunt autentice. licet in se autoritatem non habeant. que quidem scripture sunt glo. seu auctoritates talmudice. et alia scripta apud ipsos autentica."

107. Reuchlin 1511, *Augenspiegel*, in *Sämtliche Werke* 4/1:42, ll. 30–35: "wan sie wider die iuden disputirn wöllen so ziehen sie den Thalmud her für/ vnd kempffen wider sie mit dem Thalmud. Als der lobwirdig doctor der hailigen schrifft barfüsser ordens der das buch Fortalicium fidei inn Hispanien gemacht/ der... für sich vnd für vns des thalmuds wol vnd geschicklich beholffen/ als ob er die iuden wölte mit irem aigen messer erstechen."

108. Reuchlin 1511, *Augenspiegel*, in *Sämtliche Werke* 4/1:63, ll. 24–31: "Welche die syent die vß luterer mainung des cristenlichen glaubes frembde außlüt begerennt zu rechtem glaubenn zu bringen/ die sollent das mit senfften wortten vnnd nit mit rawher mainung vnnderston/ vff das nit der widerwil die ihene vertrybe/ dero gemütt wol möcht ain gütte vernunfft von der irrung abwenden. Vnd welche anders thünd/ vnd sie vnder verborgener gestaltt von gewonlichen sitten wöllent abwenden/ die mag man erkennen das sie nit gottes handel/ sunder ire aigene henndel treiben."

109. Reuchlin 1511, *Augenspiegel*, in *Sämtliche Werke* 4/1:49–50: "bapst Sixtus der vierd hab beuolhen die selben cabalischen bücher in latinische sprach zü transferirn vnd zü tolmetschen/ vnserm glauben zü sunderm nutz."

110. Reuchlin 1511, *Augenspiegel*, in *Sämtliche Werke* 4/1:63, ll. 10–18: "kan ich für war bessers nit raten nach meiner klainen verstentnus/ dan das die K. M. vmb gottes vnd vnsers cristenliches glaubes willen by den hohen schulen in teutschen landen verfüge/ das ain yegkliche vniuersitet müß x. iar zwen maister halltten die do künden vnd sollen die studenten vnd schuler inn hebraischer sprach leren vnd vnderweißen/ wie die Clementin anzaigt vnd vßweißt/ sub titulo de magistris prima. Dar zu sollen vns die iuden so in vnsern landen sitzen vnd wonen mit leihung der bücher gutwilliglich vnd nachbeürlich beholffen sein/ vff zimlich caucion vnd on iren schaden." The reference to canon law ("de magistris prima") is to *Clementines* 5, 1, 1.

111. Reuchlin 1511, *Augenspiegel*, in *Sämtliche Werke* 4/1:52, ll. 28–30: "Dan die iuden sind vnsere Capsarij librarij vnnd bibliothecarij die sollich bücher behalttenn darauß wir vnnßers glaubens zeugknus mögen stellen." The passage evokes St. Jerome's introduction to the Pentateuch.

112. Reuchlin 1511, *Augenspiegel*, in *Sämtliche Werke* 4/1:56, ll. 23–24: "Noch ist vnder denen allen [i.e., ancient translations of the Hebrew Bible] der allt text der iuden beuor geweßen on befleckt."

113. Reuchlin 1511, *Augenspiegel*, in *Sämtliche Werke* 4/1:50, l. 32–51, l. 2: "das hailig gaistlich recht sagt/ c. ut veterum librorum dis. ix. das der glaub der alltten bücher müß durch die hebraisch geschrifft gehandt habt werden/ vnd wan die wörter vnd reden rabi Salomonis der über die bibel geschriben hat vß vnserm Nicolao de Lyra der auch über die bibel geschriben hat/ cantzeliert vnd aus gethon wern/ so wölt ich das überig so der selb Nicolaus de Lyra vß seinem aigen haupt über die bibel gemacht hette gar inn wenig bletter comprehendiern vnd begreiffen."

114. Hailperin 1963 offers a comprehensive study of Rashi's impact on Nicholas of Lyra.

115. Reuchlin 1511, *Augenspiegel*, in *Sämtliche Werke* 4/1:57, ll. 27–29: "vnser apostel Paulus hat alle kunst der iuden gelernt vnnd ist by den rabin zü schul gangen/ was ist vß im worden? mer dan alle andere aposteln."

116. Reuchlin 1511, *Augenspiegel*, in *Sämtliche Werke* 4/1:51, ll. 2–19: "sollich commentarien kan vnd mag die cristenlich kirch nit von handen lasen/ dan sie behaltten die hebraische sprach inn der aigenschafft übung/ dero die hailig schrifft nit kan mangeln besunder im alten testament/ Gleich als wir nit künden noch mögen der griechischen sprach vnd irer grammaticken vnnd commentarien inn dem newen testament mangeln vnnd embern/ wie das yetzt gemelt gaistlich recht Ut veterum aus weiset. Dann ich wil das mit vrlaub vnnd züchten geredt haben/ das man inn vnßerm cristenlichen glauben gar vil doctores findt die do mangel halb der zwaier sprachen die hailgen geschrifft nit recht aus legen/ vnnd werden gar dick zü spott darab/ darumb soll mann die commentarios vnnd gloßen der menschen die ir sprach von iugent vff wol gelernt haben kains wegs vndertrucken/ sunder wa die seien zü handen bringen/ vff pflantzen vnd inn gütten eern haltten/ als brunnen daraus die recht warhait der sprachen vnd verstentnus der hailigen schrifft fleüßt/ des halb spricht das gaistlich recht in ca. ieiunium lxxvi. distinc. Vil der vnnsern haben vil gesagt das anander wider ist/ darumb wir genött vnnd gezwungen werden zü den iuden ze lauffen vnnd die warhait der kunst vil mer aus dem brunnen dan aus den abflüssen zesüchen."

117. Reuchlin 1511, *Augenspiegel*, in *Sämtliche Werke* 4/1:53, ll. 20–24: "die weil wir sy alle iar ierlichs inn vnsern kirchenn am karfreitag offenlich scheltten perfidos iudeos/ das ist glaubruchig iuden/ vnd nach rechtem teutsch die weder trawen noch glauben halten. So möchten sy daruff vnder inen sagen nach innhaltung der recht also: Sie liegen vns an/ wir hond vnßern glauben nie gebrochen."

118. Reuchlin 1511, *Augenspiegel*, in *Sämtliche Werke* 4/1:59, ll. 20–23: "Der iud ist vnsers herr gots alls wol als ich/ stat er/ so stat er seinem herrn/ fallt er/ so falltt er seinem herrn/ ain yegklicher würdt für sich selbs müssen rechnung geben. Was wöllen wir aines andern seelen vrtailn/ got ist wol so mechtig das er in mag vffrichten."

119. For the imperial mandate authorizing confiscation of Reuchlin's *Eye Glasses*, see Reuchlin, *Briefwechsel* 2:625–29 (appendix 4, 7 October 1512). See also Reuchlin, *Briefwechsel* 2:630–33 (appendix 5, 9 July 1513), for the imperial mandate for the confiscation of Reuchlin's *Defensio*.

120. The letter, dated 23 October 1514, appeared in Reuchlin 1519, ed., *Illustrium virorum epistolae*, fol. Fi^r–Fi^v.

121. See Maimon 1978, 191–220. Maimon, however, did not connect this event to the anti-Jewish agitation of the book controversy and its aftermath.

122. See Reuchlin, *Briefwechsel* 3:309–15, ll. 40ff. (no. 290, 31 August 1516), where August Stromer reports that Archbishop Albrecht rudely refused to accept *Beschyrmung* from Pfefferkorn. After Maximilian's action of February 1516, Albrecht may have decided to have nothing further to do with the persecution.

CHAPTER 7

Epigraph source: Reuchlin 1513, *Defensio*, in *Sämtliche Werke* 4/1:342, ll. 19–23: "Ita faveo Iudaeis, ut iniuriae non subiaceant et inuriam non faciant....Iniusticia enim est immanitas omnem humanitatem repellens."

  1. See Pfefferkorn 1516, *Defensio*, fol. C4ʳ, and the discussion in chapter 6.
  2. Only a few even bothered to mention well-known precedents for condemning the Talmud, in particular Innocent IV's authorization for Nicholas Donin to burn copies of the Talmud in Paris.
  3. Reuchlin 1511, *Augenspiegel*, in *Sämtliche Werke* 4/1:64.
  4. Pfefferkorn 1516, *Defensio*, D1ᵛ, in Hutten 1859–70, supplement volume 1:103–4.
  5. The report of the Freiburg commission is in Pfefferkorn 1516, *Defensio*, fol. D2ᵛ–D4ᵛ, in Hutten 1859–70, supplement volume 1:104–7. See Reuchlin, *Briefwechsel* 2:117–25 (no. 159, 10 November 1509), esp. 123 n. 18; and L. Geiger 1871, 238.
  6. See Pfefferkorn 1511, *Handt Spiegel*, fol. a1ʳ, the title: "Handt Spiegel Johannis Pfefferkorn/ wider vnd gegen die Jüden/ vnd Judischen Thalmudischen schrifftenn So/ sie vber das Cristenlich Regiment/ singen vnd lesen Welche pillich Gotslesterer/ ketzer vnd aberglauber/ des alten Newen/ vnd des Naturlichen gesetzen gezelt/ geheissen/ verthümbt vnd abgethan/ werden mögen. Darumb sich etliche cristen wider mich setzen/ anfechten Solliche artickel zů widerlegen Dargegen ich antwurdt vnd mit bescheidene reden vffgelöst hab."
  7. See Reuchlin 1511, *Augenspiegel*, in *Sämtliche Werke* 4/1:22–26, for Reuchlin's explanation that he is publishing the *Recommendation* "only to save my honor" ("allain zů rettung meiner eern," 24, l. 2) in the aftermath of Pfefferkorn's scurrilous attacks in *Magnifying Glass*.
  8. To refute accusations that professors at Cologne had written *Magnifying Glass*, Pfefferkorn would later emphasize that he wrote and published the tract in Mainz.
  9. See Pfefferkorn 1511, *Handt Spiegel*, fol. a1ᵛ, where Pfefferkorn writes that Tongern asked him "Warumb der loblich handel betreffen der Jüdische bücher halben nit entlichen seinen fürgang haben mag."
  10. See E. Martin 1994, 251.
  11. Pfefferkorn 1511, *Handt Spiegel*, fol. a4ʳ: "Mann solt wol Cristen finden/ die sprechen sie seind des teüfels mitbürger."
  12. Pfefferkorn 1511, *Handt Spiegel*, fol. c2ʳ: "So jch von den götlichen doctoribus bericht bin/ dz sie clerlich befinden/ Gregorius vnd Innocencius der virdt/ haben den Talmut verbrent oder verbrennen lassen."
  13. Pfefferkorn 1511, *Handt Spiegel*, fol. a4ʳ–a4ᵛ.
  14. See Pfefferkorn 1512, *Brantspiegell*, fol. A3ᵛ.
  15. Pfefferkorn 1511, *Handt Spiegel*, fol. a3ᵛ: "hat er doch hebraysche Grammaticam drucken lassen/ ist wol ware Getruckt aber nit gemacht Das wil ich mit jme selber beweisenn."
  16. Pfefferkorn 1512, *Brantspiegell*, fol. B4ʳff.
  17. Pfefferkorn 1512, *Brantspiegell*, fol. A3ʳ.

18. See, for example, Pfefferkorn 1511, *Handt Spiegel*, fol. d1ʳ: "die sünd des schentlichenn wüchers" (the sin of shameless usury).

19. Pfefferkorn 1511, *Handt Spiegel*, fol. c3ᵛ; see also E. Martin 1994, 251. Pfefferkorn writes that this happened "zů deütsch bey Collen an dem Reynn," which I take to mean Deutz, a village in the vicinity of Cologne where Jews were permitted to reside.

20. Pfefferkorn 1511, *Handt Spiegel*, fol. c2ᵛ–c3ᵛ. Pfefferkorn claims to have seen the doctor and his accomplices in Prague.

21. Pfefferkorn 1511, *Handt Spiegel*, fol. c3ᵛ–d4ᵛ. This story takes up eleven of the forty-seven pages of the pamphlet. It features long passages narrating the Franciscan's anti-Jewish campaign before the Jews converted him.

22. The four cases are those at Deggendorf (1337), Breslau (1453), Passau (1478), and Sternberg (1492). See Pfefferkorn 1511, *Handt Spiegel*, fol. a4ʳ.

23. Pfefferkorn 1511, *Handt Spiegel*, fol. a3ᵛ–a4ʳ: "Ist nit offembar an jrem thůn vnnd lassenn Das sie dye Cristenlichen kirchen schenden vnd lestern Als nemlich jn dem vergangenn jare zů Berlyn jn der Marck bescheen/ Das heilig hochwirdig Sacrament gemißhandelt/ geschmecht/ vnd gevneret."

24. See Pfefferkorn 1516, *Defensio*, fol. A2ᵛff., where Pfefferkorn repeats the innuendos (claiming the Berlin Jews were "justly" burned) and associates Albrecht of Brandenburg's hatred of Jews with the Berlin case.

25. For Pfefferkorn's list of articles against the Talmud, see Pfefferkorn 1511, *Handt Spiegel*, fol. b3ʳ–c1ʳ.

26. As early as 28 August 1511, Reuchlin would begin accusing Hoogstraeten of having composed Pfefferkorn's polemics. See Reuchlin, *Briefwechsel* 2:212, ll. 75–76 (no. 185, 28 October 1511).

27. Pfefferkorn 1511, *Handt Spiegel*, fol. c2ʳ.

28. In September 1515, the theology faculty at Cologne backed up their claim to having authority for censuring books by citing a special commission from Pope Sixtus IV empowering them to conduct heresy trials specifically against witches and, by extension, against all forms of heterodoxy. See Kober 1923, 116–17. This document also specifies that the faculty had been taking action against both Reuchlin and the Jews: the faculty "at its own expense and for the love of God and the Catholic faith is prosecuting this case against Reuchlin and the Jews and their accomplices" (Kober 1923, 117: "quae sui impensis amore dei et fidei catholicae hanc causam prosequitur contra Reuchlin et Judaeos et eorum complices").

29. Tongern 1512, *Articuli*, fol. H6ʳ.

30. Reuchlin, *Briefwechsel* 2:222, ll. 12–14 (no. 187, 2 January 1512): "serenissimae imperatoriae maiestati persuaderes super negocio librorum Iudaicorum, quatinus idem negocium laudabiliter per eandem Caesaream maiestatem coeptum interverteres."

31. Reuchlin, *Briefwechsel* 2:222, ll. 20ff. (no. 187, 2 January 1512): "sed et Iudaeis ipsis...occasionem praestitisti, quo amplius nos irrideant, quando inter Christianos et quidem inter eos, qui docti reputantur, te unicum invenerint, qui suam causam agat, tutetur ac defendat, quasi nec Christum neque virginem

matrem neque apostolos neque fidem nostram intemeratam blasphement aut vituperent."

32. Reuchlin, *Briefwechsel* 2:200–201 (no. 183, 26 October 1511).

33. Reuchlin, *Briefwechsel* 2:227–29 (no. 188, 4 January 1512).

34. Reuchlin 1512, *Ain clare verstentnus*, in Reuchlin, *Sämtliche Werke* 4/1:171–96.

35. Reuchlin, *Briefwechsel* 2:231–37 (no. 190, 27 January 1512).

36. Reuchlin, *Briefwechsel* 2:274–78 (no. 195, 28 February 1512); 2:278–81 (no. 196, 29 February 1512).

37. See Reuchlin, *Briefwechsel* 2:276, ll. 42ff. (no. 195, 28 February 1512).

38. Reuchlin, *Briefwechsel* 2:280, ll. 14–16 (no. 196, 29 February 1512): "te…Iudaeis eorumque perfidis et blasphemis libris et nominatim Thalmud adversantem."

39. Reuchlin, *Briefwechsel* 2:282–84 (no. 197, 11 March 1512).

40. Reuchlin, *Briefwechsel* 2:286, ll. 42–46 (no. 198, 11 March 1512): "poëtae et historici, quorum hoc tempore magna copia vivit, qui me praeceptorem quondam suum, ut par est, venerantur, qui tantam iniquitatem adversariorum perpetuae traderent memoriae et innocenter passum me describerent cum aetherna gymnasii vestri ignominia."

41. Reuchlin 1513, *Defensio*, in *Sämtliche Werke* 4/1:282, ll. 1–4: "Non enim sunt vere theologi, quibus sit credendum. Non tanto et tam precioso theologiae nomine digni, qui non theologos sed vilissimos scurras, turpissimos blacterones, infames scaenicosque detractores imitantur."

42. Reuchlin 1513, *Defensio*, in *Sämtliche Werke* 4/1:296, ll. 9–11: "Qua in re compassione quadam miserendum esset tam antiquae scholae facultatis theologicae Coloniensium, quae forte, ut annosis accidit, senio desipere incipit, delirare ac dementare."

43. Reuchlin 1513, *Defensio*, in *Sämtliche Werke* 4/1:354, l. 21: "diabologus."

44. Reuchlin 1513, *Defensio*, in *Sämtliche Werke* 4/1:300, ll. 17–18: "ut inquisitione sua illa solenni, quam cupere videntur, aurum a Iudaeis emungerent."

45. Reuchlin 1513, *Defensio*, in *Sämtliche Werke* 4/1:384, l. 1 (addressing Emperor Maximilian): "Nihil in eo invenies nisi molle, effoeminatum, puerile," and so on.

46. Reuchlin, *Briefwechsel* 2:445ff. (no. 229, ca. September 1513).

47. Reuchlin 1513, *Defensio*, in *Sämtliche Werke* 4/1:254, ll. 14–15: "Quibus libellis ex Agrippina Colonia circumfertur ubique Iudaeos non ultra esse Iudaeos, sed haereticos et hostes nostros. "

48. Reuchlin 1513, *Defensio*, in *Sämtliche Werke* 4/1:420, ll. 12–14: "Sed hoc scio, quod synagoga Iudaeorum praeceptum habet, quod et legit et inter se in festivitatibus publicat, ut omnes Iudaei debeant orare pro pace regni."

49. Reuchlin 1513, *Defensio*, in *Sämtliche Werke* 4/1:430, ll. 6–7: "quia credant omnes gentes salvari posse in sua fide."

50. Reuchlin 1513, *Defensio*, in *Sämtliche Werke* 4/1:344, ll. 19–25: "Scio, tulerunt aegre adversarii, quia eos dixi concives esse nostros. Nunc plus insaniant velim iracundia, rumpantur ilia, quia dico Iudaeos esse fratres nostros, fratres Arnoldi,

fratres omnium theologistarum Coloniensium, non tantum quod unum patrem omnium habeamus in coelis, unde omnis paternitas, verum etiam quod ex eodem nobiscum parente in terris generati sunt, qui, licet non sint nobiscum membra, tamen sunt nobiscum fratres."

51. Reuchlin 1513, *Defensio*, in *Sämtliche Werke* 4/1:332ff.

52. Reuchlin 1513, *Defensio*, in *Sämtliche Werke* 4/1:344–46: "Ecce qualis sum fautor Iudaeorum, qui detestandam perfidiam reseco et tamen in eo iniuriam illis inferri non consulo.... Fautor igitur sum, ut debeo, ut decet, ut S. Paulus, ut S. Hieronymus, ut S. Thomas de Aquino, ut pontifices, ut imperatores, ut iurisconsulti omnes doctissimi et Christianissimi, non contra ecclesiam, sed pro ecclesia.... Fautor sum, quia perversis et nocentibus mala et intolerabilia iuste perimo."

53. See Kober 1923.

54. Kober 1923, 119 (document 3). Hoogstraeten advises that no change of venue "extra provinciam" be permitted, thereby consigning the matter to his jurisdiction.

55. Kober 1923 (document 5b), 121.

56. See Reuchlin, *Briefwechsel* 2:630–33 (appendix 5).

57. Document printed in Gratius 1514, *Prenotamenta*, fol. aa6^v–bb1^r.

58. Printed in Pfefferkorn 1516, *Defensio*, fol. I2^r, in Hutten 1859–70, supplement volume 1:135: "censuimus et deliberavimus libellum ipsum pias aures christifidelium et maxime simplicium graviter offendere, multos quoque et varios articulos in fide plurimum suspectos et scandalosos, haeresim quoque sapientes et Iudaeorum inprimis perfidiae consentanteos continere."

59. Kober 1923 (document 1), 115.

60. Trusen 1998, 93, speculates that Hoogstraeten probably worried that he did not have adequate legal justification for that step.

61. *Acta iudiciorum* 1518, fol. A2^r.

62. Hoogstraeten was awarded an MA from the University of Louvain in 1485.

63. See Peterse 1995, 17; and Hoogstraeten 1507, *Defensorium fratrum mendicantium*.

64. Hoogstraeten 1510, *Tractatus magistralis*.

65. See *Acta iudiciorum* 1518, fol. A2^r–B1^r.

66. *Acta iudiciorum* 1518, fol. B1^r: "petimus per uos uenerabiles dominos Commissarios, uestramque diffinitiuam sententiam pronunciari decerni et declarari praefatum libellum Speculum Oculare Ioanni Reuchlin inscriptum haeresibus et erroribus refertum, perfidis iudaeis nimis fauorabilem, ecclesiae dei iniuriosum, ac sacris ecclesiae doctoribus irreuerentialem, ipsumque propterea scriptura seu impressoria arte per prouinciam et seu diocesim Moguntinensem multiplicatum communi hominum usui interdicendum, condemnandum, supprimendum. tollendum. ac igne publice concremandum."

67. Jerome discusses this in the context of Isaiah 5:18–19.

68. *Acta iudiciorum* 1518, fol. A2^v.

69. *Acta iudiciorum* 1518, fol. A3^r.

70. See Hailperin 1963.

71. *Acta iudiciorum* 1518, fol. A3^r.

72. *Acta iudiciorum* 1518, fol. A4^v.

73. Reuchlin 1511, *Augenspiegel*, in *Sämtliche Werke* 4/1:51, ll. 8–11: "man inn vnßerm cristenlichen glauben gar vil doctores findt die do mangel halb der zwaier sprachen die hailgen geschrifft nit recht aus legen/ vnnd werden gar dick zü spott derab."

74. Reuchlin 1511, *Augenspiegel*, in *Sämtliche Werke* 4/1:37, ll. 25–27: "Es müssen aberglauben vnd irrthumb sein darumb das die rechtglaubigen bewert erscheinen."

75. See *Acta iudiciorum* 1518, fol. A4^r.

76. Reuchlin 1511, *Augenspiegel*, in *Sämtliche Werke* 4/1:38, l. 24: "mein grundtfeste diß ratschlags."

77. Reuchlin 1511, *Augenspiegel*, in *Sämtliche Werke* 4/1:38, ll. 20–24: "So gründ ich meinen rat vff das hailig euangelium das der Thalmud nit sol verbrent werden. Dan vnser herr Jesus Cristus hat zü den iuden gesagt Johan. v.: Erfragent suchent oder erforschent die schrifften so vil ir wenen in den selben das ewig leben zü haben/ vnd die selbigen synd von mir zeugknus gebende."

78. *Acta iudiciorum* 1518, fol. A4^r.

79. Reuchlin 1513, *Defensio*, in *Sämtliche Werke*, 4/1, 264, l. 26: "haeresis expressa et explicite condemnata." See Peterse 1995, 37.

80. *Acta iudiciorum* 1518, fol. B2^v; and Trusen 1998, 95–96.

81. See Trusen 1998, 95; Peterse 1995, 36; and F. W. E. Roth 1909, 143.

82. This is based on Gratius 1514, *Prenotamenta*, fol. aa4^v, which is biased in favor of Hoogstraeten.

83. *Acta iudiciorum* 1518, fol. B3^r–B3^v.

84. See Reuchlin, *Briefwechsel* 2:456, ll. 64–70 (no. 231, 30 November 1513).

85. See Reuchlin, *Briefwechsel* 2:457, ll. 88–101 (no. 231, 30 November 1513).

86. *Acta iudiciorum* 1518, fol. C1^r.

87. On Georg von Speyer, see Remling 1852–53, 2:231–66.

88. See L. Geiger 1871, 133.

89. *Acta iudiciorum* 1518, fol. C2^r–C3^v.

90. See Peterse 1995, 40, for details.

91. Greiff and Reuchlin contended that Hoogstraeten did not have the procedural authority to make this change in the bench, and that it needed the explicit authorization of the archbishop. See Trusen 1998, 100.

92. See *Acta iudiciorum* 1518, fol. C7^v: "publice in aula ante auditorium affixit." The document ("schedulam quandam impressam") was a printed broadside. Unfortunately, no copies of the imprint have survived.

93. Kober 1923, 113, on the refusal of the archbishop of Cologne, Philipp II von Daun, to endorse the Cologne proceedings.

94. See *Acta iudiciorum* 1518, fol. C7^v–C8^r, for an apparent quotation from Pfefferkorn's broadside: "declaramus memoratum libellum haereses sapientem et errores multos continentem perfidis iudaeis plusquam deceat fauorabilem, ecclesiae dei iniuriosum, ac sacris ecclesiae doctoribus irreuerentialem...ac igni publice concremandum." The Cologne decision was also published in Gratius 1514, *Prenotamenta*.

95. *Acta iudiciorum* 1518, fol. D1ᵛ–E4ᵛ (Reuchlin's "Libellus excusatorius").

96. See Trusen 1998, 103–4, on the practices of medieval heresy proceedings. The standard practice was to consider words *"prout sonant,"* as they sound, rather than according to their context or the author's general perspective. Thus, obviously, an orthodox author could be charged with inadvertently making a heretical statement.

97. *Acta iudiciorum* 1518, fol. E4ʳ: "decerni et declarari supra memoratum libellum nullam haeresim aut errorem ab ecclesia publice damnatum, manifeste sapientem et continentem, perfidis iudaeis non plusquam deceat aut iura permittunt fauorabilem, ecclesiae dei aut sacris eiusdem doctoribus neque iniuriosum neque irreuerentialem."

98. *Acta iudiciorum* 1518, fol. F3ᵛ: "decernimus et declaramus supra memoratum libellum cum eius declaratione annexa ut praefertur nullam haeresim aut errorem ab ecclesia publice damnatum manifeste sapere aut continere, perfidis iudaeis non plus quam deceat aut iura permittant fauorabilem fore, aut ecclesiae dei seu sacris eiusdem doctoribus neque iniuriosum neque irreuerentialem esse. Et ab omnibus ipsum Oculare speculum cum eius annexa declaratione (quam in singulis coniunctam cum libello et repetitam esse uolumus) legi et publicari posse."

99. Reuchlin had the text printed as a broadside in 1514. See Reuchlin, *Briefwechsel* 3:46 n. 12. It also appeared as part of the dedication to Jacob Questenberg of Reuchlin 1515, trans., *S. Athanasius in librum psalmorum.* See Reuchlin, *Briefwechsel* 3:241–57 (no. 273, 12 August 1515).

100. Kober 1923, 114; and Trusen 1998, 105.

CHAPTER 8

Epigraph source: Reuchlin, *Briefwechsel* 3:381, ll. 31–32 (no. 300, 25 October 1516): "non Reuchlin per nos, sed nos per Reuchlin servatos et defensos intelligimus."

1. On the phenomenal growth of humanist culture in Rome, see Stinger [1985] 1998.

2. *EE* 2:74, ll. 32–38 (no. 334, 15 May 1515); and *CWE: Correspondence* 3:94: "neque enim non possum tangi Romae desyderio, quoties tantus tantarum simul commoditatum aceruus in mentem venit. Primum vrbis omnium multo celeberrimae lumen ac theatrum, dulcissima libertas, tot locupletissimae bibliothecae, suauissima tot eruditissimorum hominum consuetudo, tot litteratae confabulationes, tot antiquitatis monumenta, denique tot vno in loco totius orbis lumina." For a similar description, see *CWE: Correspondence* 3:87 (no. 333).

3. *EE* 2:80, ll. 31–34 (no. 335, 21 May 1515); and *CWE: Correspondence* 3:100–101: "et felicissimo ingenii tui solo longe bellissimus obtigit cultor, politissimus ille Politianus; cuius opera non spinosis istis ac rixosis litteris, sed veris illis nec sine causa bonis appellatis."

4. Reuchlin 1511, *Augenspiegel,* in *Sämtliche Werke* 4/1:49–50: "vnd das bapst Sixtus der vierd hab beuolhen die selben cabalischen bücher in latinische sprach zü transferirn vnd zü tolmetschen/ vnserm glauben zü sunderm nutz/ der selben bißher allain dreü zü latinischer zungen kommen sind."

5. See Reuchlin 1511, *Augenspiegel*, in *Sämtliche Werke* 4/1:49.

6. Reuchlin 1511, *Augenspiegel*, in *Sämtliche Werke* 4/1:49, ll. 23–27: "also hat sein hailigkait [i.e., Alexander VI] durch iren flyß erfunden das graff Johanns obgemeldt gütten füg seins schreibens vnd lernens inn Cabalischen büchern gehabt hat/ vnd des halb sein büch Apologia genant durch ain breve apostolicum bestettet anno domini 1493."

7. Daniel Bomberg, though a Christian, published nearly 200 Hebrew books. He depended on learned Jewish editors for all of his projects. In 1520–23, he became the first to publish complete editions of each version of the Talmud.

8. Santi Pagnini's literal translation of the Bible was not published until 1528 (during the pontificate of Clement VII), even though the research had been sponsored by Leo X.

9. See D'Amico 1983, 16–19ff.

10. See F. X. Martin 1992; O'Malley 1968; and Reeves 1992.

11. Reuchlin, *Briefwechsel* 2:427–45 (no. 228, before September 1513).

12. See Reuchlin, *Briefwechsel* 2:439 n. 2, for an explanation that Bonet de Lattes (unbeknownst to Reuchlin) may have been dead since May 1510.

13. Reuchlin, *Briefwechsel* 3:40–45, esp. ll. 87ff. (no. 238, 25 April 1514).

14. *Acta iudiciorum* 1518, fol. G 4ʳff.

15. See Reuchlin's letter to Guillaume Cop (which included a copy of the Speyer Verdict) for his concerns about Petit's activism; Reuchlin, *Briefwechsel* 3:189–96 (no. 265, after 1 March 1515).

16. See *Acta doctorum Parrhisiensium contra Speculum oculare* 1514, fol. A3ᵛ.

17. Reuchlin, *Briefwechsel* 3:67–81 (no. 242, 19 June 1514). This letter was published in *Acta doctorum Parrhisiensium* 1514 (and in Reuchlin 1519, ed., *Illustrium virorum epistolae.*)

18. L. Geiger 1871, 287ff.

19. See Reuchlin, *Briefwechsel* 3:86–90 (no. 245, 30 August 1514).

20. The condemnation was printed in *Acta doctorum Parrhisiensium contra Speculum oculare* 1514, fol. B4ʳ.

21. Pfefferkorn 1514, *Sturm*, fol. b1ʳff.

22. *Acta doctorum Parrhisiensium* was printed by Heinrich Quentel, who produced many books for the University of Cologne.

23. Friedländer 1837, 108–10.

24. This was in a letter to Cardinal Castellesi; see Reuchlin, *Briefwechsel* 3:137, ll. 17–19 (no. 256, 29 December 1514): "Bernardinus [i.e., Cardinal Carvajal] ingenio se suo preciosus iudex sublegatus ita ingesserit, ut omnibus invitis et me ignorante Iacobum adversarium ab excommunicationis vinculo absolverit."

25. For a general study of Grimani, see Paschini 1943.

26. Neither translation has survived. According to Jacques Lefèvre d'Etaples, the Cologne translation was a dangerous distortion of Reuchlin's *Recommendation* and, as such, was a reason for the Sorbonne's condemnation. See Reuchlin, *Briefwechsel* 3:86–90 (no. 245, 30 August 1514).

27. Reuchlin, *Briefwechsel* 3:316–47 (no. 291, 12 September 1516).

28. Rosinus worked diligently on Reuchlin's case and sent several letters to Stuttgart to keep Reuchlin up to date on developments. In his letter to Leo X in support of Reuchlin, Maximilian indicated that his ambassador would be representing his position on the Reuchlin case in Rome. See Reuchlin, *Briefwechsel* 3:487–89 (appendix 2, 23 October 1513).

29. On Hummelberger's concerns about investing more money in the case, see Reuchlin, *Briefwechsel* 3:286–88 (no. 283, 19 February 1516); and 3:288–91 (no. 284, 14 March 1516). In spring 1516, Reuchlin reported to Erasmus that he had just borrowed 1,000 gold ducats to cover expenses in Rome; see Reuchlin, *Briefwechsel* 3:293–96 (no. 286, 5 June 1516).

30. *Acta iudiciorum* 1518, fol. H2ᵛ–H3ʳ.

31. See Pacheco 1985.

32. See Minnich 1992, 118.

33. Both letters are dated 16 May 1515; See Hutten 1859–70, supplement volume 1:149ff. for the text of both letters.

34. See Minnich 1990. As many as 430 prelates from all over Europe are known to have participated.

35. Stow 1977, xxvi.

36. Stow 1977, 218, translation modified.

37. Stow 1977, 220, translation modified.

38. Stow 1977, 220.

39. Reuchlin, *Briefwechsel* 3:270–76 (no. 280, 24 January 1516).

40. Francis I initially tried to intervene in a letter to Leo X from spring 1515 (see Hutten 1859–70, supplement volume 1:149). He urged Leo to respect the condemnation of Reuchlin issued by the German universities and the University of Paris. See Reuchlin, *Briefwechsel* 3:316–47 (no. 291, 12 September 1516), esp. ll. 27ff., for the intercession in Bologna. Pfefferkorn printed Francis's letter in *Beschyrmung* (1516) and *Defensio* (1516).

41. Reuchlin, *Briefwechsel* 3:270–76 (no. 280, 24 January 1516).

42. Reuchlin, *Briefwechsel* 3:86–90 (no. 245, 30 August 1514); see also the letter of support from Cop in Reuchlin, *Briefwechsel* 3:284–86 (no. 244, 25 August 1514).

43. According to *Acta iudiciorum* 1518, fol. 16ʳ, and the title page (fol. A1ʳ) of Benigno 1517, *Defensio praestantissimi viri Ioannis Reuchlin*, there were eighteen commissioners; according to a letter from Bernhard Adelmann to Willibald Pirckheimer, there were twenty-six commissioners, of which nineteen voted for, and seven against, Reuchlin. See Pirckheimer, *Briefwechsel* 3:23–24 (no. 392, 15 August 1516).

44. See Minnich 1992, 82.

45. See *Acta iudiciorum* 1518, fol. 16ʳ, for a partial list.

46. Reuchlin, *Briefwechsel* 3:316–47 (no. 291, 12 September 1516), esp. ll. 80ff.

47. Reuchlin, *Briefwechsel* 3:316–47 (no. 291, 12 September 1516), esp. ll. 93–119.

48. Reuchlin, *Briefwechsel* 3:316–47 (no. 291, 12 September 1516), esp. ll. 143–47.

49. See *CWE: Correspondence* 3:85ff. (no. 333, 15 May 1515); and 3:93ff. (no. 334, 15 May 1515).

50. *EE* 2:79, ll. 204–6 (no. 334, 15 May 1515); and *CWE: Correspondence* 3:99: "Quanquam his omnibus spes est futurum vt vestra opera vir tam eximius et orbi restituatur et litteris."

51. *EE* 2:72, ll. 110–11 (no. 333, 15 May 1515); and *CWE: Correspondence* 3:90–91: "Huic omnis debet Germania, in qua primus Graecarum et Hebraicarum litterarum studium excitauit."

52. *Acta iudiciorum* 1518, fol. 16ʳ: "Qui omnes et singuli pro Ioanne Reuchlin ac eius innocentia et intemerato libro suo tulerunt sententiam absolutoriam. Praeter Magistrum palatii de ordine praedicatorum." Prierias was then *magister palatii*. See Reuchlin, *Briefwechsel* 3:340 n. 64.

53. See Reuchlin, *Briefwechsel* 3:327, ll. 174–76 (no. 291, 12 September 1516), where Reuchlin's opponents are said to have condemned the book in a limited way: "Tres aut quatuor κάκιστοι hostes contra librum dedisse feruntur, nec simpliciter, sed limitate."

54. Reuchlin, *Briefwechsel* 3:326, ll. 148–53 (no. 291, 12 September 1516).

55. Cardinal de' Medici is mentioned in Martin Gröning's report as having informed a strangely befuddled Leo that Leo had indeed issued the *mandatum de supersedendo*. See Reuchlin, *Briefwechsel* 3:326 (no. 291, 12 September 1516), ll. 156ff.

56. *Acta iudiciorum* 1518, fol. 16ᵛ: "Sic tandem inquisitor praenominatus a curia Romana ubi iam in quartum annum ad inualidandum processum Spirensem uariis modis personaliter laborauerat, uacuis manibus Coloniam rediit. Et adhuc manet aethernumque manebit sententia Spirensis in uigore et honore."

57. Leo X censured *The Letters of Obscure Men* on 15 March 1517.

58. *EE* 3:125, ll. 13–14 (no. 700, 3 November 1517); and *CWE: Correspondence* 5:179: "Video recrudescere bellum quod inprimis volebam extinctum."

59. See Rummel 1995 for a detailed history of the "humanist-scholastic debate."

60. *EE* 3:589, ll. 57–59 (no. 967, 18 May 1519); and *CWE: Correspondence* 6:367: "His persuaderi non potest quin semel collapsura sit omnis ipsorum autoritas, si sacros libros habeamus emendatiores et horum intellectum ab ipsis petamus fontibus."

61. *EE* 4:105, ll. 195–200 (no. 1033, 19 October 1519); and *CWE: Correspondence* 7:114: "sed mihi non tempero quin illud mysterium aperiam, istos longe alio tendere quam ore prae se ferant. Iampridem male habet eos efflorescere bonas literas, efflorescere linguas, reuiuiscere veteres authores, quos antehac exedebant tineae puluere opertos, mundum ad fontes ipsos reuocari. Timent suis lacunis, nolunt videri quicquam nescire, metuunt ne quid maiestati ipsorum decedat."

62. See *CWE: Correspondence* 5:84 (no. 636), for Erasmus's account of persuading Hutten not to publish the work in 1514 (when it was apparently written). See also Hutten 1859–70, 3:413–48.

63. Letter to Dietrich Zobel in Benigno 1517, *Defensio praestantissimi viri Ioannis Reuchlin*, fol. A1ᵛ–B1ʳ.

64. See Nauert 1988.

65. Reuchlin 1517, *De arte cabalistica*, fol. E5ᵛ–F3ʳ.

66. This is a major issue in Hoogstraeten 1519, *Destructio cabale*.

67. *On the Eve of the Reformation* was the title Hajo Holborn gave a popular English edition (trans. Francis Griffin Stokes) of *The Letters of Obscure Men*.

68. Gratius had also quarreled early in his career with Hermann Busch, one of the authors of *The Letters of Obscure Men*, over Busch's use of an elementary grammar by Donatus.

69. The pioneering study of authorship is W. Brecht 1904.

70. *Epistolae obscurorum virorum* 1909, ed. and trans. Stokes, 385. See Hutten 1859–70 I, no. 51, for evidence that in May 1517 Hoogstraeten was contemplating a heresy case against Erasmus for views expressed in his Bible. See also *CWE: Correspondence* 7:45.

71. *Epistolae obscurorum virorum* 1909, ed. and trans. Stokes, 385.

72. *CWE: Correspondence* 6:164–71 (no. 694, 2 November 1517). Erasmus, however, quibbled with Pirckheimer for having cast his net too broadly in his defense of Reuchlin.

73. Pirckheimer, *Briefwechsel* 3:159, ll. 434–37 (no. 464, 30 August 1517): "Hinc est, quod Vetus testamentum a similibus negligitur, Novum quasi idiotis scriptum vilipenditur, apostolorum doctrina vix leccione digna putatur; hinc, quod divus Hieronymus tanquam grammaticus contemnitur."

74. See Pirckheimer, *Briefwechsel* 3:159, ll. 436ff. (no. 464, 30 August 1517).

75. Pirckheimer, *Briefwechsel* 3:160, ll. 482–87 (no. 464, 30 August 1517): "litteras latinas, graecas et haebreas [sic] callere necesse est,...hebreas, quia in illis et Veteris et Novi testamenti mysteria cuncta deliteant."

76. Pirckheimer, *Briefwechsel* 3:151, ll. 129–30 (no. 464, 30 August 1517): "Sive igitur me Erasmistam sive nuncupent Reuchlinistam, nulla contumelia sed pocius me laude affecisse sciant."

77. Pirckheimer, *Briefwechsel* 3:160–61, ll. 482ff. (no. 464, 30 August 1517).

78. Pirckheimer, *Briefwechsel* 3:156, ll. 322–26 (no. 464, 30 August 1517): "poterant...opera multa, quae adhuc sive in cabalistica seu thalmutica doctrina recondita latebant, in lucem proferre ac ex iis, quae vel bene litteratus Capnion vel Paulus Rizius—et ipse amicus noster eruditus—praeterierant, dei ecclesiam locupletare."

79. Pirckheimer, *Briefwechsel* 3:156, ll. 326–39 (no. 464, 30 August 1517).

80. Benigno 1517, *Defensio praestantissimi viri Ioannis Reuchlin*, fol. A2^v–A3^r.

81. Melanchthon, moreover, did not express his scorn for Kabbalah until after Reuchlin's death.

82. *EE* 3:253, ll. 19–27 (no. 798, 13 March 1518); and *CWE: Correspondence* 5:347–48: "Optarim te propensiorem ad Graeca quam ista Hebraica, licet ea non reprehendam. Video gentem eam frigidissimis fabulis plenam nihil fere nisi fumos quosdam obiicere; Talmud, Cabalam, Tetragrammaton, Portas Lucis, inania nomina. Scoto malim infectum Christum quam istis neniis. Italia multos habet Iudaeos, Hispania vix habet Christianos. Vereor ne hac occasione pestis iam olim oppressa caput erigat. Atque vtinam Christianorum Ecclesia non tantum tribueret Veteri Testamento! quod, cum pro tempore datum vmbris constet, Christianis litteris pene antefertur."

83. *EE* 3:589, l. 71 (no. 967, 18 May 1519); and *CWE: Correspondences* 6:368: "Mihi sane neque Cabala neque Talmud vnquam arrisit."

84. Pirckheimer, *Briefwechsel* 3:152, ll. 156–58 (no. 464, 30 August 1517): "Quid enim virum christianum ad tantum scelus impellere debuisset, ut Iudeorum amiciciam et fidei et veritati praeferre dignum duxisset?"

85. Pirckheimer 3:156, ll. 355ff. (no. 464, 30 August 1517).

86. *Epistolae obscurorum virorum* 1909, ed. and trans. Stokes, 384 (translation slightly altered).

87. *Epistolae obscurorum virorum* 1909, ed. and trans. Stokes, 444–45.

88. See *Epistolae obscurorum virorum* 1909, ed. and trans. Stokes, 487–89 (no. 2, 47), an extremely hostile parable of a new Christian who did not convert sincerely.

89. *Epistolae obscurorum virorum* 1909, ed. and trans. Stokes, 387–88.

90. *Epistolae obscurorum virorum* 1909, ed. and trans. Stokes, 295.

91. On Benigno, see Weinstein 1970, 242–43, especially for his connections to Leo X and the Medicis.

92. See Vasoli 1992.

93. Benigno's tract, which was brought to Cologne by Martin Gröning, was printed by Count von Neuenahr in *Defensio praestantissimi viri Ioannis Reuchlin*. A facsimile reprint is in the appendix to Erdmann-Pandžić and Pandžić 1989.

94. Benigno 1517, *Defensio praestantissimi viri Ioannis Reuchlin*, fol. A1^r: "ipse primus ex ordine votum emiserat."

95. Benigno 1517, *Defensio praestantissimi viri Ioannis Reuchlin*, fol. B4^v: "Nunc Romae archiepiscopus Nazarenus existens, inter alia quae scripsi, hunc quoque tractatulum, in Ioannis Reuchlin Germani vtraque in lingua, vel potius in omni (nam et Chaldaeam et Hebraeam complectitur) facundissimi, vtraque in philosophia et diuina et humana praestantissimi, commendationem, per modum dialogi editum, ad te Inuictissime Caesar transmitto."

96. Benigno 1517, *Defensio praestantissimi viri Ioannis Reuchlin*, fol. C1^r: "Eum itaque virum, qui tantopere illustrauit, glorificauit ac magnificauit patriam, nonne ipsa patria illustrare, glorificare, et magnifacere deberet?"

97. Benigno 1517, *Defensio praestantissimi viri Ioannis Reuchlin*, fol. C1^{v}ff.

98. Benigno 1517, *Defensio praestantissimi viri Ioannis Reuchlin*, fol. D1^v–D2^r.

99. Galatino 1518, *De arcanis catholicae veritatis*. On the complex scholarly career of Galatino, see Rusconi 1992.

100. Galatino 1518, *De arcanis catholicae veritatis*, fol. a2^r.

101. See Campanini 1997, 45. Kleinhans 1926 documented Galatino's strong dependence on Martí. Rusconi 1992, 167, cites use of Pablo de Heredia in some sections.

102. See Cohen 1982, 103ff., esp. 113, on Pablo Christiani: "Friar Pablo began [i.e., at the 1263 Disputation at Barcelona] by saying that he would prove from our Talmud that the messiah of whom the prophets testify has already come."

103. See, for example, W. Frey 1985, on the anti-Judaism in *The Letters of Obscure Men*. Moreover, Reuchlin's two Kabbalistic publications would be reprinted during the sixteenth century along with Galatino's anti-Jewish works (see bibliography under

Reuchlin). An Italian Jew in the mid-sixteenth century, a certain Todros ha-Cohen, would even cite Reuchlin's Kabbalistic tracts as a reason for his conversion to Christianity (see Campanini 1999, 72).

104. The speech appears in Reuchlin 1519, ed., *Illustrium virorum epistolae*, fol. n3ᵛ–o4ʳ.

105. Reuchlin 1519, ed., *Illustrium virorum epistolae*, fol. B3ᵛ; Reuchlin, *Briefwechsel* 3:403–6 (no. 305, January to April 1517): ll. 12–15: "'Pater sancte, ego sumam mihi parteis Reuchlin et volo stare loco ipsius. Legi suas lucubrationes omneis, quas habere potui. Homini fit iniuria.' Cui pontifex post multa respondit: 'Noli curare, Poggi, non feremus, ut quicquam mali patiatur hic vir.'" The letter was written in Rome by Paulus Gereander (who matriculated at the University of Tübingen in 1514).

106. See F. Martin 1992, on the career of Giles of Viterbo.

107. M. Brecht 1991–93, 1:98–105.

108. See Secret 1959.

109. O'Malley 1968, 87.

110. O'Malley 1968, 83.

111. See Reuchlin 1519, ed., *Illustrium virorum epistolae*, fol. B4ʳ–C1ʳ; Reuchlin, *Briefwechsel* 3:369–73 (no. 297, 20 October 1516). See F. Martin 1992, 165; and O'Malley 1968, 76.

112. Reuchlin 1519, ed., *Illustrium virorum epistolae*, fol. C1ʳ; Reuchlin, *Briefwechsel* 3:448–49 (no. 312, 24 May 1517).

113. Reuchlin 1519, ed., *Illustrium Virorum epistolae*, fol. B4ʳ; Reuchlin, *Briefwechsel* 3:380–88, ll. 29–32 (no. 300, 25 October 1516): "Denique in hoc iudicio tuo, ubi hac aestate pericoloso aestu laboravimus, non te, sed legem, non Thalmud, sed ecclesiam, non Reuchlin per nos, sed nos per Reuchlin servatos et defensos intelligimus."

114. All these works are listed in the bibliography.

115. See Dörner 1999, 149–79. The dedication to Questenberg includes a reprint of the Speyer Verdict. In 1514, Reuchlin asked Questenberg to present a copy of his *Clarorum virorum epistolae* personally to Leo X; see Reuchlin, *Briefwechsel* 3:35–40 (no. 237, 20 April 1514).

116. See discussion in chapter 4. Unfortunately for Reuchlin, Adriano Castellesi's influence at Rome evaporated when he was implicated in the Petrucci plot of spring 1517. Nonetheless, Reuchlin included a tribute to Castellesi in the *Letters of Illustrious Men*, which was published in 1519, well after his fall from favor. Dörner 1999, 177, estimates that Reuclin became aware of Castellesi's exile from Rome in November 1518.

117. Reuchlin, *Briefwechsel* 3:420–28, esp. l. 159 (no. 309, before 27 March 1517): "Assilit huic meae puritati tota ferme urbs Romana."

118. Reuchlin 1519, ed., *Illustrium virorum epistolae*, fol. C1ʳ; also in Reuchlin, *Briefwechsel* 3:449–50, ll. 12–13 (no. 313, 25 May 1517): "Libros tuos Pythagoricos pontifex legit avide, ut res bonas solet."

119. During the first Roman phase, from 1514 through 1516, Hoogstraeten continued to base his case on the sixteen accusations he made originally. His formal

charges from the Mainz-Speyer phase, as formulated in the *Writ of Accusation*, remained the point of reference for Reuchlin's supporters during the trial at Rome and during the new phase following the commission's vote (1516–20). Reuchlinists published the *Writ of Accusations* in 1518 as part of the *Acts of the Trials* and again in 1518 as part of a fierce attack on Hoogstraeten, the *Letters of Three Illustrious Men*. The last named pamphlet included a terse legal brief that answered each of Hoogstraeten's charges primarily on the basis of Reuchlin's *Arguments*, the appendix to the *Eye Glasses* of 1511 (see *Epistolae trium illustrium virorum* 1518, fol. f4^v–g4^r). It probably reflects the legal strategy used before the Roman commission.

120. See Peterse 1995, 64.

121. Hoogstraeten 1518, *Apologia*, fol. a1^v: "Magorumque corpora dicere non horrent esse rusticos ex westphalia."

122. See Hoogstraeten 1518, *Apologia*, fol. a1^v–a2^r. On fol. a2^r, he labels Pirckheimer a "degenerantem."

123. Hoogstraeten 1519, *Destructio cabale*, fol. A4^r.

124. See Peterse 1995, 108–10.

125. Hoogstraeten 1518, *Apologia*, fol. Cc1^r: "At peruersi eorum libri qui sunt exteriora arma sue interioris seu interne malignitatis atque perfidie. subsunt potestati principum et ecclesie."

126. Hoogstraeten 1518, *Apologia secunda*, fol. B2^v: "[Thomas Aquinas] ait Judei sunt serui ecclesie ac perinde ipsa de rebus disponere potest."

127. Hoogstraeten 1518, *Apologia*, fol. Ll3^v: "turpiter ad iudaicum inflecteres fauorem. vt eos concives sacri scriberes imperii. quos canonicum ius dicit de iure seruituti perpetue subiectos. quosque diuus Imperator Constantinus (tamquam huius iuris executor) perpetue seruituti subiecit."

128. Hoogstraeten 1518, *Apologia*, fol. a2^v: "Quo quid iudeis dulcius. sedi vero apostolice ac christianitati ignominiosus Capnion canere potuisset."

129. Hoogstraeten 1518, *Apologia*, fol. Aa1^r: "archirabinum Capnionem." Hoogstraeten applied this title derisively in contrast to the Archbishop Benigno.

130. Hoogstraeten 1518, *Apologia*, fol. a2^v: "O dei saluatoris nostri iniuriam immo blasphemiam maximam."

131. Hoogstraeten 1518, *Apologia*, fol. a2^v: "Ait namque heu temerario ore (in hoc resuscitasse visus luem illam Arrianarum) in nouo testamento tam insufficienter quam ineuidenter expressum esse, quod Jesus Marie superbenedicte filius, sit verus deus."

132. Hoogstraeten 1518, *Apologia*, fol. Aa2^r: "Multas etiam contra Mosis legem hereses."

133. Hoogstraeten 1518, *Apologia*, fol. Bb1^r: "Refert diuinus noster Aquinas…Judeos scripsisse in Thalmud, deum aliquando peccare et a peccato purgari. Reprobatque idem turpissimam illam blasphemiam."

134. Hoogstraeten 1518, *Apologia*, fol. Aa3^v: "Multa quoque in eorum doctrinis continentur falsa. erronea. iniqua. et absurda. non diuine solum legi. sed naturali penitus repugnantia."

135. Hoogstraeten 1518, *Apologia*, fol. Cc1^r: "doctrinam Thalmudicam originem traxisse ex secta scribarum et phariseorum. eamque a christo condemnatam. perinde

et vere esse hereticam." Hoogstraeten derived this interpretation, as he says, from Jacobus de Placentia.

136. Hoogstraeten 1518, *Apologia secunda*, fol. C3ʳ (margin): "Thalmud apertior est contra christum quam pro eo."

137. Hoogstraeten 1518, *Apologia secunda*, fol. C6ᵛ: "Thalmud editus est ad resistendum fidei nostre."

138. Erasmus 1519, *Farrago nova epistolarvm Des. Erasmi Roterodami.*

139. *EE* 4:50, l. 313 (no. 1006, 11 August 1519); and *CWE: Correspondence* 7:53, l. 335: "Nomen haereseos...est inuisum."

140. *EE* 4:45, l. 82 (no. 1006, 11 August 1519); *CWE: Correspondence* 7:47, ll. 86ff. (no. 1006): "tuum potius ago negocium."

141. *EE* 4:46, ll. 136–43 (no. 1006, 11 August 1519); and *CWE: Correspondence* 7:49, ll. 144ff.: "Quin et illud erat tuae prudentiae, perpendere num libellus ille Capnionicus haberet aliquid quod pestem aliquam grauem religioni Christianae posset inferre. Nihil autem illic agitur nisi ne quid praeter aequum patiantur Iudaei. Quorsum autem attinebat tanto spiritu agere vt Iudaeos in odium adduceres? An quisquam est nostrum qui non satis execretur hoc hominum genus? Si Christianum est odisse Iudaeos, hic abunde Christiani sumus omnes."

142. *EE* 4:51, ll. 328–38 (no. 1006, 11 August 1519); and *CWE: Correspondence* 7:54, ll. 352ff. (no. 1006): "Consulueris autem non ordini modo Praedicatorio verumetiam vniuerso theologico, si quorundam maledicentiam insulsissimam autoritate tua reprimas, qui...virulentissime deblaterant in linguarum peritiam, in politiores literas; in harum inuidiam antichristos, haereses, et alias id genus tragoedias admiscentes, cum obscurum non sit quid Ecclesia debeat viris linguarum peritis, quid debeat eloquentibus. Haec studia non obscurant theologicam dignitatem sed illustrant, non oppugnant sed famulantur."

143. Reuchlin, *Briefwechsel* 3:293–96 (no. 286, 5 June 1516); and *CWE: Correspondence* 3:299–301.

144. See *CWE: Correspondence* 3:108–9, ll. 315ff. (no. 335, 21 May 1515).

145. *EE* 3:58, l. 8 (no. 636, 25 August 1517); and *CWE: Correspondence* 5:84, ll. 10–11: "cur mihi tantam conflant inuidiam?"

146. *EE* 4:105, ll. 208–11 (no. 1033, 19 October 1519); and *CWE: Correspondence* 7:114–15: "Deinde quid mihi cum causa Capnionis et Lutheri? Sed haec arte commiscuerunt, vt comuni inuidia degrauarent omnes bonarum literarum cultores."

147. *EE* 4:372, ll. 18–20 (no. 1155, 8 November 1520); and *CWE: Correspondence* 8:79: "Mihi semper studio fuit Lutheri causam a tua bonarumque literarum causa seiungere, quod ea res et nos vocaret in communem inuidiam."

CHAPTER 9

Epigraph source: Pfefferkorn 1521, *Ajn mitleydliche claeg*, fol. G1ᵛ: "Du meinst man habe yetzunt mit Martinus Lauter sovil tzo schaffen und tzo schicken. das man deiner sol vergessen. Reuchlin ych sag dir vnd glaub mir das. deiner wurt nit vergessen."

1. See Reuchlin, *Briefwechsel*, ed. L. Geiger, 321 (no. 289, 10 February 1520), printed in Böcking, supplement volume 1:441; and Pirckheimer 1940–2006, *Briefwechsel* 4:195ff. (no. 669), where Reuchlin claims to Pirckheimer that ever since receiving the mandate of supersedure from the pope, his opponents had not been pursuing the case until now (i.e., early 1520): "appelationem suam et causam non sint prosecuti usque ad haec tempora."

2. Both letters were printed in Pfefferkorn 1516, *Defensio*, fol. L2ᵛ–L3ᵛ (the letter of Charles V) and L4ʳ–L4ᵛ (letter of Adrian of Utrecht). Of the two, Charles's is the harsher condemnation of Judaism and Reuchlin's defense of Jewish writings.

3. Hoogstraeten 1519, *Apologia secunda*, fol. a1ᵛ–a2ʳ. See also L. Geiger 1871, 422.

4. Reuchlin, *Briefwechsel*, ed. L. Geiger, 307 (no. 271, 9 November 1518), printed in Reuchlin, *Briefe*, ed. Friedländer, 77.

5. Reuchlin, *Briefwechsel*, ed. L. Geiger, 321 (no. 289, 10 February 1520), printed in Hutten 1859–70, supplement volume 1:441–42: "Quia impetrarunt [i.e., his enemies] alium Iudicem loco Reverendissimi Cardinalis Grimani, qui abest a curia, et illi surrogatus nomine Dominicus de Iacobatiis, Cardinalis nuper a Leone creatus sit s. Bartolo in Insula, acutissimus, ut aiunt, iurista, coram quo volunt de apicibus iuris sophismatizare, si forte possint me ad expensas retorquere."

6. Reuchlin, *Briefwechsel*, ed. L. Geiger, 307–8 (no. 272, 12 November 1518), printed in Reuchlin, *Briefe*, ed. Friedländer, 79–80.

7. Reuchlin, *Briefwechsel*, ed. L. Geiger, 298 (no. 256, 7 May 1518): "Es mag mich nicht helfen, dass kaiser, churfürsten, fürsten, bischöffe, äbte, städte den papst gebethen haben, dass seine heiligkeit mir lasse fürderlich recht geben. Ich bitte Gott, dass er uns gnade verleihe, dass wir unterthanen uns selbst bessern, damit wir besserer häupter würdig warden."

8. Reuchlin, *Briefwechsel*, ed. L. Geiger, 311–12 (no. 278, 11 February 1519), printed in Hutten 1859–70, 1:459: "coeperunt nostrates prope multi de nostro Leone desperare, suspicantes eum non talem esse qualem omnes literaturae politioris amatores quondam fore putabant."

9. In 1518, Gratius published *Lamentationes obscurorum virorum*, which was printed with his *Epistola apologetica*, both of which answer the blistering persiflage of *The Letters of Obscure Men*. Pfefferkorn's tracts *Beschyrmung* and *Streydt puechlyn* are forceful efforts to encourage expulsions of Jews and the conviction of Reuchlin. Both were published in 1516 in the aftermath of *The Letters of Obscure Men*, although *Streydt puechlyn* responds most explicitly to *The Letters of Obscure Men*. *Streydt puechlin* also appeared in a Latin adaption, *Defensio* (1516), which is often thought to have been the work of Gratius.

10. See Nauert 1991, 50–51. In 1496, Cologne enrolled 578 new students; in 1525, new students numbered 120; and in 1535 only 54 (an all-time low).

11. *EE* 2:372, ll. 55–56 (no. 481, 31 October 1516): "Epistolae Obscurorum Virorum operae precium est videre quantopere placent omnibus." Different translation in *CWE: Correspondence* 4:481.

12. The papal imprimatur required that the printed Talmud include the *Responsa* of Felix Pratensis that castigated alleged anti-Christian passages. See Lotter 1993, 87; and Simonsohn 1988–91, 4:1837ff.

13. See the discussion in chapter 8.

14. Neuenahr 1519, *Vivat Rex Carolus*, fol. D2ʳ.

15. Neuenahr 1519, *Vivat Rex Carolus*, fol. D2ᵛ: "Unica, crede mihi, pestis est in Germania IACOBUS HOSTRATUS."

16. Neuenahr 1519, *Vivat Rex Carolus*, fol. D2ʳ: "et breui uidebis in Germania renasci Athenas." See Nauert 1988, 73.

17. See Sickingen 1519, *Eruoderung*, fol. a2ᵛ, where he states that Reuchlin took pains "to instruct me in morals during my youth" ("mich in meiner jugent sitlicher tugent zů vnterweisen"). Without explaining the details, Sickingen also claims that Reuchlin had given his parents assistance: "dz er meinen eltern offtmals gefellig dinst erzaigt" (fol. a2ᵛ).

18. Reuchlin, *Briefwechsel*, ed. L. Geiger, 318–19 (no. 285, 8 November 1519): "In medio malorum collocatus, cogito diligenter, qua via tranquilliori animo philosophari queam. Apud nos regnat pestis, regnat victoriosorum vindicta, regnat invidia, regnat bonorum oppressio, regnat concussio, praecessit fames, sequutus est gladius; concludit pestilentia. Quodque majus malum est, factione laborat tota fere nostra terra, cum plures sint qui aere alieno et paupertate premantur, quam qui abundent pecunia, et vulgi sit studium, praedari ac divitum substantiam rapere, cujus autorem, pari affectione praeditum, ducem suum, perdidere. Inde illa cogitatio, quonam modo possint Principem latronum recuperare. Quod nisi caute provideat prudens confoederatio; actum est de omnibus bonis viris atque probis, Wirtembergense territorium habitantibus." Also in Pirckheimer, *Briefwechsel* 4:112–13 (no. 631).

19. Sickingen 1519, *Eruoderung*.

20. Source for this is Reuchlin, *Briefwechsel*, ed. L. Geiger, 321 (no. 289, 10 February 1520), printed in Hutten 1859–70, supplement volume 1:441.

21. See Reuchlin, *Briefwechsel*, ed. L. Geiger, 321 (no. 289, 10 February 1520), printed in Hutten 1859–70, supplement volume 1:441–42.

22. L. Geiger 1871, 451 n. 1; and Kober 1923, 117 (a record from the minutes of the meetings of the Cologne faculty of theology).

23. L. Geiger 1891, 223–26.

24. Ribysen had known Reuchlin at least since 1502, when they corresponded (Reuchlin, *Briefwechsel* 1:372–74 [no. 117, 30 August 1502]). Reuchlin had befriended the humanist Johannes Wacker (Vigilius) at least since 1497, when he was a guest in Wacker's home in Heidelberg. In 1520, Wacker was the vicar of the bishop of Worms. See Reuchlin, *Briefwechsel* 1:304–5 n. 2.

25. Hutten 1859–70, supplement volume 1:447: "eruditio et vitae integritas fideique sinceritas."

26. Hutten 1859–70, supplement volume 1:446–47.

27. This is according to the eyewitness account of Johannes Cochlaeus from Frankfurt, in a letter of 12 June 1520 to Pirckheimer (Hutten 1859–70, 1:358–59): "the

friars...appointed five procurators in Rome—Jacob Questenberg, Johannes Coritius, Caspar Wirt, Johannes Peuer, and Jodocus Eginger—to petition the pope so that the entire case would be laid to rest for both sides so that no one's honor would be diminished."

28. L. Geiger 1871, 449. For Elector Ludwig's letter, see Reuchlin, *Briefe*, ed. Friedländer, 116–17.

29. See Kober 1923, 117, the record for 8 September 1520. This order from Leo X restoring Hoogstraeten to his offices is the best evidence that Hoogstraeten had in fact been removed from them.

30. Reuchlin, *Briefwechsel*, ed. L. Geiger, 325–26 (no. 295, 11 May 1520), printed in Hutten 1859–70, 1:461–62: "ne quid inseratur in Brevi papali quod innocentis mei honorem sive famam quovis colore possit commaculare." The letter also indicates that the agreement was achieved "with the help of the Dalbergs, other military men, many lawyers." Apparently, the family of Reuchlin's deceased patron Johannes von Dalberg (d. 1503) was still supporting him.

31. See M. Brecht 1991–93, 1:390–91. The bull was not published until 24 July 1520.

32. Kober 1923, 117: "allatae literae m. Jo. Ingewinckil prepositi s. Severini, quibus idem nuntiat et irritam declaratam sententiam Spirensem et librum Reuchlin condemnatum addito brevi apostolico, quo iubebatur Jacobus de Hochstraten, quem provincialia comitia Francofurti a prioratus Coloniensis et inquisitionis officio ad compositionem cum Reuchlini fautoribus ineundam privarant, restitui praefecturae Col. et inquisitionis muneri."

33. See Hutten 1859–70, supplement volume 2:152–53: "Speculum Oculare nuncupatum, fuisse et esse scandalosum, ac piarum aurium Christi fidelium offensivum, ac non parum impiis Iudaeis favorabilem, et propterea ab usu et de manibus Christi fidelium tollendum usumque eius inhibendum etc. cum impositione perpetui silentii eidem Iohanni et condemnationem eiusdem in expensis in huiusmodi causa tam in partibus quam Romana Curia factis, adeo ut per huiusmodi sententiam damnatio doctrinalis eiusdem Speculi Ocularis iam pridem per Facultatem Theologicam nostrae Universitatis facta, iam iustificata et approbata et confirmata extitit."

34. See Hoogstraeten 1519, *Destructio cabale*, fol. a2ʳ.

35. Pfefferkorn 1521, *Ajn mitleydliche claeg*, fol. H2ʳ: "Ja Reuchlin. hett es dir der Babst vor acht jaren gethan. so hett Martinus Lauther vnd deine jüngeren Obscurorum virorum deß nit thüren wünschen noch gedencken. weß sie jtzundt zů nachteyl Christenliches glaubens offentlichen treyben. Vnd deßselbigen alles bistu allein eyn funcken vnd auffrüster. die heilig Kirchen in ein irrung vnd aberglauben zů füren."

36. The rhymes in support of Reuchlin and Luther are the second item (clearly not written by Thomas Murner, who opposed Luther), *Ein kurtzer begriff vnbillicher frevel handlung Hochstrats*, in Murner 1521, *History Von den vier ketzren Prediger ordens*, fol. P2ᵛ–P4ʳ. The pamphlet is a curiosity for it contains a lengthy poem by Thomas Murner satirizing a recent scandal in the Dominican Order (the Jetzer

Affair, 1506ff.) as well as a brief poem against Hoogstraeten for his persecution of Reuchlin and Luther. The pamphlet, however, is also directed against Murner because he had become a strident opponent of Luther since he first published the poem on the Jetzer Affair.

37. See Ficker 1922; Hannemann [1955] 1994a; and Brod 1965, 332–37, for discussions of Reuchlin images.

38. Reuchlin, *Briefwechsel*, ed. L. Geiger, 327 (no. 298, 3 January 1521), printed in Ulmann 1872, 406–7: "Nun hat mir der Edel und Streng her franciscus von Sickingen ain Richtung und Transaction gemacht das wir nemlich der gantz ord predigermünch fur sich und die Ire uff güttlich schidlüt mit baiderteil tail wissen und willen komen und vertragen sind, derselb vertrag ist von Ine Inn gemainem Capittel zu Frankfort gehallten gelopt geschworn und versigellt Inn namen Ir und der Iren, daruff hand sie dominum Hochstraten prior Zu Cöln von seinem Inquisitorampt abgesetzt und im gebotten den friden Zu hallten und den krieg wider mich nit mer zu füren, der genent bruder Jacob Hochstratt ist aber Trüwloß und gelübdbrüchig an sinem orden und sinen öbern worden und hat all obedientz veracht und in abweßen miner procuratoren und anwellt Zu Rom Inn der Zyt der Vacantz so man sußt gewonlich nit gericht hallt hat er einen Römerspruch ußgebracht wie Zu Rom dick geschicht das alles ain Nullitet und nichtigkait sy was vor gehandelt durch min gn. H. von Spyer sy, und das man min büchlin und Rathschlag kaiserlich maiestet gegeben abthun undertrucken und verbietten soll zu leßen, des haben sie kain annder ursach gedören anzougen den es sy ergerlich und den Juden günstig, und habent heresim und ketzery laßn fallen. Nichtz dest minder wollten die brüder und Ir anhang Zu Cöln söllichen Ratschlag Im Ougenspiegel verbrennen, were der von nit von minen wegen geappellirt worden und ist Inn verbotten under derwylen nichtz usserhalb des rechtes wider mich fürzenemen by pen des Banns und II^M ducaten. Aber gnedigster her So kain gloub Inn dene lüten ist sonder alle lychtfertigkait hab ich ain Supplication an unsern allergnedigsten hern den Römischen kaiser gestellt und die hern franciscus von Sickingen obgemellt zugeschickt, die dem Rechten gemeß ist."

39. Hutten 1859–70, 1:427 (Hutten writing to Martin Bucer, 25 November 1520): "Capnion appellavit, quem Franciscus tuebitur modis omnibus."

40. L. Geiger 1871, 452.

41. Reuchlin, *Briefwechsel*, ed. L. Geiger, 327 (no. 298, 3 January 1521), printed in Ulmann 1872, 407: "Main ich, so ich ain lay und nit gaistlich sy, und der handel den glouben nit berürt sonder alls Ir urtail lut allain scandalum und ergerniß und gunst der Judischhaitt, So gehör diser handel dem Römischen kaiser Zu Alls welltlich und nit alls gaistlich."

42. Pfefferkorn 1521, *Ajn mitleydliche claeg*, fol. G1^r–G1^v.

43. Pfefferkorn 1521, *Ajn mitleydliche claeg*, fol. A4^v: "lasterer der heilgen kyrchen. eyn felscher der heilgen schryfften. eyn totsleger der selen. eyn betreger vnd verfuerer des christlichen volcks. eyn verretter des Römschen keyserlichen stoels. vnd meyn verretter. eyn aduocayt vnd patroin vur die treuloissen Juden."

44. He also included a German translation of the University of Paris's condemnation of *Eye Glasses* from 1514. See Pfefferkorn 1521, *Ajn mitleydliche claeg*, fol. F2^rff.

45. Pfefferkorn 1521, *Ajn mitleydliche claeg*, fol. G3^v–H1^v.

46. Pfefferkorn 1521, *Ajn mitleydliche claeg*, fol. H6^v.

47. Pfefferkorn 1521, *Ajn mitleydliche claeg*, fol. G1^v: "Ich smeck brait wurst."

48. Pfefferkorn 1521, *Ajn mitleydliche claeg*, fol. F4^r–F4^v (for the assertion that Reuchlin's knowledge of Hebrew is weak) and D3^v and E2^v (on the accusation that Reuchlin accepted bribes from Jews).

49. Pfefferkorn 1521, *Ajn mitleydliche claeg*, fol. D4^r: "Dann die Epistel vnd der Ratschlag seint gantz widerwertig."

50. Pfefferkorn 1521, *Ajn mitleydliche claeg*, fol. B3^v.

51. Pfefferkorn 1521, *Ajn mitleydliche claeg*, fol. D3^r–D3^v: "ist offenbar. das sie in menschlicher gedechtnuß. die jungen Christen kinder gemartyrisiert. peynget vnd getödt haben. auch das heylig sacrament an vielen enden gelestert vnnd gemißhandelt." This clearly contradicts the assertion by Oberman [1981] 1984, 69, that Pfefferkorn rejected these accusations against Jews.

52. Pfefferkorn 1521, *Ajn mitleydliche claeg*, fol. H3^r: "Pfefferkorn sag vns die vrsach/ was hastu von den Juden geschrieben. das du den Reuchlin verzurnt vnd so hitzig wider dich gearbeit hat."

53. For the entire passage, see Pfefferkorn 1521, *Ajn mitleydliche claeg*, fol. H3^r–H3^v.

54. Pfefferkorn 1521, *Ajn mitleydliche claeg*, fol. H3^r–H3^v: "das man jnen die Lasterböcher soll abthon. vnd vntertrucken. wie das Keyser Maximilian hochloblicher gedechtnuß bestanden hat."

55. Pfefferkorn 1521, *Ajn mitleydliche claeg*, fol. H3^v: "das sie vnlustig arbeit musten treyben."

56. Pfefferkorn 1521, *Ajn mitleydliche claeg*, fol. H3^v: "aber mit den wercken seindt sie ketzer vnd abtrunnige menschen. dann sie halten weder das alt noch das new testament. weder eyns noch keins. vnnd darzu fragen sie nit viel nach jrem Messias. er kum/ oder sey kummen. dann allein gelt vnd gůt ist jr Got vnd jr glaub."

57. Pfefferkorn 1521, *Ajn mitleydliche claeg*, fol. H3^v: "so solten sie gar baldt durch sich selbst vergencklich werden. vnd den Christen glauben bekennen."

58. Pfefferkorn 1521, *Ajn mitleydliche claeg*, fol. H3^v–H4^r: "Nun hatt mich mein Herr vnd mein Gott verhört mit der Synagogen zu Regenspurg. die haben Christlichen vnnd frömmiglichen dem also eyn follenstreckung gethan."

59. Pfefferkorn 1521, *Ajn mitleydliche claeg*, fol. H4^v: "Die von Regenspurg haben es kurtz vnd gůt gemacht. Also sölt jr Herren von Wormbs vnd Franckfort mit den Juden auch handeln. schleyfft. reyßt. werfft vmb. vnd brecht ab jr teufflische Synagogen. vnd löndt vnser lieben frawen zů eren ein Capellen oder Clausen darvon (wie andere Reichstetten dermassen gethan haben) bawen."

60. Pfefferkorn 1521, *Ajn mitleydliche claeg*, fol. H4^v.

61. See Lewin 1911, 22. The final agreement of 18 May 1521, which imposed a heavy tax burden on the city of Regensburg for the illegal action, did not permit Jewish resettlement. Several sources indicate that Luther himself met with the Regensburg Jews at the Diet of Worms.

62. See Reuchlin, *Briefwechsel*, ed. L. Geiger, 291 (no. 253, 5 April 1518), writing to Pirckheimer: "Et est omnino similis haeresis fratris Hieronymi Savanarolae [sic]

qui Florentiae combustus est, ut vidisse potes in confessatis et actis suis, cui fuit
etiam sub pena excommunicationis inhibitum, ne ultra praedicaret, ille autem
similiter dicebat, papae in eo non esse obediendum, et allegabat sacram scripturam."
Reuchlin is comparing Hoogstraeten's refusal to abide by the papal imposition of
silence to Savonarola's refusal to stop preaching in Florence. He made the same
comparison in a letter to Jacob Questenberg; see Reuchlin, *Briefwechsel*, ed. L. Geiger,
298–99 (no. 257, 9 May 1518), printed in Reuchlin, *Briefe*, ed. Friedländer, 70.

63. In March 1516, Johannes Lang wrote that the scholastic theologians had
no students at the University of Wittenberg, while the classes that focused on Bible
exegesis (such as Luther's) and patristic writers were full. See Hagen 1969; and
Seebaß 2006, 63.

64. On the general significance of humanism in the early career of Luther, see
Junghans 1985.

65. Pirckheimer never acknowledged *Eccius Dedolatus* as his own work. See
Eckius Dedolatus 1983.

66. See WA 2:384–85; and Hoogstraeten 1519, *Destructio cabale*, fol. ¶ʳ.

67. WA 2:386: "pestilentiorem et impudentiorem haereticum sol non vidit quam
Iacobum Hostraten." This broadside, *Scheda adversus Iacobum Hochstraten*, does not
mention the Reuchlin controversy, though it seems to refer to it generally.

68. Reuchlin, *Briefwechsel*, ed. L. Geiger, 356–58 (no. 280ª, 12 September 1519).

69. Melanchthon, *Briefwechsel* 1:265–66, ll. 20–22 (no. 130, 21 March 1521): "Ex
Ingolstadio scripsit ad me quidam amicus de Capnione satis multa. Rogat Capnio, ne
quid ad se in ista rerum tempestate scribam."

70. Reuchlin, *Briefwechsel*, ed. L. Geiger, 328–29 (no. 299, 22 February 1521),
Ulrich von Hutten writing to Reuchlin: "addis causam te ejus improbasse semper,
aegerrime tulisse quod tuum nomen in illius scriptis inveniatur, conatum etiam
abstrahere nos qui illi adhaereant.... Tibi displicet Lutheri negotium, et illud
improbas, vellesque extinctum.... Me quidem, non tantum si oppugnabis unquam
Lutheri causam, sed et si te sic pontifici Romano submittas, habebis valde abs te
dissentientem." It is possible that Reuchlin never received this letter.

71. Pirckheimer, *Briefwechsel* 3:162, ll. 567–68 (no. 464, 30 August 1517).

72. WA: *Briefwechsel* 2:36, ll. 12–13 (no. 251, 8 February 1520): "ne hac re tam sibi
quam toti vniuersitati maculam parerent."

73. See Dürer 1956, 1:86, ll. 34–36: "Es hatz awch doctor Eck, als man sagt,
öfflich zw Ingelstett ferbrennen wollen, wÿ des docter Rewleyns püchleinn
geschehen ist etwen."

74. Reuchlin, *Briefwechsel*, ed. L. Geiger (no. 291, 18 March 1520), 322.

75. WA: *Briefwechsel* 1:23–24, ll. 5–9 (no. 7, February 1514): "Nosti autem, optime
Magister, quod et ego hominem in magno habeo pretio et affectu, et iudicium meum
forte suspectum est, quia (ut dicitur) liber et neutralis non sum. Tamen, quia exigis,
dico, quod sentio: mihi prorsus nihil apparere in omni eius scripto consilio, quod
periculosum sit."

76. WA: *Briefwechsel* 1:28, l. 18 (no. 9, 5 August 1514): "innocentissimi
Capnionis."

77. See the entire passage in *WA: Briefwechsel* 1:28–29, ll. 23–31 (no. 9, 5 August 1514): "Det dominus vt cito finis fiat. Singulare tamen mihi gaudium est. ad vrbem et Apostolicam [sedem p]otius peruenisse rem quam in partibus latius illis emulis datam esse licentiam Iudicandi [Co]loniensibus Cum Roma Doctissimos homines inter Cardinales habeat, saltem plus gratiae…concedetur….Vale et ora pro me Et oremus pro Capnione nostro."

78. *WA: Briefwechsel* 1:268–69, ll. 2–28 (no. 120, 14 December 1518): "Dominus tecum, vir fortissime. Gratulor misericordiae Dei, quae in te est, vir et eruditissime et humanissime, qua tandem praevaluisti obstruere os loquentium iniqua. Fuisti tu sane organum consilii divini, sicut tibi ipsi incognitum, ita omnibus purae theologiae studiosis expectatissimum; adeo longe alia fiebant a Deo, et alia videbantur geri per vos. Eram ego unus eorum, qui tecum esse cupiebant, sed nulla dabatur occasio. Eram tamen oratione et voto tibi semper praesentissimus. Sed quod tunc negatum est socio, nunc cumulatissime tributum est successori. Invadunt dentes istius Behemoth me, si quo modo sarcire queant ignominiam, quam retulerunt ex te. Occurro et ego ipsis, longe quidem minoribus ingenii et eruditionis viribus, quam tu occurristi et prostravisti, sed non minore animi fiducia. Congredi mihi detrectant, respondere recusant, sed mera vi et violentia in me viam affectant. Vivit vero Christus, et ego perdere nihil possum, quia nihil habeo. Fracta sunt in tua firmitate non parum quidem cornua horum taurorum. Hoc enim in te egit Dominus, ut tyrannus sophistarum aliquando et tardius et mitius disceret veris theologiae studiis resistere, ac respirare inciperet Germania, scripturarum doctrina tot heu annorum centenariis non tam oppressa, quam extincta. Non erant haec initia danda pulcherrimorum studiorum per hominem parvae gratiae; sed sicut Christum (sit venia comparationi) omnium maximum montem Deus contrivit usque in pulverem mortis, verum ex hoc pulvere postea excreverunt tot magni montes, ita et tu parum attulisses fructus, nisi mortificatus in pulverem fuisses redactus, unde nunc tot surgunt proceres literarum sacrarum. Et exaudita est oratio gementis ecclesiae: Salvum me fac, Domine, quoniam defecit sanctus; diminuti sunt fideles de filiis hominum, quoniam exaltati fuerunt ad altitudines Dei vilissimi filiorum hominum."

79. *WA* 5:19–23. See Melanchthon 1519, *De rhetorica libri tres*, fol. a2ᵛ, for a similar grouping of Erasmus, Reuchlin, and Luther as a challenge to scholastic theology. In this passage, Melanchthon expresses love for logic (dialectics), while rejecting scholastic approaches to the Bible. He also praises Reuchlin for saving splendid libraries from the "sophists" who wanted to burn them: "CAPNIONEM factio ista non est passa, a flammis, ab incendio pulcherrimas bibliothecas asserentem."

80. Quoted from Oberman [1981] 1984, 18.

81. Osiander 1975–, 4:68–69: "sein durch die achtbarn und hochgelerten Johannen Reuchlin, der rechten, und Erasmen von Roterdam, der heiligen schrift doctorn, und etlich andre mer tapfere und hochberumbte männer, zum ersten die drei haubtsprachen lateinisch, kriechisch und hebraisch."

82. Junghans 1985, 91; and Seebaß 2006, 13. Junghans 1985, 92, entertains the possibility that Luther acquired Reuchlin's *Rudiments* hot off the press in 1506.

83. *WA: Tischreden* 1:525 (no. 1041): "Lingua Ebraica ist omnium optima...ac purissima, quia ab illis linguis [i.e., Latin and Greek] nihil prorsus mendicat."

84. See Raeder 1961; and Raeder 1977.

85. See *WA: Briefwechsel* 1:149–50 (no. 61, 22 February 1518), esp. 150, ll. 14–15.

86. Raeder 1977, 41–42, vividly portrays Reuchlin's concern for a grammatical literal sense of Scripture in the *Rudiments* (clearly in a way evocative of the Jewish *peshat* approach), while Luther sought a "theological grammatical sense," meaning that Christian theology should guide the interpretation of grammar in the Hebrew Bible.

87. Burnett 2004, 193, places Luther's definitive rejection of Jewish commentaries in 1542. Nonetheless, as Burnett indicates, Luther continuously used Jewish philology, while rejecting Jewish exegesis.

88. Pelikan, Hotchkiss, and Price 1996, 23–39; and Pelikan 1959.

89. See *WA* 53:647, for Luther's simultaneous rejection of Münster and Pagnini.

90. In his *Operationes in psalmos* of 1519, Luther rejected Reuchlin's Christian approach to the tetragrammaton without citing Reuchlin by name. Erasmus did the same thing in *Praise of Folly* (1511), where he ridiculed the insertion of a *shin* in the tetragrammaton.

91. Melanchthon [1532] 2001, *Elementa rhetorices*, 178: "Nec minus sunt inepti Iudaeorum Cabalistae, qui nouis uerbis repertis, mira mysteria promittunt, cum meras nugas doceant."

92. See Oberman [1981] 1984, 34, on Luther's opinion that the end of time would not necessarily experience a mass conversion of the Jews.

93. *LW* 45:200; and *WA* 11:314, l. 31–315, l. 2: "Und wenn ich eyn Jude gewesen were und hette solche tolpell und knebel gesehen den Christen glauben regirn und leren, so were ich ehe eyn saw worden denn eyn Christen."

94. *LW* 45, 229; and *WA* 11:336, ll. 22–34: "Darumb were meyn bitt und rad, das man seuberlich mit yhn umbgieng und aus der schrifft sie unterrichtet, so mochten yhr ettliche herbey komen. Aber nu wyr sie nur mit gewallt treyben und gehen mit lugen teydingen umb, geben yhn schuld, sie mussen Christen blutt haben, das sie nicht stincken, und weys nicht wes des narren wercks mehr ist, das man sie gleich fur hunde hellt, Was sollten wyr guttis an yhn schaffen? Item das man yhn verbeutt, untter uns tzu erbeytten, hantieren und andere menschliche gemeynschafft tzu haben, da mit man sie tzu wuchern treybt, wie sollt sie das bessern? Will man yhn helffen, so mus man nicht des Bapsts, sonder Christlicher liebe gesetz an yhn uben....Ob ettliche hallstarrig sind, was ligt dran? sind wyr doch auch nicht alle gutte Christen."

95. *LW* 45, 201; and *WA* 11:315, ll. 33–35: "ßo hat er doch keynem volck die heyligen schrifft, das ist das gesetz und die Propheten befolhen denn den Juden."

96. *LW* 45:200; and *WA* 11:315, l. 8: "eyn lautter geschwetz...on alle schrifft."

97. *LW* 45:201; and *WA* 11:316, ll. 1–3.

98. The passages, which were commonly used in anti-Jewish polemics or debates, are Genesis 22:18; 2 Samuel 7:12–14; and Isaiah 7:14.

99. See the bibliography in *WA* 11:308–9.

100. See *WA* 11:309–10. The first translation was by Jonas Justus (1524, two printings) and the second by Johannes Lonicer (1525).

101. See the excellent discussion of this in Lewin 1911, 33–35.

102. *LW* 45:229; and *WA* 11:336, l. 35: "Hie will ichs dis mall lassen bleyben, bis ich sehe, was ich gewirckt habe."

103. *WA: Briefwechsel* 1:23–24, ll. 32–44 (no. 7, February 1514): "Hoc tandem concludo, cum per omnes prophetas praedictum sit, Iudaeos Deum et regem suum Christum maledicturos et blasphematuros, et qui hoc non legit vel intelligit, fateor eum nondum vidisse theologiam. Ideoque praesumo Colonienses non posse scripturam solvere, quia sic oportet fieri et scripturam impleri. Et si tentaverint Iudaeos a blasphemiis purgare, hoc facient, ut scriptura et Deus mendax appareat. Sed confide Deum fore veracem, etiam invitis et frustra sudantibus mille millibus Coloniensibus. Dei enim solius hoc opus erit, ab intra operantis, non hominum, a foris tantummodo ludentium potius quam operantium. Si istae ab eis tollantur, component peiores, quia sic sunt in reprobum sensum per iram Dei traditi, ut sint secundum Ecclesiasten incorrigibiles, et omnis incorrigibilis correctione peior fit et nunquam emendatur."

104. Lewin 1911, 2ff. From the beginning Luther distinctively criticized a "Jewish" concept of the righteousness of man as opposed to the righteousness of God. Eventually, he would associated the Jewish adherence to the law as works righteousness, the basis for his trope that Catholic works righteousness was "Jewish."

105. Tongern 1512, *Articuli*, fol. Aʳ: "Hermanni Buschii Pasiphili in Judeos iudeorumque amatores preposteros Elogium."

106. See *WA* 51:195: "EIne vermanung wider die Juden," which could well be an addendum to the publication of the final sermon. It is possible that Luther delivered his final sermon on 15 February 1546, a Monday.

107. See *WA* 51:195, ll. 28–32: "Sie [i.e., the Jews] sind unsere öffentliche Feinde, hören nicht auff unsern HErrn Christum zu lestern, Heissen die Jungfraw Maria eine Hure, Christum ein Hurenkind, Uns heissen sie Wechselbelge oder mahlkelber, und wenn sie uns kondten alle tödten, so theten sie es gerne, Und thuns auch offt, sonderlich, die sich vor ertzte ausgeben."

108. *WA* 51:196, ll. 14–16: "Wollen sich die Jüden zu uns bekeren und von jrer lesterung, und was sie sonst gethan haben auffhören, so wollen wir es jnen gerne vergeben, Wo aber nicht, so sollen wir sie auch bey uns nicht dulden noch leiden." See also Oberman [1981] 1984, 113.

109. Lewin 1911, 98. Letter of 8 December 1543, Bullinger to Martin Bucer.

110. See Porchetus 1520, *Victoria Porcheti adversus impios Hebraeos*. Luther's copy of this book, with his annotations, survives. Porchetus's work was edited by the Renaissance biblical scholar Agostino Giustiniano, first professor of Hebrew at the University of Paris and also a Dominican. Giustiniano edited a polyglot edition of the Psalms in 1516, including the Hebrew text.

111. *LW* 47:277; and *WA* 53:530.

112. *LW* 47:268; and *WA* 53:522, l. 35: "eine scharffe barmhertzigkeit."

113. Luther is uninterested in cloaking his efforts to eradicate Jewry in a campaign of conversion. See, for example, *LW* 47:137, ll. 22–24: "much less do I propose to convert Jews, for that is impossible" (*WA* 53:417: "Viel weniger gehe ich damit umb, das ich die Jüden bekeren wolle, Denn das ist ummüglich [*sic*].").

114. *LW* 47:368; and *WA* 53:522, ll. 30–32: "Zu leiden ists uns nicht…damit wir uns nicht teilhafftig machen aller jrer lügen, flüche und lesterung."

115. *LW* 47:268; and *WA* 53:523, ll. 1–5: "Erstlich, das man jre Synagoga oder Schule mit feur anstecke…damit Gott sehe, das wir Christen seien."

116. *LW* 47:270; and *WA* 53:524. See, for example, *WA* 53:524, ll. 13–14: "So möcht sich etwa ein Reuterey samlen wider sie, weil sie aus diesem Büchlin lernen werden, was die Jüden sind."

117. Scheible 1993, 123, however, concluded that Melanchthon had an "enlightened, rational attitude toward Jews": "geradezu aufgeklärt-rationale Einstellung Melanchthons gegenüber den Juden."

118. See Oberman [1981] 1984, 47, for the claim that Jonas altered the meaning of Luther's tract. Like most other historians, Oberman is also inclined to disassociate Melanchthon from Luther's anti-Jewish efforts.

119. Scholars who have focused on exegetical anti-Judaism have tended to ignore the sociopolitical dimensions of Luther's anti-Semitism. See Edwards 1983, 115–42, for a discussion of Luther's anti-Judaic theology, and especially 139, for an attempt to grapple with the "theological explanation of Luther's attitude toward Jews."

120. Lewin 1911, 110.

121. For a general history of the change in papal policy, see Stow 1977.

CHAPTER 10

Epigraph source: Reuchlin, *Briefwechsel*, ed. L. Geiger (no. 301, 23 September 1521), 331: "Nunc autem ingratus et inhumanus mihi videar, nisi tuum nomen, quantum in me est, aeternitati mandandum curem."

1. See Hannemann [1955] 1994a, 101ff., for the proposal that Reuchlin was ordained at some point at the end of his life. His name appeared on a list of members of the Salve Regina confraternity in Stuttgart among a group of priests. The list, however, does not identify Reuchlin as a priest and no surviving records indicate that Reuchlin received ordination.

2. See L. Geiger 1871, 411. Pellican wrote that he discussed many things over several hours with Reuchlin, who was, however, "infirmus."

3. The announcement survives in the papers of Johannes Brassicanus. See Rhein 1994a, 283 (the entire notice): "Capnion hebraicae linguae praeceptor Cras hora xii. in aula consueta inchoabit librum Regis Judaeorum sapientissimi concionatoris De contemptu mundi. qui est a nostris inscriptus Ecclesiastes Et auditoribus suis cum discussione grammatica hebraice praelegit illum Tybingae x kal Martias Anno M.D.xxij."

4. Reuchlin, *Briefwechsel*, ed. L. Geiger (no. 303, 13 January 1522), 333: "tanquam Hebraicarum literarum protomartyr."

5. The gravestone is dated 1501, which probably indicates the year his first wife died and the year the memorial was placed in the Hospital Church.

6. Reuchlin has periodically been taken to task for the spelling of "עלם" instead of "עלום" on his gravestone. Brod 1965, 342, called the misspelling a "howler" ("so ein elementarer Schnitzer"). Possibly, Reuchlin was using an Aramaic spelling but, most likely, he left out the "ו," which is a *mater lectionis*, because that is the spelling in David Kimhi's *Sefer ha-Shorashim* and, therefore, in his own dictionary (see Reuchlin 1506, *De rudimentis hebraicis*, 394). Reuchlin defined "עלם" as "aethernitas," which would support the translation of the inscription as "eternity of the living," or "eternal life."

7. See L. Geiger 1871, 472ff., for a longer list of those who paid tribute to Reuchlin.

8. See Reuchlin, *Briefwechsel*, ed. L. Geiger (nos. 301 and 304), 330–31, 335–36, for the dedications. The first book was the 1521 edition of the Psalms in Hebrew and the second was the 1522 edition of Proverbs, Song of Songs, and Ecclesiastes in Hebrew.

9. Reuchlin, *Briefwechsel*, ed. L. Geiger (no. 301, 23 September 1521), 330–31: "Talmud opus certe magni et laboris et impensae, mihique a Summo Pontifico demandatum."

10. Wenninger 1981, 259.

11. Wenninger 1981, 258.

12. See chapter 6, on the importance of Reuchlin's use of fifteenth-century anti-Jewish polemics in his *Recommendation*.

13. See Reuchlin 1511, *Augenspiegel*, in *Sämtliche Werke* 4/1:53 (quoted in chapter 6).

14. Reuchlin 1506, *De rudimentis hebraicis*, 1; and Reuchlin, *Briefwechsel* 2:35, ll. 12–14 (no. 138, 7 March 1506): "erit necesse veterem sanctarum literarum dignitatem in novam faciem Latinis hominibus hactenus incognitam reverti."

15. See L. Geiger 1871, 233–34; and chapter 1.

16. See, for example, Reuchlin 1511, *Augenspiegel*, in *Sämtliche Werke* 4/1:42; and chapter 6.

17. See Reuchlin 1513, *Defensio*, in *Sämtliche Werke* 4/1:342; and chapter 7.

18. See Reuchlin 1517, *De arte cabalistica*, fol. O7ᵛ; and chapter 4.

19. Reuchlin 1519, trans., *Liber S. Athanasii de variis quaestionibus*, esp. fol. I3ᵛ and N1ʳ. Reuchlin quoted Maimonides' *Guide for the Perplexed* some ten times (in Hebrew with Latin translation) in his annotations to this text he attributed to Athanasius.

20. See the discussion of Hoogstraeten's *Writ of Accusation* in chapter 7.

21. In a separate context, Osiander also wrote to Elijah Levita to apologize for the violence of Luther's anti-Jewish rhetoric, although, fearing retribution, he sought to conceal that correspondence from Luther. See Lewin 1911, 99ff.

22. Oberman [1981] 1984, 35, aptly described Osiander's approach as "to confront agitation with information."

23. See Hsia 1988, 136–43, for a description of Osiander's argument, and 124–31 and 143 for Eck's reaction to it.

24. See Israel [1985] 1998, 29ff.; and Katz 1982.

25. *EE* 4:46, ll. 142–43 (no. 1006, 11 August 1519): "Si Christianum est odisse Iudaeos, hic abunde Christiani sumus omnes."

26. On Erasmus's near rejection of Hebrew Scriptures, see Augustijn 1980, 32ff.

Bibliography

PRIMARY SOURCES CONSULTED

I. Works by Johannes Reuchlin

A. Collected Works

Reuchlin, Johannes. *Sämtliche Werke*. Ed. Widu-Wolfgang Ehlers,
   Hans-Gert Roloff, and Peter Schäfer. Stuttgart-Bad Cannstadt:
   Frommann-Holzboog, 1996–.

B. Reuchlin's Correspondence

Friedländer, Gottfried, ed. *Beiträge zur Reformationsgeschichte: Sammlung
   ungedruckter Briefe des Reuchlin, Beza und Bullinger nebst einem Anhange
   zur Geschichte der Jesuiten*. Berlin: Enslin'sche Buchhandlung, 1837.

Horawitz, Adalbert, ed. *Zur Biographie und Correspondenz Johannes
   Reuchlin's*. Vienna: Karl Gerold's Sohn, 1877.

Reuchlin, Johannes. *Briefwechsel*. Ed. Matthias Dall'Asta and Gerald
   Dörner. Stuttgart-Bad Cannstadt: Frommann-Holzboog, 1999–. This
   edition of Reuchlin's correspondence is the foundation for Reuchlin
   research. Three of four planned volumes have appeared. For Reuchlin's
   correspondence after 1517, older sources are cited.

———. *Briefwechsel: Leseausgabe in deutscher Übersetzung*. Trans. into
   German by Adalbert Weh, Manfred Fuhrmann, and Georg Burkard.
   Stuttgart-Bad Cannstatt: Frommann-Holzboog. 2000–.

———. *Johann Reuchlins Briefwechsel*. Ed. Ludwig Geiger. Stuttgart:
   Litterarischer Verein, 1875.

———, ed. *Clarorum virorum epistolae latinae graecae et hebraicae variis
   temporibus missae ad Ioannem Reuchlin Phorcensem ll. doctorem*.
   Tübingen: Thomas Anshelm, 1514.

Reuchlin, Johannes, ed. *Illustrium virorum epistolae*. Hagenau: Thomas Anshelm, 1519.

Schlecht, Joseph, ed. "Briefe aus der Zeit von 1506 bis 1526." In *Briefmappe*, ed. A. Bigelmaier, St. Ehses, J. Schlecht, and Fr. X. Thurnhofer, 23–116. Münster: Aschendorffsche Verlagsbuchhandlung, 1922.

C. Other Works by Reuchlin

Ad Alexandrum Sextum pontificem maximum pro Philippo Bavariae duce Palatino Rheni, Sacri Romani Imperii electore. Venice: Aldus Manutius, 1498. Reprinted in Reuchlin, ed. *Illustrium virorum epistolae*. Hagenau: Thomas Anshelm,1519, fol. n3ᵛ–o4ʳ.

Ain clare verstentnus in tütsch vff doctor Johannsen Reüchlins ratschlag von den iuden büchern vor mals auch zu latin imm Augenspiegel vssgangen. Tübingen: Thomas Anshelm, 1512.

[*Augenspiegel*]. *Doctor Johannsen Reuchlins... Augenspiegel.* Tübingen: Anshelm, 1511.

De accentibus et orthographia linguae hebraicae. Hagenau: Thomas Anshelm, 1518.

[*De arte cabalistica*]. *Ioannis Reuchlin Phorcensis ll. doc. de arte cabalistica libri tres Leoni X. dicati.* Hagenau: Thomas Anshelm, 1517. Benzing 1955, 28–29, records six further editions.

[*De arte praedicandi*]. *Ioannis Reuchlin Phorcensis ll. doctoris liber congestorum de arte praedicandi.* Pforzheim: Thomas Anshelm, 1504.

[*De rudimentis hebraicis*]. *Principium libri Ioannis Reuchlin... de rudimentis hebraicis.* Pforzheim: Thomas Anshelm, 1506. Sebastian Münster produced a second, revised edition: Basel: Heinrich Petri, 1537.

De verbo mirifico. Basel: Johannes Amerbach, 1494. Further editions: Tübingen: Thomas Anshelm, 1514; Cologne: Eucharius Cervicornus, 1532; Lyons: Tornaesius, 1552; in Petrus Galatinus, *Opus de arcanis catholicae veritatis.* Basel: Hervagius, 1561, 552–651; in Johannes Pistorius, *Artis cabalisticae... tomus primus.* Basel: Sebastian Henricpetri, 1587, 873–979.

Defensio Ioannis Reuchlin Phorcensis ll. doctoris contra calumniatores suos Colonienses. Tübingen: Thomas Anshelm, 1513. Subsequent edition: Tübingen: Thomas Anshelm, 1514.

[*Henno*]. *Ioannis Reuchlin Phorcensis scenica progymnasmata.* Basel: Johannes Bergmann von Olpe, 1498. Benzing 1955, 11–22, records thirty-three separate editions and six further editions with *Sergius*.

[*Sergius vel caput capitis*]. *Comoedia cui nomen Sergius.* Erfurt: Wolfgang Schenk, ca. 1504. Benzing 1955, 7–10, records fifteen separate editions.

[*Tütsch missiue*]. *Doctor iohanns Reuchlins tütsch missiue. warumb die Juden so lang im ellend sind.* Pforzheim: Thomas Anshelm, 1505.

[*Vocabularius breviloquus*]. Attributed to Johannes Reuchlin. Basel: Johannes Amerbach, 1472. Benzing 1955, 1–5, records twenty-two editions of this work.

D. Works Translated by Reuchlin

Athanasius. *S. Athanasius in librum psalmorum.* Tübingen: Thomas Anshelm, 1515.

Athanasius (attributed). *Liber S. Athanasii de variis questionibus.* Hagenau: Thomas Anshelm, 1519.

Constantinus magnus Romanorum imperator. Tübingen: Thomas Anshelm, 1513.

Ezobi, Joseph. *Rabi Joseph Hyssopaeus Parpinianensis poeta dulcissimus ex hebraica lingua in latinam traductus.* Tübingen: Thomas Anshelm, 1512.

Hippocrates. *De praeparatione hominis.* Tübingen: Anshelm, 1512.

Homer (attributed). *Homeri Batrachomiomachia.* Vienna: Winterburger, ca. 1510. Benzing 1955, 32–33, records four further editions.

Proclus. *Sermo Procli Cyzicensis episcopi.* Tübingen: Ulrich Morhart, 1529.

Psalms. *Ioannis Reuchlini Phorcensis ll. doctoris in septem psalmos poenitentiales hebraicos.* Tübingen: Thomas Anshelm, 1512. 2nd ed.: Wittenberg: Klug, 1529.

E. Works Edited by Reuchlin

Aeschines and Demosthenes.... *Graeciae excellentium oratorum Aeschines et Demosthenis orationes adversariae.* Hagenau: Thomas Anshelm and Johannes Setzer, 1522.

Xenophon. Ξενοφῶντος. Ἀπολογία Σωκράτους. Hagenau: Thomas Anshelm and Johannes Setzer, 1520. Includes *Apology of Socrates, Agesilaus,* and *Hiero.*

F. Modern Translations and Editions of Works by Reuchlin

[*De arte cabalistica*]. *L'Arte Cabbalistica (De arte cabalistica).* Trans. into Italian by Giulio Busi and Saverio Campanini. Florence: Opus Libri, 1995.

[*De arte cabalistica*]. *On the Art of the Kabbalah.* Trans. Martin Goodman and Sarah Goodman. Lincoln: University of Nebraska Press, [1983] 1993.

["Ratschlag ob man den iuden alle ire bücher nemmen/ abthün vnnd verbrennen soll"]. *Gutachten über das jüdische Schrifttum.* Ed. and trans. Antonie Leinz-von Dessauer. Konstanz and Stuttgart: Thorbecke, 1965.

["Ratschlag ob man den iuden alle ire bücher nemmen/ abthün vnnd verbrennen soll"]. *Recommendation Whether to Confiscate, Destroy and Burn All Jewish Books.* Trans. Peter Wortsman. New York: Paulist, 2000.

II. Works by Other Authors

Acta doctorum Parrhisiensium ... contra speculum oculare Ioannis Reuchlin Phorcensis, una cum sententia eiusdem libelli condemnativa ad ignem. Cologne: Quentel, 1514.

Acta iudiciorum. Hagenau: Thomas Anshelm, 1518.

Adriani, Matthäus. *Libellus hora faciendi pro domino.* Tübingen: Thomas Anshelm, 1513.

Bebel, Heinrich. [*Carmina*]. Reutlingen: Michael Greyff, 1496.

Benigno, Giorgio. *Defensio praestantissimi viri Ioannis Reuchlin.* Cologne: Eucharius Cervicornus, 1517.

Cellarius, Johannes. *Isagogicon in hebraeas litteras.* Hagenau: Thomas Anshelm, 1518.

Celtis, Conrad. *Der Briefwechsel des Konrad Celtis.* Ed. Hans Rupprich. Munich: Beck, 1934.

Corpus iuris canonici. Ed. Emil Friedberg. 2 vols. Leipzig: Tauchnitz, 1879–81.

Deutsche Reichstagsakten unter Maximilian I. Ed. Heinz Angermeier and Reinhold Seyboth. Gottingen: Vandenhoeck und Ruprecht, 1989–.

Dürer, Albrecht. *Dürer: Schriftlicher Nachlaß*. Ed. Hans Rupprich. 3 vols. Berlin:
    Deutscher Verein für Kunstgeschichte, 1956.

Epistolae obscurorum virorum. Ed. and trans. Francis Griffin Stokes. London: Chatto
    and Windus, 1909.

Erasmus, Desiderius. *Collected Works of Erasmus*. Toronto: University of Toronto
    Press, 1974–.

———. *Farrago nova epistolarum Des. Erasmi Roterodami*. Basel: Froben, 1519.

———. *Opus epistolarum Des. Erasmi*. Ed. P. S. Allen, H. M. Allen, and H. W. Gannod.
    8 vols. Oxford: Clarendon, 1906–58.

[Frankfurt am Main]. Institut für Stadtgeschichte Frankfurt am Main.
    "Bürgermeisterbuch," 1508.

———. "Bürgermeisterbuch," 1509.

———. "Juden Akten 438."

———. "Juden Akten 655."

———. "Juden Akten 779."

———. "Reichstagsakten 25."

———. "RS II, nr. 250."

———. "RS II, nr. 294."

———. "RS III, nr. 530."

Galatino, Pietro. [*De arcanis catholicae veritatis*]. *Opus toti Christianae rei publicae
    maxime utile de arcanis catholicae veritatis contra obstinatissimam Iudaeorum
    nostrae tempestatis perfidiam*. Ortona Mare: Gershom Soncino, 1518.

Germania Judaica. Vol. 3, *1350–1519*, in three parts. Ed. Arye Maimon, Mordechai
    Breuer, and Yacov Guggenheim. Tübingen: Mohr, 1987–2003.

Die geschicht vnnd bekantnüß des getaufften Juden genannt Johannes Pfefferkorn.
    Strasbourg: Johannes Knobloch, 1514.

Giles of Viterbo. *Scechina e libellus de litteris hebraicis*. Ed. François Secret. Rome:
    Centro Internazionale di Studi Umanistici, 1959.

Graetz, Heinrich. "Aktenstücke zur Confiscation der jüdischen Schriften in
    Frankfurt a. M. unter Kaiser Maximilian durch Pfefferkorns Angeberei."
    Monatsschrift für Geschichte und Wissenschaft des Judenthums 24 (1875): 289–300.

Gratius, Ortwin. *Lamentationes obscurorum virorum... Epistola apologetica Ortwini
    Gratii*. Cologne: Quentel, 1518.

———. [*Prenotamenta*]. *Hoc in opusculo. contra speculum oculare Ioannis Reuchlin
    Phorcensis. hec in fidei et ecclesie tuitionem continentur prenotamenta Ortwini
    Gratii*. Cologne: Quentel, 1514.

Hoogstraeten, Jacob. [*Apologia*]. *Ad sanctissimum dominum nostrum Leonem papam
    decimum, ac divum Maxemilianum imperatorem semper augustum. Apologia
    reverendi patris Iacobi Hochstraten*. Cologne: Quentel, 1518.

———. [*Apologia secunda*]. *Ad reverendum dignissimum patrem d. Ioannem
    Ingewinkel...Apologia secunda reverendi patris Iacobi Hochstraten*. Cologne:
    Quentel, 1519.

———. *Defensorium fratrum mendicantium*. Cologne: Quentel, 1507.

———. *Destructio cabale, seu cabalistice perfidie ab Ioanne Reuchlin Capnione
    iampridem in lucem edite*. Cologne: Quentel, 1519.

———. *Erronee assertationes in oculari speculo Io. Reuchlin*. Rome: Giaccomo Mazzocchi, 1517.

———. [*Tractatus magistralis*]. *Ad reverendissimum... Philippum sancte ecclesie Coloniensis episcopum. Tractatus magistralis*. Cologne: Martin von Werden, 1510.

Hutten, Ulrich von. *Opera quae reperiri potuerunt omnia*. Ed. Edward Böcking. 5 vols. and 2 supplement vols. Leipzig: Teubner, 1859–70.

Joseph of Rosheim. *The Historical Writings of Joseph of Rosheim: Leader of Jewry in Early Modern Germany*. Trans. and ed. Chava Fraenkel-Goldschmidt. Leiden: Brill, 2006.

Keen, Ralph. *A Melanchthon Reader*. New York: Peter Lang, 1988.

Kober, Adolf. "Urkundliche Beiträge zum Reuchlinschen Streit: ein Gedenkblatt zum 30. Juni 1922." *Monatsschrift für Geschichte und Wissenschaft des Judenthums* 67, N.F., 31(1923): 110–22.

Kracauer, Isidor. "Actenstücke zur Geschichte der Confiskation der hebräischen Schriften in Frankfurt a. M." *Monatsschrift für Geschichte und Wissenschaft des Judenthums* 44(1900): 114–26, 167–77, 220–34.

———. "Die Konfiskation der hebräischen Schriften in Frankfurt a. M. in den Jahren 1509 und 1510." *Zeitschrift für die Geschichte der Juden in Deutschland* 1 (1887): 230–48.

———. "Rabbi Joselmann de Rosheim." *Revue des Etudes Juives* 16 (1885): 84–105.

———. "Verzeichniss der von Pfefferkorn 1510 in Frankfurt a. M. confiscierten jüdischen Bücher." *Monatsschrift für Geschichte und Wissenschaft des Judenthums* 44 (1900): 320–459.

Luther, Martin. *Luthers Werke: Kritische Gesamtausgabe*. Weimar: Böhlau, 1883–.

———. *Luther's Works: The American Edition*. Ed. Jaroslav Pelikan and Helmut Lehmann. 55 vols. St. Louis and Philadelphia: Concordia and Fortress, 1955–86.

Melanchthon, Philipp. [*De rhetorica libri tres*]. *Philippi Melanchthonis de rhetorica libri tres*. Basel: Froben, 1519.

———. *Elementa rhetorices*. Ed. and trans. Volkhard Wels. Berlin: Weidler Buchverlag, [1532] 2001.

———. *Melanchthons Briefwechsel*. Ed. Heinz Scheible. Stuttgart-Bad Cannstatt: Frommann-Holzboog, 1991–.

———. *Oratio continens historiam Ioannis Capnionis*. In *Opera quae supersunt omnia*, vol. 11:999–1010. Braunschweig: Schwetschke, [1552] 1843.

Münster, Sebastian. *Dictionarium hebraicum*. Basel: Froben, 1523.

Murner, Thomas. *History Von den vier ketzren Prediger ordens*. Strasbourg: Johann Prüß the Younger, 1521.

———. *Ritus et celebratio phase iudeorum*. Frankfurt: Beatus Murner, 1512.

Nauclerus, Johannes. *Memorabilium omnis aetatis et omnium gentium chronici commentarii*. 2 vols. Tübingen: Thomas Anshelm, 1516.

Neuenahr, Hermann von, ed. *Epistolae trium illustrium virorum ad Hermannum Comitem Nuenarium. Eiusdem responsoria una ad Ioannem Reuchlinum, et altera ad lectorem. Item, libellus accusatorius fratris Iacobi de Hochstraten. contra oculare speculum Ioannis Reuchlin. defamationes eiusdem Iacobi. Item, defensio nova Ioannis Reuchlin ex urbe Roma allata*. Hagenau: Thomas Anshelm, 1518.

———. *Vivat Rex Carolus*. Cologne: n.p., 1519.

Olin, John C., ed. *Christian Humanism and the Reformation: Selected Writings of Erasmus, with The Life of Erasmus by Beatus Rhenanus.* New York: Fordham University Press, 1975.

Osiander, Andreas. *Gesamtausgabe.* Ed. Gerhard Müller and Gottfried Seebaß. Gütersloh: Gerd Mohn, 1975–.

Paul of Burgos [Pablo de Santa Maria]. *Scrutinium scripturarum.* Mantua: Johannes Schallus, 1475.

Pellican, Conrad. *Das Chronikon des Konrad Pellikan.* Ed. Bernhard Riggenbach. Basel: Bahnmaier, 1877.

———. *De modo legendi et intelligendi hebraea.* Strasbourg, 1504.

Pfefferkorn, Johannes. *Ajn mitleydliche claeg vber alle claeg.* Cologne: Servas Krufffter, 1521. Kirn 1989, 204, records a second edition from 1521.

———. *Allen vnd yglichen geistlichen vnd weltlichen,* 1510. In Spanier 1934, 581–87.

———. *Beschyrmung Johannes Pfefferkorn.* Cologne: n.p., 1516.

———. [*Brantspiegell*]. *Abzotraiben und aus zuleschen eines vngegrunten laster buechleyn mit namen Augenspiegell… Dar gegen ich meyn vnschult allen menschen gruntlich tzu vernemen vnd tzu vercleren in desem gegenwyrdigen buechgelgyn genant Brantspiegell gethan hab.* Cologne: Herman Gutschaiff, 1512.

———. *Defensio Ioannis Pepericorni contra famosas et criminales obscurorum virorum epistolas.* Cologne: Heinrich von Neuß, 1516.

———. *Handt Spiegel.* Mainz: Johannes Schöffer, 1511.

———. [*Der iuden beicht*]. *Ich heyß eyn buchlijn der iuden beicht.* Cologne: Johannes Landen, 1508.

———. [*Der iuden peicht*]. *Ich heyss ain büchlein der iuden peicht.* Augsburg: Jörg Nadler, 1508. Kirn 1989, 202, records two further editions of this pamphlet from 1508.

———. [*Der iuden beicht,* Latin translation of]. *Libellus de iudaica confessione.* Cologne: Johannes Landen, 1508. 2nd ed.: Nuremberg: Weissenburger, 1508.

———. *Jn lob vnd eer dem Allerdurchleuchtigsten Großmechtigsten Fursten vnd heren hern Maximilian.* Cologne: Heinrich von Neuß, 1510. Another edition: *Zu lob vnd Ere.* Augsburg: Erhard Öglein, 1510.

———. [*Jn lob vnd eer,* Latin translation of]. *In laudem et honorem illustrissimi maximique principis et domini Maximiliani.* Cologne: Heinrich von Neuß, 1510.

———. [*Der Juden Spiegel,* 1st version]. *Der Joeden spiegel.* Cologne: Johannes Landen, 1507.

———. [*Der Juden Spiegel,* 1st version]. *Der Juden Spiegel.* Nuremberg: Wolfgang Huber, 1507.

———. [*Der Juden Spiegel,* 1st version, Latin translation of]. *Speculum adhortationis iudaice ad Christum.* Cologne: Martin von Werden, 1507. Another edition: Speyer: Konrad Hist, 1507.

———. [*Der Juden Spiegel,* 2nd version]. *Der Juden Spiegel.* Cologne: Martin von Werden, 1508.

———. [*Der Juden Spiegel,* 2nd version, Latin translation of]. *Speculum adhortationis iudaice ad Christum.* Cologne: Martin von Werden, 1508. Kirn 1989, 201, records a second edition of the Latin translation.

———. [*Der Juden veindt*]. *Ich bin ein buchlin. der Juden veindt ist mein namen.* Cologne: Johannes Landen, 1509. 2nd ed., Augsburg: Erhard Öglein, 1509.

———. [*Der Juden veindt*, Latin translation of]. *Hostis iudeorum.* Cologne: Heinrich von Neuß, 1509.

———. *Streydt puechlyn.* Cologne: Heinrich von Neuß, 1516.

———. *Sturm Johansen Pferfferkorn vber vnd wider die drulosen Juden. anfechter des leichnams Christi. vnd seiner glidmossen. Sturm vber eynen alten sunder Johann Reuchlin. zuneiger der falschen Juden.* Cologne: Quentel, 1514.

———. [*Wie die blinden Juden yr Ostern halten*]. *In disem buchlein vindet yr ein entlichen furtrag. wie die blinden Juden yr Ostern halten.* Cologne: Johannes Landen, 1509. 2nd ed.: Augsburg: Erhard Öglein, 1509.

———. [*Wie die blinden Juden yr Ostern halten*, Latin tranlation of]. *In hoc libello comparatur absoluta explicatio quomodo ceci illi iudei suum pascha servent.* Cologne: Heinrich von Neuß, 1509.

Pirckheimer, Willibald. *Eckius Dedolatus.* Ed. and trans. Niklas Holzberg. Stuttgart: Reclam, 1983.

———. *Willibald Pirckheimers Briefwechsel.* Ed. Emil Reicke, Josef Pfanner, Helga Scheible, and Dieter Wuttke. 7 vols. Munich: Beck, 1940–2009.

Porchetus. *Victoria Porcheti adversus impios hebraeos.* Paris: Aegidius Gourmont and Franciscus Regnault, 1520.

Regesten zur Geschichte der Juden in der Reichsstadt Frankfurt am Main von 1401–1519. Ed. Dietrich Andernacht. 3 vols. Hannover: Hahnsche Buchhandlung, 1996.

Rhenanus, Beatus. *Briefwechsel des Beatus Rhenanus.* Ed. Adalbert Horowitz and Karl Hartfelder. Hildesheim: Olms, [1886] 1966.

[Rosenthaliana]. Bibliotheca Rosenthaliana MS 388. Sixteenth-century manuscript with copies of documents from the Jewish community of Frankfurt. Ed. in Kracauer 1900a.

Schwarz, Peter. *Contra perfidos iudaeos de conditionibus veri messiae.* Esslingen: Conrad Fyner, 1475.

———. *Stern des Meschiah.* Esslingen: Conrad Fyner, 1477.

Sefer Yetzirah. Trans. Knut Stenring. New York: KTAV, [1923] 1970.

Sforno, Ovadiah. *Pentateuch Commentary.* Ed. and trans. Raphael Pelcovitz. Brooklyn, N.Y.: Mesorah, 1987.

Sickingen, Franz von. *Eruoderung vnd verkundung: des Edeln vnd vestn Francisco von Sickingen/ zů Eberbürg/ an vnd wider Prouincial prioren vnd Conuenten Prediger ordens teutscher nation vnd sunderlichen Brüder Jacoben von der hochstraten/ auch prediger ordens/ von wegen vnd namen/ des hochgelerten vnd weitberümbten hern Johann Reüchlins baider Rechten doctor/ seiner erlangten Executorial halben.* Landshut: Johann Weißenburger, 1519. This pamphlet was also printed twice in Strasbourg in 1519.

Simonsohn, Shlomo. *The Apostolic See and the Jews.* 8 vols. Toronto: Pontifical Institute of Mediaeval Studies, 1988–91.

Tanner, Norman, and Giuseppe Alberigo, ed. *Decrees of the Ecumenical Councils.* 2 vols. London: Sheed and Ward, 1990.

Tongern, Arnold van. *Articuli sive propositiones de iudaico favore nimis suspecte ex libello theutonico domini Ioannis Reuchlin...extracte.* Cologne: Quentel, 1512.

Victor of Carben. *Opus aureum ac novum...in quo omnes iudeorum errores manifestantur.* Cologne: Heinrich Neuß, 1509.

The Zohar. Trans. Harry Sperling and Maurice Simon. 5 vols. London: Soncino, 1931–34.

The Zohar. Trans. and ed. Daniel Matt. Stanford: Stanford University Press, 2004–.

SECONDARY SOURCES CONSULTED

1495—Kaiser Reich Reformen der Reichstag zu Worms. 1995. Koblenz: Landesarchivverwaltung der Stadt Worms.

Abel, Wolfgang von, and Reimund Leicht. 2005. *Verzeichnis der Hebraica in der Bibliothek Johannes Reuchlins.* Ostfildern: Thorbecke.

Ackermann, Markus Raphael. 1999a. *Der Jurist Johannes Reuchlin (1455–1522).* Berlin: Duncker und Humblot.

———. 1999b. "Johannes Reuchlin und die italienische Rechtswissenschaft." In *Reuchlin und Italien,* ed. Gerald Dörner, 133–48. Stuttgart: Thorbecke.

Alberts, Hildegard. [1955] 1994. "Reuchlins Drucker Thomas Anshelm unter besonderer Berücksichtigung seiner Pforzheimer Presse." In *Johannes Reuchlin 1455–1522,* ed. Manfred Krebs, 205–65. Sigmaringen: Thorbecke.

Amelung, Peter. 1972. "Reuchlin und die Drucker seiner Zeit." *Schwäbische Heimat* 23:168–77.

———. 1986. "Wann starb Herzog Eberhard im Bart?" *Zeitschrift für Württembergische Landesgeschichte* 45:319–26.

Angermeier, Heinz. 1984. *Die Reichsreform 1410–1555: Die Staatsproblematik in Deutschland zwischen Mittelalter und Gegenwart.* Munich: Beck.

———. 1994. "Reuchlin, Württemberg und das Reich." *Historisches Jahrbuch* 114:381–95.

———. 1998. "Reuchlin als Politiker." In *Reuchlin und die politischen Kräfte seiner Zeit,* ed. Stefan Rhein, 53–63. Sigmaringen: Thorbecke.

Augustijn, C. 1980. "Erasmus und die Juden." *Nederlands Archief voor Kerkgeschiedenis,* n.s., 60:22–38.

Aulinger, Rosemarie. 1980. *Das Bild des Reichstages im 16. Jahrhundert: Beiträge zu einer typologischen Analyse schriftlicher und bildlicher Quellen.* Göttingen: Vandenhoeck und Ruprecht.

Awerbuch, Marianne. 1993. "Über Juden und Judentum zwischen Humanismus und Reformation. Zum Verständnis der Motivation von Reuchlins Kampf für das jüdische Schrifttum." In *Reuchlin und die Juden,* ed. Arno Herzig, Julius H. Schoeps, and Saskia Rohde, 189–200. Sigmaringen: Thorbecke.

Backes, Martina. 1992. *Das literarische Leben am kurpfälzischen Hof zu Heidelberg im 15. Jahrhundert: Ein Beitrag zur Gönnerforschung des Spätmittelalters.* Tübingen: Niemeyer.

Baer, Yitzhak. 1961–66. *A History of the Jews in Christian Spain.* Trans. Louis Schoffman. 2 vols. Philadelphia: Jewish Publication Society of America.

Barham, Francis. 1843. *The Life and Times of John Reuchlin, or Capnion, the Father of the German Reformation*. London: Whittaker and Co.

Baron, Salo Wittmayer. 1969. *A Social and Religious History of the Jews*. Vol. 13, *Inquisition, Renaissance and Reformation*. New York: Columbia University Press.

Bauch, Gustav. 1901. *Die Anfänge des Humanismus in Ingolstadt: Eine litterarische Studie zur deutschen Universitätsgeschichte*. Munich and Leipzig: Oldenbourg.

———. 1904. "Die Einführung des Hebräischen in Wittenberg." *Monatsschrift für Geschichte und Wissenschaft des Judenthums* 48:22–32, 77–86, 145–60, 283–99, 328–40, 461–90.

Becht, Hans-Peter, ed. 1989. *Pforzheim in der frühen Neuzeit: Beiträge zur Stadtgeschichte des 16. bis 18. Jahrhunderts*. Sigmaringen: Thorbecke.

Becht, Hans-Peter, D. Le Maire, and Stefan Rhein. 1986. *Johannes Reuchlin Phorcensis (1455–1522): Ein humanistischer Gelehrter. Eine Ausstellung des Stadtarchivs Pforzheim im Reuchlinhaus Pforzheim vom 12. Dezember 1986 bis zum 9. Januar 1987*. Pforzheim: n.p.

Béhar, Pierre. 1993. "Tradition und Innovation in der Weltanschauung von Reuchlin und Agrippa von Nettesheim." In *Mittelalterliche Denk- und Schreibmodelle in der deutschen Literatur der frühen Neuzeit*, ed. Wolfgang Harms and Jean-Marie Valentin, 149–60. Amsterdam: Rodopi.

Beierwaltes, Werner. 1994. "Reuchlin und Pico della Mirandola." *Tijdschrift voor filosophie* 56:313–36.

Ben-Sasson, Haim Hillel. 1966. "Jewish-Christian Disputation in the Setting of Humanism and Reformation in the German Empire." *The Harvard Theological Review* 59:369–90.

Bentley, Jerry H. 1983. *Humanists and Holy Writ*. Princeton: Princeton University Press.

Benzing, Josef. 1955. *Bibliographie der Schriften Johannes Reuchlins im 15. und 16. Jahrhundert*. Vienna: Walter Krieg Verlag.

Bietenholz, Peter G. 1985. "Erasmus und die letzten Lebensjahre Reuchlins." *Historische Zeitschrift* 240:45–66.

Bietenholz, Peter G., and Thomas B. Deutscher, ed. 1985–87. *Contemporaries of Erasmus: A Biographical Register of the Renaissance and Reformation*. 3 vols. Toronto: University of Toronto Press.

Black, Crofton. 2006. *Pico's "Heptaplus" and Biblical Hermeneutics*. Leiden: Brill.

Blau, Joseph L. [1944] 1965. *The Christian Interpretation of the Cabala in the Renaissance*. Port Washington, N.Y.: Kennikat.

Bleicher, Thomas. 1972. *Homer in der deutschen Literatur (1450–1740): Zur Rezeption der Antike und zur Poetologie der Neuzeit*. Stuttgart: Metzler.

Blumenkranz, Bernhard. 1946. *Die Judenpredigt Augustins*. Basel: Helbing und Lichtenhahn.

Bock, Ernst. 1927. *Der schwäbische Bund und seine Verfassungen (1488–1534): Ein Beitrag zur Geschichte der Zeit der Reichsreform*. Breslau: Marcus.

Bonfil, Robert. [1991] 1994. *Jewish Life in Renaissance Italy*. Trans. Anthony Oldcorn. Berkeley and Los Angeles: University of California Press.

Bonjour, Edgar. 1960. *Die Universität Basel: Von den Anfängen bis zur Gegenwart, 1460–1960*. Basel: Helbing und Lichtenhahn.

Brann, Noel L. 1984. "Pre-Reformation Humanism in Germany and the Papal Monarchy: A Study in Ambivalence." *Journal of Medieval and Renaissance Studies* 14:159–85.

Brecht, Martin. 1991–93. *Martin Luther*. Trans. James L. Schaf. 3 vols. Minneapolis: Fortress.

Brecht, Walter. 1904. *Die Verfasser der Obscurorum Virorum Epistolae*. Strasbourg: Trübner.

Breuer, Mordechai. 1972. "Frankfurt am Main." *Encyclopaedia Judaica* 7:83–92.

Brod, Max. 1965. *Johannes Reuchlin und sein Kampf: Eine historische Monographie*. Stuttgart: Kohlhammer.

Browe, Peter. 1935. "Die Judengesetzgebung Justinians." *Analecta Gregoriana* 8:109–46.

———. 1938a. "Die Judenbekämpfung im Mittelalter." *Zeitschrift für katholische Theologie* 62:197–231.

———. 1938b. "Die religiöse Duldung der Juden im Mittelalter." *Archiv für katholisches Kirchenrecht* 118:3–76.

———. 1942. *Die Judenmission im Mittelalter und die Päpste*. Rome: Saler.

Burnett, Stephen. 2004. "Reassessing the 'Basel-Wittenberg Conflict': Dimensions of the Reformation-Era Discussion of Hebrew Scholarship." In *Hebraica Veritas?*, ed. Allison P. Coudert and Jeffrey S. Shoulson, 180–201. Philadelphia: University of Pennsylvania Press.

———. 2005. "'Spokesmen for Judaism': Medieval Jewish Polemicists and Their Christian Readers in the Reformation Era." In *Reuchlin und seine Erben: Forscher, Denker, Ideologen und Spinner*, ed. Peter Schäfer and Irina Wandrey, 41–51. Ostfildern: Thorbecke.

Busi, Giulio. 1999. "Die Kabbala als eine symbolische Option." In *Reuchlin und Italien*, ed. Gerald Dörner, 57–67. Stuttgart: Thorbecke.

Campanini, Saverio. 1997. "Le prefazioni, le dediche, e i colophon di Gershom Soncino." In *L'attività editoriale de Gershom Soncino 1502–1527*, ed. Giuliano Tamani, 31–58. Cremona: Edizioni dei Soncino.

———. 1999. "Reuchlins jüdische Lehrer aus Italien." In *Reuchlin und Italien*, ed. Gerald Dörner, 69–85. Stuttgart: Thorbecke.

Carl, Horst. 1998. "*Triumvir Sueviae*—Reuchlin als Bundesrichter." In *Reuchlin und die politischen Kräfte seiner Zeit*, ed. Stefan Rhein, 65–86. Sigmaringen: Thorbecke.

Carlebach, Elisheva. 2001. *Divided Souls: Converts from Judaism in Germany, 1500–1750*. New Haven: Yale University Press.

Catholy, Eckehard. 1969. "Die Entfaltung der Komik im humanistischen Drama lateinischer Sprache bei Johannes Reuchlin." In *Das deutsche Lustspiel: Vom Mittelalter bis zum Ende der Barockzeit*, ed. Eckehard Catholy, 94–112. Stuttgart: Kohlhammer.

Christ, Karl. 1924. *Die Bibliothek Reuchlins in Pforzheim*. Leipzig: Harrassowitz.

Classen, Carl Joachim. 1997. *Zu Heinrich Bebels Leben und Schriften*. Göttingen: Vandenhoeck und Ruprecht.

Cohen, Jeremy. 1982. *The Friars and the Jews: The Evolution of Medieval Anti-Judaism.* Ithaca: Cornell University Press.

Cohn, Henry. 1971. "The Early Renaissance Court in Heidelberg." *European Studies Review* 4:295–322.

Coing, Helmut. 1964. *Römisches Recht in Deutschland.* Mediolani: Typis Giuffrè.

Dall'Asta, Matthias. 1999. "Bücher aus Italien." In *Reuchlin und Italien,* ed. Gerald Dörner, 23–43. Stuttgart: Thorbecke.

D'Amico, John F. 1982. "Paulo Cortesi's Rehabilitation of Giovanni Pico della Mirandola." *Bibliothèque d'Humanisme et Renaissance: Travaux et Documents* 44:37–51.

———. 1983. *Renaissance Humanism in Papal Rome: Humanists and Churchman on the Eve of the Reformation.* Baltimore: Johns Hopkins University Press.

Dan, Joseph. 1993. "The Emergence of Jewish Mysticism in Medieval Europe." In *Mystics of the Book: Themes, Topics, and Typologies,* ed. R. A. Herrera, 57–95. New York: P. Lang.

———. 1997. *The Christian Kabbalah: Jewish Mystical Books and Their Christian Interpreters.* Cambridge, Mass.: Harvard College Library.

Darlow, Thomas Herbert, and Horace Frederick Moule. 1903–11. *Historical Catalogue of the Printed Editions of Holy Scripture in the Library of the British and Foreign Bible Society.* 4 vols. London: British and Foreign Bible Society.

Davies, Martin. 1995. *Aldus Manutius: Printer and Publisher of Renaissance Venice.* London: The British Library.

Decker-Hauff, Hansmartin. [1955] 1994. "Bausteine zur Reuchlin-Biographie." In *Johannes Reuchlin 1455–1522,* ed. Manfred Krebs, 83–107. Sigmaringen: Thorbecke.

———. 1966. *Geschichte der Stadt Stuttgart.* Stuttgart: Kohlhammer.

Deutsch, Yaacov. 2004. "Polemical Ethnographies: Descriptions of Yom Kippur in the Writings of Christian Hebraists and Jewish Converts to Christianity in Early Modern Europe." In *Hebraica Veritas?,* ed. Allison P. Coudert and Jeffrey S. Shoulson, 202–33. Philadelphia: University of Pennsylvania Press.

Dibbelt, Hermann. 1938. "Reuchlins griechische Studien: Ein Beitrag zur Geschichte der deutschen Geistesbildung." *Das Gymnasium* 49:16–26.

Diemling, Maria. 1999. "'Christliche Ethnographien' über Juden und Judentum in der Frühen Neuzeit: Die Konvertiten Victor von Carben und Anthonius Margaritha und ihre Darstellung jüdischen Lebens und jüdischer Religion." PhD diss., Universität Wien.

———. 2006. "Anthonius Margaritha on the 'Whole Jewish Faith': A Sixteenth-Century Convert from Judaism and his Depiction of the Jewish Religion." In *Jews, Judaism and the Reformation,* ed. Dean Bell and Stephen Burnett, 303–33. Leiden: Brill.

Distel, Theodor. 1895. "Die erste Verdeutschung des zwölften Lukianischen Totengesprächs nach einer urtextlichen Handschrift von Johann Reuchlin (1495)." *Zeitschrift für vergleichende Litteraturgeschichte,* N.F., 8:408–17.

Dörner, Gerald. 1998. "Reuchlin, Johannes (1455–1522)." *Theologische Realenzyklopädie* 29:94–98.

Dörner, Gerald. 1999. "Jacob Questenberg—Reuchlins Briefpartner an der Kurie." In *Reuchlin und Italien*, ed. Gerald Dörner, 149–79. Stuttgart: Thorbecke.

Dörner, Gerald, and Stefan Rhein. 1997. "Der Reuchlin-Briefwechsel—auf dem Weg zu einem neuen Reuchlinbild." In *Editionsdesiderate zur Frühen Neuzeit*, ed. Hans-Gert Roloff, 121–39. Amsterdam: Rodopi.

Dougherty, M. V., ed. 2008. *Pico della Mirandola: New Essays*. Cambridge: Cambridge University Press.

Eckert, Willehad Paul. 1964. "Das Verhältnis von Christen und Juden im Mittelalter und Humanismus: Ein Beitrag zur Geistes- und Kulturgeschichte." In *Monumenta Judaica. 2000 Jahre Geschichte und Kultur der Juden am Rhein*, ed. Konrad Schilling, 1:131–98. Cologne: Joseph Melzer Verlag.

———. 1970. "Nikolaus von Kues und Johannes Reuchlin." In *Nicolò Cusano agli Inizi del Mondo Moderno*, ed. Giovanni Santinello, 195–209. Florence: Sansoni.

———. 1989. "Die Universität Köln und die Juden im späten Mittelalter." In *Die Kölner Universität im Mittelalter: Geistige Wurzeln und soziale Wirklichkeit*, ed. Albert Zimmermann, 488–507. Berlin: Walter de Gruyter.

Edwards, Mark U. 1983. *Luther's Last Battles: Politics and Polemics, 1531–46*. Ithaca: Cornell University Press.

Ehrstine, Glenn. 1998. "Scaenica Faceta: The Choral Odes of Johannes Reuchlin's Scaenica Progymnasmata (1497)." In *Acta Conventus Neo-Latini Bariensis*, ed. Rhoda Schnur, J. F. Alcina, John Dillon, Walther Ludwig, Colette Nativel, Mauro de Nichilo, and Stephen Ryle, 235–41. Tempe: Medieval and Renaissance Texts and Studies.

Engel, Josef, ed. 1979. *Mittel und Wege früher Verfassungspolitik*. Stuttgart: Klett-Cotta.

Erdmann-Pandžić, Elisabeth von, and Basilius Pandžić. 1989. *Juraj Dragišić und Johannes Reuchlin: Eine Untersuchung zum Kampf für die jüdischen Bücher mit einem Nachdruck der "Defensio praestantissimi viri Joannis Reuchlin" (1517) von Georgius Benignus (Juraj Dragišić)*. Bamberg: Slavische Philologie der Universität Bamberg.

Ernst, Fritz. [1933] 1970. *Eberhard im Bart: Die Politik eines deutschen Landesherrn am Ende des Mittelalters*. Darmstadt: Wissenschaftliche Buchgesellschaft.

Esser, Manfred. 1987. "Ungehaltene Rede vom wundertätigen Wort." *Allmende* 16/17:73–95.

Evans, G. R. 1985. "The 'Ars Praedicandi' of Johannes Reuchlin (1455–1522)." *Rhetorica* 3:99–104.

Fabisch, Peter. 1984. "Silvester Prierias (1456–1523)." In *Katholische Theologen der Reformationszeit*, ed. E. Iserloh, 1:26–36. Münster: Aschendorff.

Farge, James K. 1985. *Orthodoxy and Reform in Early Reformation France: The Faculty of Theology of Paris, 1500–1543*. Leiden: Brill.

Feilchenfeld, Ludwig. 1898. *Rabbi Josel von Rosheim: Ein Beitrag zur Geschichte der Juden in Deutschland im Reformationszeitalter*. Strassburg: Heitz.

Festschrift der Stadt Pforzheim zur Erinnerung an den 400. Todestag Johannes Reuchlins. 1922. Pforzheim: Riecker.

Ficker, Johannes. 1922. "Das Bildnis Reuchlins." In *Festschrift der Stadt Pforzheim zur Erinnerung an den 400. Todestag Johannes Reuchlins*, 276–94. Pforzheim: Riecker.

Finke, Karl Konrad. 1972a. "Johannes Reuchlin als Richter des Schwäbischen Bundes." *Schwäbische Heimat* 23:152–59.

———. 1972b. *Die Tübinger Juristenfakultät 1477–1534: Rechtslehrer und Rechtsunterricht von der Gründung der Universität bis zur Einführung der Reformation.* Tübingen: Mohr.

Flade, Paul. [1902] 1972. *Das römische Inquisitionsverfahren in Deutschland bis zu den Hexenprozessen.* Aalen: Scientia Verlag.

Foa, Anna. [1992] 2000. *The Jews of Europe after the Black Death.* Trans. Andrea Grover. Berkeley and Los Angeles: University of California Press.

Förstel, Christian. 1999. "Die griechische Grammatik im Umkreis Reuchlins: Untersuchungen zur 'Wanderung' der griechischen Studien von Italien nach Deutschland." In *Reuchlin und Italien*, ed. Gerald Dörner, 45–56. Stuttgart: Thorbecke.

Fouquet, Gerhard. 1983. "St. Michael in Pforzheim: Sozial- und wirtschaftsgeschichtliche Studien zu einer Stiftskirche der Markgrafschaft Baden." In *Pforzheim im Mittelalter: Studien zur Geschichte einer landesherrlichen Stadt*, ed. Hans-Peter Becht, 107–69. Sigmaringen: Thorbecke.

Fraenkel-Goldschmidt, Chava, ed. and trans. 2006. *The Historical Writings of Joseph of Rosheim.* Trans. Naomi Schendowich. Leiden: Brill.

Freimann, Aron, and Isidor Kracauer. 1929. *Frankfurt.* Trans. Bertha S. Levin. Philadelphia: Jewish Publication Society of America.

Freudenthal, Max. 1931. "Dokumente zur Schriftenverfolgung durch Pfefferkorn." *Zeitschrift für die Geschichte der Juden in Deutschland* 4:227–32.

Frey, Siegfried. 1979. "Das Gericht des Schwäbischen Bundes und seine Richter 1488–1534." In *Mittel und Wege früher Verfassungspolitik*, ed. Josef Engel, 224–81. Stuttgart: Klett-Cotta.

———. 1989. *Das württembergische Hofgericht (1460–1618).* Stuttgart: Kohlhammer.

Frey, Winfried. 1985. "Die 'Epistolae obscurorum virorum'—ein antijüdisches Pamphlet?" *Archiv Bibliographia Judaica* 1:147–72.

———. 1990. "Der 'Juden Spiegel': Johannes Pfefferkorn und die Volksfrömmigkeit." In *Volksreligion im hohen und späten Mittelalter*, ed. Peter Dinzelbacher and Dieter R. Bauer, 177–93. Paderborn: Ferdinand Schöningh.

Friedman, Jerome. 1983. *Most Ancient Testimony: Sixteenth-Century Christian Hebraica in the Age of Renaissance Nostalgia.* Athens: Ohio University Press.

Friedrich, Udo. 1998. "Johannes Reuchlin am Heidelberger Hof: Poeta—Orator—Paedagogus." In *Reuchlin und die politischen Kräfte seiner Zeit*, ed. Stefan Rhein, 163–85. Sigmaringen: Thorbecke.

Frings, Udo. 1979. "Reuchlins Komödie 'Scaenica Progymnasmata' ('Henno')." In *Impulse für die lateinische Lektüre*, ed. Heinrich Krefeld, 223–55. Frankfurt: Hirschgraben.

Funkenstein, Amos. 1971. "Basic Types of Christian Anti-Jewish Polemics in the Later Middle Ages." *Viator* 2:373–82.

Gebhardt, Bruno. 1886. *Adrian von Corneto: Ein Beitrag zur Geschichte der Curie und der Renaissance*. Breslau: Preuss und Jünger.

Geiger, Abraham. 1870. "Reuchlin und das Judenthum." *Jüdische Zeitschrift für Wissenschaft und Leben* 8:241–63.

Geiger, Ludwig. 1868. *Über Melanthons "oratio continens historiam Capnionis": Eine Quellenuntersuchung*. Frankfurt: Baer.

———. 1869a. "Johannes Pfefferkorn: Ein Beitrag zur Geschichte der Juden und zur Charakteristik des Reuchlin'schen Streites." *Jüdische Zeitschrift für Wissenschaft und Leben* 7:193–309.

———. 1869b. "Maximilian I in seinem Verhältnisse zum Reuchlin'schen Streite." *Forschungen zur deutschen Geschichte* 9:205–16.

———. 1870. *Das Studium der hebräischen Sprache in Deutschland vom Ende des XV. bis zur Mitte des XVI. Jahrhunderts*. Breslau: Schletter.

———. 1871. *Johann Reuchlin: Sein Leben und seine Werke*. Leipzig: Duncker und Humblot.

———. [1875] 1962. *Johann Reuchlins Briefwechsel*. Hildesheim: Georg Olms Verlagsbuchhandlung.

———. 1876. "Zur Geschichte des Studiums der hebräischen Sprache in Deutschland." *Jahrbücher für deutsche Theologie* 21:190–223.

———. 1889. "Johannes Reuchlin." *Allgemeine Deutsche Biographie* 28:785–99.

———. 1891. "Ungedrucktes von und über Reuchlin." *Zeitschrift für vergleichende Litteraturgeschichte und Renaissance-Litteratur*, N.F., 4:217–26.

Gerber, Jane S. 1992. *The Jews of Spain: A History of the Sephardic Experience*. New York: Free Press.

Gerschmann, Karl-Heinz. 1969. "Zu Johannes Pfefferkorns 'Übersetzung' der Evangelien." *Zeitschrift für Religions- und Geistesgeschichte* 21:166–71.

Glodny-Wiercinski, Dorothea. 1971. "Johannes Reuchlin—Novus Poeta?" *Germanisch-Romanische Monatsschrift*, N.F., 21:145–52.

Goldbrunner, Hermann. 1966. "Reuchliniana." *Archiv für Kulturgeschichte* 48:403–10.

Goshen-Gottstein, Moshe. 1993. "Reuchlin and His Generation." In *Reuchlin und die Juden*, ed. Arno Herzig, Julius H. Schoeps, and Saskia Rohde, 151–60. Sigmaringen: Thorbecke.

Graecogermania: Griechischstudien deutscher Humanisten. 1989. Edited by Dieter Harlfinger and Reinhard Barm. Weinheim and New York: VCH Acta Humaniora.

Graetz, Heinrich. [1853–76] 1891–98. *History of the Jews*. Edited by Bella Löwy. 6 vols. Philadelphia: Jewish Publication Society of America.

Graf, Klaus. 1998. "'Aus krichsscher sprach in das swebischs teutschs gebracht.' Bemerkungen zu Reuchlins Patriotismus." In *Reuchlin und die politischen Kräfte seiner Zeit*, ed. Stefan Rhein, 205–24. Sigmaringen: Thorbecke.

Greive, Hermann. 1978. "Die hebräische Grammatik Johannes Reuchlins *De rudimentis hebraicis*." *Zeitschrift für die alttestamentliche Wissenschaft* 90:395–409.

Grimm, Heinrich. 1956. "Ulrich von Hutten und die Pfefferkorn-Drucke." *Zeitschrift für Religions- und Geistesgeschichte* 8:241–50.

Grözinger, Karl E. 1993. "Reuchlin und die Kabbala." In *Reuchlin und die Juden*, ed. Arno Herzig, Julius H. Schoeps, and Saskia Rohde, 175–87. Sigmaringen: Thorbecke.

Güde, Wilhelm. 1981. *Die rechtliche Stellung der Juden in den Schriften deutscher Juristen des 16. und 17. Jahrhunderts*. Sigmaringen: Thorbecke.

Gundersheimer, Werner L. 1963. "Erasmus, Humanism, and the Christian Cabala." *Journal of the Warburg and Courtauld Institutes* 26:38–52.

Hacke, Daniela, and Bernd Roeck, ed. 2002. *Die Welt im Augenspiegel: Johannes Reuchlin und seine Zeit*. Stuttgart: Thorbecke.

Hagen, Kenneth. 1969. "An Addition to the Letters of John Lang: Introduction and Edition." *Archiv für Reformationsgeschichte* 69:27–32.

Hägler, Brigitte. 1992. *Die Christen und die 'Judenfrage' am Beispiel der Schriften Osianders und Ecks zum Ritualmordvorwurf*. Erlangen: Palm und Enke.

Hailperin, Herman. 1963. *Rashi and the Christian Scholars*. Pittsburgh: University of Pittsburgh Press.

Haller, Johannes. 1927–29. *Die Anfänge der Universität Tübingen 1477–1537*. 2 vols. Stuttgart: Kohlhammer.

Hannemann, Kurt. [1955] 1994a. "Das Bildnis Reuchlins—Ein Nachtrag und eine Nachbetrachtung." In *Johannes Reuchlin 1455–1522*, ed. Manfred Krebs, 173–96. Sigmaringen: Thorbecke.

———. [1955] 1994b. "Reuchlin und die Berufung Melanchthons nach Wittenberg." In *Johannes Reuchlin 1455–1522*, ed. Manfred Krebs, 108–38. Sigmaringen: Thorbecke.

Hartfelder, Karl, ed. 1883–84. *Deutsche Übertsetzungen klassischer Schriftsteller aus dem Heidelberger Humanistenkreis*. Heidelberg: Heidelberger Gymnasium.

Herrmann, Klaus. 2005. "Das Reuchlin-Bild bei Ludwig Geiger." In *Reuchlin und seine Erben: Forscher, Denker, Ideologen und Spinner*, ed. Peter Schäfer and Irina Wandrey, 211–50. Ostfildern: Thorbecke.

Herzig, Arno. 1993. "Die Juden in Deutschland zur Zeit Reuchlins." In *Reuchlin und die Juden*, ed. Arno Herzig, Julius H. Schoeps, and Saskia Rohde, 11–20. Sigmaringen: Thorbecke.

Herzig, Arno, and Saskia Rohde. 1996. "Reuchlin, Johannes." Trans. Susan M. Sisler. *Oxford Encyclopedia of the Reformation* 3:425–26.

Herzig, Arno, Julius Schoeps, and Saskia Rohde, ed. 1993. *Reuchlin und die Juden*. Sigmaringen: Thorbecke.

Hesslinger, Helmo. 1970. *Die Anfänge des schwäbischen Bundes: Ein Beitrag zur Geschichte des Einungswesens und der Reichsreform unter Kaiser Friedrich III*. Stuttgart: Kohlhammer.

Hieronymus, Frank. 1979. "Einbandschnipsel." In *Totum me libris dedo: Festschrift zum 80. Geburtstag von Adolf Seebaß*, ed. Alain Moirandat, Heide Spilker, and Verena Tammann, 65–107. Basel: Haus der Bücher.

———. 1992. *Ἐν Βασιλεία πόλει τῆς Γερμανίας: Griechischer Geist aus Basler Pressen*. Basel: Universitätsbibliothek Basel.

Hillerbrand, Hans J. 1993. "Vom geistigen 'Holocaust' zur rechtlichen Toleranz. Bemerkungen zum Thema Johannes Reuchlin und die Reformation." In *Reuchlin und die Juden*, ed. Arno Herzig, Julius H. Schoeps, and Saskia Rohde, 109–22. Sigmaringen: Thorbecke.

Hirsch, Samson R. 1896. "Johann Reuchlin, the Father of the Study of Hebrew among Christians." *The Jewish Quarterly Review* 8:445–70.

Hofmann, Udo. 1981. "Via compendiosa in salutem: Studien zu Jakob von Hochstratens letzten kontroverstheologischen Schriften (1525–1526)." 2 vols. PhD diss., Universität Tübingen.

Holstein, Hugo. 1888. *Johann Reuchlins Komödien: Ein Beitrag zur Geschichte des lateinischen Schuldramas.* Halle: Verlag der Buchhandlung des Waisenhauses.

———. 1890. "Reuchlins Gedichte." *Zeitschrift für vergleichende Litteraturgeschichte,* N.F., 3:128–36.

Hommel, Hildebrecht. 1938. "Der Würzburger Athenäus-Codex aus Reuchlins Besitz." *Neue Heidelberger Jahrbücher,* N. F., 88–104.

Horawitz, Adalbert. 1877. *Zur Biographie und Correspondenz Johannes Reuchlins.* Vienna: Karl Gerolds Sohn.

Hossfeld, Max. 1907–8. "Johannes Heynlin aus Stein." *Basler Zeitschrift für Geschichte und Altertumskunde* 6:309–56; 7:79–431.

Hsia, R. Po-chia. 1988. *The Myth of Ritual Murder: Jews and Magic in Reformation Germany.* New Haven: Yale University Press.

Hsia, R. Po-Chia, and Hartmut Lehman, ed. 1995. *In and Out of the Ghetto: Jewish-Gentile Relations in Late Medieval and Early Modern Germany.* Cambridge: Cambridge University Press.

Huey, Caroline. 2000. "Hans Folz and the Creation of Popular Culture." PhD diss., University of Texas.

Ickert, Scott. 1987. "Defending and Defining the *Ordo Salutis*: Jacob van Hoogstraten vs. Martin Luther." *Archiv für Reformationsgeschichte* 78:81–97.

Idel, Moshe. 1988. *Kabbalah: New Perspectives.* New Haven: Yale University Press.

———. 1993. Introd. to *On the Art of the Kabbalah,* by Johann Reuchlin, trans. Martin Goodman and Sarah Goodman, v–xxix. Lincoln: University of Nebraska Press.

———. 2008. "Johannes Reuchlin: Kabbalah, Pythagorean Philosophy and Modern Scholarship." *Studia Judaica* 16:30–55.

Irigoin, Jean. 1977. "Georges Hermonyme de Sparte, ses manuscripts et son enseignement à Paris." *Bulletin de l'Association Guillaume Budé:* 22–27.

Irtenkauf, Wolfgang. 1962. "Bausteine zu einer Biographie des Nikolaus Basellius." *Zeitschrift für Württembergische Landesgeschichte* 21:387–91.

Israel, Jonathan I. [1985] 1998. *European Jewry in the Age of Mercantilism 1550–1750.* London: Littman Library.

Jones, G. Lloyd. 1982. *The Discovery of Hebrew in Tudor England.* Manchester: Manchester University Press.

Junghans, Helmar. 1985. *Der junge Luther und die Humanisten.* Weimar: Hermann Böhlaus Nachfolger.

Kalkoff, Paul. 1920. *Ulrich von Hutten und die Reformation: Eine kritische Geschichte seiner wichtigsten Lebenszeit und der Entscheidungsjahre der Reformation (1517–1523).* Leipzig: Haupt.

Katholische Theologen der Reformationszeit. 1984–. Edited by Erwin Iserloh. 6 vols. Münster: Aschendorff.

Katz, David S. 1982. *Philo-Semitism and the Readmission of the Jews to England.* Oxford: Clarendon.

———. 1994. *The Jews in the History of England, 1485–1850.* Oxford: Clarendon; New York: Oxford University Press.

Kaufmann, David. 1901. "Die Verbrennung der Talmudischen Litteratur in der Republik Venedig." *The Jewish Quarterly Review* 13:533–38.

Kaufmann, Thomas. 2006. "Luther and the Jews." In *Jews, Judaism and the Reformation,* ed. Dean Bell and Stephen Burnett, 69–104. Leiden: Brill.

Kedar, Benjamin Z. 1979. "Canon Law and the Burning of the Talmud." *Bulletin of Medieval Canon Law,* n.s., 9:79–82.

Kirn, Hans-Martin. 1989. *Das Bild vom Juden im Deutschland des frühen 16. Jahrhunderts dargestellt an den Schriften Johannes Pfefferkorns.* Tübingen: Mohr.

Kisch, Guido. 1961. *Zasius und Reuchlin: Eine rechtsgeschichtlich-vergleichende Studie zum Toleranzproblem im 16. Jahrhundert.* Konstanz: Thorbecke.

———. 1970. *The Jews in Medieval Germany: A Study of Their Legal and Social Status.* New York: KTAV.

———. 1978. *Forschungen zur Rechts- und Sozialgeschichte der Juden in Deutschland während des Mittelalters.* Sigmaringen: Thorbecke.

Kittelson, James M. *Wolfgang Capito: From Humanist to Reformer.* Leiden: Brill, 1975.

Kleinhans, Arduinus. 1926. "De vita et operibus Petri Galatini, O. F. M., scientiarum biblicarum cultoris (c. 1460–1540)." *Antonianum* 1:145–79, 327–56.

Klepper, Deana Copeland. 2007. *The Insight of Unbelievers: Nicholas of Lyra and Christian Reading of Jewish Text in the Later Middle Ages.* Philadelphia: University of Pennsylvania Press.

Kober, Adolf. 1923. "Urkundliche Beiträge zum Reuchlinschen Streit: Ein Gedenkblatt zum 30. Juni 1922." *Monatsschrift für Geschichte und Wissenschaft des Judenthums,* N.F., 31:110–22.

Kothe, Irmgard. 1938. *Der fürstliche Rat in Württemberg im 15. und 16. Jahrhundert.* Stuttgart: Kohlhammer.

Kracauer, Isidor. 1885. "Rabbi Joselmann de Rosheim." *Revue des Etudes Juives* 16:84–105.

———. 1887. "Die Konfiskation der hebräischen Schriften in Frankfurt a. M. in den Jahren 1509 und 1510." *Zeitschrift für die Geschichte der Juden in Deutschland* 1:230–48.

———. 1891. "Pfefferkorn et la confiscation des livres hébreux à Francfort en 1510." *Revue des Etudes Juives* 22:112–18.

———. 1900a. "Actenstücke zur Geschichte der Confiskation der hebräischen Schriften in Frankfurt a. M." *Monatsschrift für Geschichte und Wissenschaft des Judenthums* 44:114–26, 167–77, 220–34.

Kracauer, Isidor. 1900b. "Verzeichniss der von Pfefferkorn 1510 in Frankfurt a. M. confiscierten jüdischen Bücher." *Monatsschrift für Geschichte und Wissenschaft des Judenthums* 44:320–459.

———. 1911–27. *Die Geschichte der Juden in Frankfurt am Main.* 2 vols. Frankfurt: Kauffmann.

Krause, Eduard. 1889. *Der Weißenburger Handel (1480–1505).* Greifswald: J. Abel.

Krauss, Samuel, ed. 1902. *Das Leben Jesu nach jüdischen Quellen.* Berlin: S. Calvary.

Krebs, Manfred. [1955] 1994a. *Johannes Reuchlin 1455–1522.* Rev. Hermann Kling and Stefan Rhein. Sigmaringen: Thorbecke.

———. [1955] 1994b. "Reuchlins Beziehungen zu Erasmus von Rotterdam." In *Johannes Reuchlin 1455–1522,* ed. Manfred Krebs, 139–55. Sigmaringen: Thorbecke.

———. [1955] 1994c. "Ein unbekannter Brief Reuchlins." In *Johannes Reuchlin 1455–1522,* ed. Manfred Krebs, 197–204. Sigmaringen: Thorbecke.

Kremer, Hans-Jürgen. 1997. *"Lesen, Exercieren und Examinieren": Die Geschichte der Pforzheimer Lateinschule vom Mittelalter zur Neuzeit.* Ubstadt-Weiher: Verlag Regionalkultur.

Kristeller, Paul Oskar. 1961. *Renaissance Thought.* New York: Harper and Brothers.

———. 1971. "A Little-Known Letter of Erasmus, and the Date of His Encounter with Reuchlin." In *Florilegium Historiale,* ed. John Gordon Rowe and W. H. Stockdale, 51–61. Toronto: University of Toronto Press.

Kuhn, Werner. 1971. *Die Studenten der Universität Tübingen zwischen 1477 und 1534: Ihr Studium und ihre spätere Lebensstellung.* 2 vols. Göppingen: Kümmerle.

Lamey, Jacob. 1855. *Johann Reuchlin: Eine kurze Darstellung seines Lebens.* Pforzheim: Flammer.

Landfester, Rüdiger. 1972. *Historia Magistra Vitae: Untersuchungen zur humanistischen Geschichtstheorie des 14. bis 16. Jahrhunderts.* Geneva: Droz.

Langmuir, Gavin I. 1990a. *History, Religion, and Antisemitism.* Berkeley and Los Angeles: University of California Press.

———. 1990b. *Toward a Definition of Antisemitism.* Berkeley and Los Angeles: University of California Press.

Laufs, Adolf. 1994. "Johannes Reuchlin—Rat und Richter: Erste Bausteine für eine juristische Biographie." In *Aus südwestdeutscher Geschichte: Festschrift für Hans-Martin Maurer,* ed. Wolfgang Schmierer, Günter Cordes, Rudolf Kieß, and Gerhard Taddey, 296–306. Stuttgart: Kohlhammer.

———. 1995. "Frieden durch Recht—der Wormser Reichstag 1495." *Juristische Schulung* 8:665–71.

———. 1998. "Johannes Reuchlin—Jurist in einer Zeitenwende." In *Reuchlin und die politischen Kräfte seiner Zeit,* ed. Stefan Rhein, 9–30. Sigmaringen: Thorbecke.

Lea, Henry Charles. [1906–7] 1966. *A History of the Inquisition of Spain.* 4 vols. New York: American Scholar.

Leinkauf, Thomas. 1999. "Reuchlin und der Florentiner Neuplatonismus." In *Reuchlin und Italien,* ed. Gerald Dörner, 109–32. Stuttgart: Thorbecke.

Leutner, Karl. 1957. *Deutsche auf die wir stolz sind.* Berlin: Buchhandlung des Waisenhauses.

Levi, Anthony. 2002. *Renaissance and Reformation: The Intellectual Genesis*. New Haven: Yale University Press.

Lewin, Reinhold. 1911. *Luthers Stellung zu den Juden*. Berlin: Trowitzsch und Sohn.

Lexikon für Theologie und Kirche. 1930–38. Ed. Michael Buchberger. 10 vols. Freiburg: Herder.

Limor, Ora, and Israel Jacob Yuval. 2004. "Skepticism and Conversion: Jews, Christians, and Doubters in *Sefer ha-Nizzahon*." In *Hebraica Veritas?*, ed. Allison P. Coudert and Jeffrey S. Shoulson, 159–80. Philadelphia: University of Pennsylvania Press.

Lorenz, Sönke. 2009. "Reuchlin and the University of Tübingen." In *Ideas and Cultural Margins in Early Modern Germany: Essays in Honor of H. C. Eric Midelfort*, ed. Majorie Elizabeth Plummer and Robin Barnes, 149–63. Surrey: Ashgate.

Lotter, Friedrich. 1993. "Der Rechtsstatus der Juden in den Schriften Reuchlins zum Pfefferkornstreit." In *Reuchlin und die Juden*, ed. Arno Herzig, Julius H. Schoeps, and Saskia Rohde, 65–88. Sigmaringen: Thorbecke.

Lowry, Martin. 1979. *The World of Aldus Manutius: Business and Scholarship in Renaissance Venice*. Oxford: Blackwell.

Ludwig, Walther. 1995. "Graf Eberhard im Bart, Reuchlin, Bebel und Johannes Casselius." *Zeitschrift für Württembergische Landesgeschichte* 54:34–60.

Maier, Johann. 1978. *Jesus von Nazareth in der talmudischen Überlieferung*. Darmstadt: Wissenschaftliche Buchgesellschaft.

Maimon, Arye. 1978. "Der Judenvertreibungsversuch Albrechts II. von Mainz und sein Mißerfolg (1515/1516)." *Jahrbuch für Westdeutsche Landesgeschichte* 4:191–220.

Markish, Simon. 1986. *Erasmus and the Jews*. Chicago: University of Chicago Press.

Martin, Ellen. 1994. *Die deutschen Schriften des Johannes Pfefferkorns: Zum Problem des Judenhasses und der Intoleranz in der Zeit der Vorreformation*. Göppingen: Kümmerle.

Martin, Francis X. 1979. "The Writings of Giles of Viterbo." *Augustiniana* 29:141–93.

——. 1992. *Friar, Reformer, and Renaissance Scholar: Life and Work of Giles of Viterbo, 1469–1532*. Villanova, Pa.: Augustinian.

Maurer, Hans-Martin. 1994. *Eberhard und Mechthild: Untersuchungen zu Politik und Kultur im ausgehenden Mittelalter*. Stuttgart: Kohlhammer.

Maurer, Wilhelm. [1955] 1994. "Reuchlin und das Judentum." In *Johannes Reuchlin 1455–1522*, ed. Manfred Krebs, 267–76. Sigmaringen: Thorbecke.

——. 1967–69. *Der junge Melanchthon zwischen Humanismus und Reformation*. 2 vols. Göttingen: Vandenhoeck und Ruprecht.

Mayerhoff, Ernst Theodor. 1830. *Johann Reuchlin und seine Zeit*. Berlin: Stuhr.

Meier-Oeser, Stephan. 1989. *Die Präsenz des Vergessenen. Zur Rezeption der Philosophie des Nicolaus Cusanus vom 15. bis zum 18. Jahrhundert*. Münster: Aschendorff.

Mellinkoff, Ruth. 1993. *Outcasts: Signs of Otherness in Northern European Art of the Late Middle Ages*. 2 vols. Berkeley and Los Angeles: University of California Press.

Mensching, G. 1989. "Die Kölner Spätscholastik in der Satire der *Epistolae obscurorum virorum*." In *Die Kölner Universität im Mittelalter: Geistige Wurzeln und soziale Wirklichkeit*, ed. Albert Zimmermann, 508–23. Berlin: Walter de Gruyter.

Merchavia, Chen. 1965. "The Talmud in the *Additiones* of Paul of Burgos." *Journal of Jewish Studies* 16:115–34.

———. 1970. *The Church versus Talmudic and Midrashic Literature (500–1248)*. Jerusalem: Mosad Beyalikh.

Mertens, Dieter. 1994. "Eberhard im Bart und der Humanismus." *Eberhard und Mechthild*, ed. Hans-Martin Maurer, 35–81. Stuttgart: Kohlhammer.

———. 1995. "Württemberg." In *Handbuch der baden-württembergischen Geschichte*, ed. Hansmartin Schwarzmaier, 2:1–163. Stuttgart: Klett-Cotta.

———. 1998. "Reuchlins Landesherr Eberhard im Bart: Variationen zum Thema 'Politik und Humanismus.'" In *Reuchlin und die politischen Kräfte seiner Zeit*, ed. Stefan Rhein, 225–49. Sigmaringen: Thorbecke.

Meyer, Carl S. 1969. "Erasmus and Reuchlin." *Moreana* 24:65–80.

Michael, Wolfgang F. 1963. *Frühformen der deutschen Bühne*. Berlin: Selbstverlag der Gesellschaft für Theatergeschichte.

———. 1971. *Das deutsche Drama des Mittelalters*. Berlin and New York: de Gruyter.

Minnich, Nelson H. 1990. "Lateransynoden II." *Theologische Realenzyklopädie* 20:489–92.

———. 1992. "Prophecy and the Fifth Lateran Council (1512–1517)." In *Prophetic Rome in the High Renaissance Period*, ed. Marjorie Reeves, 63–87. Oxford: Clarendon, 1992.

Molitor, Stephan. 1995. *1495: Württemberg wird Herzogtum: Dokumente aus dem Hauptstaatsarchiv Stuttgart zu einem epochalen Ereignis*. Stuttgart: Hauptstaatsarchiv Stuttgart.

Monnerjahn, Engelbert. 1960. *Giovanni Pico della Mirandola: Ein Beitrag zur philosophischen Theologie des italienischen Humanismus*. Wiesbaden: Steiner.

Nagel, Fritz. 1963. "Profectio Cusana: Reuchlin und Nikolaus von Cues." *Ruperto Carola* 15:88–95.

———. 1976. "Johannes Reuchlin und Nicolaus Cusanus." *Pforzheimer Geschichtsblätter* 4:133–57.

Nägele, Anton. 1935. "Dr. Ludwig Vergenhans im Dienste der Grafen und Herzöge von Württemberg." *Württembergische Vierteljahreshefte für Landesgeschichte* 41:32–83.

Nauert, Charles G. 1971. "Peter of Ravenna and the 'Obscure Men' of Cologne: A Case of Pre-Reformation Controversy." In *Renaissance: Studies in Honor of Hans Baron*, ed. Anthony Molho and John A. Tedeschi, 609–40. Firenze: Sansoni.

———. 1973. "The Clash of Humanists and Scholastics: An Approach to the Pre-Reformation Controversies." *Sixteenth Century Journal* 4:1–18.

———. 1988. "Graf Hermann von Neuenahr and the Limits of Humanism in Cologne." *Historical Reflections/Reflexions Historiques* 15:65–79.

———. 1990. "Humanist Infiltration into the Academic World: Some Studies of Northern Universities." *Renaissance Quarterly* 43:799–812.

————. 1991. "Humanists, Scholastics, and the Struggle to Reform the University of Cologne, 1523–1525." In *Humanismus in Köln/Humanism in Cologne*, ed. James V. Mehl, 39–76. Vienna: Böhlau.

Newman, Jane O. 1986. "Textuality versus Performativity in Neo-Latin Drama: Johannes Reuchlin's *Henno*." *Theatre Journal* 38:259–74.

Newman, Louis Israel. [1925] 1966. *Jewish Influence on Christian Reform Movements.* New York: AMS.

Noe, Alfred. 1999. "Vom 'Neuen Athen' zum Gottesstaat: Die florentinische Kulturpolitik zur Zeit von Reuchlins Italienreisen." In *Reuchlin und Italien*, ed. Gerald Dörner, 87–108. Stuttgart: Thorbecke.

Oberman, Heiko A. 1963. *The Harvest of Medieval Theology: Gabriel Biel and Late Medieval Nominalism.* Cambridge, Mass.: Harvard University Press.

————. [1981] 1984. *The Roots of Anti-Semitism.* Trans. James I. Porter. Philadelphia: Fortress.

————. 1983. "Three Sixteenth-Century Attitudes to Judaism: Reuchlin, Erasmus and Luther." In *Jewish Thought in the Sixteenth Century*, ed. Bernard Dov Cooperman, 326–64. Cambridge, Mass.: Harvard University Center for Jewish Studies.

————. 1993. "Johannes Reuchlin: Von Judenknechten zu Judenrechten." In *Reuchlin und die Juden*, ed. Arno Herzig, Julius H. Schoeps, and Saskia Rohde, 39–64. Sigmaringen: Thorbecke.

O'Malley, John. 1968. *Giles of Viterbo on Church and Reform.* Leiden: Brill.

————. 1969. "Fulfillment of the Christian Golden Age under Pope Julius II: Text of a Discourse of Giles of Viterbo, 1507." *Traditio* 25:265–338.

Opitz, Eckardt. 1993. "Johannes Reuchlin und Josel von Rosheim: Probleme einer Zeitgenossenschaft." In *Reuchlin und die Juden*, ed. Arno Herzig, Julius H. Schoeps, and Saskia Rohde, 89–108. Sigmaringen: Thorbecke.

Overdick, Renate. 1965. *Die rechtliche und wirtschaftliche Stellung der Juden in Südwestdeutschland im 15. und 16. Jahrhundert dargestellt an den Reichsstädten Konstanz und Esslingen und an der Markgrafschaft Baden.* Konstanz: Thorbecke.

Overfield, James H. 1971. "A New Look at the Reuchlin Affair." *Studies in Medieval and Renaissance History* 8:165–207.

————. 1984. *Humanism and Scholasticism in Late Medieval Germany.* Princeton: Princeton University Press.

Pacheco, Arsenio. 1985. "Carvajal, Bernardino López de." *Contemporaries of Erasmus* 1:274–75.

Parente, James A. Jr. 1992. "Empowering Readers: Humanism, Politics, and Money in Early Modern Germany Drama." In *The Harvest of Humanism in Central Europe: Essays in Honor of Lewis W. Spitz*, ed. Manfred P. Fleischer, 263–80. St. Louis: Concordia.

Paschini, Pio. 1943. *Domenico Grimano: Cardinale di San Marco.* Rome: Edizioni di Storia e Letteratura.

Paulus, Nikolaus. 1903. *Die deutschen Dominikaner im Kampf gegen Luther (1518–1563).* Freiburg i. Br.: Herdersche Verlagshandlung.

Pazi, Margarita. 1993. "Max Brod über Reuchlin." In *Reuchlin und die Juden*, ed. Arno Herzig, Julius H. Schoeps, and Saskia Rohde, 213–24. Sigmaringen: Thorbecke.

Pelikan, Jaroslav. 1959. *Luther the Expositor*. St. Louis: Concordia.

Pelikan, Jaroslav, Valerie R. Hotchkiss, and David Price. 1996. *The Reformation of the Bible/The Bible of the Reformation*. New Haven: Yale University Press.

Peters, Edward. 1988. *Inquisition*. New York: Free Press.

Peterse, Hans. 1995. *Jacobus Hoogstraeten gegen Johannes Reuchlin: Ein Beitrag zur Geschichte des Antijudaismus im 16. Jahrhundert*. Mainz: Zabern.

———. 1998. "Reuchlins Stellung zur Kirche und Theologie seiner Zeit." In *Reuchlin und die politischen Kräfte seiner Zeit*, ed. Stefan Rhein, 147–62. Sigmaringen: Thorbecke.

Pflüger, Johann Georg Friedrich. [1862] 1989. *Geschichte der Stadt Pforzheim*. Pforzheim: Otto Riecker.

Pforzheimer Reuchlinpreis 1955–93: Die Reden der Preisträger. 1994. Heidelberg: Winter.

Plöchl, Willebald M. 1955. *Geschichte des Kirchenrechts*. 2 vols. Vienna: Verlag Herold.

Poland, Franz. 1899. *Reuchlins Verdeutschung der ersten olynthischen Rede des Demosthenes (1495)*. Berlin: Emil Felber.

Posch, A. 1930. "Accolti, Pietro." In *Lexikon für Theologie und Kirche* 1:104.

Preisendanz, Karl. [1955] 1994. "Die Bibliothek Johannes Reuchlins." In *Johannes Reuchlin 1455–1522*, ed. Manfred Krebs, 35–82. Sigmaringen: Thorbecke.

Price, David. 1992. "Hans Folz's Anti-Jewish Carnival Plays." *Fifteenth-Century Studies* 19:209–28.

———. 1997. "Johannes Reuchlin," *Dictionary of Literary Biography* 179:231–40.

———. 2003. *Albrecht Dürer's Renaissance: Humanism, Reformation and the Art of Faith*. Ann Arbor: University of Michigan Press.

———. 2008. "Reuchlin and Rome: The Meaning of Rome in the Controversy over Jewish Books, 1510–1520." In *Topographies of the Early Modern City*, ed. Arthur Groos, Hans-Jochen Schiewer, and Markus Stock, 97–117. Göttingen: V&R Unipress.

Rabe, Horst. 1989. "Die politische Verfassung: Reich, Territorien und Reichsstädte." *Reich und Glaubensspaltung Deutschland 1500–1600*, ed. Horst Rabe, 69–96. Munich: Beck.

Raeder, Siegfried. 1961. *Das Hebräische bei Luther, untersucht bis zum Ende der ersten Psalmenvorlesung*. Tübingen: Mohr.

———. 1977. *Grammatica theologica: Studien zu Luthers "Operationes in Psalmos."* Tübingen: Mohr.

Raz-Krakotzkin, Amnon. 2007. *The Censor, the Editor, and the Text: The Catholic Church and the Shaping of the Jewish Canon in the Sixteenth Century*. Philadelphia: University of Pennsylvania Press.

Reeves, Marjorie, ed. 1992. *Prophetic Rome in the High Renaissance Period*. Oxford: Clarendon.

Reeves, Sarah. 1984. "Gansfort, Wessel." *Theologische Realenzyklopädie* 12:25–28.

Reichert, Klaus. 2005. "Die zwei Gesichter des Johannes Reuchlin." In *Reuchlin und seine Erben: Forscher, Denker, Ideologen und Spinner*, ed. Peter Schäfer and Irina Wandrey, 25–40. Ostfildern: Thorbecke.

Reinhardt, Volker. 1999. "Einheit und Vorrang der Kulturen: Reuchlin im Spannungsfeld von deutschem und italienischem Humanismus." In *Reuchlin und Italien*, ed. Gerald Dörner, 11–21. Stuttgart: Thorbecke.

Rembaum, Joel. 1982. "The Talmud and the Popes: Reflections on the Talmud Trials of the 1240s." *Viator* 13:203–23.

Remling, Franz Xaver. 1852–53. *Urkundenbuch zur Geschichte der Bischöfe zu Speyer.* 2 vols. Mainz: Kirchheim und Schott.

Rhein, Stefan. 1987. "Johannes Reuchlin: Anmerkungen zu seiner Rezeption im 19. Jahrhundert." *Badische Heimat* 67:310–20.

———. 1988. "Reuchlin, Melanchthon und die Theologie." In *Melanchthonpreis: Beiträge zur ersten Verleihung 1988*, ed. Stefan Rhein, 61–70. Sigmaringen: Thorbecke.

———. 1989. "Johannes Reuchlin als Dichter: Vorläufige Anmerkungen zu unbekannten Texten." In *Pforzheim in der frühen Neuzeit: Beiträge zur Stadtgeschichte des 16. bis 18. Jahrhunderts*, ed. Hans-Peter Becht, 51–80. Sigmaringen: Thorbecke.

———. 1990. "Religiosità individuale e riforma della società: Un contributo alla theologia di Johannes Reuchlin." In *Homo sapiens—Homo humanus*, ed. Giovannangiola Tarugi, 2:421–33. Florence: Olschki.

———. 1993a. "Johannes Reuchlin (1455–1522): Ein deutscher 'uomo universale.'" In *Humanismus im deutschen Südwesten: Biographische Profile*, ed. Paul Gerhard Schmidt, 59–75. Sigmaringen: Thorbecke.

———. 1993b. "Johannes Reuchlin." In *Deutsche Dichter der frühen Neuzeit (1450–1600): Ihr Leben und Werk*, ed. Stephan Füssel, 138–55. Berlin: Schmidt.

———. 1993c. "Der jüdische Anfang: Zu Reuchlins Archäologie der Wissenschaften." In *Reuchlin und die Juden*, ed. Arno Herzig, Julius H. Schoeps, and Saskia Rohde, 163–74. Sigmaringen: Thorbecke.

———. 1994a. "Reuchliniana I. Neue Bausteine zur Biographie Johannes Reuchlins." In *Johannes Reuchlin 1455–1522*, ed. Manfred Krebs, 277–84. Sigmaringen: Thorbecke.

———. 1994b. "Reuchliniana II: Forschungen zum Werk Johannes Reuchlins." In *Johannes Reuchlin 1455–1522*, ed. Manfred Krebs, 285–301. Sigmaringen: Thorbecke.

———. 1994c. "Reuchliniana III: Ergänzungen." In *Johannes Reuchlin 1455–1522*, ed. Manfred Krebs, 303–25. Sigmaringen: Thorbecke.

———. 1995. "Familie Reuchlin: Ein genealogischer Ausflug in die Zeit des Humanismus und der Reformation." *Ettlinger Hefte* 29:63–71.

———, ed. 1998. *Reuchlin und die politischen Kräfte seiner Zeit.* Sigmaringen: Thorbecke.

Rice, Eugene F. Jr. 1985. *Saint Jerome in the Renaissance.* Baltimore: Johns Hopkins University Press.

Ries, Rotraud. 1995. "German Territorial Princes and the Jews." In *In and Out of the Ghetto*, ed. R. Po-chia Hsia and Hartmut Lehmann, 215–45. Cambridge: Cambridge University Press.

Rödel, Walter G. 2002. "Geburt, Hochzeit, Tod: Reuchlins Familienverhältnisse vor dem Hintergrund der demographischen Struktur seiner Zeit." In *Die Welt im Augenspiegel: Johannes Reuchlin und seine Zeit*, ed. Daniela Hacke and Bernd Roeck, 17–28. Stuttgart: Thorbecke.

Roling, Bernd. 2007. *Aristotelische Naturphilosophie und christliche Kabbalah im Werk des Paulus Ritius*. Tübingen: Max Niemeyer.

Roloff, Hans-Gert. 1998. "Sozialkritik und Komödie: Reuchlin als Komödienautor." In *Reuchlin und die politischen Kräfte seiner Zeit*, ed. Stefan Rhein, 187–203. Sigmaringen: Thorbecke.

Roscoe, William. 1805–6. *The Life and Pontificate of Leo the Tenth*. 4 vols. Philadelphia: Lorenzo.

Roth, Cecil. 1959. *The Jews in the Renaissance*. Philadelphia: Jewish Publication Society of America.

Roth, Ferdinand Wilhelm Emil. 1909. "Der Kampf um die Judenbücher und Reuchlin vor der theologischen Fakultät zu Mainz 1509–1513." *Der Katholik* 89:139–44.

———. 1915. "Johann Reuchlin vor der theologischen Fakultät zu Mainz, 1511–1513." *Hessische Chronik* 4:145–48.

Roth, Ulli. 2002. "Die philologische Freiheit des Humanisten Johannes Reuchlin: Interpretation und Edition von Reuchlins Übersetzung der Psalmen 110–115." *Daphnis* 31:55–105.

Ruderman, David B. 1988. *Kabbalah, Magic, and Science: The Cultural Universe of a Sixteenth-Century Jewish Physician*. Cambridge, Mass.: Harvard University Press.

Rummel, Erika. 1995. *The Humanist-Scholastic Debate in the Renaissance and Reformation*. Cambridge, Mass.: Harvard University Press.

———. 2002. *The Case against Johann Reuchlin*. Toronto: University of Toronto Press.

———. 2006. "Humanists, Jews, and Judaism." In *Jews, Judaism, and the Reformation in Sixteenth-Century Germany*, ed. Dean Phillip Bell and Stephen G. Burnett, 3–31. Leiden: Brill.

Rupprich, Hans. [1955] 1994. "Johannes Reuchlin und seine Bedeutung im europäischen Humanismus." In *Johannes Reuchlin 1455–1522*, ed. Manfred Krebs, 10–34. Sigmaringen: Thorbecke.

Rusconi, Roberto. 1992. "An Angelic Pope before the Sack of Rome." In *Prophetic Rome in the High Renaissance Period*, ed. Marjorie Reeves, 157–87. Oxford: Clarendon.

Schäfer, Peter. 2005. "'Adversus cabbalam' oder: Heinrich Graetz und die jüdische Mystik." In *Reuchlin und seine Erben: Forscher, Denker, Ideologen und Spinner*, ed. Peter Schäfer and Irina Wandrey, 189–210. Ostfildern: Thorbecke.

Schäfer, Peter, and Irina Wandrey, ed. 2005. *Reuchlin und seine Erben: Forscher, Denker, Ideologen und Spinner*. Ostfildern: Thorbecke.

Scheible, Heinz. 1987. "Reuchlin, Johann." In *Contemporaries of Erasmus: A Biographical Register of the Renaissance and Reformation*, ed. Peter Bietenholz, 3:145–48. Toronto: University of Toronto Press.

———. 1988. "Reuchlins Bedeutung für den Toleranzgedanken." In *Konstanten für Wirtschaft und Gesellschaft: Festschrift für Walter Witzenmann*, ed. Jolanda Rothfuß, 2:274–85. Konstanz: Labhard.

———. 1989. "Melanchthons Pforzheimer Schulzeit: Studien zur humanistischen Bildungselite." In *Pforzheim in der frühen Neuzeit: Beiträge zur Stadtgeschichte des 16. bis 18. Jahrhunderts*, ed. Hans-Peter Becht, 9–50. Sigmaringen: Thorbecke.

———. 1993. "Reuchlins Einfluß auf Melanchthon." In *Reuchlin und die Juden*, ed. Arno Herzig, Julius H. Schoeps, and Saskia Rohde, 123–49. Sigmaringen: Thorbecke.

———. 1997. *Melanchthon: Eine Biographie*. Munich: Beck.

Schiffmann, Konrad. 1929. *Johannes Reuchlin in Linz*. Linz: Steurer.

Schmidt, Paul Gerhard, ed. 1993. *Humanismus im deutschen Südwesten: Biographische Profile*. Sigmaringen: Thorbecke.

Schmidt-Biggemann, Wilhelm. 1999. "Christian Kabbala: Joseph Gikatilla (1247–1305), Johannes Reuchlin (1455–1522), Paulus Ricius (d. 1541), and Jacob Böhme (1575–1624)." In *The Language of Adam/Die Sprache Adams*, ed. Allison P. Coudert, 81–121. Wiesbaden: Harrassowitz.

———. 2007. "Was ist christliche Kabbala?" In *Topik und Tradition*, ed. Thomas Frank, Ursula Kocher, and Ulrike Tarnow, 265–86. Göttingen: V&R Unipress.

Schoeps, Julius H. 1993. "Der Reuchlin-Pfefferkorn-Streit in der jüdischen Historiographie des 19. und 20. Jahrhunderts." In *Reuchlin und die Juden*, ed. Arno Herzig, Julius H. Schoeps, and Saskia Rohde, 203–12. Sigmaringen: Thorbecke.

Scholem, Gershom. [1941] 1995. *Major Trends in Jewish Mysticism*. Schocken: New York.

———. 1969. *Die Erforschung der Kabbala von Reuchlin bis zur Gegenwart*. Pforzheim: Im Selbstverlag der Stadt.

———. 1988. *From Berlin to Jerusalem*. Trans. Harry Zohn. New York: Schocken.

Schwaab, Emil. 1913. *Historische Einführung in das Achtzehngebet*. Gütersloh: Bertelsmann.

Schwab, Hans-Rüdiger. 1998. *Johannes Reuchlin Deutschlands erster Humanist: Ein biographisches Lesebuch*. Munich: Deutscher Taschenbuch Verlag.

Seckel, Emil. 1898. *Beiträge zur Geschichte beider Rechte im Mittelalter*, vol. 1. Tübingen: Laupp.

Secret, François. 1959. *Egidio da Viterbo: Scechina e libellus de litteris hebraicis*. Rome: Centro Internazionale di Studi Umanistici.

———. 1964a. *Les kabbalistes chrétiens de la Renaissance*. Paris: Dunod.

———. 1964b. *Le Zôhar chez les kabbalistes chrétiens de la Renaissance*. Paris: Mouton.

Seebaß, Gottfried. 2006. "Reuchlin und die Reformation." *Neue Beiträge zur Pforzheimer Stadtgeschichte* 1:53–65.

Seppelt, Franz Xaver. 1957. *Das Papsttum im Spätmittelalter und in der Renaissance von Bonifaz VIII. bis zu Klemens VII*. Munich: Kösel.

Setzler, Wilfried. 1979. *Kloster Zwiefalten: Eine schwäbische Benediktinerabtei zwischen Reichsfreiheit und Landsässigkeit*. Sigmaringen: Thorbecke.

Sexauer, Ottmar. [1955] 1994. "Pforzheim zur Zeit Reuchlins—Ein Kulturbild." In *Johannes Reuchlin 1455–1522*, ed. Manfred Krebs, 156–72. Sigmaringen: Thorbecke.

Shulvass, Moses A. [1955] 1973. *The Jews in the World of the Renaissance*. Leiden: Brill.

Sicherl, Martin. 1963. *Zwei Reuchlin-Funde aus der Pariser National Bibliothek*. Wiesbaden: Verlag der Akademie der Wissenschaften und der Literatur.

———. 1978. *Johannes Cuno: Ein Wegbereiter des Griechischen in Deutschland*. Heidelberg: Winter.

———. 1985. "Pseudodositheana." In *Catalepton: Festschrift für Bernhard Wyss*, ed. Christoph Schäublin, 182–202. Basel: Seminar für Klassische Philologie der Universität Basel.

———. 1993. "Johannes Reuchlin als Begründer des Griechischen in Deutschland." *Gymnasium* 100:530–47.

———. 1994. "Neue Reuchliniana." In *Graeca recentiora in Germania: Deutsch-griechische Kulturbeziehungen vom 15. bis 19. Jahrhundert*, ed. Hans Eideneier, 65–92. Wiesbaden: Harrassowitz.

Smith, Frank Dabba. 1995. "The Reuchlin Controversy." *Journal of Progressive Judaism* 4:77–88.

Spanier, M. 1934. "Pfefferkorns Sendschreiben von 1510." *Monatsschrift für Geschichte und Wissenschaft des Judenthums* 78:581–87.

———. 1935. "Zur Charakteristik Johannes Pfefferkorns." *Zeitschrift für die Geschichte der Juden in Deutschland* 6:209–29.

Spitz, Lewis W. 1956. "Reuchlin's Philosophy: Pythagoras and Cabala for Christ." *Archiv für Reformationsgeschichte* 47:1–20.

———. 1957. *Conrad Celtis: The German Archhumanist*. Cambridge, Mass.: Harvard University Press.

———. 1963. *The Religious Renaissance of the German Humanists*. Cambridge, Mass.: Harvard University Press.

Stälin, Christoph Friedrich von. 1856–73. *Wirtembergische Geschichte*, vols. 3 and 4. Stuttgart: Cotta.

Stern, Selma. 1959. *Josel von Rosheim: Befehlshaber der Judenschaft im Heiligen Römischen Reich Deutscher Nation*. Stuttgart: Deutsche Verlags-Anstalt.

———. 1965. *Josel of Rosheim: Commander of Jewry in the Holy Roman Empire of the German Nation*. Trans. Gertrude Hirschler. Philadelphia: Jewish Publication Society of America.

Stievermann, Dieter. 1979. "Der Augustinermönch Dr. Conrad Holzinger—Kaplan, Rat und Kanzler des Grafen bzw. Herzogs Eberhard d. J. von Württemberg am Ende des 15. Jahrhunderts. " In *Mittel und Wege früher Verfassungspolitik*, ed. Josef Engel, 356–405. Stuttgart: Klett-Cotta.

———. 1989. *Landesherrschaft und Klosterwesen im spätmittelalterlichen Württemberg*. Sigmaringen: Thorbecke.

———. 1998. "Johannes Reuchlin als Jurist und Rat in württembergischen Diensten." In *Reuchlin und die politischen Kräfte seiner Zeit*, ed. Stefan Rhein, 31–51. Sigmaringen: Thorbecke.

Stinger, Charles L. [1985] 1998. *The Renaissance in Rome*. Bloomington: Indiana University Press.

Stintzing, Roderich von. 1880. *Geschichte der deutschen Rechtswissenschaft*. Munich and Leipzig: R. Oldenbourg.

Stow, Kenneth R. 1977. *Catholic Thought and Papal Jewry Policy, 1555–1593*. New York: Jewish Theological Seminary of America.

Straus, Raphael. 1939. *Regensburg and Augsburg*. Trans. Felix Gerson. Philadelphia: Jewish Publication Society of America.

Synan, Edward A. 1965. *The Popes and the Jews in the Middle Ages*. New York: Macmillan.

Talmage, Frank Ephraim. 1975. *David Kimhi: The Man and the Commentaries*. Cambridge, Mass.: Harvard University Press.

Tänzer, Aron. 1937. *Die Geschichte der Juden in Württemberg*. Frankfurt: Kauffmann.

Tewes, Götz-Rüdiger. 1999. "Zwei Fälle—ein Kläger. Das Netzwerk der Feinde Reuchlins und Luthers." In *Reuchlin und Italien*, ed. Gerald Dörner, 181–97. Stuttgart: Thorbecke.

Theologische Realenzyklopädie. 1976–. Ed. G. Krause, G. Müller, and H. Balz. Berlin: de Gruyter.

Toch, Michael. 1997. "Wirtschaft und Geldwesen der Juden Frankfurts im Spätmittelalter und in der Frühen Neuzeit." In *Jüdische Kultur in Frankfurt am Main*, ed. Karl E. Grözinger, 25–46. Wiesbaden: Harrassowitz.

Trachtenberg, Joshua. 1943. *The Devil and the Jews: The Medieval Conception of the Jew and Its Relation to Modern Antisemitism*. New Haven: Yale University Press.

Treu, Martin. 1998. "Johannes Reuchlin, Ulrich von Hutten und die Frage der politischen Gewalt." In *Reuchlin und die politischen Kräfte seiner Zeit*, ed. Stefan Rhein, 133–45. Sigmaringen: Thorbecke.

Trusen, Winfried. 1987. "Johannes Reuchlin und die Fakultäten: Voraussetzungen und Hintergründe des Prozesses gegen den 'Augenspiegel.'" In *Der Humanismus und die oberen Fakultäten*, ed. Gundolf Keil, Bernd Moeller, and Winfried Trusen, 115–57. Weinheim: VCH.

———. 1998. "Die Prozesse gegen Reuchlins 'Augenspiegel.' Zum Streit um die Judenbücher." In *Reuchlin und die politischen Kräfte seiner Zeit*, ed. Stefan Rhein, 87–131. Sigmaringen: Thorbecke.

Tschech, Erna. 1971. "Maximilian und sein Verhältnis zu den Juden." PhD diss., University of Graz (Austria).

Ulmann, Heinrich. 1872. *Franz von Sickingen*. Leipzig: S. Hirzel.

Vasoli, Cesare. 1992. "Giorgio Benigno Salviati (Dragisic)." In *Prophetic Rome in the High Renaissance Period*, ed. Marjorie Reeves, 121–56. Oxford: Clarendon.

Vernet, André. 1961. "Les manuscripts grecs de Jean de Raguse." *Basler Zeitschrift für Geschichte und Altertumskunde* 61:75–105.

Viellard-Baron, Jean-Louis. 1979. "Platonisme et Kabbale dans l'Œuvre de Johannes Reuchlin." In *XVIIIe Colloque International de Tours: L'Humanisme Allemand (1480–1540)*. Munich: Fink, 159–67.

Vocht, Henry de. 1934. *Monumenta Humanistica Lovaniensia: Texts and Studies about Louvain Humanists in the First Half of the XVIth Century*. Louvain: Uystpruyst.

———. 1951. *History of the Foundation and the Rise of the Collegium Trilingue Lovaniense 1517–1550*, vol. 1. Louvain: Bibliothèque de l'Université.

Walde, Bernhard. 1916. *Christliche Hebraisten Deutschlands am Ausgang des Mittelalters*. Münster: Aschendorff.

Weil, Gérard, E. 1963. *Élie Lévita: Humaniste et Massorète*. Leiden: Brill.

Weinstein, Donald. 1970. *Girolamo Savonarola*. Princeton: Princeton University Press.

———. 1972. "In Whose Image and Likeness? Interpretations of Renaissance Humanism." *Journal of the History of Ideas* 33:165–76.

Weislinger, Johann Nikolaus. 1730. *Huttenus delarvatus*. Augsburg: M. and T. Wagner.

Wels, Volkhard. 2000. *Triviale Künste: Die humanistische Reform der grammatischen, dialektischen und rhetorischen Ausbildung an der Wende zum 16. Jahrhunderts*. Berlin: Weidler.

Wenninger, Markus J. 1981. *"Man bedarf keiner Juden mehr": Ursachen und Hintergründe ihrer Vertreibung aus den deutschen Reichsstädten im 15. Jahrhundert*. Vienna: Böhlaus Nachfolger.

Whittaker, John. 1977. "Greek Manuscripts from the Library of Giles of Viterbo at the Biblioteca Angelica in Rome." *Scriptorium* 31:212–39.

Wickes, William. 1970. *Two Treatises on the Accentuation of the Old Testament*. With a prolegomenon by Aron Dotan. New York: KTAV.

Widmann, Hans. "Zu Reuchlins Rudimenta Hebraica." In *Festschrift für Josef Benzing zum sechzigsten Geburtstag: 4. Februar 1964*, ed. Elisabeth Geck and Guido Pressler, 492–98. Wiesbaden: Pressler.

Wiesflecker, Hermann. 1971–86. *Kaiser Maximilian I*. 5 vols. Munich: Oldenbourg.

Willms, Johannes. 1978. "Eine deutsche Humanistenbibliothek—Die Bibliotheca Reuchliniana." *Bücherfreunde, Büchernarren: Entwurf zu einer Archäologie der Leidenschaft*, 61–77. Wiesbaden: Harrassowitz.

Wilms, Hieronymous. 1941. *Der Kölner Universitätsprofessor Konrad Köllin*. Cologne: Albertus Magnus Verlag.

Wilpert, Paul, ed. 1966. *Judentum im Mittelalter: Beiträge zum christlich-jüdischen Gespräch*. Berlin: Walter de Gruyter.

Winter, Jakob, and August Wünsche, ed. [1894] 1965. *Die jüdische Literatur seit Abschluß des Kanons*. 3 vols. Hildesheim: Olms.

Wirszubski, Chaim. 1989. *Pico della Mirandola's Encounter with Jewish Mysticism*. Cambridge, Mass.: Harvard University Press.

Wohlfeil, Rainer. 1993. "Die Juden in der zeitgenössischen bildlichen Darstellung." In *Reuchlin und die Juden*, ed. Arno Herzig, Julius H. Schoeps, and Saskia Rohde, 21–35. Sigmaringen: Thorbecke.

Worstbrock, Franz Josef. 1970. "Zur Einbürgerung der Übersetzung antiker Autoren im deutschen Humanismus." *Zeitschrift für deutsches Altertum* 99:45–81.

——. 1976. *Deutsche Antikerezeption 1450–1550*. Boppard am Rhein: Boldt.

Wyss, Bernhard. 1970. "Pseudodositheus bei Reuchlin: Zur Basler Handschrift F II 54." *Museum Helveticum* 27:273–87.

Yates, Frances A. 1979. *The Occult Philosophy in the Elizabethan Age*. London: Routledge and Kegan Paul.

Zambelli, Paola. 1969. "Agrippa von Nettesheim in den neueren kritischen Studien und in den Handschriften." *Archiv für Kulturgeschichte* 51:264–95.

——. 2007. *White Magic, Black Magic in the European Renaissance*. Leiden: Brill.

Zeydel, Edwin H. 1970. "Johannes Reuchlin and Sebastian Brant: A Study in Early German Humanism." *Studies in Philology* 67:117–38.

Zier, Hans Georg. 1982. *Geschichte der Stadt Pforzheim von den Anfängen bis 1945*. Stuttgart: Theiss.

Zika, Charles. 1974. "The Place of Johannes Reuchlin in the Renaissance Occult Tradition." Ph D diss., University of Melbourne.

——. 1976. "Reuchlin's 'De verbo mirifico' and the Magic Debate of the Late Fifteenth Century." *Journal of the Warburg and Courtauld Institutes* 39:104–38.

——. 1976–77. "Reuchlin and Erasmus: Humanism and Occult Philosophy." *The Journal of Religious History* 9:223–46.

——. 1998. *Reuchlin und die Okkulte Tradition der Renaissance*. Sigmaringen: Thorbecke.

Zimmer, Eric. 1980. "Jewish and Christian Hebraist Collaboration in Sixteenth-Century Germany." *The Jewish Quarterly Review* 71:69–88.

Zimmermann, Albert, ed. 1989. *Die Kölner Universität im Mittelalter: Geistige Wurzeln und soziale Wirklichkeit*. Berlin: Walter de Gruyter.

Index

Printed in the USA/Agawam, MA
June 25, 2020

757084.011